SUNY at Sixty

SUNY scholarly conferences

SUNY at Sixty

The Promise of
the State University of New York

Edited by
John B. Clark, W. Bruce Leslie,
and Kenneth P. O'Brien

Published by State University of New York Press, Albany

© 2010 State University of New York

For information, address State University of New York Press, Albany, NY
www.sunypress.edu

Production by Kelli W. LeRoux
Marketing by Fran Keneston

Library of Congress Cataloging-in-Publication Data

SUNY at sixty : the promise of the State University of New York / edited by,
    John B. Clark, W. Bruce Leslie, Kenneth P. O'Brien.
      p.   cm.
Includes bibliographical references and index.
    ISBN 978-1-4384-3303-5 (hardcover : alk. paper)—
    ISBN 978-1-4384-3302-8 (pbk. : alk. paper)
    1. State University of New York—History.
2. Higher education and state—New York (State)—History. I. Leslie, William Bruce.
II. Clark, John B. III. O'Brien, Kenneth Paul.
LD3839.S86 2010
378.747–dc22

2009046609

10 9 8 7 6 5 4 3 2

This book is dedicated to the SUNY family of students, faculty, staff, and administrators past, present, and future; who embody that special academic community of which we are so proud to be a part.

We especially want to remember Martin L. Fausold and Sanford H. Levine, two distinguished colleagues and pioneers of SUNY history. Hopefully, this book will serve as a fitting legacy to their memory.

THE STATE UNIVERSITY of NEW YORK

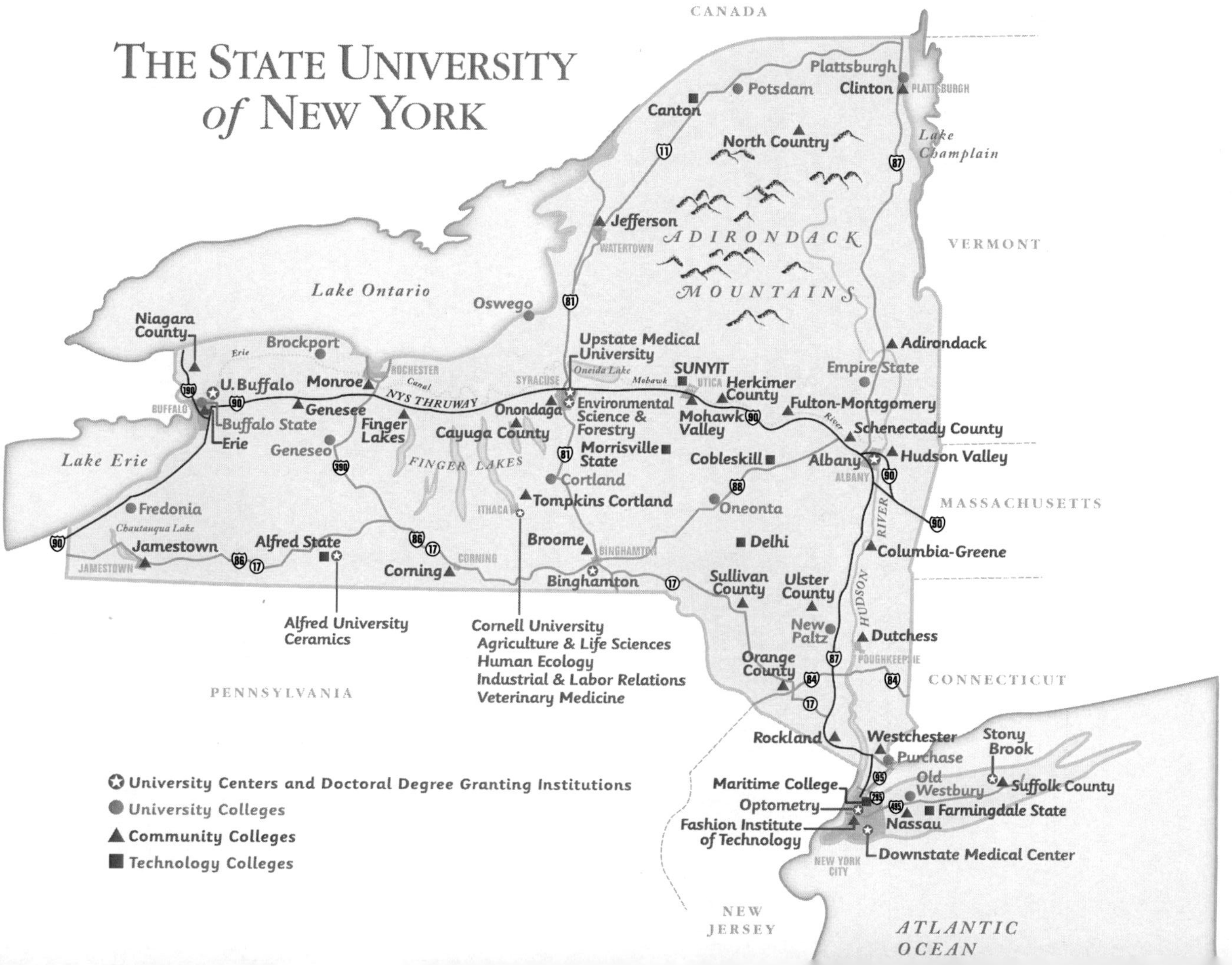

CANADA

VERMONT

MASSACHUSETTS

CONNECTICUT

NEW JERSEY

PENNSYLVANIA

ATLANTIC OCEAN

Lake Ontario

Lake Erie

Lake Champlain

Chautauqua Lake

Oneida Lake

Cayuga Lake

FINGER LAKES

ADIRONDACK MOUNTAINS

HUDSON RIVER

Mohawk River

Erie Canal

NYS THRUWAY

Cities/Labels:

Plattsburgh · Potsdam · Canton · Jefferson · North Country · Clinton · Oswego · Brockport · Niagara County · U. Buffalo · Buffalo State · Erie · Fredonia · Jamestown · Genesee · Monroe · Finger Lakes · Geneseo · Alfred State · Corning · Cayuga County · Onondaga · Upstate Medical University · Environmental Science & Forestry · SUNYIT · Herkimer County · Morrisville State · Cortland · Tompkins Cortland · Broome · Binghamton · Cobleskill · Delhi · Oneonta · Sullivan County · Orange County · Ulster County · New Paltz · Empire State · Fulton-Montgomery · Schenectady County · Hudson Valley · Albany · Columbia-Greene · Adirondack · Mohawk Valley · Poughkeepsie · Dutchess · Rockland · Westchester · Purchase · Maritime College · Optometry · Fashion Institute of Technology · Downstate Medical Center · New York City · Stony Brook · Old Westbury · Farmingdale State · Nassau · Suffolk County

Callout labels:

Alfred University Ceramics

Cornell University
Agriculture & Life Sciences
Human Ecology
Industrial & Labor Relations
Veterinary Medicine

Legend:

University Centers and Doctoral Degree Granting Institutions

- ⊛ University Centers and Doctoral Degree Granting Institutions
- ● University Colleges
- ▲ Community Colleges
- ■ Technology Colleges

Table of Contents

Acknowledgments

This book culminates two decades of hard work by SUNY faculty and staff to sustain the mystic chords of memory that bind us across this massive educational enterprise. In the late 1980s, Professor Martin Fausold of Geneseo assembled volunteers from across SUNY to start preserving our history—just when the founding generation was leaving us. He ignited a fire that briefly burned brightly, then smoldered, and finally burst into flame at a conference celebrating SUNY's 60th Anniversary at the University of Albany on April 3–5, 2009. Professor Fausold did not live to see this consummation of his work, but he would have taken particular satisfaction from the participation of SUNY's newly-appointed chancellor, Nancy Zimpher.

We were delighted that two former chancellors of SUNY, Clifton R. Wharton Jr. and D. Bruce Johnstone, addressed the conference and have revised their comments for this book. We also valued the presence and remarks of former chair of the Board of Trustees, Donald Blinken, and the current chair Carl T. Hayden.

The "SUNY and the Promise of Public Higher Education in America" conference, with over sixty presentations in twenty sessions, plus two keynotes, was a tribute both to the system and to the loyalty of so many who have shaped it. But there was also the "tough love" of academic analysis, especially by the six distinguished historians of higher education whom we brought from outside SUNY to keep us honest.

We would like to have included all of the conference presentations in this book, as well as the insightful comments of moderators and commentators, but demands of space required selection, which we based on thematic development and balance. However, we are delighted that SUNY Press is making the other contributions available online at www.sunypress.edu. We thank all of the nearly 100 conference participants, as well as 200 attendees for making the conference memorable.

Staff from SUNY System Administration and the University at Albany turned a potential logistical nightmare into three smoothly-orchestrated and very productive days. In particular, we thank Curtis Lloyd, Yvette Roberts, Maggie Clairmont, Zulaika Rodriguez, and Bill Hedberg who were with us through the whole process. Ben Weaver, Pierre Radimak, and Carol Donato, among others, stepped in during the frantic run-up to the conference and played essential roles. We also thank President George Philip of the University of Albany and SUNY Provost Risa Palm for making their staff available and providing important guidance. The president of the SUNY Faculty Senate, Carl Wiezalis, provided support from the conception of the conference. We thank the members of the Program Committee, especially Henry Steck, Jim Ketterer, and Geoff Williams. Professor Douglas Skopp of Plattsburgh was with us at critical moments.

Beyond the customary thanks to a book's editors, we owe a deeper debt to Gary Dunham and Jane Bunker of SUNY Press. They attended the conference and then inspired us to assemble this volume with their commitment that our university press serve the SUNY community.

Through the years leading up to the conference, successive administrations at Brockport and Geneseo offered support far beyond kind words that kept the project alive.

Finally, we thank Carolyn Clark, Tessa Harding, and Diane O'Brien for their love and support, offering this volume as compensation for those long periods when the conference and the book manuscript took us away mentally and physically.

Foreword

Chancellor Nancy L. Zimpher

It was my great good fortune to attend the conference celebrating the 60th anniversary of the State University of New York in April 2009, two months after being appointed the twelfth chancellor of SUNY, and two months before I would begin my service. As a result, I was automatically thrust into the process of looking back at SUNY's history while being captivated by the process of looking forward.

This exercise is critical, not only for the benefit of the historical record and for an infusion of scholarship on SUNY's history; it is also a necessary step in the process of authoring SUNY's future.

The conference and this chronicle of its proceedings are a testament to SUNY's breadth and depth of scholarly and historic resources. Not insignificantly, this book is also perhaps an instant classic for students of SUNY's fascinating political history.

Perhaps not surprisingly, the chapters written by former Chancellors Clifton Wharton and Bruce Johnstone were particularly relevant to my own daily questions and long-range plans; I especially appreciate Bruce's valuable perspective that many of today's problems were also yesterday's:

> And while each time has its own special challenges—and the current ones are genuinely formidable—I suspect that the ones that Clifton Wharton and I faced and the ones looming before Chancellor-elect Zimpher have more in common than in difference. Many of these challenges are deeply rooted in SUNY's history, and this is why we must learn from each other and why this scholarly conference on SUNY's history is so important.

To that end, each of the authors offers a unique piece of SUNY's historical puzzle, and each is a valuable contribution to this compendium.

For me, the headline that rises to the top of these twenty-seven essays is the fact that widespread outrage over ethno-religious discrimination gave birth to SUNY (with help from Governor Thomas Dewey's political aspirations). The level of political pressure and the accelerated level of demand after World War II led to a situation in which SUNY's creation became inevitable.

That SUNY was born, in large measure, of a movement to end discrimination and provide equal educational opportunities is no small footnote of history. Indeed, this mandate to offer high quality, accessible, affordable higher education to all New Yorkers—and others around the nation and the world—remains central to SUNY's mission. I believe we are meeting that mandate with great success.

As more than one contributor to this collection acknowledges, it is an unwieldy task to assign a single identity to a system with 64 campuses, 7,669 degree programs, 87,000 faculty members and 440,000 students. But if one were required to assign a singular identity, its watchword would be *diversity*.

This is not a new phenomenon. As Cliff Wharton writes in his essay of recollections, "capitalizing on SUNY's rich diversity was my first vision."

That's why, true to its roots, SUNY's diversity is its identity and its stock-in-trade. My new favorite SUNY metaphor is one penned by Joel Rosenthal in his essay on college histories of SUNY campuses: "That string of jewels on the glittering necklace of SUNY." Each campus sparkles on its own, but as a whole, SUNY possesses a value far greater than the sum of its parts.

We have focused a great deal of attention on diversity of students, not just from a wide array of ethnic and racial backgrounds, but from across the globe, and this initiative is central to raising SUNY's profile around the world, simultaneously gathering greater resources and preparing students for the global economy in which we live.

But we need to be careful not to become complacent and satisfied that our diversity is in and of itself enough. We need to find a way to capture and leverage those relationships by building connections that form a *functional* diversity.

We have achieved excellence—to a degree that it is no longer accurate to call SUNY higher education's best-kept secret. The word is out. That is why we are seeing enrollments climb at an astounding rate. But how do we make sure we can meet the demand in a way that will be sustainable and that will maximize SUNY's positive impact for students and for our communities?

Our critical and timely task is to continue to provide a vast range of opportunities for our diverse and growing student population, provide economic stimulus for our communities, and develop new synergies between our campuses and industry, all the while making sure we are doing the human capital development that will create the future workforce for New York and beyond.

But as chronicled in this collection, we have faced many challenges in the past on the way to meeting our goals, and the future will be no different.

In the current environment of shrinking public resources, there will be a need for even more creativity, ingenuity, inventiveness, and innovation in creating the SUNY that will provide the network of opportunities and investments to spur economic development and recovery.

At this writing, we have initiated a comprehensive strategic planning process that will develop the roadmap for SUNY for the coming decade, a process that is engaging every campus and a wide range of stakeholders in re-visioning SUNY's future.

I believe SUNY is poised for a renaissance that will make the next chapters a very exciting part of our history, not just for SUNY but for all of higher education. I believe we can create a new model for state systems, one that is based on greater collaboration, partnerships, and innovation.

I agree with Cliff Wharton that "education is society's investment in itself—and its future. The taxpaying public must look at this spending as a means of empowerment and not a luxury or consumer product. Until society recognizes the fact that higher education contributes to future growth, we will continue to neglect this decisive key to our nation's future."

Fortunately, as this collection illustrates, we have an opportunity to expand SUNY's reach and positive influence here in New York, to create many more opportunities for individuals, families, and communities, to play a pivotal role in New York's economic recovery, and to serve as a model of higher education for the nation and the world.

It is my hope that *SUNY at Sixty: The Promise of the State University of New York* will find its way to the nightstands and bookshelves of every policymaker and lawmaker in New York. I believe that if they have the benefit of this diversity of voices on SUNY's past, they will be in a much better position to make decisions that will strengthen SUNY for the future.

Each of the authors in this volume is a treasured resource, and there are countless others who have participated in the past and current making of SUNY's history. I especially want to thank John Clark, Bruce Leslie, and Ken O'Brien for undertaking the large task of compiling and editing this book; and of course, Gary Dunham and Jane Bunker and their outstanding team at SUNY Press for pushing this critical project forward.

The wealth of knowledge, experience, and vision put forth in these chapters bolsters my already-high confidence that we at the State University of New York can proceed with a greater understanding of where we came from, putting us in good stead as we move forward and create the next chapters in SUNY's history. I am honored to have a front-row seat in that process and I look forward to the journey that will be recorded in future volumes.

Introduction: Taking Stock of New York's State University after Six Decades

The State University of New York testifies to New Yorkers' deep commitment to and investment in public higher education. Its sixty-four campuses dot the state from eastern Long Island into Manhattan, north up the Hudson Valley into the Adirondack mountains to the Canadian border, west to Niagara Falls and Lake Erie, nearly to the Ohio border. As America's largest comprehensive university, SUNY incorporates community colleges, colleges of technology, university colleges, research universities, medical schools, and health science centers, and includes specialized campuses in fields as diverse as optometry, ceramics, horticulture, fashion, forestry, and maritime training. SUNY has awarded nearly 3 million degrees and enrolls nearly 440,000 students who are served by 87,000 faculty and staff and supported by a budget over $10 billion.

Yet, like America's other state university systems, SUNY attracts little affection or scholarly interest. As Clark Kerr, author of California's iconic 1960 Master Plan lamented, "the rise of the multicampus system ... has been the subject ... of almost complete neglect."[1] Even though fifty state systems have driven the American experiment in mass higher education and their combined students, faculty, and staff outnumber the population of most countries, their history is little studied. With SUNY's size and accomplishments, its low profile in scholarly and policy literature is especially startling. One scholar recently commented on the "surprisingly sparse scholarly literature on New York's public universities and the SUNY system."[2]

This volume, and the SUNY 60th Scholarly Conference held at the University at Albany in April 2009 that gave birth to it, reduces the deficit by exploring some of the paths taken by the State University of New York in its

---

[1]Clark Kerr. *The Great Transformation in Higher Education, 1960–1980*. Albany: SUNY Press, 1991, 251.

[2]Nancy Diamond. Review of Politics and Higher Education in New York State–A Case Study, by Sidney Gelber. *History of Education Quarterly* 43 (Spring, 2003), 148–151.

many manifestations on the way to becoming America's largest comprehensive university. First, please follow us on a brief historical tour.

I.   A Guided Tour through SUNY's First Six Decades

SUNY's creation was inextricably bound in the legendary 1948 presidential campaign, etched in American memories by President Harry S. Truman's improbable comeback victory over Governor Thomas E. Dewey. For higher education in New York State, the events leading up to the election day surprise have quite a different significance. Returning GIs' unpredicted desire for post-secondary education, concerns about the post-war economy, Dewey's national ambitions, and New York's intense ethno-religious political tensions, framed the debates that shaped the State University of New York.

Despite the backing of Governor Dewey at the height of his political power and New York's dubious distinction of being the only state without a state university, SUNY's creation was bitterly contested. New York State offers a contradictory educational past. On one hand, all of its educational institutions are overseen by the oldest educational umbrella organization in the country, the University of the State of New York (bearing the confusing acronym "USNY"), which was founded in 1784 to administer the former Kings College (renamed a more patriotic "Columbia"). On the other hand, New York was arguably the last to create a state university. USNY's powerful Board of Regents had often made New York a national leader in elementary and secondary education. In higher education, however, its record was less impressive. While the Regents continued to champion New York's impressive array of private colleges and universities, they dampened discussions of public higher education. New York City created public colleges, most notably the City College of New York (founded in 1847), but the only state-supported institutions of higher education were small normal schools and agricultural and technical institutes spread throughout the state.

By the 1930s, serious questions were being asked about private institutions' ability to meet the rising demand for post-secondary education. World War II and the impending return of veterans made new answers imperative. In order to head off a possible state system, the Regents offered a tepid response and private colleges opened state-aided temporary institutions that were to close after the flood of former GIs waned. As Syracuse University's chancellor, William Tolley, frankly warned Commissioner of Education George Stoddard, "We ought to guard against the danger of temporary agencies becoming permanent institutions. We do not want an embryo of a state university ... which would be difficult to liquidate."[3]

---

[3]Amy M. Gilbert. *ACUNY: The Associated College of Upper New York: a Unique Response to an Emergency in Higher Education in the State of New York*. Ithaca: Cornell University Press, 1950, 24.

Tolley's fears might not have become reality if several forces in post-war New York had not intersected with the veterans' return. The revelations of the Holocaust made discrimination, particularly anti-Semitism, a burning issue, especially in New York. Documentation of discrimination in New York's elite private colleges and universities touched off a firestorm. Meanwhile, as Governor Dewey contemplated another presidential run, he could not ignore President Truman's Commission on Higher Education. Yet any plans to reform the Empire State's post-secondary education risked alienating some critical segment of New York's electorate. Finally, after bitter conflicts and painful compromises, legislation was passed. Governor Dewey interrupted his Wisconsin primary campaign to fly back to Albany and, with a flourish of his pen, launch SUNY on April 4, 1948.

After the high drama surrounding SUNY's birth, its first decade was quite quiet. The compromises necessary to get legislative approval inevitably restricted the infant enterprise. The obstacles thrown in its path are even reflected in an anomaly in SUNY's seal. The "1948" inscription hides the reality that the legislation Dewey signed contained a poison pill that prohibited the system from operating for a year. Therein lies a telling tale. Opponents spent that year trying to stuff the genie back in the bottle by placing SUNY under the unfriendly Board of Regents. The Condon-Barrett bill was defeated in March, 1949, but only after another bitter legislative fight. Finally, on April 5, 1949, President Alvin Eurich, SUNY's first president and former acting president at Stanford University, was able to summon the leaders of New York's thirty-two state-operated campuses to Albany and began to operate SUNY.

The new system was modest by later standards, enrolling a total of 32,000 students in its first year, an average of only one thousand per campus. The heart and face of the system were eleven State Teachers Colleges and six Agricultural and Technical Institutes. There were also five Institutes of Applied Arts and Sciences with uncertain futures and three GI colleges slated for eventual closure. Also included were seven colleges contracted out to three private universities, Alfred, Cornell, and Syracuse.

The guiding principle was that SUNY would only "supplement" the private colleges and universities. Dewey's motivation to create SUNY had been to overcome a record of discrimination, especially in existing medical programs. Beyond that, however, his vision for SUNY was limited. At a 1950 SUNY symposium on the "Functions of a Modern University," he stressed "that the State University shall work in cooperation with our priceless private colleges and universities. There must be no competition between them. They must supplement each other with neither weakening the other." He further dampened educational ambitions with his claim that machinists and taxi drivers earned more than lawyers. "To regard a college degree as a guaranteed ticket to security in earnings, is an illusion which I think all of us should join together in shattering."[4]

The compromises that secured the original passage of the SUNY legislation, and then the defeat the Condon-Barrett bill, further limited SUNY. Opponents of SUNY's independence from the Regents prevented the creation of a permanent Board of Trustees until 1954.[5] There were informal bans on teaching liberal arts or training secondary teachers in academic subjects (except at Albany), engineering except at the Maritime Academy, and a prohibition on raising private funds. Significantly, doctoral programs and research were also out of bounds. SUNY's second president, William Carlson (1952–58), chafed at these limitations and campaigned to create a flagship university. He covertly commissioned the Blegen Report, which opened with the line "State University is an academic animal without a head" and predictably called for a flagship. Incurring the wrath of the chairman of the SUNY Board, Frank Moore, and Governor Averill Harriman, Carlson was summarily dismissed.

SUNY seemed destined to remain a modest collection of institutions. But then stars realigned and SUNY was soon transformed. The launch of Sputnik, the election of Nelson Rockefeller as governor, the approaching waves of "baby boomers," and the lapse of the ban on teaching liberal arts intersected to liberate SUNY from the mantra to "only supplement the private colleges."

Rockefeller's Heald Commission drew up a blueprint outlining a very different kind of university. Former state teachers colleges would become liberal arts colleges, community colleges would rapidly expand, and students would help support the expansion by paying tuition for the first time. Most dramatically, SUNY faculty would undertake significant scholarly research, not at Blegen's single flagship, but at four university centers offering doctoral programs, spread across the state at Stony Brook, Binghamton, Albany, and Buffalo. Finally, SUNY would be an independent force, freed from the restrictions of the earlier compromises and from the Regents' interference.

Carlson's successor, Thomas Hamilton (1959–62), did not fit the Rockefeller mold and left for the more peaceful University of Hawaii. The following nearly two-year interregnum permitted unique gubernatorial influence until Rockefeller found his chancellor. Samuel Gould was a former chancellor in the University of California system, whose leader, Clark Kerr, had shaped the model state system. The Rockefeller-Gould dynamic launched SUNY into what many remember as its "golden age."

---

[4]Quotations from State University of New York, Functions of a Modern University. Albany: 1950, 30–31. Richard Norton Smith. *Thomas E. Dewey and His Times*. Simon & Schuster, 1982, 472–3. Sidney Gelber "Politics and Public Higher Education in New York: Stony Brook–A Case Study." *History of Schools & Schooling*, Vol. 11. New York: Lang, 2001, 69–73.

[5]Oliver C. Carmichael. *New York Establishes a State University*. Nashville: Vanderbilt University Press, 1955, 311–312.

As "baby boomers" swelled enrollment and public and private support for research grew, SUNY rapidly expanded. In addition to developing the research centers and diversifying the missions of the former teachers colleges and "ag and techs," new four-year and community colleges were opened and intercampus programs launched. Gould's picture on the front of the January 12, 1968 *Time* magazine, accompanied by a laudatory story on SUNY, confirmed the transformation.

Almost as quickly as the "golden years" began, however, they ended. Ironically, the very beneficiaries of the growth helped end it. The combination of the civil rights movement being supplanted by "black power," the baby boom morphing into a New-Leftish counter-culture, and the consensus-shattering Vietnam War brought chaos to the campuses, which peaked with massive protests following the Kent State shootings in Spring 1970. Chancellor Gould resigned for his health and much of the public and legislature resented students' seeming ingratitude. Finally, a disenchanted Governor resigned in 1973.

Gould's successor, Ernest Boyer (1970–77), grasped what proved to be a poisoned chalice. Declining public, gubernatorial, and legislative support, as well as an economy spiraling downward, taking New York City's crumbling finances with it, destroyed both budgets and hopes. As Governor Hugh Carey (1975–83) famously pronounced, "the days of wine and roses are over." Soon, the scary term "retrenchment" entered the SUNY vocabulary. Boyer was no doubt relieved to accept President Carter's invitation to become Commissioner of Education.

Even without wine and roses, SUNY remained a prodigious educational engine of approximately one-third of a million students on sixty-four campuses, which had awarded 650,000 degrees by Boyer's departure. But the tone was anything but expansive. The number of students plateaued as the baby boomers graduated and the proportion of youth entering higher education temporarily dipped.

Not surprisingly, SUNY's priorities shifted from growth to efficient management of existing resources. Boyer's successor, Clifton Wharton Jr. (1978–87), brought stability during the longest chancellorship in SUNY's history. *The Challenge and the Choice*, a report commissioned by Wharton, became a blueprint for reducing bureaucratic inefficiency, and SUNY gained significant freedom from Albany's restrictive budgetary rules. Under his successor, Bruce Johnstone (1988–1994), budgets began to recover and relative tranquility returned.

But Johnstone's departure and the defeat of Governor Mario Cuomo (1983–95) tossed SUNY into controversy once again. Governor George Pataki (1995–2007) appointed a number of new members to the Board of Trustees who believed SUNY needed major changes, to make it both more efficient and educationally effective. The Board's 1995 report, *Rethinking SUNY*, recommended cost efficiencies and it later adopted a system-wide general education curriculum that sparked heated debate on SUNY campuses. Another difficulty was the lack of stable and prolonged leadership at the chancellor level. After Johnstone's departure in 1994, seven individuals led SUNY on a permanent or a temporary basis in the fifteen years preceding the appointment of Chancellor Nancy Zimpher in June 2009. Only Chancellor Robert King's tenure (2000–05) offered any continuity in the period.

Governor Eliot Spitzer's (2007–08) election briefly inspired comparisons to Rockefeller and hopes for another "Golden Age," with a lavishly-funded SUNY driving New York's economic revival. His blue-ribbon Commission on Higher Education could dream expansively of a New York State led into a prosperous future by its private colleges and universities, CUNY, and especially SUNY. Those dreams were soon shattered, rudely replaced by worries about surviving a national economic collapse.

Our attention to SUNY's administrative and political leaders should not obscure the more important realities "on the ground" across sixty-four campuses. Through periods of feast and famine, SUNY has educated millions of students, shaped a skilled workforce, and created an informed citizenry for the State and beyond. Some of SUNY's characteristics were imprinted at birth; in other ways, the founders would have trouble recognizing their creation in its maturity.

II. Twenty-Seven Ways to Understand SUNY

For all its accomplishments, SUNY has not quite won the hearts and minds of New Yorkers. Buoyed by the belief that disseminating a useful past can increase public and scholarly appreciation, a determined group of historians, archivists, and others interested in SUNY's heritage have worked for many years to preserve SUNY's history and promote its historical self-awareness. The 60th anniversary provided an opportunity to focus their efforts, galvanize others, and utilize the talents of some nationally-known scholars in the history of higher education. Thus, on April 3–5, 2009, about 100 participants and 200 attendees gathered at the University at Albany to celebrate the 60th anniversary of President Eurich calling together the thirty-two campus leaders to launch SUNY.

The twenty-seven papers in this book began as presentations at the conference and then matured with the benefit of the understandings that developed there. Unfortunately, space permitted inclusion of less than half of the presentations, omitting much worthy scholarship. These are available on-line at http://www.sunypress.edu/ConferenceProceedings.aspx. We thank all of the conference participants and numerous SUNY System Administration and University at Albany staff who made the conference possible.

The ten chapters offer a variety of perspectives on SUNY as a whole and its parts. Chapters 1 and 7 examine its founding and demographic diversity. Chapters 2, 3, 4, and 5 offer institutional case studies organized in terms of the sectors of this "comprehensive university." Chapter 6 offers perspectives from significant reports, while chapter 8 provides an international view. Chapter 9 provides important retrospective glances by two former chancellors, and in the final set, historians and archivists look "back to the future." Introductions place each chapter's articles in broader historical and thematic contexts.

We are pleased that this book and the conference preceding it showcase the complexity and scope that make SUNY the nation's largest comprehensive university. The authors of the twenty-seven articles range across SUNY from non-teaching professionals at community and comprehensive colleges, to faculty in varied disciplines across the system, to former chancellors. This SUNY mix is leavened with six nationally-known historians of higher education from outside SUNY. Thus, many wrote out of loyalty to the system they have committed careers to, often applying analytical tough love to their professional family. Others approached their subject from a more detached scholarly vantage.

SUNY's complexity makes sweeping judgments about its history nearly impossible. But we confidently assert that, although contemplating the past appears to be a luxury in troubled times, the sense of identity and perspective provided by a search for a useful past is fundamental to charting a successful future.

As SUNY's longest serving chancellor, Clifton Wharton Jr., warned:

> "those of us who are today a part of SUNY's continuing history ... are too busy grappling with the problems of the present to spend much time on the past.
>   This is a mistake I think."[6]

---

[6] *Sixty-four Campuses: The State University of New York to 1985.* Albany: Office of University Affairs and Development, 1985, vii.

The Empire State Creates a University

Introduction

Sanford H. Levine, State University of New York

Sixty years have passed since the creation of the State University of New York. Sixty years is a short period in the history of higher education, but it was a crucial period in the development of public higher education in the state of New York.

Today we celebrate the magnificent accomplishment of that creation, the State University of New York (SUNY), the nation's largest comprehensive system of public higher education. SUNY currently serves more than 438,000 students on sixty-four geographically-dispersed, state-operated, statutory and community college campuses, and boasts more than 2.4 million alumni. These campuses provide access to almost every field of academic and professional study at the associate's, bachelor's, master's, doctoral, and certificate levels of study.

This accomplishment has been achieved, moreover, while challenges and debates have surrounded New York's balance of public and private higher education. Issues of balance and level of support continue to surface because they are rooted in the fundamental political and social dynamics of SUNY's creation.

In broad historical perspective, the creation of SUNY did not occur in the absence of conflicts, differing attitudes, and political and religious cross-currents (see Ottman, *Forging SUNY in New York's Political Cauldron, infra*). Unlike the other states, the New York experience was the result of years of public policy debate over the extent of the State's role in the direct delivery of higher education. Simply stated, other states desired to create major public institutions of higher education; New York did not.

Many factors contributed to this. These included New York's unique response to the 1862 Federal Morrill Land-Grant Act by designating Cornell University, a private university, as the state's land-grant institution with four later-developed "contract" or statutory units; the New York State Board of Regents' strong support of private colleges and universities throughout the

1

state; long-term state funding to a small number of teacher-training colleges and other limited-scope two- and four-year schools; the initiation of state scholarship aid in 1913, which could be utilized at any private and public institution; and the differing religious positions on governmental interference in private educational practices.

In the period in the 1940s that led up to SUNY's formal establishment, several additional factors were also present. These new realities, among many, included the introduction of federal policy affecting higher education (see Hutcheson, *Shared Goals, Different Politics, and Differing Outcomes: The Truman Commission and the Dewey Commission, infra*), the problem of accommodating large numbers of returning veterans from World War II who sought educational opportunity with the support of the federal GI Bill, the continuing aspirations and presidential campaigns of sitting Governor Thomas E. Dewey, and pressing concerns that government must play a role in ending discrimination in admission to higher education for those traditionally bypassed or excluded arbitrarily (see Wechsler, *The Temporary Commission Surveys Biased in Admissions, infra*).

In New York, these complexities became the focus of the reports of the Temporary Commission on the Need for a State University (1946–48), and in many ways, the basis of the recurring charges given to the several commissions, committees, and task forces examining the direction of SUNY and State support of higher education over the past sixty years, including the recent New York State Commission on Higher Education (2007–08).

The concerns take many forms but they fall generally into three principal areas:

SUNY and the Private Institutions and the New York State Board of Regents. What role does a comprehensive system of public higher education play in New York's historical arrangement of private institutions, the special nature of the Cornell University-State relationship, and the broad policy-making responsibilities of the New York State Board of Regents? What are the requirements for fiscal and legal support for public and private higher education and the responsibilities of the governor and legislature for providing that support? Do these requirements differ among the state-operated campuses, the statutory colleges, and the locally-sponsored community colleges of SUNY?

SUNY and the State. How does a comprehensive system of public higher education fit into the structure of New York State government with its multi-layered and often-competing oversight and regulatory agencies? What are the essential requirements for effective management authority for the system and the individual campuses?

SUNY and "Federalism" and the Campuses. How should a comprehensive system of public higher education be effectively governed as a centralized/decentralized institution, while recognizing the need to maintain the broad diversity of individual campus missions and initiatives that are the system's strengths?

The creation of the SUNY system in 1948 answered many of these complex questions. As in any political consensus, some solutions were reached, some compromises made, and some issues left unresolved. Even as the governor signed the pieces of legislation that created the system and its companion Fair Educational Practices Act, many opposing interests were at work attempting to change and redirect the conclusions reached. These challenges were not ultimately successful, however, and on April 5, 1949, the leaders of the pre-existing state-operated colleges convened under the SUNY umbrella to launch New York's public university.

From that beginning to the present time, the State University of New York system has passed through various periods of growth, redefinition, transformation, and re-examination. As previously noted, some of the same principal questions, particularly related to state funding support and management authority, have continued to be addressed and readdressed by the SUNY trustees, chancellors, presidents, and the state's policy-makers. Many new initiatives for SUNY and the City University of New York (CUNY) have resulted from these studies, while others did not bring forward satisfactory proposals. At the same time, the 60th anniversary of SUNY's creation is celebrated for the scope of the institution's major accomplishments. It is clear that the university's new leadership has a fresh opportunity to chart the evolving course of SUNY's future.

I. Shared Goals, Different Politics, and Differing Outcomes: The Truman Commission and the Dewey Commission

Philo Hutcheson, Georgia State University

American presidential campaigns have often been intriguing (and indeed, even filled with intrigue), as different candidates maneuver for media attention and political support while avoiding political harm. The 1948 Harry Truman— Thomas Dewey election had its own curious twists, highlighted, no doubt, by the famous photograph of a smiling Harry Truman holding a *Chicago Tribune* with the headline, "Dewey Wins!" Yet there is another curious twist, not meriting such memories as a headline error by a major newspaper, but nevertheless one of remarkable historical and contemporary proportions. Harry Truman and Thomas Dewey both appointed commissions to examine higher education at a time when less than five percent of the nation's population had earned a bachelor's degree and the nation was still struggling to return to a peacetime economy after years of intense focus on winning a global war.

Both commissions had a sustained impact on the direction of higher education. This paper examines what they shared in perspectives and recommendations, where they differed, and what the general outcomes were.

President Harry Truman appointed the President's Commission on Higher Education in July 1946 and the commission issued all but its statistical report in December 1947, with the printing and distribution of the six volumes spread across the fall of 1947 through the spring of 1948. The commission met seven times from July 1946 through November 1947, with sub-committees on each of five topics usually meeting when the full commission met. The commission members agreed upon the topics at the first meeting, selecting as themes the responsibilities of higher education, ways and means of providing higher education to all, organization and expansion of higher education, financing higher education, and providing personnel for higher education.[1] The report of the commission, *Higher Education for American Democracy*, is widely recognized for its apparent impact on a variety of areas of higher education, such as the widespread usage of the term "community college" and the argument that 49 percent of young Americans were intellectually capable of some college-level work, suggesting the possibility of mass higher education. The commission also recommended provision of federal financial aid for college students based on financial need, much broader than such targeted programs as the Servicemen's Readjustment Act of 1944 (the "GI Bill"). The report also urged that all students be allowed to use these scholarships, regardless of their institution's type or control.

In February 1946, Governor Thomas Dewey spoke to New York's state legislature about the need to examine the state's system of higher education and shortly thereafter, the legislature passed a bill authorizing a committee, the Temporary Commission on the Need for a State University (this in an era when clever acronyms were unnecessary), to examine and recommend action in regard to undergraduate, graduate, and professional education in New York. The commission included fifteen members, as well as ten *ex officio* members from the state government; Governor Dewey and the legislature completed the appointment of the members in July 1946. The commission approved three committees to examine specific topics of concern—barriers to college access, facilities, and organization and finance—and a large staff reported on those topics. The commission first met in October 1946. The committees did not meet until January 1947, when the full commission had its next meeting; they and a small group of commission members met during the winter, spring, and

---

[1]"Tentative List of Factual Data for the President's Commission on Higher Education," in Goodrich C. White Papers, Box 17, folder 6, Special Collections and Archives, Robert W. Woodruff Library, Emory University. These topics became the titles, in slightly revised form, of the final report. See *Higher Education for American Democracy: A Report of the President's Commission on Higher Education*. New York: Harper & Brothers, 1948.

summer of 1947. The third full meeting of the commission did not occur until September 1947, followed by a final meeting in January 1948, and publication of their report a month later.[2]

After years of examining and re-examining the 1947 President's Commission on Higher Education, I am startled to see the similarities between the starting points for the "President's Commission" and the "Temporary Commission." There are indeed differences, but those have less to do with the topics addressed than the political contexts of the two commissions.

Specifically, four issues were paramount for both commissions, and only the fifth was solely the province of the 1947 President's Commission. In the case of one of the similarities, a report from New York City Mayor Fiorello LaGuardia's Committee on Unity, titled "Report on Discrimination in Institutions of Higher Learning," generated considerable discussion by both Commissions. In both Commissions—perhaps surprisingly, for both President Truman and Governor Dewey—there was a strong commitment, at least for the time, to overcoming patterns of discrimination in institutions of higher education.

The second similarity is hardly surprising; both commissions addressed the unanticipated and remarkable influx of veterans into higher education under the aegis of the GI Bill. While recent scholarship indicates that by and large those veterans were either enrolled in college before their enlistment in the armed services or would have been likely to attend college if they had not served in the armed services, nevertheless the sheer number of GIs enrolling at colleges and universities placed serious pressure on institutions of higher education.

The third similarity reflects in part both the first and second, yet also serves as a reminder that planning had come to higher education; both commissions examined structures and systems of higher education in order to increase access and efficiency. Both commissions favored community colleges as one key institutional means to increasing access and efficiency.

The fourth similarity is probably the most buried in historical terms. Both commissions offered substantial discussion about the need for more students in medical and health professions schools.

Finally, the one striking difference between the two commissions is the sustained discussion of general education apparent in the 1947 President's Commission report. The Temporary Commission in contrast, offers almost no such discussion. In great part, this difference reflects the decision of the President's Commission to focus its work on societal needs and higher education, rather than more narrowly on the needs of higher education, while

---

[2]Oliver Cromwell Carmichael Jr., *New York Establishes a State University: A Case Study in the Processes of Policy Formation*. Nashville, TN: Vanderbilt University Press, 1955.

the Temporary Commission had more immediate pressures given that the State of New York did not have a state university, the last state without such an institution.

The politics, however, differed. Obviously, the politics differed as a matter of the executive's political party; Truman was a Democrat and Dewey was a Republican. Furthermore, the 1947 President's Commission operated in the federal environment, while the Temporary Commission was in a state environment. Yet I find that the most striking difference between the two political settings was not simply the federal and state issue, but more specifically that the 1947 President's Commission was reporting to the president in an environment where the role of federal support of higher education was ambiguous. Other than targeted programs serving national needs, even such substantial ones as the GI Bill, there was no clear role for the federal government. There was even the caution that the United States Constitution did not mention education and the 10th Amendment declared that any issue not mentioned in the Constitution was under the purview of the states. In contrast, the New York Democrats had already pushed for a bill authorizing a state university, several interest groups wanted a state university, and obviously the State of New York had the constitutional authority to create a state university. Hence, the immediate outcomes for the two reports differed, although the impact of both reports, in different terms over different periods of time, was substantial.

As a matter of clarification, I want to distinguish between the work and impact of presidential commissions in the past and the present. Some interesting works on presidential commissions in the past ten or fifteen years make reasonable arguments that such commissions are not especially effective. While the effects of the 1947 President's Commission were not as direct as those of the Temporary Commission, many scholars distinguish between the effects of Truman's Commission of the late 1940s from those of later ones.[3] It is very important to remember that presidential commissions then operated in a very different environment. Today there are over 2,000 White House staff members, so policy creation and implementation in the federal executive branch goes

---

[3]As a rather thorough sample of those citations, see Arthur M. Cohen and Florence B. Brawer, *The American Community College, 3rd ed.* (San Francisco: Jossey-Bass Publishers, 1996) and George B. Vaughan, *The Community College in America: A Pocket History* (Washington, D.C.: American Association of Community and Junior Colleges, 1982). On financial aid and state planning, see Richard Freeland, *Academia's Golden Age: Universities in Massachusetts, 1945–1970* (New York: Oxford University Press, 1992), 70–119; on general education, Frederick Rudolph *Curriculum: A History of the American Undergraduate Course of Study Since 1636* (San Francisco: Jossey-Bass Publishers, 1977), 264. For overall discussions of the impact of the President's Commission, see Laurence E. Gladieux and Thomas R. Wolanin, *Congress and the Colleges: The National Politics of Higher Education* (Lexington, Mass.: D.C. Heath and Company, 1972), xi, Thomas R. Wolanin, *Presidential Advisory Commissions: Truman to Nixon* (Madison: University of Wisconsin Press, 1975), 20–21, and David W. Breneman and Chester E. Finn Jr., *Public Policy and Private Higher Education* (Washington, D.C.: The Brookings Institution, 1978).

through a very different process than in 1947, when all staff members could fit into one room, and, frankly, Harry Truman didn't really have a chief of staff (although one White House staff member, John Steelman, was convinced that he held that role). So in very real terms, we can expect there to be more definite outcomes from presidential commissions in the past than in the present.

Two characteristics reinforced the similarities. One, as noted, is the context of various national conditions of the time, specifically raised awareness about the horrors of discrimination (an awareness that would somewhat fade to judicial decisions in the Eisenhower years), and the need to educate veterans. The other characteristic almost suggests the need for a casual reference to C. Wright Mills and "the power elite." As Figure 1 indicates, a number of commission members, as well as staff members, either served on both commissions or worked within the policy boundaries of groups connected to or influential on both commissions. In some ways this would not be surprising, as the circles of men and some women working on policy issues in higher education were understandably small in the late 1940s. Nevertheless, when I began to compare those people involved in both commissions, I could not help but wonder if the muse of history had written that it would be so, so that a historian of education decades later could take pleasure in a remarkably unusual, important, but simple discovery. In the vernacular, a bunch of people with a whole lot of experience in working with each other are not very likely to provide very different outcomes while working on two groups that have similar goals. Figure 1 displays the interconnections between the two commissions, some of which would be more hidden than clear without the research that I have done on the 1947 President's Commission. There were twenty-eight members of the 1947 President's Commission, as well as six additional staff members, and there were fifteen members of the Temporary Commission, as well as ten *ex officio* members, and six staff members. Of particular note are those Temporary Commission members who were active in the American Council of Education; the chair of the President's Commission, George Zook, was president of the council, and several members of the President's Commission had been or were active in the council.

The shared experiences even run a little deeper, as Algo Henderson was not only a staff member for the Temporary Commission, but also associate commissioner of education for New York, appointed in November 1947 by Francis Spaulding, the Commissioner of Education. Furthermore, Bishop Oxnam was a member of the State Committee for Equality in Education, which was active in lobbying the Dewey Commission, as was Rabbi Stephen Wise.[4]

---

[4]"Spaulding Names Educator as Aide," New York Times, November 22, 1947, 13, and "Highlights of the Report of the Presidential Commission on Higher Education," (New York: State Committee for Equality in Education, December 1947), back cover.

FIGURE 1　Members, Staff Members, and Important Actors for the 1947
President's Commission and the Temporary Commission, Including Shared
Experiences.

President's Commission	Temporary Commission	Shared Experiences
George Zook (chair)	Owen Young (chair)	
Sarah Blanding	Sarah Blanding	
O.C. Carmichael	O.C. Carmichael (vice-chair)	Chair of Board of Trustees, State University of New York
Alvin Eurich		Appointed President, State University of New York, 1948
Algo Henderson	Algo Henderson (staff)	
Rabbi Stephen S. Wise		Testified, Temporary Commission
George Stoddard		NY Commissioner of Education, 1940–1942
Ordway Tead		Chair, NYC Board of Higher Education
	Edmund Day	Substantial ACE experience
	Floyd Reeves (staff)	Substantial ACE experience
	Francis Spaulding (*ex officio*)	Substantial ACE experience
Arthur Compton	John E. Burton	
Henry Dixon	Rev. Robert I. Cannon, S.J.	
Milton Eisenhower	Joseph Carlino	
John Emens	Betty Hawley Donnelly	
Douglas Freeman	Ganno Dunn	
Msgr. Frederick Hochwalt	George Edmund Haynes	
Lewis Jones	Alvin S. Johnson	
Horace Kallen	Paul Klapper	
Fred Kelly	George Mintzer	
Murray Lincoln	Walter Rothschild	
T.R. McConnell	George Whipple	

President's Commission	Temporary Commission	Shared Experiences
Earl McGrath	Benjamin Feinberg (*ex officio*)	
Martin R.P. McGuire	Oswald Heck (*ex officio*)	
Agnes Meyer	Lee Mailler (*ex officio*)	
Harry Newburn	Elmer Quinn (*ex officio*)	
Bishop G. Bromley Oxnam	D. Mallory Stephens (*ex officio*)	
F.D. Patterson	Arthur Wicks (*ex officio*)	
Mark Starr	William Wallin (*ex officio*)	
Harold Swift	David Berkowitz (staff)	
Goodrich White	Philip Cowen (staff)	
Rabbi Stephen Wise	Robert Leigh (staff)	
Francis Brown (staff)	John Rodell (staff)	
A.B. Bonds (staff)	E. Franklin Frazier (consultant)	
Newton Edwards (consultant)	Paul Studenski (consultant)	
Fred Kelly (consultant)		
L.D. Haskew (consultant)		
James Allen (consultant)		

Nevertheless, I do not want to overstate the shared membership characteristics, as there are other reasons for similarities between the two reports. For example, I have learned through examination of the sole transcription of any of the Truman Commission meetings that two members, Agnes Meyer and Horace Kallen, were consistently the most fervent in raising the issue of racial equality and the need for the Commission to address that issue. Hence, shared membership does not necessarily suggest the emphasis on racial equality issues. Furthermore, the report of the Truman Commission, *Higher Education for American Democracy*, specifically cites the report of Mayor LaGuardia's Committee on Unity. (An additional impetus for the President's Commission, and cited in its report, is the report of Truman's Committee on Civil Rights, *To Secure These Rights*, a compelling and unbelievably frank statement issued in 1947 on the sad state of affairs in race relations in the United States.) In addition, the Truman Commission report indicated in the second volume, "Equalizing and Expanding Individual Opportunity," that "State legislation which places explicit and uniform obligation upon all institutions of higher learning is currently being urged in New York State, Pennsylvania, Massachusetts, and New Jersey."[5] So, oddly, what is perhaps the most compelling of the themes of the two commissions, deeply rooted in democratic achievements and failures—educational access regardless of, in the terms of the time, race, creed, or color—is a shared goal, rather than simply a direct expression by members of both commissions.

Some of the commission members on the list of shared appointments or experiences do not appear to have been particularly active in the work of the Truman Commission, although there are important exceptions. For example, Ordway Tead was not only a commission member, but also the staff writer for the second volume of the report, "Equalizing and Expanding Individual Opportunity." Furthermore, George Zook made sure that all commission members voted on the proposals for dividing the work of the commission as well as the final report, so while some members dominated one or another aspect of discussion during commission meetings, the decision regarding the language of the report rested with all members. Temporary Commission members did not necessarily vote on various aspects of their report until its final version. Finally, it is clear in the case of both commissions that the staff director made a consistent and concerted effort to keep all members informed.

Both commissions deeply felt the need to increase access regardless of race, creed, or color. And in both cases, I am confident that part of that need derived from another similarity—the understanding that veterans had returned home after years in the trenches and had succeeded in college. This success proved that access ought to be extended. War-hardened and older, veterans pushed both professors and Joe College students academically. This understanding has reached mythical dimensions, as a number of scholars have recently concluded that many of those veterans were college-bound or in college prior to joining a branch of the armed services. Thus, the access provided by the GI Bill may not have been as functionally important as we like to think.[6]

There are two nuances to note distinguishing their discussions of access to higher education. First, the President's Commission went through a debate over the need to create access rapidly, rather than through "gradualism," a term especially popular in the South and resting on assumptions of goodwill, particularly among whites. Those advocating rapid access won the debate, although

---

[5]On Meyer and Kallen, see University Archives, President, John R. Emens, President's Commission on Higher Education-Transcripts of Proceedings, December 10, 1946, Box 4, Folder 123, Ball State University. Higher Education for American Democracy. New York: Harper & Brothers, 1948, Vol 2, 37–38 on the Committee on Unity, 27 on state legislation.

[6]Daniel A. Clark, "'The Two Joes Meet. Joe College, Joe Veteran': The G.I Bill, College Education, and Postwar American Culture," *History of Education Quarterly* 38 (Summer 1998): 165–189. Robert C. Serow, "Policy as Symbol: Title II of the 1944 GI Bill," *The Review of Higher Education* 27 (Summer 2004): 481–499.

the four dissenters wrote a dissent published in the President's Commission report, one of two dissenting statements (despite internal dissension, there were no published dissenting statements for the Temporary Commission report). The Temporary Commission, one might say, stayed the course, although ensuing debate in the state legislature raised a range of objections to a sweeping bill on non-discrimination in higher education.

Second, the issue of access permeates the President's Commission report—in fact, at times, the report has a radical tone, even when read in contemporary terms. Interestingly, the report specifically advises colleges and universities to implement curricular and extracurricular programs to advance understanding of different cultures and races in the United States and internationally, what we would easily, if not automatically, call today, "diversity programming." In contrast, while undergirding the report of the Temporary Commission and clearly providing an impetus for the commission and the report's goals, including in legislation following the Temporary Commission's report, the need for access is not described in the glowing or consistent terms of the President's Commission. Nevertheless, the similarity of the two reports in regard to the need for access is by far the more substantial characteristic.

Veterans brought more than the question of college success into the discussion. They also highlighted enrollment pressures, which raised the issue of institutional arrangements to meet those pressures. And in both commission reports, I think that the most interesting conclusion, and indeed one with different outcomes in each case, is the argument for the community college. It seems absolutely clear that the late 1940s mark a time when the junior college, becoming the community college, was perceived as the means for achieving the access goals expressed in the arguments of national and institutional leaders. They were the primary means for providing some form of access to higher education for large numbers of students. However, the President's Commission not only praised the community college as the place where so many college students (approximately 13 percent, as the remaining 36 percent were likely capable of four years of college) could succeed, but it also offered substantial discussion of the need to organize higher education in systematic form in every state. In fact, the Commission dedicated a seventy-four-page volume of its report to the issue of organizing higher education. The Temporary Commission did not dedicate as many pages to its recommendations, but the political hue and cry over the initial recommendation to create access through locally-supported community colleges, rather than a central four-year institution, resulted in enough paper to far exceed the seventy-four pages of the President's Commission. The result, in the final report of the Temporary Commission and the legislation, was both community colleges and a specific four-year institution. (Curiously, the initial suggestion for that four-year institution was to take over Syracuse University, a suggestion that did not meet with much acclaim in the state legislature, even though Syracuse officials were interested in the proposal.) Hence, both commissions offered praise and support for community colleges, but recognized that college access would require both four- and two-year institutions.

The considerable difference in the amount of discussion about general education is partially accounted for by the different charges to the commissions. President Truman asked his commission to "reexamine our system of higher education in terms of its objectives, methods, and facilities; and in light of the social role it has to play." Clearly then, the President's Commission had reason to expound, as it did, on the importance of general education—and it did so with the understanding that such an education would be instrumental in overcoming totalitarian governments abroad and prejudices within the nation, thereby reinforcing the focus on access and equity. The commission decision to focus on societal needs only reinforced the need for such discussion. Nevertheless, as with the 1945 statement by the Harvard faculty on general education, typically known as the "Harvard Redbook," there was very little impact in terms of the college curriculum and general education.

As for the Temporary Commission, Governor Dewey's charge was equally directive and far more specific; the commission was to investigate whether or not to establish a state university. The charge did not include such broad-reaching questions as the "social role" of the state university. So however much educators love to debate issues of general education, those on the Temporary Commission had a far more specific goal that suggested little about general education.

An even more intriguing aspect of the differences stems from the different politic contexts. After years spent years slogging through discussions about the report of the President's Commission, I have learned that scholars loved to cite the report for over three decades. Yet there was virtually no discussion among U.S. Senators or Congressional representatives. Nor did President Truman propose legislation reflecting the major recommendations of the President's Commission, although he asked the Bureau of the Budget to examine the costs of a federal financial aid program, urged passage of a bill for federal aid to schools in 1948, and asked for the establishment of a Department of Health, Education, and Security, which would have centralized many federal higher education programs in one agency, a recommendation of the President's Commission. (In all fairness to President Truman, he faced a Republican-controlled Congress, the need to re-build Europe, the increasingly threatening Communist nations of the Soviet Union and the People's Republic of China, and an economy suffering from conversion to peacetime production and consumption, as well as a serious housing shortage. Proposing a new federal scholarship program under the cloud of Constitutional uncertainty would have been an unlikely, if not unwise, political choice.)

The considerable debates among educators following the publication of *Higher Education for American Democracy* (such members as Ordway Tead and Oliver Carmichael weighed in on those debates), however, are mere ripples in a pond compared to the lake effect of New York State legislators, state officials, interest groups, and newspaper editorials. There are repeated reports in the *New York Times* regarding the amount and degree of pressure on the Temporary Commission, the legislature, the governor, and members of the state executive branch, which stand in welcome political relief to the relative quiet accorded the report of the President's Commission among politicians and officials at the federal level. Perhaps a sole example suffices here. While there were occasional media reports about the President's Commission, there were no leaks—except perhaps one—regarding the work of the President's Commission. And while it probably helped to have an accomplished journalist (Agnes Meyer) on the commission offering specific advice about working with the newspaper reporters, nevertheless the commission was able to manage its relationship with the press.

This was not so for the Temporary Commission. In fact, there were angry exchanges among commission members about the leaks to the press and in one instance a commission member, John Burton (Governor Dewey's budget director), apparently blind-sided the commission by releasing his own version of the organization of community colleges and the state university, focusing financial support for the community colleges on local, rather than state entities. He shifted his recommendations in later versions and to a degree, his later version of community college financing proved to be the winning one.

Some aspects of the President's Commission discussions and report were grounded in sharp exchanges, as those resulting in the two dissenting statements, one on desegregation and gradualism, and the other on federal support for capital outlays for public higher education. Nevertheless, the overall tone of the commission meetings was deliberative. The tone of the Temporary Commission was at times sharp, if not divisive, although the political bickering led to political compromise. Some members of the Temporary Commission were deeply opposed to local financing of community colleges, but John Burton eventually won a partial compromise on that financing recommendation by agreeing to support the development of two medical centers. The President's Commission also attended to education in the health professions, within however, the broader context of the need of certain occupations for more college-educated personnel (including, for example, teaching and engineering, as well as the health professions). Its recommendations were not for specific medical centers, but rather for the expansion of existing facilities and more effective use of those facilities.

Thus, the two commissions shared many goals, but experienced different political settings. The outcomes were in an immediate sense different, but over the long term, they shared important characteristics.

A. The Outcomes

Scholars have noted that President Truman and Governor Dewey likely recognized the possible competition between their two higher education commissions and records of the Truman Commission indicate that its members were indeed aware of the work of the Dewey Commission. As for any political capital gained in the ensuing presidential campaign, other than both executives' clear support for anti-discrimination efforts if not legislation, there does not appear to be the mark of higher education. Matters such as the economy and fears about Communist influence at home and abroad were more pressing for the candidates and the electorate; if anything, the anti-discrimination issue itself was fractured by the Dixiecrats who walked out of the Democratic Party and ran their own presidential ticket.

What, then, of the specific outcomes? In the case of the Truman Commission, it is difficult to draw a direct line from the Commission's report to specific outcomes. Nevertheless, many scholars have argued that *Higher Education for American Democracy* had a substantial impact on two highly-important characteristics of United States higher education: the community college and federal financial aid. The former argument is difficult to sustain in direct terms because the extraordinary growth of community colleges began in the 1960s (by the late 1960s, state and local governments were establishing community colleges at literally the rate of one per week). Yet it was the President's Commission that popularized the term "community college." Suggestions for that name had already appeared in the 1930s in such publications as the *Journal of Higher Education*. The insistence of many community college leaders that the President's Commission had an impact may well be born out by the actions of state education agencies and elected officials in the 1950s. In regard to federal financial aid, the chronological gap is even longer, as it was not until 1965 that the Higher Education Act became law and authorized federal scholarships based on need, without the limitations that characterized previous federal laws, such as the GI Bill and the 1958 National Defense Education Act. Language again comes into play here, as the President's Commission, the first ever federal commission appointed to solely examine higher education, proposed a massive federal scholarship program for undergraduates, and there is considerable evidence that the proposal engaged policymakers up to the passage of the 1965 Higher Education Act.[7]

As for the Dewey Commission, it had a specific and immediate legislative response. In March 1948, the New York state legislature passed three bills, one

[7] On community colleges, see Vaughan, *The Community College in America*, as an example of the popularization of the term and see *Community College Journal of Research and Practice* 23 (January-February 1999), Special Issue on Focus on America, Part V for discussion of the establishment of community colleges in Midwestern states. On federal financial aid, see Gladieux and Wolanin, *Congress and the Colleges*, as well as Breneman and Finn, *Public Policy and Private Higher Education*. For an assessment of the early engagement of educators and policymakers in response to the Truman Commission Report, see Philo A. Hutcheson, "The 1947 President's Commission on Higher Education and the National Rhetoric on Higher Education Policy," *History of Higher Education Annual* 2002, vol. 22, (2003): 91–107.

to establish the state university, one to establish community colleges, and one prohibiting educational discrimination based on race, religion, creed, color, or national origin (with the proviso that church-related institutions could select on the basis of their faiths). Obviously, the Temporary Commission's report resulted in one of the two largest systems of public higher education in the United States, a system marked both by multiple points of access and substantial research production. Thus, in many important ways, these two commissions, within different contexts and different emphases, came to very similar recommendations. Despite differences in politics and immediate outcomes, in both cases we must credit the two commissions for reinforcing the early post-World War II movement toward mass higher education, a distinct characteristic of United States higher education in comparison to virtually all other nations.

II. Forging SUNY in New York's Political Cauldron

Tod Ottman, SUNY Albany

On April 4, 1948, New York Governor Thomas E. Dewey signed legislation creating the State University of New York (SUNY) and banning discrimination in college admissions.[8] Dewey commented that these bills "bring about now the establishment of a State University system and lay the groundwork for its expansion." His prediction was accurate; by 2009 SUNY has grown to sixty-four campuses serving more than 438,000 students with a budget over $10 billion, making it America's largest comprehensive system of public higher education.[9]

Dewey's action, while commendable, was long overdue in the Empire State's history of higher education. In fact, New York was one of the last in

---

[8]As a result of space limitations, only a shortened set of notes is provided here. For a fuller analysis of SUNY's birth and a complete set of accompanying citations see Chapter 4, "Creating A State University: New York State Higher Education Policy, 1910–1948," in Tod Ottman, "'Government that has both a heart and a head: The Growth of New York State Government During the World War II Era, 1930–1950'" (University at Albany, SUNY, PhD diss., 2001). I would like to thank the following people for their generous support, encouragement, advice and time throughout all phases of this project: Dick Andrees, Peter Eisenstadt, James D. Folts, Richard F. Hamm, Karl S. Kabelac, Bruce Leslie, Kathleen Pakenham, Carl Peterson, Harold S. Wechsler, Dan S. White, and Julian E. Zelizer. Together, they have helped me in countless ways. Moreover I am also thankful to the New York State Archives Partnership Trust for supporting this research with a Larry J. Hackman Research Residency.

[9]"Governor Signs 4 Bills to Set Up State University," *New York Herald Tribune*, April 5, 1948; State of New York, Public Papers of Thomas E. Dewey. Albany, 1948, 229; www.suny.ed/About_suny/fastfacts/index.cfm; www.suny.edu/about_suny/index.cfm.

the country to create a state-wide public university system. Although New York was the nation's most populous and wealthiest state, with New York City as its cultural center, the state's public provision for public higher education was among the most limited in the country. Then World War II's political aftermath pushed New York into a significantly more expansive higher education policy. For over a century, New York's higher education policy had largely consisted of public subsidies to private colleges, a policy which, by the 1930s, no longer met New Yorkers' demand for post-secondary education. But the private colleges within the state fiercely protected the status quo and successfully resisted change until after World War II.

A. The Public Subsidization of the Private Colleges

Before the war, the concept of public higher education in New York State existed in a policy backwater. Few organizations in New York State exhibited any interest in higher education and neither the legislature nor the public at large took much notice. Through the 1920s and 1930s, education in general was barely mentioned in the state Democratic and GOP party platforms and higher education was omitted entirely. With so little public concern, New York's private colleges, represented by the Association of Colleges and Universities of the State of New York (ACUSNY), were the key players in state higher education decision making. Consequently, the interests of the private colleges and the state became so intertwined as to make them indistinguishable. Through the Great Depression, the Board of Regents and the State Education Department (SED) always consulted ACUSNY before making decisions affecting higher education.[10]

Private colleges could exercise such influence in state higher education policy because New York State lacked a public university. Unlike states that had established public universities, beginning with Georgia in 1785, New York relied almost exclusively on private colleges and provided substantial public subsidies to them, beginning with grants to Columbia College in 1787 and continuing in several different forms over the next century and a half. By the eve of World War II, nearly eighty private colleges in the State of New York—including the two "Ivy League" universities of Columbia and Cornell—benefited from public subsidies.[11]

By the Great Depression, New York needed to expand its post-secondary educational opportunities because high school attendance mushroomed from 314,615 students in 1926 to 477,665 in 1933, as the economic depression drove

---

[10]E.R. Van Kleeck to Francis T. Spaulding, August 8, 1946, New York State Archives (NYSA)-B0459, Box 16, File: "Van Kleeck."

[11]Paul Scudiere, "A Historical Survey of State Financial Support of Private Higher Education in New York." University at Albany SUNY, Ed.D. diss., 1975.

many high school graduates with poor employment prospects to continue their schooling. And by the 1930s, employers increasingly demanded workers with specialized skills. Thus, between 1925–26 and 1939–40, New York's college enrollment increased 81 percent, from 107,770 to 195,596.[12]

The demand for post-secondary education, however, was even greater. SED official Harlan H. Horner conducted a survey in 1934, which revealed that each year at least 10,000 high school graduates who desired post-secondary education could not attain it because New York lacked inexpensive alternatives. In 1937, another study found Horner's estimate "too conservative" and raised it to 15,000. Such ominous figures, however, had little policy impact, as ACUSNY members scoffed at Horner's endorsement of junior colleges.[13]

The state did support limited public higher education. It operated eleven tuition-free Normal Schools dedicated to teacher training that enrolled approximately 9,000 students. New York City ran its own colleges, as well; City College of New York (CCNY), founded in 1847, expanded by the late 1930s to four tuition-free college centers with a combined enrollment of well over 50,000 students. But neither system satisfied demand. For example, CCNY, which admitted only city residents and received no state aid, was in such financial straits that by the late 1930s that the college raised admission standards expressly to cut enrollments and contain costs.[14]

Under ACUSNY's influence, New York's higher education policymakers wanted to meet the state's new needs with old solutions. At ACUSNY's annual conference in 1936, Livingston Farrand, the retiring president of Cornell University, called for "extending State scholarships." President Dixon Ryan Fox of Union College seconded Farrand's call, claiming, "It would serve the State well to triple the ... general university scholarships." Two years later, the Regents issued a report that also officially embraced scholarship expansion and argued against "the establishment of any state-wide system of 'junior colleges,' or of a state university." The report urged doubling the number of scholarships from 3,000 to 6,000 and tripling the value of each award from $100 to $300 to fully meet rising college tuition and living expenses, with no mention of the projected annual addition of 10,000 to 15,000 students.[15]

---

[12]The Reminiscences of Harry Gideonse, 1961, Columbia Oral History Project, 118; Temporary Commission on the Need for a State University TCNSU Report, "Trends of College Enrollment," July 1947, p. 3, NYSA-A0614, Box 1, File 31.

[13]Regents Inquiry Staff Report, August 31, 1937, p. 67a, NYSA-A2027, Box 13, File 2; Abbott, Government Policy, 147.

[14]Betsey C. Corby, "The Centralization of Educational Administration in the New York State Normal Schools." University at Buffalo, SUNY, PhD diss., 1993, 95; Gideonse, Reminiscences, 114–115.

[15]"Farrand Urges A Scholarship System in State," New York Herald Tribune, October 29. 1936; Luther Gulick, Education for American Life New York: 1938, 59.

B.   Effects of War: the Veteran Tidal Wave and Ethno-Religious Discrimination

Then, the Second World War unleashed two forces that overwhelmed the status quo. First, the more than 1.5 million veterans who returned to the Empire State in the winter of 1945 and spring of 1946 could now freely attend college through the federal Serviceman's Readjustment Act (the "GI Bill"), and second, the war had produced a greatly heightened sensitivity to ethnic and religious discrimination.

America's tradition of governmental benefits for veterans forced the State of New York to implement a comprehensive higher education policy review. In January 1946, Governor Thomas E. Dewey's annual message to the state legislature outlined a litany of new postwar programs focused on the demands of veterans and New York's conversion to peacetime. Dewey committed the state to an expansive new public housing program, construction of a massive new arterial highway system, and an exploration into the need for a state university.[16]

A few months before Thomas E. Dewey's legislative message, an SED official noted a "tidal wave of veterans" returning back to New York, many seeking a higher education. In December 1945, SED received data from Army separation counselors predicting that perhaps as many as 330,000 of New York's 1.5 million returning veterans would eventually seek post-secondary education within the state. Moreover, it forecast that at least 11,200 veterans would immediately seek a full-time four-year college education. In June 1946, SED drastically revised this estimate upwards to more than 100,000.[17]

Regarding past patterns of discrimination, public revelation in early 1946 of the long-standing "quota system" in the state's private colleges exploded into a public firestorm. Outraged, new political players, including civic, minority, and liberal groups and politicians, thrust themselves into previously-closed higher education policy discussions. These groups, building on the rhetoric of the recent conflict between democracy and fascist racism, boldly advocated much more through-going solutions than those previously contemplated by the state's higher education policymakers.

By a quota system, New York's private historically Protestant colleges had restricted the numbers of Jews, Catholics, Italians, Slavs, and African Americans. This policy was first formally implemented by Columbia University in 1919 to curtail the rising number of Jewish students. Columbia devised new admission criteria that stressed an individual's social characteristics, rather than academic record, as most relevant to selection. Candidates were asked their place of birth, their racial and religious background (including parents'

---

[16]Public Papers of Thomas E. Dewey, 1946. Albany: 1947. 9–32.

[17]Hillis Miller and John S. Allen. *Veterans Challenge the Colleges.* New York: King's Crown Press, 1947. 1, 4–12.

religion), their parents' occupations and birthplaces, and were required to pro-vide a photograph and submit to an interview.[18] Once established at Columbia, the quota system was quickly implemented in most of New York State's other private colleges.

An investigation of admissions policies in 1947 documented that the majority of New York's colleges asked for the applicant's religion, as well as a picture on application forms. Forty-five percent of the schools asked for the maiden name of the applicant's mother, and 41 percent required the birthplace of the applicant's parents. Some required data on the nationality of the appli-cant (twenty percent) and the parent (thirteen percent), the applicant's race (20 percent), and parents' religion (11 percent). Such information was nor-mally sought most by the state's most prestigious colleges. Columbia, Cornell, St. Lawrence, Colgate, and Union all required an applicant's photo and all but one required the mother's maiden name, parents' birthplaces, and applicant's religion. The results of these policies were firm quotas for Jews and almost total exclusion for blacks. Of the above five colleges, in 1946, Cornell, Columbia, and Union kept their Jewish enrollments at between 10 and 15 percent; Col-gate and St. Lawrence kept the proportion under 5 percent. Only about one-half of 1 percent of New York's 1946 college student population was African American.[19]

On January 22, 1946, a front-page article in the *New York Times* publicly revealed the operation of a quota system by colleges within New York City that had been documented by Mayor William O'Dwyer's Committee on Unity. Although the article did not identify the institutions investigated, it quickly became known that the medical schools of both Columbia and Cornell were key perpetrators. As a remedy, the mayor's committee called for the establish-ment of a state university.

Discrimination in higher education would be a central political issue in New York for the next two years. The day after the *Times* story broke, the American Jewish Congress (AJC) and the New York State Teachers Guild called for revoking the tax exemption of higher education institutions that discriminated.[20] New York City Democrats in the state legislature joined the attack. One day after the story appeared, the Democratic state legislative leader of Manhattan, Senator Francis J. Mahoney, a liberal Catholic, and Brooklyn

---

[18]Harold S. Wechsler. *The Qualified Student: A History of Selective College Admission in America*. New York: Wiley, 1977. 155–157.

[19]"Discrepancies in Admission Policies," NYSA-A0614, Box 1, File 23; Survey Data Sheet, NYSA-A3036, Box 2, File: "Application Blank Study;" Survey Data Sheet, NYSA-A3036, Box 3, File: "Jewish Student Census, 1946–1947;" "Distribution of Minority Group Students," NYSA-A0614, Box 1, File 25.

[20]"Bias in Colleges Against City Youth Charged in Report." *New York Times*, January 23, 1946; "Mayor May Crack Down on Quota System in City Schools." PM, February 1, 1946.

Democratic Assembly leader Irwin Steingut, the leading representative of the powerful Brooklyn Jewish voting bloc, submitted bills proposing a bias-free state university. Public pressure within New York City to create a public University for New York State became intense.

Since New York City and its ethnic groups were the electoral linchpin to carrying the state in a presidential election, Thomas E. Dewey moved to satisfy these downstate interests. Therefore, in consultation with GOP leaders, in early February Dewey proposed the creation of a one-year commission to investigate the charges of admissions discrimination and explore the need for a state university.[21] On July 14, 1946, Governor Dewey released the names of his thirty appointees to the Temporary Commission on the Need for a State University, popularly known as the "Young Commission."

Political considerations were central to Dewey's selections, which represented key downstate Jewish, Catholic, and Black interests, as well as the Democrats and the private colleges. For the first time, interests outside New York's closed circle of traditional educational policymakers of ACUSNY and the Regents had key roles in higher education policymaking. To chair his commission, Dewey chose Owen D. Young, longtime chairman of the General Electric Corporation, a prominent state and national Democrat, and as a longstanding member of the Board of Regents (1934–45), a force in New York State educational policy. Other members included: Joseph Carlino, a New York City attorney and prominent figure in the state's Italian community; Alvin S. Johnson, the retired president and co-founder of the New School; George Mintzer, chief counsel to the American Jewish Committee; Father Robert Gannon, Fordham University President and the current head of ACUSNY; and five state politicians, including Steingut.[22]

Coming on the heels of a war seen as a struggle against racism and ethnic and religious repression, some liberals drew pointed parallels between the policies of the recently vanquished Third Reich and the admissions practices of New York's colleges. Max Lerner, a leading political columnist and lifelong critic of discrimination, attacked New York's private colleges for judging applicants on "the principles of Hitler's racist state." He embraced the idea of a public university in New York that would "create islands of refuge from the Nazi racism in our privately endowed colleges."[23]

---

[21]"Dewey Urges Year Study of State University." *New York Herald Tribune*, February 5, 1946.

[22]"Owen D. Young is Appointed to Head University Survey." *New York Times*, July 14, 1946; Untitled Lists, University of Rochester, Thomas E. Dewey Papers (UR-TEDP), Series 10, Box 30, File 10.

[23]"Racism at the Grassroots," PM, January 24, 1946; "The Classroom is Ours," PM, January 31, 1946.

Others drew similar connections. Alvin Johnson, after successfully championing New York State's 1945 Ives-Quinn anti-discrimination employment law, moved on to discrimination in education. While he was serving on the Young Commission, Johnson helped found the New York State Committee Against Discrimination in Education (NYSCADE) in the fall of 1946 to fight the quota system. Johnson dramatically stated, "I know that ninety percent of the people of the State are ashamed of the fact that New York stands out as the great leader of discrimination, the great Hitler State of America."[24]

Politicians also linked New York's colleges to Nazism. Former Governor Herbert Lehman, the nation's leading Jewish political figure, running for the US Senate in the fall of 1946, charged that "a menacing and inexcusable departure has been made from American democratic tradition, and one of the worst features of European culture has foisted itself upon the American educational system."[25]

Between 1946 and 1948, the issue of ethnic discrimination dominated the discussions of a state university. A later study by the American Jewish Committee concluded that the immediate postwar years (1946–50) were a defining period in the permanent diminution of anti-Semitism in America. Following the destruction of Hitler's legions, hatred toward Jews was no longer acceptable in the nation, especially in New York State. This postwar change inevitably led to the elimination of the quota system and it ultimately transformed New York's system of higher education.[26]

C. Democratic Cohesiveness and Presidential Politics

While the war advanced greater toleration toward Jews, the Empire State's ethno-religious groups sharply disagreed over the direction of higher education, leading to serious tension within New York's Democratic Party, as Jews and Catholics, two of the New Deal coalition's core constituencies, often came to loggerheads over the state's higher education policy. As long as Democrats failed to agree on the future direction of higher education policy, Governor Dewey and the Republicans could remain aloof. Thus, there was little progress in 1947. But in early 1948, Dewey backed a major policy innovation. Gearing up for his second run for the White House, he needed to woo downstate ethnic

---

[24]Alvin S. Johnson to Thomas E. Dewey, September 24, 1946, UR-TEDP, Series 4, Box 90, Folder 14.

[25]"Speech at NYSCADE," September 23, 1946, Columbia University, Herbert H. Lehman Papers, Speech File 1946–1949, Drawer 243.

[26]Charles Herbert Stember, et. al. *Jews in the Mind of America*. New York: Basic Books, 1966. 121–122, 128, 131.

votes. Thus, the Republican Governor backed a major expansion in New York's provision for public higher education.

The Young Commission had moved slowly, not completely staffing its research team until January 1947, just a month before the Commission's one-year tenure was to expire. With Dewey's support, the legislature extended the Commission's life for another year. In the spring of 1947, it began to formulate policy recommendations on improving access to higher Education.[27]

In contrast to the Young Commission's glacial pace, the Jewish community's effort to enact legislation to ban discrimination in the colleges was moving forward rapidly. By mid-1946, Alvin Johnson's NYSCADE was working to raise public awareness of the quota system. Prominent Jewish New Yorkers joined NYSCADE, including former Governor Lehman, Stephen S. Wise of the AJC, and Assistant Secretary of Defense Anna M. Rosenberg, as well as other nationally-known figures, such as Franklin D. Roosevelt Jr. Besides providing key organizational support, the AJC funded NYSCADE's campaign to ban the quota system. Johnson and the AJC worked closely to draft a bill that would "liberate," in the words of Johnson, "our [educational] institutions from the Hitlerite influence," a rhetorical flourish that was often repeated.[28]

In January 1947, Assemblyman Bernard Austin (D-Brooklyn) and Senator Walter J. Mahoney, a Catholic, (R-Buffalo) introduced NYSCADE's bill, soon dubbed "Austin-Mahoney" into both legislative houses.[29] To build public support for Austin-Mahoney, the AJC and NYSCADE sponsored rallies in February and the first week of March 1947. In response to AJC publicity efforts, Assembly Speaker Oswald D. Heck (R-Schenectady) predicted that Austin-Mahoney stood "a good chance for passage."[30]

Attempts by New York State's Jewish community to enact Austin-Mahoney, however, drew a pointed response from the Archdiocese of New York. This split between Catholics and Jews over educational policy was just one more incident in the complex, even tempestuous, relationship between these

---

[27]"University Survey to Go On," *New York Times*, February 15, 1947.

[28]Address by Dr. Alvin Johnson, February 11, 1947, YU-ASJP, Box 12, File 203.

[29]Alvin S. Johnson to Alexander Pekelis, May 27, 1946, Yale University, Alvin S. Johnson Papers (YU-ASJP), Box 5, File 95; Alvin S. Johnson to Will Maslow, December 11, 1946, University of Nebraska at Lincoln, Alvin S. Johnson Papers (UNL-ASJP), Box 20, File 3; Copy of "Austin-Mahoney" bill, University at Albany, SUNY, Association of Colleges and Universities of the State of New York Papers, Series 5, Box 2, File: "Education Practices Bill 1947."

[30]"State Law to Ban College Bias Seen." *New York Times*, February 26, 1947.

groups during this period within the New York State Democratic organization.[31]

The Catholic Archdiocese asked legislators to defeat Austin-Mahoney, arguing that the proposed legislation gave the state, not the parent, responsibility for education, which contradicted Catholic doctrine. In the words of the Archdiocese, Austin-Mahoney was "un-American" and contained "passages that infringe on the fundamental rights of parents." Moreover, the Church stated that Austin-Mahoney would "seriously affect the freedom of all educational institutions in the State."[32]

Despite Archdiocesean opposition, the AJC and Alvin Johnson pushed forward. NYSCADE dubbed the first week of March "Austin-Mahoney Week" by collecting signatures, passing out handbills, and holding rallies in Manhattan's Garment District, replete with loudspeakers and sound trucks. Then on March 1, 3, and 4, NYSCADE, the AJC, and the Jewish War Veterans, staged three all day sit-ins in the state Capitol in Albany, demanding Austin-Mahoney's passage.[33]

The Archdiocese responded on March 2 by stepping up its attack, blasting Austin-Mahoney as a "communistic" bill that "will permit future encroachments on the parental function of education."[34] The Archdiocese's opposition to Austin-Mahoney was also grounded in a concern that the legislation would affect the traditional Catholic colleges' openly preferential treatment to Catholics.

With such strong opposition from the Archdiocese, Austin-Mahoney was not passed and negotiations between the contending parties continued. The Catholic Church in New York politics was, in the words of Warren Moscow, the *New York Times'* political reporter in Albany, a lobby of such "great influence" that it could "effectively veto legislation it believes detrimental" to its interests. Thus, on March 4, as more than 400 AJC and NYSCADE protestors were holding their last state capitol sit-in, Senator Mahoney, the co-sponsor of Austin-Mahoney, withdrew his support from the bill, noting the Archdiocese's opposition.[35]

In the summer of 1947, the commission's researchers, who uncovered widespread and discriminatory practices, presented their findings to the

---

[31]Ralph Papaleo, "The Democratic Party in Urban Politics in New York State, 1933–1938." St. John's University, PhD diss., 1978.

[32]"State Catholics Oppose Bill on Education Bias." *New York Herald Tribune*, February 27, 1947.

[33]"Capitol Marchers Back Bias Bill." *New York Sun*, March 3, 1947.

[34] "Gives Catholic Stand on Bill." *New York Sun*, March 3, 1947.

[35]Warren Moscow, *Politics in the Empire State.* New York: Knopf, 1948, 45–46, 201; Statement of Walter Mahoney, March 4, 1947, NYSA-A3036, Box 2, File: "Public Opinion Clippings."

Commission. Although Jews applied at twice the rate of non-Jews to colleges within the state, Commission researchers found that Jews were rejected five times more frequently. In particular, New York City Jews were rejected nine times more often.[36]

And for all groups, access to higher education promised to get worse. From 1900 to 1940, New York college enrollment, according to Commission findings, increased by a factor of seven to 196,000, and by 1946 had reached 269,000 students. Yet by New York colleges' own estimates, for 1946, their physical capacity was only 172,800 students. Therefore the colleges were already exceeding their maximum capacity by an astounding 64 percent, or 96,200 students. Even worse, the Commission projected that college enrollment in New York would spiral by 1960 to 360,000, more than double the colleges' capacity.[37]

These worrisome figures, however, did not initially sway the commission. Its private college faction opposed any anti-discrimination measure because they thought that without restrictions on Jewish enrollment, the state's private colleges would be "flooded" with Jewish students. Moreover, they saw the establishment of a state university as a direct economic threat, increasing competition and threatening the existing public subsidies. They used their role on the commission to prevent such measures, measures that they viewed as being pushed by Jewish agitators. Father Gannon, for example, had earlier written (during the political fallout following the *Times* article that led to Dewey creating the Young Commission), "Our stand is-appoint a committee, see that it has intelligent members and depend on the eloquence of the situation to prevent the creation of this absurdly expensive Jewish university."[38]

The political situation outside the Young Commission, moreover, was equally bleak. By spring of 1947, Governor Dewey had also turned against building a state university campus. When Dewey appointed the commission, he privately made it clear to key members that he fully supported an anti-discrimination measure banning the quota system, a position he maintained throughout the period, but a state university was another matter. When Dewey learned in the spring of 1947 that the commission estimated it would cost $100 million to construct a single site state university, he responded that building such a campus "was thinking in terms which were too large."[39]

---

[36]TCNSU Meeting Minutes, August 26, 1947, p. 78–80, NYSA-A0614, Box 30, File 60.

[37]"Trends of College Enrollment in New York State," NYSA-A0614, Box 1, File 31.

[38]Alvin S. Johnson to Robert Walrmsley, February 6, 1948, YU-ASJP, Box 7, File 122; Robert I. Gannon to William F. Cahill, January 28, 1946, Fordham University, Robert I. Gannon Papers, Box 3, File 26.

[39]Alvin S. Johnson to Thomas E. Dewey, September 19, 1946, YU-ASJP, Box 2, File 31; Oliver Cromwell Carmichael, *New York Establishes A State University: A Case Study in the Processes of Policy Formation.* Nashville: Vanderbilt University Press 1955, 115–116.

Hence, the Young Commission's initial policy recommendations, fitting the governor's wishes, were very modest. In August 1947, the commission proposed the creation of a "state university system" rather than a more costly single-campus university. This "system" was to consist of two-year community colleges spread throughout New York, with the state funding initial construction and with annual operating expenses split evenly between the localities and Albany. One public medical and dental school was also proposed.

Dewey, however, even saw this proposal as too expensive, and at a commission meeting in September, his budget director, John E. Burton, severely criticized the fiscal extravagance of its recommendations as a "raid upon the Treasury to break the state budget." To cut costs, Burton rejected out of hand the need for a state medical school. Moreover, Burton refused to accept state responsibility in paying for community colleges; for the budget director, all costs, both initial construction and later operational expenses, were to be borne on the local level.[40]

On the quota system, however, a breakthrough was achieved. Following Austin-Mahoney's initial defeat in March, the AJC and NYSCADE immediately redrafted the bill for legislative resubmission. To win Archdiocese support, religious institutions were now exempted from this new bill, which reduced Catholic opposition. This was followed by another event of equal significance, which assured Austin-Mahoney's passage. In the fall of 1947, commission chairman Young decided to back legislation outlawing the quota system. He pressed for a resolution of this matter in early October, when he boldly appointed a subcommittee consisting of commission members Gannon and George Mintzer of the AJC to work out a compromise. Mintzer admitted that "[a]t first glance this looked like a hopeless task." But under pressure from Young, and after a "good deal of horse trading," in Gannon's words, a compromise was reached and then approved by a unanimous commission vote in late October. With this new anti-discrimination measure, the quota issue was effectively resolved.[41]

On the larger issue of creating a state university, if the events through most of 1947 pushed the Young Commission toward modest policy proposals, presidential politics soon pushed in the opposite direction. In December 1947, President Harry S. Truman's Commission on Higher Education released a report recommending a massive new federal aid package to the nation's colleges, calling upon the federal government to expend $135 million (a figure to

[40]TCNSU Staff Memo, August 27, 1947, NYSA-A3036, Box 4, File: "Edmund E. Day 2;" Carmichael, 137–138.

[41]Theodore Leskes to Alvin S. Johnson, August 15, 1947, UNL-ASJP, Box 20, File 3; George J. Mintzer to Thomas E. Dewey, November 5, 1947, UR-TEDP, Series 5, Box 125, File 2; Edmund E. Day to Owen D. Young, November 28, 1947, Colgate University, Everett Needham Case Papers, Box 17, File: "Discrimination 1947–1948."

rise to $1 billion by 1960) annually for 300,000 scholarships. In comparison, the Young Commission's plans suddenly looked woefully inadequate.[42]

These recommendations profoundly affected discussions in New York. Two weeks after the Truman Commission's report, in a confidential memo to the Young Commission, budget director Burton endorsed a set of higher education proposals completely at variance with the Administration's former position. The Administration now called for a large, single-site public university and also backed a public medical school. The expenses of establishing both institutions, moreover, were to be fully borne by Albany. Finally, in a retreat from the Administration's position that the state should not contribute funds for community colleges, the budget director pledged New York to pay 50 percent of the costs to construct a large county-based community college system. Once built, Burton promised that Albany would cover one third of the colleges' annual operating expenses. He may have indeed viewed the original Young Commission plan as a "raid upon the Treasury," but the Administration's new plan stood at a whopping $156 million.[43]

Throughout his political career, Dewey had persistently wooed Jewish voters. His December plan for a state university was in tune with Jewish voters' desires. Considering that the governor had to carry the city if he hoped to win the state in his upcoming presidential campaign, New York City Jews—particularly Brooklyn's one million strong Jewish voting bloc—had to be satisfied. In the past, the governor had criticized presidents Franklin Roosevelt's and then Harry Truman's foreign policies toward Palestine and promised to do more for European-Jewish refugees. He had been the first presidential candidate to promise a Jewish homeland in Palestine and in his 1946 gubernatorial reelection, he made strong pro-Zionist statements. In 1948, he attacked President Truman's support of the United Nation's plan to place Israel in a federal union with Transjordan, forcing Truman to distance himself from the proposal.[44]

No explicit evidence has been found tying the Dewey Administration's policy reversal on higher education to attract Jewish voters. Yet considering the timing of the governor's proposals and his reversal following the release of the Truman Commission's reports, the conclusion seems likely that political considerations were central to his calculations. Contemporary observers thought so, as well. Edward Saveth of the AJC characterized the "gangbuster's" turnabout this way: "If in 1948 in the national political arena, Dewey were to

---

[42]"Scholarship Plan, $135,000,000 Cost, Urged for Nation." *New York Times*, December 22, 1947.

[43]John E. Burton to TCNSU Members, December 31, 1947, NYSA-A3036, Box 4, File: Untitled.

[44]Robert Silverberg. *If I Forget Thee O'Jerusalem: American Jews and the State of Israel*. New York: Morrow, 1970. 246–248, 264, 314, 318, 436–439.

cross swords with Truman on the issue of education, it [was] important that he have a lance of stronger material than the report that the [Young] Commission provided."[45]

Following the governor's presentation of his December plan, the various interests on the Young Commission spent the two weeks before the last meeting of January 12, 1948, jockeying for position. Dewey's confidential plan had been leaked to the *New York Times*. Yet once public, Dewey's plan did not satisfy Democrats. On January 10, commission member and Assembly Minority Leader Stanley Steingut publicly called for two more public medical schools, as well as three separate dental schools, and four schools of nursing, in addition to the governor's recommendations. With the Democrats and the GOP now in a race to outdo each other, New York State's private colleges were in a very uncomfortable position.[46]

Young Commission members Edmund Day and Father Gannon were willing to acquiesce on one public medical school, but the private colleges would not accept the establishment of a large public university (which both political parties now endorsed). At the commission's final meeting on January 12, Day and Gannon made this unambiguously clear. As the Cornell president put it, "I realize the time has come when there is a high premium on compromise," but on creating a "monolithic [state] university ... I'm not ready to compromise on that particular point." Echoing President Day, Gannon told the commission that ACUSNY also completely opposed a state university. Fearing a complete collapse in negotiations and desiring to issue a unanimous report, Owen D. Young implored commission members to compromise. Therefore, bowing to Gannon and Day, the commission only recommended a community college system. In return, however, Day and Gannon agreed that a final determination on a large single-site state university would be made later by the new community colleges' trustee board. Moreover, Gannon and Day also accepted two public medical schools and endorsed the anti-discrimination measure drafted the previous October. Having laboriously achieved unanimity, the Young Commission transmitted its recommendations to Governor Dewey in early February 1948, concluding its tortuous life.[47]

On March 5, 1948, three separate bills embodying many of the Young Commission's recommendations were drafted by the governor's office and were introduced into the legislature under bipartisan sponsorship. The first

---

[45]Carmichael, 166.

[46]"Higher Education System in State Called Inadequate." *New York Times*, January 2, 1948; "Democrats Offer University Plan," New York Times, January 11, 1948.

[47]TCNSU Meeting Minutes, January 12, 1948, p. 12, 13, NYSA-A0614, Box 3, File 68; "University Plan Given to Dewey; Adds $125 Million to State Plant," *New York Herald Tribune*, February 17, 1948.

two bills established SUNY and its community college system; the last bill was a fair educational practices measure. Yet following legislative submission, Dewey's proposals encountered fierce resistance from ACUSNY and the New York State Board of Regents. The private colleges and the Regents publicly attacked the governor's measures because Dewey drafted the bills empowering himself to make all appointments to the new SUNY Board of Trustees, going far beyond the commission's recommendations. With sole appointment power, Dewey appointees would decide whether to create a large, single-site state university. In time, the measures would end the Regents' and ACUSNY's domination over higher education policy, a supremacy the two groups had enjoyed since 1904.[48]

Despite their objections, there was little ACUSNY and the Regents could do. Strong public feeling backed SUNY's creation, and both the governor and the Democratic and GOP legislative leadership were out to satisfy these public sentiments, rather than the vested interests of the private colleges. In a joint statement released on March 9, Democratic and GOP leaders dismissed the Regents' criticism of the governor's bills, stating, "the people of our State want a State University and a State University system now. After two years of debate, the time has come for action." Opposed by both the governor and the legislative leaders, the Regents' position was hopeless. Consequently, on March 10, all three measures passed the Senate, each by a vote of 53 to 1. Two days later they also cleared the Assembly. On April 4, 1948, Dewey signed the legislation, establishing SUNY and banning discrimination in higher education.[49]

Admittedly, the SUNY created in 1948 was quite modest. In the face of determined ACUSNY resistance, the Young Commission failed to create a large single-site public university, and Dewey and the SUNY Board of Trustees exhibited little desire for expansion. When Dewey left the governor's office in 1954, SUNY had a modest annual budget of $43 million. But in the next decade, under the executive stewardship of liberal Republican Nelson Rockefeller (1959–71), SUNY would grow into America's largest comprehensive public university system. When Rockefeller left office in 1971, SUNY's annual budget had grown to an immense $1.1 billion. The base upon which

---

[48]"State University, Anti-Bias School Law Go to Legislature with Dewey Support," *Knickerbocker News* (Albany), March 5, 1948; Owen D. Young to Thomas E. Dewey, March 10, 1948, UR-TEDP, Series 5, Box 289, File 4; William J. Wallin to Thomas E. Dewey and Legislative Leaders, March 8, 1948, NYSA-15080-78, Box 18, File: "State University Bill—Letters."

[49]Thomas E. Dewey to Frank E. Gannett, March 22, 1948, UR-TEDP, Series 10, Box 18, File 14; "Statement By Senator Feinberg, Speaker Heck, Senator Quinn, Assemblyman Steingut," March 9, 1948, NYSA-15080-78, Box 16, File: "State University;" "Governor Signs 4 Bills to Set Up State University," *New York Herald Tribune*, April 5, 1948.

Rockefeller built his "proudest achievement" was established as a consequence of both the aftermath of World War II and electoral politics.[50]

D. Conclusion

Since the late eighteenth century, higher education policy in the Empire State had consisted of generous public subsidies to the state's private colleges. By the 1930s, however, this approach no longer adequately provided post-secondary education. The cultural and ideological changes resulting from the Second World War brought higher education into the public limelight and successfully challenged the private colleges' dominance, permanently reshaping higher education in New York. The Board of Regents, SED, and ACUSNY were unable to stem the tide. In the end, even the Young Commission proved irrelevant as presidential politics determined the ultimate outcome.

III. The Temporary Commission Surveys Bias in Admissions

Harold S. Wechsler, New York University

On March 12, 1948, the New York state legislature passed three major laws intended to increase access to higher education in the state; two of these laws created SUNY and authorized localities to open state-aided community colleges. The third—the Fair Educational Practices Act (FEPA)—attempted to remedy racial and ethnic discrimination in the admissions policies practiced by at least some of New York's private colleges and universities since World War I. The fate of European Jews in World War II, the state politics of race relations, and growing evidence of admissions discrimination prompted a coalition of minority groups, led by the AJC, to demand an end to racial and ethnic bias. FEPA (also known as the Quinn-Olliffe law) was New York State's response.

Contemporaries viewed FEPA as an essential complement to the SUNY and community college laws. Racial, religious, and ethnic discrimination by private colleges, charged minority group representatives, necessitated a non-discriminatory state university. But absent an anti-discrimination law, they continued, providing a public alternative would allow private institutions to maintain, even strengthen, racial and religious barriers.

This essay focuses on the research supporting the Quinn-Olliffe law. The Temporary Commission on the Need for a State University, which proposed the three laws, commissioned research on the use of racial and religious criteria

---

[50]Peter D. McClelland and Alan L. Magdovitz. *Crisis in the Making: The Political Economy of New York Since 1945*. Cambridge: Cambridge University Press, 1981. 164–165.

in determining admission to the private colleges. David S. Berkowitz, author of the key study, gained unprecedented access to statistics compiled by these colleges.[51] Placed on the defensive by the evidence of discrimination that he uncovered, New York's private colleges shifted from outright opposition to acceptance of both anti-discrimination legislation and the inevitability of a public university.

Accusations that the state's private colleges employed quotas or other discriminatory barriers against black, Catholic, and Jewish applicants had circulated since the early 1920s. Eyebrows were raised after World War I when Columbia University, with its rapidly-growing Jewish undergraduate contingent, adopted a selective admissions policy. Applicants filled out an eight-page application asking for race, religion, mother's maiden name, and a photograph. They also were interviewed and took a "psychological exam"—the parent of the SATs.[52] Columbia used the information from this admissions procedure to identify African Americans, Italian Americans, and Jews, and to limit their presence in its undergraduate college and medical school.

Concern about the use of invidious admissions criteria increased in 1922 when Harvard President Abbott Lawrence Lowell proposed to limit the proportion of Jews admitted to the freshman class. The ensuing firestorm ended only when a faculty committee rejected the proposal.[53] Harvard officials, having learned the price of candor, covertly implemented a quota in 1926.

So did private colleges in New York State. Syracuse University, for example, worked throughout the 1930s to assure "the steady and persistent reduction in the percentage of Jewish students in the University." "The present percentage is 12%," the admissions director wrote in 1932. "There have been very numerous complaints brought to me by students and members of the staff that this percentage is far too great for the best interests of the University. I feel that next year the percentage should be brought below 10% and in five years should be brought to a total of 5% and never to exceed it in the future. This would be

---

[51]This essay is adopted from a speech delivered at the SUNY 60th Anniversary Scholarly Conference. Thanks to John Clark, Lynn D. Gordon, Sanford Levine, and W. Bruce Leslie for their comments on an earlier draft. David S. Berkowitz, with Supplementary Studies by E. Franklin Frazier and Robert D. Leigh, *Inequality of Opportunity in Higher Education: A Study of Minority Group and Related Barriers to College Admission*, Legislative Document 1948, No. 33. Albany, NY: Williams Press, Inc., 1948.

[52]Harold S. Wechsler, *The Qualified Student: A History of Selective College Admission in America: 1870–1970*. New York: Wiley-Interscience, 1977. Chapter 7.

[53]Marcia G. Synnott. *The Half-Opened Door: Discrimination and Admissions at Harvard, Yale, and Princeton, 1900–1970*. Westport, CT: Greenwood Press, 1979, and Jerome Karabel. *The Chosen: The Hidden History of Admission and Exclusion at Harvard, Yale, and Princeton*. Boston: Houghton Mifflin Harcourt, 2005.

one of our strongest factors in securing the type of student which we desire."[54] Having no access to these archives, contemporaries had to find another way to translate suspicions into evidence. The Temporary Commission on the Need for a State University provided an opportunity to investigate the use of invidious admissions criteria by New York's private colleges and universities.

The arguments for and against opening a state university and passing a fair education practices act were inter-related. After World War II, private colleges claimed to have room for most returning GIs. But, responded the AJC and its allies, a private college might deny admission to a Jewish, black, or Italian applicant based on race or ethnicity, even if it had room. Opposition to expanding public higher education weakened as citizens became aware of admissions policies that discriminated against racial and religious minorities. The problem was not only that colleges discriminated, but also that they denied having such policies, and that the New York State Board of Regents—known historically for its strong support of private higher education—failed to enforce equal treatment of all applicants and that the state's public higher education sector was underdeveloped.[55]

As early as mid-1945, local student groups initiated anti-discrimination efforts on many campuses; the nascent National Students Association, and some faculty and institutional groups soon picked up the ball.[56] So did President Harry S. Truman, whose Commission on Higher Education devoted a volume of its report to denouncing racial and ethnic quotas and suggesting ways of overcoming such barriers to college attendance.[57]

The political campaign to end admissions discrimination in New York State's private colleges began in the summer of 1945. AJC assembled a coalition of minority defense groups, initiating a multi-pronged approach by suing the New York City Tax Commission. The commission, AJC charged, granted Columbia University a tax exemption, yet the university, they alleged, denied the use of its facilities to otherwise qualified applicants because of race, color, or

---

[54]Frank N. Bryant to Charles Wesley Flint, November 14, 1932, Records of the Chancellor's Office: Chancellors Flint and Graham, 1922–1942, Syracuse University Archives, RG 1, Box 1, "A-Al to Admissions" "Admissions, 1931–33" file.

[55]A 1939 report commissioned by the Regents stated, "New York is adequately supplied with private colleges, universities and public and private professional schools though it does not have a state university." The report recommended that 'no additional state funds should be spent this generation to set up new colleges or independent professional schools." *Regents' Inquiry into the Character and Cost of Public Education in the State of New York*, Luther H. Gulick, director, *Education for American Life: A New Program for the State of New York*. New York: McGraw-Hill, 1938. 59.

[56]Eugene G. Schwartz. *American Students Organize: Founding the National Student Association After World War II: An Anthology and Sourcebook*. Westport, CT: Praeger, 2006.

[57]President's Commission on Higher Education. *Higher Education for American Democracy*, vol. 2. Washington, DC: Government Printing Office, 1947.

religion, an action forbidden to tax-exempt educational corporations.[58] The suit failed. The proper remedy, said the court, assuming the plaintiff could demonstrate discrimination, was to admit the aggrieved students, not to remove the tax exemption. But AJC, not expecting to win the suit, had received the desired publicity.[59]

In 1946, the New York City Mayor's Committee on Unity, established as a response to the Harlem race riots of 1943, conducted public hearings on admissions discrimination by the city's private colleges. These hearings embarrassed several ill-prepared deans, who lost their memories when confronted with evidence of discriminatory admissions practices. The committee's report heightened demands for greater unbiased access to private medical and liberal arts education, and expanded public higher education opportunities.[60]

Not trusting public exposure, humiliation, and promises by the private colleges to do better, the AJC and its allies turned to the New York state legislature. Bipartisan anti-discrimination legislation, introduced by Democratic Assemblyman Bernard Austin, a Jew, and Republican Senator Walter J. Mahoney, a Catholic, in 1946 and 1947, received as much or even more attention than the deliberations over the state university. Trainloads of Austin-Mahoney supporters went to Albany in February and March 1947. Momentum for passage increased until New York City Coadjutor Archbishop James Francis McIntyre publicly denounced the bill as "after a Communistic pattern" because he believed state regulation of private colleges could jeopardize the independence of Catholic higher education in the state.[61] Now, unwilling to risk a vote, the sponsors withdrew their bills, pending the recommendations of the Temporary Commission. By themselves, the state's private colleges and universities—represented by ACUSNY—might not have resisted the momentum, since competition for students had weakened their ability to collaborate. "The Catholics saved us," said Columbia's Acting President Frank D. Fackenthal.

---

[58]The 1754 Kings College (later Columbia) charter prohibited the Anglican college authorities from excluding "any person of any religious denomination whatever from equal liberty and advantage of education, or from any of the degrees, liberties, privileges, benefits, or immunities of the said college, on account of his particular tenets in matters of religion." John B. Pine, comp., *Columbia College—Charters, Acts and Official Documents*. New York: Columbia College, 1895. 10–24; David C. Humphrey, *From Kings College to Columbia: 1746–1800*. New York: Columbia University Press, 1976. 48, 69.

[59]Goldstein v. Mills et al. (Trustees of Columbia University in the City of New York), Supreme Court, September, 1945, 185 Misc. 851, 57 NYS (2nd) 810, affirmed 62 NYS 2d 619 (1946). Reprinted in Oliver Carmichael Jr. *New York Establishes a State University*. Nashville, TN: Vanderbilt University Press, 1955.

[60]New York City, "Mayor's Committee on Unity Report on Inequality of Opportunity in Higher Education." New York: City of New York, 1946.

[61]"Archbishop Scores Anti-Bias Measure; McIntyre Says Church Finds the Austin-Mahoney Bill Communistic in Pattern." *New York Times.* March 3, 1947, 3.

AJC and its allies believed they could strengthen their argument for a public university—while also reducing barriers to private colleges—by demonstrating that private colleges practiced admissions discrimination. Anecdotal and fragmentary evidence would not suffice. But the professional research staff hired by the Temporary Commission found a way to obtain the needed data. Floyd Reeves, a professor of higher education at the University of Chicago, directed the staff. Well-known and respected by all parties, Reeves had consulted on the 1938 Regents Inquiry into the Character and Cost of Public Education in New York and had coauthored the inquiry's study of adult education. In his new role, he commissioned several studies of higher education in New York State, including three on minority student access.[62]

An agreement among Reeves, ACUSNY, and the Temporary Commission to survey the admissions patterns of the association's members resulted in *Inequality of Opportunity in Higher Education*, the key report. Concerned that the commission might conduct a more intrusive inquiry—or that it might rely upon data compiled by the minority defense groups[63]—ACUSNY offered to collaborate as long the commission guaranteed institutional anonymity when reporting results.[64] Reeves commissioned Berkowitz, a historian at Emerson College in Boston, to conduct the study. Berkowitz personally coded the questionnaires after removing all identifying marks. He and Cornell President Edmund Ezra Day, representing the association, possessed the only keys to institutional identities.

---

[62]The studies included Floyd W. Reeves, Algo D. Henderson, and Philip A. Cowan. "Matching Needs and Facilities in Higher Education," Legislative Document 1948, No. 31 (Albany, NY: Williams Press, Inc., 1948); Paul Studenski, assisted by Edith T. Baikie. "Costs and Planning of Higher Education." Legislative Document 1948, No. 34 (Albany, NY: Williams Press, Inc., 1948); George St. J. Perrott, John T. O'Rourke, Lucy Petry, and E. Richard Weinerman, Education for the Health Services, Legislative Document 1948, No. 32 (Albany, NY: Williams Press, Inc., 1948). Such studies were not unprecedented, though critics found the treatment of higher education in the multi-volume Regents Inquiry (1938) inadequate. The Rapp-Coudert Commission report, known mainly for its inquiry into radical activity on the campuses of the municipal colleges, included statistical data on their academic and financial status. *University of the State of New York, Regents' Inquiry into the Character and Cost of Public Education in the State of New York* (New York: McGraw-Hill, 1938), and New York (State) Legislature, Joint Committee on the State Education System, Report of the New York City Sub-Committee of the Joint Legislative Committee on the State Education System, transmitted to the Legislature March 17, 1944, Legislative Document 1944, no. 60 (Albany, NY: Williams Press, Inc., 1944).

[63]See, for example, Edwin J. Lukas and Arnold Foster. *Study of Discrimination at Colleges of New York State.* New York: American Jewish Committee and Anti-Defamation League of B'nai B'rith, 1950.

[64]"This plan protected the large institutions and made identification of the small ones more difficult." Edmund E. Day, "Final Report of the Committee on Cooperation with the Temporary Commission on the Need for a State University," David E. Berkowitz Papers, Series A3036, New York State Education Department Library.

Published in summer 1948, *Inequality of Opportunity in Higher Education* became the largest study of minority group barriers to that point. But Berkowitz had circulated the key results of his study in mid-1947, in time to influence the deliberations of the Temporary Commission. Seven of the 206 responding units, he noted, admitted racial discrimination; eighteen units exercised religious preference.[65] "Among the nonsectarian schools," Berkowitz wrote, "two liberal arts colleges reported restrictions on Jews, Catholics, and Protestants, and one a limitation on Negroes. One nonsectarian junior college reported a limitation on Jews and one stated that limitations on Negroes 'may be considered in the future.' One each of nonsectarian schools of business administration, physical education, and home economics reported limitations on Jews, Catholics, and Protestants."[66]

Evidence of discrimination went beyond self-reports. Berkowitz employed an "index of bias in selection" to assess the admissions practices of fourteen upstate colleges. Colleges close to New York City received the bulk of applications from Jewish students, so the index measured the ratio of applications to acceptances. The published tables replaced the names of the surveyed colleges with letters to assure institutional anonymity.

Fortunately for historians, Berkowitz left his copy of the key among the documents now housed in the New York State archives.[67] That's how we know that Hofstra—a Long Island commuter college—alone among the 14 sampled units, accepted a larger proportion of Jewish than Gentile applicants.[68] Acceptance rates for Jewish candidates elsewhere ranged from seven percent at Colgate (thirty-two percent for non-Jews) to fifty-three percent at Adelphi (sixty-three percent for non-Jews). Union College (17/47), the men's and women's colleges at the University of Rochester (13/46 and 15/64, respectively), and Elmira College (13/60) joined Colgate in the high bias category (Table 1).[69]

The temperate language in the published report did not negate the force of the findings. "The general experience of 3,039 Jewish applicants to fourteen non-sectarian liberal arts colleges in the upstate area in the Fall of 1946,"

---

[65]Berkowitz, et al., *Inequality of Opportunity in Higher Education*, 92–93. Reporting by unit helped to maintain the anonymity of large and therefore identifiable universities.

[66]Ibid., 95.

[67]David S. Berkowitz Papers, A 3036, New York State Archives, Box 4, "Code Inventory" file.

[68]Berkowitz collected data on Jewish enrollments for almost all colleges and universities in New York State. But the archives only provide statistics on the ratio of applications to admissions for the colleges listed in Table 1.

[69]The two notes appeared in the published table.

TABLE 1

Applications and Acceptances for Jewish and Non-Jewish Students in 14 Nonsectarian Privately Controlled Liberal Arts Colleges in Upstate New York, Fall 1946[70]

| College | Number of Applications and Acceptances | | | | Percent of Applications Accepted | | Index of Bias in Selection[b] |
| | Jewish | | Non-Jewish[a] | | | | |
	Applications	Acceptances	Applications	Acceptances	Jewish	Non-Jewish[a]	
Hofstra (A)	662	493	1,567	1,079	75%	70%	93
Sarah Lawrence (B)	227	50	462	117	22	25	114
Adelphi (C)	493	262	892	559	53	63	119
Hobart (D)	120	51	679	384	43	57	133
Hamilton (E)	183	19	1,028	156	10	15	150
Wells (F)	63	24	276	178	38	65	171
William Smith (G)	72	28	234	157	39	67	172
Russell Sage (H)	127	27	165	65	21	39	186
Skidmore (I)	233	52	700	293	22	42	191
Union (J)	150	26	614	291	17	47	277
University of Rochester-Men (K)	250	32	727	331	13	46	354
University of Rochester-Women (L)	122	18	284	181	15	64	427
Colgate (M)	241	16	1,297	409	7	32	457
Elmira (N)	96	12	220	131	13	60	462
Total	3,039	1,110	9,115	4,331	37%	48%	130

[a]Excluding Negro students.
[b]Based on the ratio of the percent of non-Jewish to the percent of Jewish applications accepted.

Sources: Berkowitz, Inequality of Opportunity in Higher Education, 108. Code sheets are located in the David S. Berkowitz Papers, A 3036, New York State Archives, Box 4, "Code Inventory," file. Capital letters next to the names of colleges refer to the published codes.

[70]The "percent of applications accepted" excluded African-American students. The index of bias was based on the ratio of the percent of non-Jewish to the percent of Jewish applications accepted.

Berkowitz wrote, "makes it clear that no equality of treatment in the selection of Jewish and non-Jewish candidates existed in these 14 colleges as a whole."[71]

The private colleges said little about the report. ACUSNY head Father Robert I. Gannon, the president of Fordham University, personally opposed all anti-discrimination legislation. But by fall 1947 he would not answer in the affirmative when asked whether McIntyre's March denunciation implied opposition by the church hierarchy to all anti-discrimination legislation. According to Shad Polier, representing the AJC, McIntyre met with him and Joseph Proskauer, a prominent attorney, and president of the American Jewish Committee, after the Archbishop's denunciation of the Austin-Mahoney bill. McIntyre initially opposed a revised version of the bill allowing denominational colleges to grant religious preferences. "It's a good bill," Proskauer replied, "I write enough for you, don't I?"[72] The key parties negotiated compromise legislation in October 1947 and FEPA passed the legislature the following March with virtually no substantive revisions.

The FEPA negotiations created a climate allowing the private colleges and the AJC-led coalition to agree on state university and community college legislation based on Temporary Commission proposals in early 1948. But the Board of Regents proved a reluctant partner to the negotiations, since the legislation transferred operating authority for the state's teachers colleges from the board to a new state university governing board. The failure of the Regents to protect some of the state's citizens compromised its ability to object to the transfer in 1948. The failure also placed the Regents on the defensive in 1949, when the board attempted to retake control of the new university via the Condon-Barrett bill.

The legislature turned back the latter attempt in March 1949 for two reasons. First, the state's private colleges remained neutral after receiving a promise from SUNY officials that the university would wait ten years before adding liberal arts curricula to the teachers colleges.[73] Second, newspapers republished a damaging statement made by Regents Chancellor William Wallin at the

---

[71]Berkowitz et al., Inequality of Opportunity in Higher Education, 126. "High academic requirements prevent the admission of many qualified youth, policies of geographic priorities create barriers, and Negroes find it extremely difficult to obtain within the State access to professional education in certain fields," wrote Floyd Reeves in his introduction to the study. "Even though Jewish students as a whole have the highest rate of college attendance of any group in the State they feel the burden of discriminatory practices in certain institutions" (Floyd Reeves, "Foreword," in Ibid., 7).

[72]Author's interview with Shad Polier, February 2, 1972; Wechsler, The Qualified Student, Ch. 8.

[73]Judith Glazer, "Nelson Rockefeller and the Politics of Higher Education in New York State," History of Higher Education Annual, 9 (1989), 87–114. Glazer's sources included an interview she conducted with Martha Downey, SUNY board secretary, Albany, May 28, 1982, and Ronald Gross and Judith Murphy, "New York's Late-Blooming State University," Harper's 233 (December, 1966), 93.

1938 New York State Constitutional Convention. "I rise to speak on behalf of discrimination as a liberty which I think ought to be enjoyed by everyone in this State," stated Wallin, then Regents vice chancellor. "In the matters of education," he continued, "it ought to be open to any institution to bar from it, provided it is not a public institution, to bar from entering into it, those it sees fit to forbid entering."[74] Wallin disowned his remarks, saying he supported and would enforce FEPA. But, critics asked, with how much enthusiasm? And by extension, how would the Regents govern the fledgling state university if the board assumed control?

The Regents lost direct control of the state's existing higher education operating units, while, ironically, gaining responsibility for enforcing FEPA. The law's administrator—a State Education Department employee—represented the state to the colleges. But he also represented the citizens' demand for civil rights to the leadership of the State Education Department and to the Regents. Once appointed, the FEPA administrator worked to eliminate controversial questions from admissions forms, conducted nine applicant-initiated investigations, and commissioned a statistical study.[75] Critics accused the administrator of weak enforcement during his tenure in office, though demands for strict adherence to the compromise legislation limited his discretion. In the 1960s, the enforcement office used its powers to promote racial integration on the elementary and secondary school level in hot spots such as White Plains and New Rochelle.

We don't know the number of Black, Catholic, and Jewish students who changed their career plans or abandoned higher education because private New York colleges practiced discrimination. Thanks to David Berkowitz, we do know that many qualified minority students who had applied to upstate colleges were denied access—at least to their first choices. These rejections occurred at a time when the same colleges argued against a public university, claiming they had room for more students. We also know from his data that "the rate of college attendance, that is, the number of students enrolled in college per 100 youth of college age, is nearly twice as high in New York City as it is in the upstate area."[76] This differential existed despite a high degree of academic selectivity in admission to New York City's municipal colleges.

---

[74] New York (State) Constitutional Convention, Revised Record of the Constitutional Convention of the State of New York, April fifth to August twenty-sixth, 1938, Edward J. Adamson and Maurice Jay Levin, eds. Albany, NY: J.B. Lyon Company, 1938. 1142–1144. Reprinted in Carmichael Jr., New York Establishes a State University, appendix 18, 387–388.

[75] Theodore Bienenstok and Warren W. Coxe. Decrease in College Discrimination: A Repeat Study and Comparison of Admission of High School Graduates to Colleges in New York State in 1946 and in 1949. Albany, NY: University of the State of New York, State Education Department, Division of Research, 1950.

[76] Berkowitz et al., Inequality of Opportunity in Higher Education, 145.

The problems associated with minority student access helped politicians to address a larger problem. The initial reluctance of Governor Thomas Dewey to support a state university, notes one historian, stemmed from having to "ask the predominantly Protestant upstate rural New Yorkers to support a state university because minority groups in urban areas were discriminated against in their demands for higher education."[77] But in hindsight, increased access to public higher education after World War II for all students in New York resulted from the sacrifices of earlier applicants whose race, religion, or nationality had hindered or blocked their admission to the private colleges of the state.

---

[77]Carmichael Jr., *New York Establishes a State University*, 47.

The Building Blocks of SUNY

Introduction

Douglas R. Skopp, Distinguished Teaching Professor of History, Emeritus and College Historian, SUNY Plattsburgh

If we compare SUNY to a fleet at sea, its university colleges and colleges of technology would be its battleships: rough and ready, purposeful, adroit in responding to crises, and indispensable for the vitality and integrity of the entire fleet. Its community colleges would be like ships of varying size harbored throughout the SUNY sea, essential in providing fundamental services and able to meet specific, localized needs; its specialized campuses would correspond to the flotilla's uniquely-tasked ships, each with its own special focus; and SUNY's university centers would be like aircraft carriers, dwarfing the other vessels and receiving a proportionally greater share of resources because of their paramount, complex missions. All must sail the same political waters, face the same economic storms, and have the same common purpose on behalf of the state's citizens. But on-board responses to commands from SUNY System Administration would be handled differently, depending upon the ship's location, the skill and particular interests of the captain and crew, and the support of the local community.

These campus decisions have become milestones in the histories of SUNY's university colleges, colleges of technology, and community colleges. When they were launched in the 19th and early 20th centuries, they "sailed" under the authority of New York State's Department of Education, most notably under the indefatigable eye of Commissioner Hermann Cooper in the 1930s and 1940s. Since SUNY's establishment in 1948, all its units have grown and flourished—some more, some less—with understandable pride in their past and hope for smoother waters and greater opportunities ahead.

SUNY's various campuses have varied histories for three main reasons: leaders who made daring decisions that separated them from their peers; shifting enrollment patterns and curricular changes that required each unit's administration, faculty, and staff to respond, occasionally with great hardship, creativity, and flexibility; and uneven fortunes, geographically, economically, and politically in their host communities.

Not told here, but worthy of further attention, is the constructive role, in general and with local variations, that has been played by SUNY's faculty and staff collective bargaining units in the creation of a healthy and socially responsible institution of higher learning. Just as there have been strong, determined leaders within SUNY, there have been comparable, self-sacrificing leaders in its unions. With diminishing resources and differing priorities, conflicts between "labor" and "management" may well be expected, but in SUNY's case, these conflicts, while temporarily turbulent, have resulted in constructive resolutions and have done much to promote the integrity and well being of the entire system. This is especially important since centrifugal forces have caused many campuses to seek greater independence that has led to competition with each other for resources and students as they cultivated their separate identities.

The four papers in this section detail the variations on some of these common themes, with attention to the factors that occasioned them. To a great extent, their stories reflect the inspiring stories of all the other units of their type within SUNY.

Tim Nekritz describes SUNY Oswego's path, from its pioneering foundation by Edward Austin Sheldon, the father of teacher education in the United States, to its declining fortunes in the 1930s and a devastating fire in 1941. Oswego's transformation in 1942, along with all the other former normal and training schools in New York, gave it the edge its graduates needed in competition with would-be teachers from the state's private colleges and universities. Oswego's President Ralph W. Swetman had counterparts elsewhere in the state, for example in Plattsburgh's President Charles Ward. Oswego Teachers College distinguished itself by opening its doors to a group of refugees from Hitler's Europe at the end of World War II.

Ken O'Brien and Bruce Leslie's article gives us an appreciation of the liberal arts curricula at SUNY Brockport, a much needed corrective to the negative reputation heaped on teachers colleges and the nation's public education in general in the wake of the Soviet Union's launching of Sputnik in 1957. Based upon extensive questionnaires and oral histories, as well as documentary evidence, they argue that Brockport's transition to become a multi-purpose, liberal arts college while retaining its professional studies components was a distinct success. As such, it seems to have been somewhat more harmonious than SUNY Plattsburgh's, where tensions between the older education faculty and the newer liberal arts faculty ruffled some feathers. One way both institutions bridged the divide was by creating Honors Programs. Importantly, both campuses enjoyed the support of their local communities in turbulent periods of expansion and social change.

Wayne Mahood's focus is SUNY Geneseo, challenged by declining enrollment and decimating budgets in the early 1970s until it "re-invented" itself as a nationally renowned, highly selective liberal arts college by emphasizing its ivied walls, creative faculty, and intellectual atmosphere. Credit must go to Geneseo's visionary president Robert W. MacVittie and his administrative team, as they tackled the institution's problems head-on. Geneseo's Five Year Plan in 1975 empowered a powerful steering committee and three task-forces, all involving faculty—in hindsight, a wise and decisive step in the school's ultimate success. Mahood's inspiring story of Geneseo's transformation is best appreciated within the context of SUNY's other university colleges (and their envious faculties) that chose a different path to cope with diminished enrollment and budget shortfalls.

Joseph Petrick gives us a kaleidoscopic view of the path taken by New York's original six schools of agriculture as they transformed and expanded into today's SUNY's Colleges of Technology. As with SUNY's other units, statewide mandates and economic concerns, coupled with local conditions, required dynamic, imaginative leadership and continuing commitment to public service. Their individual successes and unique missions are writ large in their respective histories.

Taken together, the histories of all of SUNY's sectors display a complex mosaic of aspirations and accomplishments in which the sum is greater than any of its parts. Their collective accomplishment provides important gems for SUNY's crown.

I. SUNY Oswego: From Recovery and Refugees to Re-Invention and Revival

Tim Nekritz, SUNY Oswego

Today's SUNY Oswego helped launch an educational revolution when formed in 1861. The "Oswego Method" was soon known nationally and internationally, due to the work of Edward Austin Sheldon (1823–1897) who incorporated "object-teaching" (i.e., lessons using objects, charts, illustrations, and more active learning instead of rote memorization) into the Oswego school district. The teachers he trained were prized and poached by other school districts.

He responded by establishing a practice school where students received training in education while teaching current students. The resulting Oswego Training School, which Sheldon later billed "the first Teachers Training School ever organized in America,"[1] paved the way for later, more progressive methods, while graduating thousands of teachers.

---

[1] Edward Austin Sheldon, *Autobiography of Edward Austin Sheldon*, ed. Mary Sheldon Barnes. New York. Ives-Butler Company 1911. p. 137–8. Shortly after Oswego proved successful, normal schools (later SUNY institutions) were organized or reorganized under the Oswego Method at Brockport, Buffalo State, Cortland, Geneseo, New Paltz, and Potsdam. Oswego graduates also founded institutions or led educational efforts across the growing United States as well as other countries including Brazil, Japan, and the Philippines.

Yet despite the renown of the Oswego Method and the influence of its graduates across the country and even the world, Oswego—like so many others—entered the 1940s facing severe economic and social challenges. Despite its heritage, Oswego Normal School struggled to attract students and maintain adequate budgets in the battered economy of the Great Depression. Attempts to upgrade Oswego from a normal school to a degree-granting teachers college were frustrated until 1941; by then another crisis overshadowed everything else. Soon millions of young men were fighting tyranny abroad while Oswego and other colleges were fighting for survival on the home front.

The first blow, the passing of a civilian draft in 1940, virtually erased the industrial arts division, long a strength of the campus. With so many called into the military, Oswego had only forty-one male students remaining "and the state was seriously considering closing the college," George Pitluga, a political science professor, recalled. But college President Ralph W. Swetman rallied his Oswego troops, saying everyone would have to pitch in to save the campus. "Among other things, faculty members, at their own expense, traveled all over the state recruiting students, necessarily female."[2]

Swetman traveled to Washington, D.C. and landed an important asset: a program to train a 300-person Air Force contingent that "saved the homestead," Pitluga said. The crisis established a collaborative spirit, "a pervading sense that faculty and administration must work together to save the college," he noted. "It was *our* college, not *the* college."[3]

After the war, local Congressman Hadwin C. Fuller extolled Oswego's contributions to the war effort in a speech to the House of Representatives. Praising the college's "service to community, state and country," Fuller said that during World War II "every member of the faculty was engaged in some civic activity connected to the promotion of the war," providing first-aid training, civilian leadership (including the city's air-raid warden), and spearheading local war-bond drives and Red Cross activities. He pointed out that this was in addition to the seven faculty and some 300 students interrupting academic careers to serve the country.[4]

The "constant enrollment of 300 prospective pilots, bombardiers and navigators" filled that hole, however, thanks to Swetman securing the 324th College Training Detachment of the U.S. Army Air Corps for fifteen months.[5]

---

[2]Dorothy Rogers, *SUNY College at Oswego: Its Second Century Unfolds.* Oswego: State University College at Oswego Auxiliary Services, 1968, p. 34.

[3]Ibid.

[4]Hon. Hadwin C. Fuller, "The Oswego State Teachers College, Mother of All Teachers Colleges" to the U.S. House of Representatives, July 18, 1946, reprinted in *Congressional Quarterly*.

[5]Ibid.

When the industrial arts enrollment sunk to a graduating class of nineteen, Swetman convinced cadets' wives and men who were declared physically unfit for service to enroll. The college's remaining industrial arts faculty and students constructed model airplanes to serve the Navy's needs, and some of its faculty members turned their teaching attention to bolstering the know-how of pre-flight cadets.[6]

But before the U.S. even entered the cauldron of war, 1941 brought a local day of infamy, January 18, when a serious fire struck Sheldon Hall, its first and signature building, whose cornerstone was laid in 1911. What President Ralph W. Swetman described as a "disastrous fire" whose origin was never learned, gutted the building's auditorium. With Sheldon Hall and Park Hall, the industrial arts building, as the only two buildings on campus, Swetman and other administrators contacted local officials, alumni, and friends of education to arrange meetings and conduct a letter-writing campaign to state officials for funding.[7]

A booklet titled "What Oswego Normal Needs: Restoration and Extension," used to rally support, spelled out three funding targets. The college hoped to secure $11,000 from Governor Herbert H. Lehman's supplemental budget to clean the building and immediately replace needed equipment. They hoped for $15,900 from the state legislature's supplemental budget to restore needed equipment, such as the Sheldon Memorial Organ, a grand piano, seats, and drapery once the auditorium was reconstructed.[8]

Most ambitiously, administrators wanted the legislature to pass a special bill allocating "$310,000 for restoration of the auditorium, repair of the main building and extension of existing facilities which are necessary to meet the increased requirements of the state program for the preparation of teachers." The booklet asked for support of Assembly Bill No. 1411, Introductory 1238.[9]

A.   Victory on Campus

As the country entered World War II, Oswego and eight newly-minted colleges operationalized a hard-fought victory to convert from normal schools into bachelor's degree-granting teachers' colleges. When Swetman assumed the presidency of Oswego Normal School in 1933, the state's Commissioner of Education Hermann Cooper challenged him to convert it from a three-year teacher-training school to a four-year degree-granting institution with full college status.[10]

---

[6]Rogers, p. 37–38.

[7]Letter from Ralph W. Swetman to Earl B. Mowry, Mayor of Mexico, February 6, 1941.

[8]"What Oswego Normal Needs: Restoration and Extension" booklet, 1941, p. 2.

[9]Ibid.

[10]"Teachers College Bill Is Approved." *Oswego Palladium-Times*. April 13, 1942.

The nine-year battle gained momentum during the college's 75th anniversary observances in 1936, but winning the upgraded recognition proved difficult. The state legislature approved it three times, only to have Governor Lehman veto the measure three times. The normal schools appealed to the Board of Regents, securing this important pillar of support. As Swetman noted in a letter to Regent John Lord O'Brien, the normal schools "sincerely hope[d] that the action on the part of the Board of Regents in granting the degree will be the additional evidence necessary to persuade the Governor to sign."[11]

The effort finally bore fruit on a Monday morning, April 13, 1942, when Lehman signed the bill to convey degree-granting power to the teachers' colleges of Oswego, as well as future SUNY brethren Brockport, Cortland, Fredonia, Geneseo, New Paltz, Oneonta, Plattsburgh, and Potsdam. "The graduates will now have the prestige of the degree in applying for positions anywhere in or out of the state, equality in salary schedules, and full recognition of their work in graduate schools," Swetman said.[12]

Logistically, those running normal schools, like Swetman, would no longer go by the title "principal," but instead would be called "college presidents." Salaries for presidents would be between $6,000 and $7,500 (raising the former upper limit of $6,500), with annual raises of $250 until they reached the upper level. Salary ranges were similarly set for deans ($5,000 to $6,000), professors ($4,000 to $5,000), assistant professors ($3,000 to $4,000) and, insultingly, women's deans ($3,000 to $4,000). In a final semantic move, the law "changes the title of those attending the Normal schools from 'pupils' to 'students.'"[13]

Graduates were pleased, as at least two alumni—G. Merwin Prindle of Utica and Louis J. People, chair of the Boy's Industrial Department in Woodrow Wilson Vocational High School in Jamaica, New York—wrote to say how happy they were to see their hard-earned four-year diplomas ... but both asked if the name on the sheepskin could be changed from the outdated Oswego Normal School to Oswego State Teachers College.[14]

Aulus Sanders, the longtime influential chair of the Art Department, said of the measure: "We had a resurgence in spirit. I think it boosted the morale of not only the students but certainly the faculty." He told of "a celebration in Albany when this went off, and practically the entire faculty went down there." He talked of the pride in Oswego "being called a college instead of a three- or

---

[11] Letter from Swetman to John Lord O'Brien, State Education Department, January 23, 1942.

[12] "Teachers College Bill Is Approved."

[13] Ibid.

[14] Letter from G. Merwin Prindle to Swetman, undated; letter from Louis J. People to Swetman and Registrar Harold D. Alford, May 4, 1943.

four-year institution," adding that, despite the school's notable tradition, "we weren't a college until the degree-granting privilege was granted."[15]

While many young men hoped to start or continue their studies after the war, not all were fortunate enough to do so. An Armistice Day service in 1944 honored ten students or alumni who had lost their lives in service—Lt. John Clements, Lt. Joseph Dahlstrom, Lt. James Diment, Lt. Charles Duell, Lt. William English, Lt. John Lockwood, Ens. Frank Parrish, Lt. Wilford Frass, Lt. James Ruddick, and Lt. Albert A. Verber. Two others—Sgt. Joseph Hennessey and Lt. Robert Rogers—were prisoners of war and another two, Lt. Francis McAllister and Cpl. Clifford Ruth, missing in action.[16] A total of 530 past and present members of the college family were serving at that time.[17] At the ceremony, the Oswego *Palladium-Times* quoted Marion Davis as hoping those serving would not toil or die in vain, imploring the effort must bring lasting peace. "We must have a world free and safe from war, and strong in democracy," Davis said in her address.[18]

The aforementioned efforts to recruit students, especially from New York City, bore fruit. The team of Golden Romney and James Moreland visited city schools to speak to students about what an Oswego education could do for their futures. "For a while we were bringing in more people from New York City than any other teachers' college upstate," Sanders said.[19]

For her part, 1948 graduate Virginia Lyon said a visit from the towering Romney and the shorter Moreland—"Mutt and Jeff," she called them with a laugh—was instrumental in her attending Oswego. Lyon recalled one day in high school when she was called to the office where, given her expressed interest in teaching, two men from Oswego's Teachers College wanted to speak to her.[20]

Between their pitch for Oswego and Romney and Moreland's jokes about each other's height differential, "I was entranced," Lyon said. "I'd never seen teachers like that—so happy-go-lucky. And I figured if the rest of the school was like that, it was terrific." After making an eight-hour drive up to see the school, Lyon said: "This is it."[21]

---

[15] Aulus Sanders, interview with Jeffrey Levine on January 23, 1979. SUNY Oswego Special Collections, Penfield Library.

[16] "College Holds Armistice Day Rites Thursday." *Palladium-Times*. November 10, 1944. p. 5.

[17] Ibid.

[18] "College Holds Armistice Day Rites Thursday."

[19] Sanders, interview.

[20] Interview with Virginia Lyon, June 7, 2008.

[21] Ibid.

Once arriving, she found classes were small and the teachers friendly. "That's one thing that sticks out in my mind," Lyon remembered. "They were helpful. They were happy to see you. There was a lot of esprit de corps among the faculty. I learned a lot."[22]

Because of the war, she did not see many men in her studies. "The only men that were here were 4F ones, meaning they were not up to being in the service," she said. Men constituted such a small part of the choir that she remembered the director addressing the group as: "Sopranos, altos and men."[23]

The college continued to recruit faculty. An October 12, 1944 account in the *Palladium-Times* reported a jaunty get-together to welcome eight new teachers. James Moreland acted as toastmaster and introduced them to the crowd, where each new faculty member "made a brief speech of acknowledgement, which on inspection proved to be the same speech repeated eight times."[24]

The new faculty—Beulah A. Counts, Stella Cullen, Ruth H. Davis, Eva Hampton, Esther Hibbard, Hester Hoffman, Thomas Miller, and Rupert Stroud—further entertained by mounting "a melodrama of the last century." Audience members were serenaded with songs popular during the melodrama's time period while waiting for the stage to be set. The resulting stage performance was "a bombastic presentation" which "delighted the faculty, their wives, and friends, and demonstrated that the new members not only had a large measure of ability, but had devoted a large amount of time to the working out [of] their sketch."[25]

B.   Cauldron to Classroom

While the Oswego State Teachers College likely resembled many other institutions of the time, its community had a unique war-influenced distinction: the Fort Ontario Emergency Refugee Shelter, where 982 refugees of war-torn Europe were relocated. These visitors—mostly Jewish—interacted with the community and its college in many ways.

When Eleanor Roosevelt visited the camp, she asked David Levy, one of the refugees, how he was enjoying America. "I love America, and I love the camp," Levy replied. "But I want to go to college." The famous first lady queried the shelter's director, Joseph Smart, on what would be necessary for the refugees to go to college, telling him: "I hope you find a way."[26] A series

---

[22]Ibid.

[23]Ibid.

[24]"Dinner Held by College Faculty." *Oswego Palladium-Times*. October 12, 1944, p. 2.

[25]Ibid.

[26]Ruth Gruber, *Haven: The Untold Story of 1,000 World War II Refugees, Fiftieth Anniversary Edition*. Brooklyn: Safe Haven Publication, 1998, p. 162.

of letters between Swetman and Smart and federal and local officials show the steps required to make it possible, and ultimately, many refugees were embraced within Oswego's college walls.

Smart reported in a January 6 letter to Swetman that there were a dozen refugees interested in attending, and they were voluntarily performing "a reasonable amount of work at the Shelter without compensation so that they will pay their way as most American young people do." Various charitable organizations were raising the funds, though Smart asked that Swetman make a tuition concession in charging the students the rate for residents to make it workable.[27]

A letter from Smart in February 1945 indicates that ten students would be allowed to attend,[28] though later correspondence only lists nine enrolled as Oswego State Teachers College students: Jetta Handel, Tina Korner, Mira Lederer, David Levy, brothers Alexander and Rajko Margulis, Walter Maurer, Vadim Mikailov, and Samuel Romano. Ralph Swetman sent a letter to Edward Huberman of the shelter in June 1945, reporting that six of the nine refugees had higher grade-point averages than the 2.20 mean for the student body.[29]

Swetman's letter noted that star pupils included Alexander Margulis, with a 3.80 GPA, Samuel Romano with a 3.53, and Rajko Margulis, holding a 3.20. Given that many of the refugees had to adjust to a new culture and language along with the pressure of schoolwork, Swetman emphasized that the shelter should be proud of all students for their college participation.[30]

Upon departing the camp, the Margulis brothers sent Swetman a thank-you note indicating how much the college and community did for them:

> Leaving this country, we desire to express to you once more our deep gratitude for all the kindness you have showed us. We shall never forget the friendly atmosphere we enjoyed while attending the Oswego State Teachers College .... [W]e know that we have sincere friends in Oswego who tried their best, as you did to help us .... It was really a pleasure to study in a school led by you.[31]

Some of the center's youngest members benefited from the college as well. In a September 1944 letter, Swetman responded very positively to a federal representative about twenty-eight children allocated to the Campus School. "We shall be very happy to have them with us," Swetman wrote and added

---

[27]Letter from Joseph H. Smart to Ralph W. Swetman, January 6, 1945.

[28]Letter from Smart to Swetman, February 7, 1945.

[29]Letter from Swetman to Edward Huberman, June 14, 1945.

[30]Ibid.

[31]Letter from Alexander and Rajko Margulis to Swetman, August 21, 1945.

that "They represent a very professional challenge to us and also an excellent opportunity for our college students to become intimately acquainted with practical idealism."[32]

The college and the refugee center also engaged in cultural exchanges. The visitors gladly showcased their talent on campus, such as a musical act led by refugee George Sternberg. "The exceptional applause on the part of the students indicated how cordially you were received," Swetman wrote to Sternberg. While expressing the "great musical satisfaction" he took from a duo performing a Mozart selection, Swetman also asked Sternberg if the musicians would consider returning for a music appreciation event in the future.[33]

Swetman also thanked Smart for a theatrical performance called "The Proposal" given by a refugee troupe. "Given in a language strange to most of our students, the facility of facial expressions and physical gestures, proved that the art of pantomime rises above language barriers," Swetman said, "and we assure you that each step in the development of the comedy was enjoyed by the audience and appreciated to the full." In addition to the praise of the faculty and college students, Swetman explained that the sixth, seventh, and eighth grade students at the Campus School enjoyed the show and every eighth-grader "wrote me a letter expressing their appreciation.[34]

In turn, the college also supplied entertainment for the refugees. A letter from Swetman to Huberman mentions a recital on campus by visiting artist Miss Nelson, a dancer of some renown, which several refugees attended. Swetman reported that Nelson "will be very happy to accept your kind invitation to give a dance recital [at Fort Ontario] for your group" on the following Saturday.[35] And college representatives gladly shared their knowledge at the shelter. Aulus Sanders, chair of the Art Department, gave a series lectures at the center in November 1944, on topics such as "Art in America." In addition to the lessons on the country's art culture, the *Palladium-Times* noted: "Listening to the lectures given in English, and participating in the discussion also help the advanced students of English to improve their knowledge and use of the spoken language."[36]

One piece of the historical record deserves to be set straight. A CBS miniseries titled "Haven" on the experience of the refugees in Oswego portrayed many members of the community as anti-Semitic and showed they had to overcome prejudice. Historical records and the memories of refugees show

---

[32]Letter from Swetman to Lester K. Ade, September 1, 1944.

[33]Letter from Swetman to George Sternberg, October 29, 1945.

[34]Letter from Swetman to Smart, February 23, 1945.

[35]Letter from Swetman to Smart, August 2, 1945.

[36]"To Hold Forum at Refugee Shelter." *Oswego Palladium-Times.* November 29, 1944, p. 7.

differently. The refugees and shelter officials spoke frequently for community organizations and received warm welcomes. Paul Bokros, a teen when the refugees arrived in the Port City, recalled hundreds of Oswego residents greeting and waving at them when they arrived. "Our stay (in Oswego) was responsible for the tremendous success we all achieved," he said in 2001.[37] Success stories were many, including the Margulis brothers entering Harvard Medical School together and Alex later working on a team at the University of California Medical Center that developed the CAT scan.[38]

Other refugees denied that any bigoted or unwelcome behavior shown in the miniseries ever occurred.[39] Perhaps their attitude was best summed up by Albert Schimel, whom Swetman singled out for performing a stirring solo in a musical presentation at the college. As Schimel prepared to leave camp, he wrote to Oswego's president, "We never forget the kind reception we always had in your Institute."[40]

C.   The Boys Come Home

With the war coming to an end, millions of men would return home to a nation needing to transition to a peacetime economy but without enough immediate jobs for its veterans. To help the transition, as well as use the power of education to uplift its citizens, Franklin D. Roosevelt signed the Servicemembers' Readjustment Bill of 1944, which became popularly known as the GI Bill. The initiative paid for the education of returning servicemen and would reinvigorate the education system while altering the American landscape.

Hundreds of the 7.8 million veterans who took advantage of the GI Bill came to Oswego State Teachers College. Sanders noted a change in the post-war students. "Before the war, these young men took it easy in school," he recalled. "But when they came back, they knew what they wanted. They were serious about their work. They were beginning to get married and they were serious about their future."[41]

One of those veterans, David J. Kidd, arrived in Oswego with his wife, Barbara, and more of an interest in studies than college tomfoolery. He told of watching freshmen forced to wear frosh caps and receiving gentle hazing from upperclassmen. "Very few students who were veterans participated in these

---

[37]Tim Nekritz, "'Haven' Refugee 'Appalled' at Miniseries Embellishment." *Oswego Palladium-Times.* February 13, 2001, p. 1.

[38]Gruber, *Haven*, p. 222.

[39]Nekritz, "Ex-refugees: 'Haven' Series Tarnishes Port City's Image." *Oswego Palladium-Times.* February 16, 2001, p. 1.

[40]Letter from Albert Schimel to Swetman, January 8, 1946.

[41]Sanders, interview.

freshmen activities, but it was not because we were anti-social." Kidd recalled. "We were older, and being married, we had family and housing responsibilities to think about."[42]

Married veterans like Kidd received a monthly $90 check (plus $15 for each child); unmarried vets collected $75 monthly, and the GI Bill covered one month of tuition for every month of military service. He remembered that "in addition to the monthly allotment check, the GI Bill paid for textbooks, supplies and student fees. Even yearbooks were covered."[43]

The influx of new students under the GI Bill, while welcome on all fronts, posed great logistical challenges to the college. New York State's Board of Regents raised quotas for teachers' colleges, allowing them to admit more students to address a looming need for elementary school teachers. Oswego could admit 250 freshmen into the elementary education program and another 125 in industrial arts.[44] The influx of learners resulted in an unusually large mid-term enrollment increase of 100 to 937 students in February 1947, split almost evenly into 470 in elementary and 467 in industrial arts. In all, 569 men—more than 350 of them veterans—enrolled and 368 women, a dramatic gender reversal from wartime.[45]

January and February 1947 found the college pleading with anyone in the city who had a spare room, especially for 100 female students. "The need for rooms for girls is so critical," Dean of Women Dorothy Mott told the *Palladium-Times*, "that we will attempt to furnish any empty rooms available in the city with the necessary furniture and fittings if the householder will agree to rent the rooms and furnish the heat."[46]

President Swetman tapped the "Committee of Four," faculty members Mott, James Hastings, William Reynolds, and Willard Allen, to solve the immediate student housing challenge. The scramble for temporary housing found the college working with the city to house some faculty and veterans in Fort Ontario, which had been vacated by the refugees.[47] While the Fort could accommodate 124 GIs, who paid a $4 weekly or $17.50 monthly rent for any

---

[42]David J. Kidd, "Splinter Village: 1947–1949". 2005, p. 23.

[43]Idem, p. 43.

[44]"Freshman Quota at College Next Fall Set at 375." *Oswego Palladium-Times.* January 18, 1947, p. 12. Oswego's 250 quota was one of the highest of the state colleges. Buffalo was allowed 300; Cortland and New Paltz 250; Brockport, Geneseo and Oneonta 200; Fredonia 175; Potsdam 150; Plattsburgh 125.

[45]"Registration of 937 Students at College, Record." *Oswego Palladium-Times.* February 7, 1947, p. 4.

[46]"College Ready to Furnish Rooms for Its Students." *Oswego Palladium-Times.* February 1, 1947, p. 10.

[47]Kidd, p. 9.

of the sixty-two two-person units,[48] this was nowhere near enough to meet the demand.

Fortunately, Swetman and his Committee of Four had already applied for surplus military barracks, each converted to hold four apartments to house World War II veterans teaching or studying at Oswego.[49] In all, twenty-five structures came to the campus from Camp Shanks, a base near Poughkeepsie, which had housed World War II troops waiting to ship out through New York City.[50] Construction of the relocated barracks began in spring 1947, with the houses open for living by June.[51] Simple and fairly rough in nature, the buildings soon became known as Splinter Village. The end apartments held two bedrooms, while the middle two were one-bedroom units. In all units, the bedrooms were 10 feet by 11 feet, living rooms 10 feet by 15 feet, kitchens a square 10 feet by 10 feet and bathrooms a cozy 5 feet by 6 feet.[52]

For his modest one-bedroom apartment, David Kidd paid $18 per month, with no charge for utilities. Barbara Kidd's job as a bookkeeper in Randolph's Jewelry Store in downtown Oswego paid the minimum wage of 50 cents an hour, or $20 per week. "Car payments, car insurance and maintenance were the most expensive items in our budget, but gasoline was cheap at less than 20¢ per gallon," Kidd remembered.[53]

Art professor Dr. Robert Steinen, who joined the Oswego faculty in 1946 and was a reserve artillery officer, noted, "When the buildings were constructed at Camp Shanks around 1941, they were built for a useful expectancy of five years." However, Splinter Village was used until in 1957 when permanent residence halls started coming online, and four others were converted to classroom structures and used throughout the 1960s.[54] The remnants of Splinter Village, known as buildings 500 and 700, lasted until the late 1960s; the former housing classrooms and faculty offices, the latter a gym and rec hall before becoming a theatre. These supposedly temporary structures became a part of campus lore while servicing more than two decades of students.[55]

The college also bought or leased properties off campus, including the purchase of Hillcrest Hall, a fading west-side orphanage, to house around

---

[48]"Barracks Ready at Fort Ontario for GI Students." *Oswego Palladium-Times*. February 3, 1947, p. 4.

[49]Kidd, p. 9.

[50]Untitled news release, c. 1968.

[51]Kidd, p. 23.

[52]Idem, p. 17.

[53]Idem, p. 23–25.

[54]Untitled news release, c. 1968.

[55]Ibid.

seventh students. More notably, the college purchased "a city poor house out of town about two miles," as home to about eighty students. "It would take considerable renovation, but there was over 100 acres of property, a beautiful winding brook dam, pond, buildings—it was just choice property," President Foster S. Brown recalled. Thus, the area now known as Fallbrook became part of Oswego's campus.[56]

D.   Boom Time

Leadership changed hands as enrollment began mushrooming. President Swetman retired in 1946, due to health problems. After Dean Thomas Miller served as acting president through fall 1947, Harvey M. Rice assumed the helm as Oswego's fifth president. It fell to him to address a new opportunity and challenge: Oswego's transition as part of the new State University of New York.[57] Oswego was one of the thirty-two institutions, and one of the eleven teachers colleges, among the founding members of what was destined to become the country's largest comprehensive university.

Just as SUNY represented a plan for a larger, more vital state education system, the campus itself was rapidly expanding to meet demand. When Foster S. Brown assumed the presidency in 1952, he noted the campus had only three permanent buildings: "Old Main," now known as Sheldon Hall; "the Industrial Arts building," (Park Hall); and the Lonis-Mackin-Moreland complex, the first residence halls coupled with a student union, constructed in 1951. The Brown years would see ever-rising student enrollment and an unprecedented building boom.

The foundation of the SUNY system and state focus on meeting student demand proved pivotal. In May 1957, Brown touted a state bonding issue to some 200 delegates of the Central District Spring Conference of parent-teacher associations having a meeting on campus. With 1,700 students studying at Oswego that year, a population expected to rise to 1,900 in the fall, Brown argued that the college's "present auditorium will not even accommodate our freshman class" while "[c]lasses are being held in temporary World War I and World War II buildings." In addition to three dormitories, the Lee Hall plant and physical education building, and the planned new home for the Campus School, "we need two additional dormitories, a science building and an auditorium."[58]

---

[56]Oral history by Dr. Foster S. Brown, October 1978, transcribed by Douglas Eckert in July 1980.

[57]Rogers, p. 42.

[58]"Dr. Brown Urges P-TA to Support Bond Referendum." *Oswego Palladium-Times.* May 29, 1957.

Brown urged PTA representatives to tell their members "about the crucial situation facing these schools and ask them to help provide sufficient educational facilities by voting for the bond issue in the fall."[59] Underscoring the mushrooming education market, an item one column to the right in the *Palladium-Times* told of Oswego State Teachers College graduates who had accepted fall positions at schools in Baldwinsville, Hannibal, Oswego, Phoenix, Pulaski, and Red Creek.[60]

A headline in the *Palladium-Times* two weeks later called the college a "Beehive of Activity" as three buildings representing $3,791,000 of investment continued construction. The largest was Lee Hall, which would hold the central heating plant and new gym, "a $2,225,000 giant under contract to John W. Rouse Co. of Governeur." The same firm also worked on an $854,000 dormitory that would become Johnson Hall. Next door, Oswego's Peter Raby Co. had broken ground the previous day, June 10, on the $682,000 dining facility now called the Lakeside Dining Center.[61]

The paper billed the dormitory as the first of five 200-bed facilities planned to meet student housing demands, "while other buildings coming up there are a 700-foot-long classroom building, a library, a science building and an auditorium." While existing appropriations supported some of the work, "others depend upon the favorable outcome of this year's state university bond issue referendum."[62]

When New York voters approved the bond issue, the campus could look forward to more growth. Oswego joined other SUNY institutions "expanding its plants and programs to make room for a record number of high school graduates who will be leaving the state's secondary schools in the next few years."[63]

President Brown anticipated 2,000 students enrolling for fall 1958.[64] They would be met with new buildings, a new library, a new classroom building, and a new residence hall, Johnson Hall, to which two more dormitory buildings, Lee and Lakeside, would be quickly added.

The 1960s saw the opening of twenty-nine buildings in all. High-rise residence halls with names drawn from Iroquois heritage (Onondaga, Cayuga, Seneca, and Oneida) and Pathfinder Dining Center comprised "New Campus"

---

[59]Ibid.

[60]"OSTC Seniors Get Positions For Fall." *Oswego Palladium-Times.* May 29, 1957.

[61]"OSTC Beehive of Activity, Three Buildings Rising." *Oswego Palladium-Times.* June 11, 1957.

[62]Ibid.

[63]"1,700 Students For Spring Term At Oswego State." *Oswego Palladium-Times.* February 6, 1958.

[64]Ibid.

and housed more students than even attended Oswego in the early 1940s. Two other towering residence halls, Hart and Funnelle, stood in the middle of campus, flanking Cooper Dining Hall. Mary Walker Health Center attended to the needs of an on-campus student community that now far exceeded 3,000.

Less than a quarter-century after a seemingly never-ending Great Depression and the depletion of students due to World War II threatened Edward Austin Sheldon's pioneering institution, the sky now seemed the limit for Oswego as Rockefeller-era money poured in. But while the demographic surge of "baby boomers" and the national GI Bill had pumped lifeblood into Oswego and colleges everywhere, much of the credit for the college's survival belongs to local initiative. The work of President Swetman and a small but dedicated core kept the college from folding when the war called away a substantial number of young people. And their welcome to a small band of refugees distinguishes Oswego's home front experience.

Then the rise of the State University of New York, providing centralized direction and enhanced funding, underpinned Oswego's educational boom. Some struggles continued as faculty and students made the most of cramped facilities, but their efforts laid the basis for the modern SUNY Oswego. Even as one more economic crisis impacts higher education in the 21st century, Oswego can take comfort from the knowledge that it has survived far worse crises in the nearly 150 years since Sheldon's Oswego Method brought fame to a new institution on the eastern shore of Lake Ontario.

II. Rescuing the State Teachers College from History's Scrapheap

Kenneth P. O'Brien and W. Bruce Leslie, The College at Brockport, State University of New York

How many today remember the specter cast by Sputnik? Perhaps few, but in the 1950s, it brought an American generation's childhood to an abrupt end. Suddenly school children weren't just reading *Dick and Jane*; they had been challenged to out-achieve Ivan and Ivanova. While many may have enjoyed the evening ritual of going out to watch a beeping ball pass overhead, the World War II generation was gripped by a moral panic. How could the land of old scowling men and hefty women shot-putters have beaten the Americans into space? A few suggested that the Soviets had better German scientists than we had. The Republicans blamed Dewey—John, not Thomas—while the Democrats blamed Eisenhower. And almost everyone blamed the schools. Suddenly our math and science classes took on new meaning, as young students were exhorted to shape up both mentally and physically.

Professional educators, the teaching profession, and teacher training were routinely condemned, with "state teachers colleges" becoming leading suspects. Under attack, these colleges soon changed their names with undue haste and embarrassing rapidity. Although most states had sponsored "state teachers colleges," they (or at least that designation) soon disappeared, little lamented in the decade after Sputnik, pounded by exposes of their presumed academic failings. The State Teachers College (STC) became an embarrassing episode in the history of American higher education, one best forgotten. College marketing departments routinely airbrushed the name from pictures and at least one college sandblasted it into oblivion.[65] Even today, the *New York Times* occasionally attacks "colleges of education," long after their official demise.[66]

Historians, perhaps reluctant to go down a road not taken, have written little about the institutions that educated 10 percent of American college students and trained about 20 percent of teachers in the 1950s. John Thelin's recent survey of American higher education omits teachers colleges entirely.[67] More strangely, James Fraser's history of teacher preparation briefly discusses the pre–World War II evolution of "normal schools" into "teachers colleges," but mistakenly dismisses the latter's postwar role with the assertion that "such single-purpose schools virtually disappeared from the American scene in the decade after World War II."[68] Although a relatively short-lived institution, this report of STCs' death is greatly exaggerated. More than 200 operated in the 1950s and many teachers colleges continued training teachers as their primary mission well into the 1960s before morphing into the workhorses of mass higher education in many state systems: public comprehensive colleges and regional universities. Even today, SUNY's former state teachers colleges award a majority of the extensive system's baccalaureate degrees.

Understanding the nature of these institutions is critical to both comprehending SUNY's early development and recognizing the vital public service these largely forgotten, often misunderstood, institutions performed. Toward these ends, this study examines Brockport State Teachers College (BSTC) in the post–World War II decades.

---

[65]Karen Hallman, "Normal School to State College: Transitions in the 20th Century". History of Education Society Annual Meeting, 2004.

[66]For instance an editorial "Rising Above the Gathering Storm." *New York Times* (Jan. 24, 2006). "Many education colleges have become diploma mills …"

[67]John Thelin. *A History of American Higher Education*. Baltimore: Johns Hopkins Press, 2004.

[68]James Fraser. *Preparing America's Teachers: A History*. New York: Teachers College Press, 2007.

Brockport State Teachers College, its name from 1941 to 1959 and a teachers college in reality into the late 1960s,[69] was one of eleven "upstate" state teachers colleges that were founding members of SUNY.[70] As such, they constituted one-third of the State University of New York's original institutions and the most prominent sector of SUNY for more than a decade after its creation. Then, the post-Sputnik calumny, coupled with the Baby Boom, forced them to slowly transition into multi-purpose colleges by the mid-to late 1960s. Today, ten are classified as "University Colleges" by SUNY, while Albany has become one of the system's four doctoral university centers.

In the two decades after World War II, BSTC remained an average-sized SUNY teachers college whose president was a protégé of SUNY's guardian angel of state teachers colleges, Herman Cooper.[71] Like most SUNY teachers colleges, the Brockport campus was in a village, in this case on the Erie Canal within 20 miles of Rochester. Thus, Brockport provides a reasonably representative case study for SUNY, and probably even more widely.[72] As such, it provides a useful vehicle for revisiting the state teachers college story, their development in the post-war era, the withering criticisms directed at them, and their subsequent transformation.

A.   State Teachers Colleges Under Attack

Admiral Hyman G. Rickover launched the post-Sputnik attack on American education, decrying progressive education's supposedly pernicious effects and

---

[69]Of the eleven teachers colleges that joined SUNY at its creation in 1948, nine were named "State Teachers College," most receiving that name in 1941, and Albany and Buffalo each a "State College for Teachers." In 1959, all eleven were renamed "State University Colleges of Education." "Education" was dropped from the titles in 1961 and 1962, although training teachers remained the primary mission for most into the mid-1960s and even the early 1970s.

[70]The other ten were in Albany, Buffalo, Cortland, Fredonia, Geneseo, New Paltz, Oneonta, Oswego, Plattsburgh, and Potsdam. In their first year in SUNY, they enrolled 11,965 students.

[71]New York State converted its three-year "normal schools" into four-year "state teachers colleges" in 1941 and gathered them under the State University of New York (aka SUNY) mantle in 1948. But meaningful conversion to college life could not begin until World War II concluded and SUNY's creation had little effect on the colleges in first decade. Thus, we use 1946 as our beginning date and cover two decades in which teacher training remained the central focus until the arrival of President Albert W. Brown in 1965. For simplicity, we anachronistically use SUNY colleges throughout the 1940s to refer to their future relationship.

[72]We base our study of Brockport's State Teachers College decades (c.1945–1965) not only on catalogues, student publications, and administrative records, but also on faculty oral histories and over 450 alumni questionnaires we have administered. We have also directed a large number of undergraduate and graduate student research papers on the State Teachers College years. The result, we believe, is an unusually rich set of archival resources, especially for a public college.

calling for more rigor, especially in science and mathematics.[73] But he was not the first. Most prominent among the critics before him was Arthur Bestor, whose provocatively titled *Educational Wastelands* had garnered considerable publicity when it was published a half dozen years earlier.[74]

Most damaging to their reputation, James Koerner's widely-read examination of teacher training, *The Miseducation of American Teachers*, strongly criticized teachers colleges' curriculum. His study claimed that whereas states required an average minimum of twenty-three credit hours of education courses for students preparing to teach in elementary schools, colleges required an average of thirty-five credits in courses he called sub-standard. His study of 435 transcripts of students preparing for elementary education at thirty-two institutions found that they averaged fifty Education credits. Worse in his view, students at teachers' colleges averaged fifty-five credits in education (versus fifty in universities and thirty-seven in liberal arts colleges), which computes as 46 percent of their college curriculum.[75]

Though some defended the quality and necessity of the education courses from Koerner's attacks, few challenged his seemingly well-researched assessment. His charges have been repeated for decades, especially the claim that future teachers spent—and still spend—about half their time on pedagogy courses.[76] In a rare dissent, Christopher Lucas later questioned "whether educationists for their part truly deserved the calumny heaped on them by their academic colleagues."[77]

When the first students ascended the stairs into Brockport's new (and only) building in 1941, they passed under "State Teachers College" etched on the portico over the entrance. That title accurately reflected the main mission, which, like that of nine of the other ten SUNY state teachers colleges, was to prepare elementary school teachers; the resulting certification included the

---

[73]H.G. Rickover. *Education and Freedom*. New York: Dutton & Co., 1959.

[74]Arthur E. Bestor. *Educational Wastelands*. Urbana, Ill.: University of Illinois Press, 1953.

[75]James Koerner. *The Miseducation of American Teachers*. Baltimore: Penguin, 1965. 118–139. First published in 1963.

[76]In 1981 a critic claimed that future teachers "are required by law to serve time, often as much as one half of their undergraduate program, in the classes of the teacher-trainers." Richard Mitchell, *The Graves of Academe*. Boston: Little-Brown, 1981; 15. A decade later, another claimed that colleges of education offered "three or four years of concentration on pedagogy to students barely out of high school, whose general education was slighted .... All of them knew more about how to teach than what to teach." Rita Kramer, Ed. *School Follies: The Miseducation of America's Teachers*. New York: Free Press, 1991; 6–7.

[77]Christopher Lucas, Lucas. *Teacher Education in America: Reform Agendas for the Twenty-First Century*. New York: St. Martin's Press, 1997; 73. Lucas summarizes the post-World War II critics including Bestor's and Koerner's books and the more moderate Conant report on pp. 67–80.

first two years of the six-year high school curriculum, in other words, junior high school.[78]

Given the post-Sputnik critiques and the institution's name, the first postwar catalogue surprisingly proclaimed the College's aim to be "providing both a sound liberal education and a specialized professional education for young people carefully selected to become future teachers in the public schools."[79] In the mid-1950s, the statement was slightly revised to provision of "a broad cultural program in arts and science, plus a professional sequence in education ...."[80]

Did such declarations reflect curricular and intellectual reality? In fact, the curriculum that returning veterans and other Brockport students encountered in the years after World War II did include a broad range of studies in the "general elementary education" curriculum. Every semester, except during the semester of "practice teaching," students took a course each in English and social studies. In addition, they took six semesters of science and mathematics, five semesters of "liberal-cultural electives," and two each of art and music. They also studied a semester of industrial arts and six credits of health.

In each of those seven semesters, the students took only one education course. Freshmen studied Child Development, followed by a year-and-a half of Child and the Curriculum, the latter echoing the title of John Dewey's classic book, and finished with a senior Seminar in Elementary Education. Including the practice teaching semester, thirty-six of the 128 credits (28 percent) were taken in Education, far less than the fifty-five credits or the 46 percent of the curriculum Koerner computed from student transcripts. It is even slightly below the percentage he cited for liberal arts colleges.

Admittedly, our figures may overstate Brockport's liberal arts as it classified the nine credits of Industrial Arts and of Health Education" as "Liberal-Cultural," whereas Koerner included them in the professional category. Even switching those, Brockport students' professional courses constituted 32 percent of total credit hours, rather than Koerner's 46 percent.

On the other hand, Koerner's tally of required academic courses underestimates Brockport's practice. He claimed that elementary education students from teachers colleges in his survey averaged only twenty-five credits (or 21 percent of 120) of English, math, and science. Brockport students were required to take thirty-nine (or 30 percent of 128) and no doubt, most took more as electives. In total, Koerner's figures predicted considerably more

---

[78]The same was true for nine other SUNY State Teachers Colleges: Buffalo, Cortland, Fredonia, Geneseo, New Paltz, Oneonta, Oswego, Plattsburgh, and Potsdam. Only the New York State College for Teachers at Albany trained secondary teachers.

[79]Brockport State Teachers College, *Bulletin: General Catalogue Issue, 1946–47*, 1.

[80]State University of New York, Teachers College at *Brockport, General Catalogue, 1954–1956*, 23.

professional courses at Brockport, and fewer arts and sciences, than students actually encountered.[81]

By the time of Sputnik, Brockport's General Elementary Education curriculum had changed little since World War II. Required education credits remained at thirty-six, though a somewhat larger number of electives was permitted. Given that among the categories of electives were "Education, Psychology and Philosophy," "Health and Physical Education," and "Industrial Arts," it is possible that some students could have approached the figures Koerner cited as typical. But it is unlikely that many did so.[82] Koerner's charge—one that has stuck with generations—that teachers colleges devoted nearly half of their curricula to professional courses in education, is simply not sustained by an examination of Brockport's elementary education program.[83]

Brockport's claim to offer a broad curriculum was, in fact, reasonably accurate. The extent to which it could fully lay claim to a liberal education depends on the balance of breadth and depth in the definition. It certainly passed the breadth test, though without the depth offered by a liberal arts college "major."

In *The Education of American Teachers*, written in the same year as Koerner's *Miseducation*, former Harvard President James Conant reached a conclusion similar to our own, that the general education in teachers colleges was equivalent to that in liberal arts colleges, perhaps even a little more desirable given its limitation on students' choice. A more moderate and denser study than Koerner's, its findings have been largely forgotten.[84]

The final word should go to the students of the time. Looking back over five decades, the lack of curricular choice and depth is the one recurring alumni complaint in responses to our questionnaires. And a few also criticized the quality of classroom courses on education. But many praised the breadth of their preparation and that praise seems warranted.

B.　Transition to the Multipurpose College

In 1958, two important events occurred, marking what would become the transformation of Brockport State Teachers College to the State University College at Brockport. The first, which was identified as a "watershed" by the

---

[81]Brockport State Teachers College, Bulletin: General Catalogue Issue, 1947–48. Koerner, Miseducation, Ch.V.

[82]State University of New York, Teachers College at Brockport, General Catalogue, 1956/7–1958/9, 34–47.

[83]We have also looked at the programs at two other SUNY Teachers Colleges for the period, Cortland and Plattsburgh, which, while not identical to Brockport, are quite similar.

[84]James Conant. *The Education of American Teachers*. New York: McGraw-Hill, 1963.

college's historian, was the appointment of the Heald Committee by University President Thomas Hale Hamilton and newly elected Governor Nelson Rockefeller.[85] Charged to re-examine the need for and role of higher education in the state, the Committee issued its findings in November 1960, calling for a revision of the State University's 1950 Master Plan by a vast expansion of public higher education, including the immediate conversion of the state's eleven Colleges of Education into liberal arts colleges.[86] This report to the Board of Regents and Governor Nelson Rockefeller fundamentally changed the scope, nature, and extent of New York's state university.

The second event escaped public notice, but it is instructive for our purposes. During a collegial lunchtime discussion between an older member of the teaching faculty, philosopher Howard Keifer, and a younger colleague, Miles Morgan, a newly minted PhD in English, Keifer wondered what his colleague planned for his newly-completed dissertation. When informed that Morgan intended to drop the work, a surprised Kiefer asked, "What do you care about?," which led to an exchange about the possibility of creating honors education at Brockport. According to Dr. Kiefer, "After about an hour's discussion we decided to offer a team taught honors course to the students we selected on what we were interested in."[87]

Kiefer took the lead, preparing the proposal and presenting it to Vice President Gordon Allen. A year later, in spring 1959, Kiefer and Morgan, along with two professors from the Social Science Department, offered the first honors course, "Great Ideas and the American Experience." Designed as a cross-disciplinary seminar, the four professors team-taught the course, into which they invited selected juniors and seniors. Meeting once a week for three hours in seminar style, the professors took on the additional course load at no extra pay.

Eventually, additional faculty from the arts, sciences, and political science were incorporated into the program. Other honors courses taught during this period included: Greek Foundations of Western Culture (involving faculty from the arts, history, literature, and philosophy); The Renaissance: Dawn of a New Era (the arts, literature, science, and political science); and The Romantic Movement (art, literature, and music). Although documentation of the honors courses is sparse, surviving student recollections note the extraordinary

---

[85]Wayne W. Dedman, *Cherishing This Heritage*. New York: Appleton-Century-Crofts, 1969; 279.

[86]Committee on Higher Education, "Meeting the Increased Demand for Higher Education in New York State; a Report to the Governor and the Board of Regents." November, 1960; 27–28.

[87]Kiefer, Howard E.. "Letter to Mark A. Anderson." Available from the SUNY Brockport Honors Program Office. July 29, 1979. Much of what follows is a reworked portion of a fine paper by Holly Hellenbrook on the Honors Program at the College at Brockport, which is available at the College Archives.

commitment of the faculty in the program and the rigor with which these very liberal subjects were pursued.

The College Honors Program in the late 1950s, before the real fallout from Sputnik or even the public plans for SUNY's expansion, stands as compelling evidence of the presence of liberal arts education at this state teachers college. While the college's curriculum in general could not yet match their ambitions, it soon would, once the Heald Committee's recommendations had worked their way through the political maze, with Rockefeller's strong support and public funding for an incredibly ambitious building program transformed the physical campuses of the state university.

Once approved, the mandates of the Heald Committee quickly worked their way onto campuses, including Brockport, through the major revision to the system's Master Plan of 1950. The 1960 plan became the blueprint for the rapid expansion of New York's state university that shaped the system for decades to come, with the Colleges of Education becoming Colleges of Arts and Sciences and the establishment of university centers, which were authorized to award doctoral degrees. At Brockport, the acceptance of the report created an unprecedented building program to serve the influx of students, as well as the organization of a large faculty Curriculum Committee, which was charged with creating a new liberal arts curriculum. Meeting for long hours between 1961 and 1963, the committee extensively examined existing programs at other colleges before recommending a small number of new academic majors in the "Division of the Liberal Arts," which were to take their place alongside Brockport's traditional programs in teacher preparation.[88] The college accepted students into the new programs in the fall of 1963, but in an interesting manner. Following state guidelines, these were upper division transfer students from the state's rapidly expanding community colleges. Two years later, the college admitted the first freshmen not committed to becoming teachers.

That same fall, 1965, a new president, Albert W. Brown, arrived from Eastern Michigan University with a mandate for change from the SUNY System Administration and a vision that was consistent with its emphasis on liberal arts programs. The programs instituted in 1963 had remained small in size in their first years; that soon changed as the college, just like the others in SUNY, began to develop traditional academic majors, dividing 1963's "Liberal Arts Program" into six "schools" that administered more than two dozen traditional liberal arts academic majors by 1970.

---

[88]"State University of New York College at Brockport, Proposed Curriculum in Liberal Arts," February 18, 1963. College Archives, Drake Memorial Library, The College at Brockport. The Brockport programs were in Early Childhood, General Elementary, Secondary Education, and Health and Physical Education, just as they had been for a decade.

Beyond the specific number and nature of liberal arts courses and programs, the period is characterized by a consistent cadre of the faculty who provided the leadership for the transition. It was the same faculty and professional administrative staff who hired the hordes of younger faculty, mostly in the burgeoning liberal arts disciplines, who flooded into SUNY in general—into Brockport specifically—with more than 100 being hired for fall 1969, followed by another 150 new faculty hires in 1970. The older members of the faculty designed the curriculum and shepherded the institution through what in retrospect was a remarkably smooth process, with little evidence of smoldering territorial disputes about the shape of the new degree programs.

But, this paper is focused on the extent of liberal arts coursework within teacher education programs at the state teachers college at Brockport in the 1950s, not the transformation to the new curricula. What happened to those programs during this expansion and to some extent, redirection, of the college curriculum? Again, we have found consistency. In 1960, for example, the undergraduate catalog lists thirty-six credits—including the twelve-credit practicum in practice teaching—of the 130 needed for the degree, in professional education courses for the elementary education program. Five years later, the number had shrunk by one to thirty-five credits, which in either case represents a tad less than 25 percent of the total number of credits in the degree program. And five years later still, after the Brown "revolution," the number had shrunk to thirty credits, but that was in a 120 credit degree, or the same 25 percent.[89]

Additionally, the Brockport education curricula *after* the 1960s offers supporting evidence for our argument about the extent of the curricular continuities between what usually have been seen as two distinct, even warring, kinds of institutions, state teachers colleges and liberal arts colleges, in the three decades after World War II.[90] President Brown's work with the faculty curriculum committee to expand the liberal arts majors had affected the education programs as well; all baccalaureate degree candidates, including those preparing to become elementary school teachers, were required to complete an academic major in a traditional discipline. Education courses were incorporated into certification programs to be taken in addition to the major, a pattern that persists at Brockport to the present day.

To conclude, our case study uncovers surprising continuities in the transition from the postwar state teachers colleges of the 1950s to the comprehensive college of the late 1960s and subsequent decades. There is scant evidence of

---

[89]These numbers have been taken from the Undergraduate Catalogs for 1959–60, 1965–66, and 1969–70. In each program, students could also take a reasonable number of electives, but in looking at the course offerings, it is unlikely that many would have been in Education.

[90]For this latter period, we make no claim beyond the College at Brockport, since it remains one of the few SUNY colleges to offer childhood education preparation through certification programs that are separate from, and additional to, the academic majors.

battles raging among the faculty, and the critical place that professional and pre-professional programs and majors continue to play in the college offers additional evidence for seeing the process as evolutionary, not revolutionary. Thus, while generalizations based on a single case are suspect, we would argue that the state teachers colleges were probably scapegoated unfairly after Sputnik; they provided a broad (though not deep) liberal arts curriculum with about as many pedagogy courses as are typical today for teacher education. Moreover, we suggest that state teachers colleges played such a critical role in the maturation of SUNY's university colleges that they deserve to be rescued from "history's scrapheap." At least that was the case for Brockport.

III. "A Touch of New England in Western New York": The Transformation of SUNY Geneseo

Wayne Mahood, SUNY Geneseo

This paper examines a success story: how SUNY Geneseo, a struggling state teachers college, transformed itself into a nationally-ranked institution.

The SUNY system, created in 1948, made its mark in the 1960s. Its ascent is usually attributed to Governor Nelson Rockefeller (1959–73), whose ambitions matched his personal wealth, and by the appointment of equally ambitious Dr. Samuel B. Gould to head the State University of New York in 1964. The rare combination of Rockefeller's and Gould's personalities and ambitions aimed to put SUNY at the forefront of public higher education. Initially they were helped by money—state and federal—which flowed as never before.[91]

However by the 1970s, Chancellor Gould was retired and demographers expressed misgivings about SUNY's future. The baby boom was ending, and there were disturbing omens of an economic slowdown. In fact, Governor Rockefeller grimly forecasted that the 1971–72 academic year would be one of "austere operation." As if on cue, that year Geneseo added fewer than twenty faculty, a sizeable drop from the fifty to sixty to which the college was acclimating, because of SUNY "growth curtailment." Plans for more than 250 SUNY building projects costing $340,000,000, including $9,300,000 at Geneseo, were suspended. Dormitory and classroom construction to accommodate the 8,000 students Geneseo anticipated by 1980 was out of the question. Likewise, plans for a new education building (projected for 1973 completion) and a library

[91]The author thanks Dr. Bruce Leslie, professor of history, SUNY Brockport, and Arthur Hatton, former vice president for college advancement, SUNY Geneseo, for reading and reacting to this paper. Ironically, Gould, then Antioch College president, was Geneseo's commencement speaker in May 1957, when he looked ahead to "The Teacher in the World Tomorrow."

addition (also 1973) were shelved. Unfortunately, this was only the beginning of difficult times for Geneseo and its sister schools.[92]

In 1973 Geneseo President Robert W. MacVittie protested a budget that "'decimated'" allocations to the school. A year later the picture was even bleaker. At the school's 1974 convocation, MacVittie declared that the State Education Department predicted dramatic public school enrollment declines for the next decade and a half because of the drop in age cohorts. Even more severe budget cuts followed Governor Hugh Carey's January 1975 inaugural address, wherein he famously declared that "the days of wine and roses are over." The state's debt had quadrupled over the previous ten years, its economy had steeply declined, and its major city was headed for bankruptcy.[93]

A. Geneseo Responds

Complying with SUNY's charge for each campus to submit a Master Plan from which SUNY would develop its statewide five-year plan, in 1975 President MacVittie appointed a fifteen-member steering committee and three separate task forces. The task forces were to examine instruction and personnel, research, and public service. A projected enrollment decline of at least 17 percent between 1980 and 1990 meant Geneseo could lose more than thirty faculty by 1984. Faculty were asked to help plan those cuts if the worst scenario was realized.[94]

B. Enrollment Crisis

Still, despite the troubling signs, no one at Geneseo really anticipated such a dire result. Yes, there had been a moderate decline from the 1972 peak of 6400 applications, but the administrators, faculty, and staff were totally unprepared for the disastrous 18 percent decline in the applications for the fall of 1977. Already coping with a sharp spike in oil and gasoline prices that began with the Arab oil embargo in 1973, which other SUNY schools also experienced, Geneseo could now lose up to thirty-one full-time equivalent faculty (FTE).[95]

---

[92]"MacVittie Raps Cuts By State for Geneseo," *Rochester Times-Union*, February 23, 1973; "College Tightens Belt," *Livingston County Leader*, August 23, 1972; "Cuts Put College in Dormitory Bind," *Rochester Times-Union*, January 21, 1972; "From the President," *Geneseo Compass*, February 12, 1971; Letter to Charles Fake, SUNY Assistant Director of Facilities Planning, from Donald Pebbles, Geneseo Facilities Program Coordinator, January 15, 1970, President's Papers, 1969–1970.

[93]Edmund J. McMahon. "Déjà Vu All Over Again: The Right Way to Cure New York's Looming Budget Gap." *Civic Report*, No. 9 (October 2002).

[94]*Geneseo Compass*, January 13, 1975; Interview of Dr. Bruce Ristow by Martin L. Fausold, July 8, 1997.

[95]*Geneseo Compass*, November 21, 1973; *The Lamron*, September 16, October 28, 1977; James McNally, *Fact Book 1980–1981*. Geneseo, New York: Office of Institutional Research, SUNY Geneseo; 17.

Fortunately, the enrollment crisis in the fall of 1977 was temporarily ameliorated when the governor and SUNY Central gave Geneseo a one-year reprieve from staff cuts. In part, this rewarded MacVittie's stewardship, which had been recognized by SUNY's recent renewal of him. But the underlying problem—coping with a severe drop in applications—remained, and the school's efforts to distinguish itself were also in jeopardy.

Geneseo responded with a three-pronged attack on its sagging enrollment. First, it plugged the hole in the dike by lowering admission criteria and admitted as many applicants as possible (resulting in an 88 percent acceptance rate). This was a real risk, for the college could have been perceived as having an "open-admission" policy, prompting the dreaded phrase "anyone can get in." But that was not the message the college wanted to deliver; it was a temporary expedient—a one-time gamble.[96]

Second, the college formed a committee to recommend long-term college priorities. Third, it established a task force to study and improve recruitment and retention practices. The recruitment and retention committee's work eventually set Geneseo on a path that led to national prominence.[97]

However, the path was not as smooth or as well defined as it seems in hindsight. Rather, as educators Christopher Morphew and J. Douglas Toma note, Geneseo's turnabout resulted from a number of sometimes halting steps.[98]

In July 1977 presidential assistant Dr. Frank Kemerer was named director of college enrollment policy and planned to examine current recruitment practices, suggest new strategies, and recommend "a realistic enrollment goal." Kemerer recommended consolidating admissions, financial aid, and career planning under one administrator (ultimately Vice President for Student Affairs David A. Young). This was followed by a retreat (the "College Planning Workshop") at Rensselaerville, New York, where forty-two faculty and administrators examined what the college was doing and where it was going. Back on campus that September, a college-wide faculty meeting focused solely on the school's mission. Should Geneseo be "pure" liberal arts? Should there be more "career-oriented options"? Or was the answer more "minors"? Marketing Geneseo was discussed, too. Kemerer, William Caren, acting director of admissions, and Arthur Hatton, then director of college relations, were charged with engineering the turnaround. However, MacVittie warned the

---

[96]William Caren, intrerview by James McNally and Wayne Mahood, January 3, 2005; McNally, *Fact Book 1980–1981*, 17.

[97]Caren, interview.

[98]Christopher C. Morphew and J. Douglas Toma, "Becoming a Public Liberal Arts College: Two Case Studies of Bucking the Trend," paper presented at the European Association for Institutional Research, Barcelona, Spain, September 2004, 13.

faculty and staff that this was long range planning, that the turnaround would take at least five years.[99]

The third prong of the attack on the enrollment crisis was a priorities committee charged with drafting a plan for reducing faculty, should it be necessary. The "hatchet committee," as many viewed it, submitted a draft proposal on February 18, 1978, recommending six levels of cuts, some severe. Fortunately, Geneseo reached its enrollment targets in the ensuing years, rendering the bleakest scenarios moot.[100]

The key to Geneseo's turnaround was recruitment. The college had to sell itself to prospective students, and fortunately, it had something to sell. It was located in a bucolic Genesee Valley village that had staked its future by investing in the college a century earlier. It benefited from healthy town-gown relations. Typically, faculty lived in the village and served in various public offices.

Further, the elements of a quality institution, including a range of undergraduate and graduate programs, were already in place. The college was successfully shifting from a single-purpose teachers college to a liberal arts-based, multiple-purpose college with a faculty from "quality doctoral-granting institutions." Changing the college's mission had required wresting control of secondary education certification programs from teacher education, culling "unnecessary" electives, adding a BS in Accounting (for which there was growing demand), and instituting a core curriculum not unlike those at prestigious liberal arts colleges. At the heart of the revised core curriculum, initiated by Vice President for Academic Affairs Thomas S. Colahan, were two four-hour courses labeled Humanities I and II, with content analogous to those at St. John's at Annapolis and Columbia College.[101]

One of Colahan's models was City College of New York, a public university with an unusually high number of Nobelists. Given SUNY Central's control over budget, the key to change was strengthening the curriculum and

---

[99]"MacVittie appoints task force on student recruitment," *Geneseo Compass*, April 22, 1977; "Student recruitment and retention discussed," Ibid., September 16, 1977; "Tuesday's Faculty Meeting Discusses Enrollment Crisis," Ibid., September 16, 1977; "Student Enrollment Declines, College Admissions Revised," Ibid., September 9, 1977; Frank Kemerer, "Enrollment Policy and Planning," July 5, 1977, Presidents' Papers, College Archives; News Release, July 8, 1977, Presidents' Papers, College Archives; Letter from President Robert W. MacVittie to Wayne Mahood, November 24, 1987.

[100]"College priorities committee draft report," *Geneseo Compass*, May 5, 1978. Education actually was taking a larger hit, for it also lost the assistant dean. Christopher C. Morphew, J. Douglas Toma, Cora Z. Hedstrom, "The Public Liberal Arts College: Case Studies of Institutions That Have Bucked the Trend Toward 'Upward Drift'... and the Implications for Mission and Market," paper presented at the Association for the Study of Higher Education, Richmond, Virginia, November 2001, 4.

[101]Robert W. MacVittie, interview by Martin L. Fausold and Wayne Mahood, June 26, 1989.

allocating faculty lines. That meant upgrading the undergraduate programs and examining faculty scholarship. Tenure and promotion were no longer "automatic;" department heads were on notice to demonstrate tougher standards. (According to Vice President Colahan, the "only way" to "make a better faculty is … by non-renewal of term appointments."[102])

One decision MacVittie made that possibly could have backfired was to remove responsibility for admissions from Colahan. A Columbia University PhD who was lured from a deanship at his alma mater, Colahan was hired for his liberal arts background. Unfortunately, he had what might be dubbed a "Field of Dreams" approach to admissions. That is, build the curriculum and hire the faculty—which he was doing—and "they (the students) will come." However, the 1977 shortfall clearly proved him wrong. Yet, MacVittie managed not to alienate Colahan, who continued to provide the necessary academic guidance. So William Caren, the new director of admissions, was to report *"directly"* [italics in original] to the president, who intended to demonstrate" his "interest [in] and authority" over admissions, not to vice president Colahan. This was a critical decision.[103]

Importantly, MacVittie realized the "entire campus" had to become "seriously involved." According to Arthur Hatton, later vice president for college advancement, the "very extensive" recruitment plan was designed to increase visibility and name recognition with key constituencies: prospective students, their parents, and alumni. Since feedback sought from many high school guidance counselors around the state indicated that Geneseo was still widely viewed as a "teachers college," a central challenge was to change that perception to more accurately reflect how the college had changed. That also meant developing courses or majors that would more directly lead to jobs, which surveys of prospective students revealed they wanted. But that could adversely affect the goal to make Geneseo a truly liberal arts school.

Nonetheless, Colahan asked Assistant Vice President Virginia Kemp to develop proposals for "practical, vocational minors to augment the liberal arts majors." The results were urban studies (sociology and geography), biochemistry (biology and chemistry), which attracted an unusual number of applicants with the highest SATs, and computer science majors. Additionally, about this time, the Department of Economics was transformed into the Department of Economics and Management Science, then the Department of Economics, Accounting, and Business, and finally into the School of Business. Importantly, the faculty bought into the changes, albeit at times reluctantly when the changes seemed to threaten their disciplines. Moreover, this was done while

---

[102]Thomas S. Colahan, interview by Martin L. Fausold, April 15, 1997.

[103]Letter from President Robert W. MacVittie to Wayne Mahood, November 24, 1987.

the faculty was being reduced from 309 to about 250, that is, from a student faculty ratio of 15:1 to 20:1.[104]

One seemingly mundane, but critical decision by MacVittie was to assign four state cars to the Admissions Office for October-December and March-May and MacVittie made his personal car available when he wasn't using it.[105] Such seemingly minor innovations were important, as SUNY colleges "had almost no flexible funds, and transfer of funds from one function to another was not allowed" at the time. The schools could call themselves whatever they liked (as long as SUNY was in the title), prepare their own calendars, develop curricula, establish campus administrative structure, etc., but budget decisions were limited. So MacVittie took advantage of what flexibility he had to distinguish Geneseo. Again, this was important to Geneseo's turnaround.[106]

Next, the admissions office, traditionally a two-person operation, was beefed up. Two 1978 graduate students were recruited to serve as admissions interns. Faculty and administrators visited schools and made phone calls with unparalleled intensity. The Student Association helped finance four-color recruitment brochures. Almost twice as many prospective students were interviewed in October 1977 than the prior year. Still, more was needed, what admissions director Caren dubbed "hyperbole." That is, Geneseo had to stretch the truth a bit—make the case that it was special and in demand. In short, Geneseo would adopt the trappings of a selective private college. Fortunately, Geneseo already enjoyed many of those.[107]

Even earlier, in 1971, when he anticipated the state's diminished funding, President MacVittie took another key initiative, not unlike private colleges and universities, creating the Geneseo Foundation as an institutionally-related agency to attract private support from alumni and friends to provide much-needed funding for student scholarships, faculty research, and travel to professional conferences. MacVittie also hired a vice president for college relations to foster development activities with money budgeted by Governor Carey for this purpose when SUNY was doing virtually nothing in this regard. This was followed in 1982 with the launching of an annual President's Donor Recognition Dinner to thank donors and recognize individuals for generous support and outstanding service to the college or community. By 2004,

---

[104]Bruce Ristow, email to author, March 18, 2009.

[105]Ibid.; comments by Arthur Hatton to the Geneseo History Committee, October 10, 2006; Letter from Robert W. MacVittie to Wayne Mahood, November 24, 1987.

[106]Letter from Robert W. MacVittie to Wayne Mahood, November 24, 1987.

[107]Ibid.; Caren interview; memo from President MacVittie to Dr. Van Quaal, July 14, 1977, Presidents' Papers, College Archives; memo from Dr. Frank Kemerer to President MacVittie, November 1,1977; Morphew, Toma, & Hedstrom, "The Public Liberal Arts College ...," 26.

the Foundation was providing over $1 million a year to support faculty and student projects.[108]

While Geneseo was putting itself on solid footing, its future was threatened by other changes forced on the college and on MacVittie's successor, Edward Jakubauskas, who arrived in 1979. Even though Jakubauskas resolved to make the college "the very best it can be" -and applications had increased 38 percent over the previous year, he was required under Governor Hugh Carey's executive budget to "eliminate another 27 positions by March 1981."[109]

To the state budget office, the most obvious way for Geneseo to absorb the cuts was to close the campus school, thus eliminating seventeen full-time and two part-time positions. This had been recommended earlier by then SUNY Chancellor Ernest Boyer, as the village did not need two elementary schools after a new K-12 school opened in 1974. Reluctantly, President Jakubauskas decided to shut down the venerable campus school. But this caused a serious rift in town-gown relations. After the decision was announced at a heavily-attended and acrimonious community meeting, a group of campus school supporters immediately but unsuccessfully sought to overturn the decision. "Oh boy. Oh, the hate mail. The violent phone calls and all that," Jakubauskas recalled almost two decades later. His departure from Geneseo may have been hastened by the reactions to this decision.[110]

Still more draconian cuts were demanded by the governor's 1982 executive budget, which "sliced" forty-six more positions from Geneseo and froze or eliminated other items. Jakubauskas complained that the budget cuts had transformed SUNY "from a tax-supported to a tax-assisted University." While the line may not have been originally from him, it delivered the message.[111]

Another momentous decision—also reached reluctantly—was to close Geneseo's School of Library and Information Science. For many, it was Geneseo and had been for almost eighty years. But the School's closing could

---

[108]Bruce Ristow, interview by Martin L. Fausold, July 8, 1997; Arthur Hatton's report to the President's "Cabinet," October 15, 1980, Presidents' Papers, College Archives; http://foundation. geneseo.edu/privsupp.shtml.

[109]*Geneseo Compass*, September 7, 1979; *Rochester Times-Union*, March 11, 1979; President's Annual Report to the College Council, September 19, 1980, Presidents' Papers, College Archives; *Geneseo Compass*, January 29, 1982; Interview of President Jakubauskas by Martin L. Fausold, August 18, 1998.

[110]*Geneseo Compass*, March 6, 1981. Plattsburgh also was told to close its campus school. Most of the rest of the campus schools had closed when instructed to do so by Chancellor Boyer in the early 1970s.

[111]*Geneseo Compass*, January 29, 1982, March 1983; interview of President Jakubauskas by Martin L. Fausold, August 18, 1998; *Geneseo Compass*, January 29, 1982. In 1983, new governor Mario Cuomo and the legislature tried to ameliorate the situation by announcing a plan to offer retirement incentives for personnel over age fifty-five.

be justified by its enrollment decline. Given the college's mission to serve undergraduates, its library school," the smallest accredited School of Library Science in the country," simply had to go, freeing up lines to institute a computer science program. However unpopular his decisions to eliminate two venerable parts of the college were, Jakubauskas had the support of the college "Priorities Committee." These decisions allowed the college to allocate additional resources to strengthen undergraduate programs.[112]

It was not all that hard to persuade the bulk of the faculty, whose departments would benefit from the lines freed up. The education faculty had been fighting a rearguard action for close to decade, and the Library School had isolated itself from the rest of the campus.

Importantly, SUNY Geneseo's "central core" was to be liberal arts courses "balance[d] by selected professional offerings [teacher education, accounting, speech pathology and audiology] that are built upon a liberal arts foundation." Geneseo's duty was to offer "a selected and limited number of high quality ... programs in areas that have a critical mass of resources of faculty, equipment, and support systems." With the exception of the computer science program, funded through the positions saved by closing the library school, no new programs were "planned or desired."[113]

The focus was to be on the opportunities Geneseo already offered. The college should tell the "Geneseo story," or, in the words of a distinguished teaching professor, "promote ourselves." It had grounds to do so. In 1983, only five years after it faced a devastating applications decline, Geneseo admitted only 49 percent of applicants, making it as selective as some well-known private liberal arts colleges. Re-allocation of lines—shifting faculty lines from low- to high-demand departments—though old to VPAA Colahan, was the new buzzword. Mathematics, physics, computer science, and language skills gained lines, while drama, dance, art, health and physical education, chemistry, and special education took reductions.[114]

Also, Geneseo was admitting a "different" student from those in the past. Not only were their SATs and high school averages higher, they differed from their earlier counterparts socioeconomically. By 1983, for example, interest

---

[112]*Geneseo Compass*, February 6, 1981; interview of Assistant Vice President Bruce Ristow by Martin L. Fausold, July 8, 1997; *Geneseo Compass*, November 6, 1981; Morphew and Toma, "Becoming ...", 10.

[113]Draft Budget and Planning Statement for 1982–83 to 1985–86, Presidents' Papers, College Archives.

[114]Annual Report 1984–85, Presidents' Papers, College Archives; *The Lamron*, October 19, 1984; *The Lamron*, February 22, 1985. Geneseo's acceptance rates and entering students' average SAT scores have been challenged by those who assert that Geneseo does not count Access Opportunity Program or Special Talent students, and there were times when the critics may have had some justification for their complaint.

in teaching by entering freshman had declined from 21.2 percent in 1967 to 15.4. Student interest in studying business had risen from less than 1 percent in 1967 to 26.9 percent in 1983. Their fathers' educational attainment had increased from 10 percent college graduates in 1967 to 30 percent in 1983. Parental income had risen from 0 percent above $30,000 in 1967 to 15 percent earning $50,000 or more. While those numbers do not take inflation into account, they indicate Geneseo was attracting students more representative of liberal arts colleges. The competition for students was no longer the State College at Buffalo or Oneonta—it was more likely Colgate or Hobart William Smith.[115]

C.   A "Success Story"

The first public notice that Geneseo was recreating itself was a 1985 Associated Press article, which reported that "Geneseo is everything one might expect in a private college." It lay "high above the Genesee Valley cornfields ... the picture of a comfortable private school." But reporter Peter Coy "advised the reader that it was not a private college; it was public." Geneseo's "success story" derived from the fact that it was among the most selective in the SUNY system. Geneseo not only competed with the privates, it had done so despite "a retrenchment period for SUNY in which Geneseo had lost 104 faculty and staff jobs."[116]

The hype coupled with the curricular changes were starting to pay off. Faced with the disastrous 1977 enrollment shortfall and caught up in the "transformative environment" which led many public colleges to become "universities" or larger comprehensive colleges, Geneseo bucked the trend. While it could have been tempted to admit more students and gamble on receiving greater funding, the college had opted to retain its small size and primarily undergraduate status and to adapt the privates colleges' techniques to "become the public alternative to the small selective private college." And it regularly told the "Geneseo story" to college counselors in high schools throughout the state, touting each entering class as the "brightest" yet and citing SAT scores, high school averages, and career aspirations.[117]

---

[115]James McNally, Geneseo Freshman Class Profiles: 1967 to 1983. Geneseo, New York: Office of Institutional Research, SUNY Geneseo; Report 84–5.

[116]"Geneseo in the News," undated article from the Associated Press New York State wire, Presidents' Papers, College Archives.

[117]Christopher Morphew, et al., "The Public Liberal Arts College ...," 4; Caren interview, January 3, 2005; "Class of '84 Termed 'Brightest in Years,'" Geneseo Compass, September 5, 1980, for example. Two other colleges bucked the trend: Truman State (once Northeast Missouri State College at Kirksville) and the College of New Jersey (nee Trenton State). The latter owes its transformation in part to Dr. Gordon Goewey, formerly music department head and graduate dean at Geneseo.

AP reporter Coy's article about SUNY and Geneseo ushered in head-turning accolades. The November 25, 1985 *U.S. News & World Report* ranked Geneseo seventh best of four-year liberal arts and professional schools in the East. Four years later, Geneseo beat out nearby Rochester Institute of Technology, Ithaca College, and fellow SUNY unit, the University at Buffalo, to place third among the top regional colleges and universities in the North. Factors weighed in the ranking were selectivity, faculty quality, academic excellence, retention, and—of all things—financial resources. Meanwhile, the May 1986 *Money* magazine called Geneseo one of "Ten Public Colleges with an Ivy Twist." The school's science departments were "noteworthy academically," while education, music, and philosophy were "humanities standouts." Then in 1991 *Money's Guide to the Best College Buys in America*, which combined private and public schools, ranked Geneseo twenty-eighth of one hundred. Three years later, Geneseo was fifteenth and the only four-year SUNY school ranked in the top one hundred. The higher ranking was attributed to graduation and retention rates and the percent of budget spent on academic quality.[118]

Better yet, on November 12, 1990, the *New York Times* profiled Geneseo. With its "ivy-covered buildings ... [which] soar startlingly out of the surrounding cornfields," Geneseo was "becoming one of the nation's most selective, highly regarded public colleges." In fact, a SUNY administrator called Geneseo's achievement a "marvel." "Increasing [institutional] quality" along with low tuition were the keys. And the students themselves were different—more affluent, but unwilling to spend money on Ivies like Cornell and Brown.

By Geneseo's own measures it was succeeding. Between 1979 and 1987, Geneseo enrolled 300 National Merit Scholars, had its first Carnegie/CASE Professor of the Year for New York, and a bootstrap operation led Geneseo to outrank better-known schools such as Johns Hopkins and Haverford for being "wired" (campus computer access) and later for being wireless. In 1986, for the sixth consecutive year, Geneseo was the first SUNY unit to close freshman applications with 6,800 applicants, the most of any SUNY arts and science college.[119]

Importantly, unlike the "major institutions" in the area (Rochester Institute of Technology and the University of Rochester), which had "launched expensive public relations campaigns," the March 29, 1987 Rochester *Democrat and Chronicle* wrote that Geneseo had "quietly"—and inexpensively—succeeded.

---

[118]*Geneseo Compass*, October 13, 1989; *Geneseo Scene*, Winter 1986, Summer 1991; *The Lamron*, September 8, 1994.

[119]Yahoo Internet Life, May 1998, May 1999, May 2000, May 2001; News Release, "SUNY Geneseo Ranks Among Top 'Unwired' Colleges in the U.S.," April 22, 2004; *Geneseo Scene*, Winter 1986; *The Lamron*, February 20, 1987; Annual Report, 1991–1992, Presidents' Papers, College Archives. *The Geneseo Scene*, Summer 1991, reported that the class of 1995 (1991 freshmen) had a high school average of 92.7, with an SAT mean of 1173.

The next steps in the transformation were taken by Dr. Carol C. Harter, a dynamo succeeding Jakubauskas, who became president of much larger Central Michigan University. Harter not only sought more cosmopolitan and ethnically- and socially-diverse faculty and students, she wanted to advance Geneseo's standing, while purging the campus of any signs of its teachers college past, e.g., eliminating any campus signs referring to "State," as in "Geneseo State." Importantly, Harter launched an ambitious—and ultimately successful— capital campaign to support faculty and student research, raising $7,000,000 and building momentum for subsequent efforts to enhance private support.

In the 1990s, Geneseo was also helped by being offered greater campus autonomy. A SUNY initiative, titled "Rethinking SUNY," afforded the various campuses the opportunity to distinguish themselves. One result was Geneseo calling itself "a public liberal arts college." (That is not a distinction any more—if it ever was—for the College Board labels all the SUNY four-year colleges public liberal arts colleges.[120])

By 1994, when Harter turned the presidency over to her provost, Christopher C. Dahl, to become president of the University of Nevada at Las Vegas, Geneseo was being recognized regularly. For example, in his 1996 guide to colleges, former *New York Times* education editor Edward Fiske wrote, "What a great place to start the rest of your life." Rankings then and later in *U.S. News & World Report, Money Magazine, Kiplinger's,* and *Time* supported Fiske's appraisal.

These rankings were supported by the quality of the students and faculty. For example, Michelle Morse, a dual biology-music major was named to *USA Today's* 1997 All-USA College Academic First Team. Geneseo can claim more than fourteen Goldwater awardees, a number of Mellon Scholars, and Dr. My Hang Huynh, a MacArthur Foundation awardee. Dr. Huynh, a 1991 graduate and Vietnam refugee, who received the so-called "genius grant" in 2007, was one of five siblings to obtain undergraduate degrees at Geneseo.

The faculty have proved their merit, as well. Even before the turnaround, one faculty member had earned the rank of Distinguished University Professor. Two faculty have been named Carnegie/CASE Professor of the Year in New York, four have been recognized as SUNY Distinguished Professors, fourteen were recognized as Distinguished Teaching Professors, seventy have received the Chancellor's Award for Excellence in Teaching, three have been awarded the Chancellor's Research Recognition Award, and two were honored by the Haimo Award for Distinguished College Teaching.

Perhaps the crowning achievement occurred in 2003, when Geneseo learned it would "shelter" "the most prestigious honor society in the country." The charter for a Phi Beta Kappa chapter had been granted to Geneseo—one

---

[120]Morphew and Toma, "Becoming ...," 18.

of only seven out of forty-one applications that year—making it the only public undergraduate institution in the state with a chapter.

D. Conclusion: Six Keys to Successful Institutional Change

A historian of education has observed that "Geneseo is a remarkable story of a public college finding a niche." Three times threatened with extinction, Geneseo, a multi-purpose college, has many of the trappings of a private liberal arts college. Careers of its alumni, many with modest family backgrounds, testify to Geneseo's success. They range from public school teachers to school superintendents, from television producers to commercial airline pilots and an army brigadier general, from college presidents to a presidential speech writer, from business CEOs to public office holders.

It took a concentrated, even audacious, effort to achieve the welcome recognition. Professors Christopher C. Morphew and J. Douglas Toma claimed it "required setting an overarching strategy after reading the external environment—and recalibrating both style and substance to embrace it in a disciplined manner both over the short and long term." According to Morphew and Toma, the steps that transformed Geneseo were leadership, perceived selectivity, the lower cost of a public college, a clear message to college counselors, a disciplined approach, and attention to faculty hiring.[121]

1. Leadership

President MacVittie took a chance, sought advice from subordinates, and acted decisively. Facing an enrollment shortfall that could have been devastating, he reallocated resources to focus on recruitment and—at the risk of failure—elected to stay small and become selective. Importantly, MacVittie took charge of recruitment and admissions. He recognized that the turnaround had to be a campus-wide effort—faculty, staff, and students were invited to and were willing to help.

2. Perceived Selectivity

Geneseo emulated the more prestigious private colleges. This wasn't all that hard to do, for the college had a product to sell; it was small and located in an historic valley, it had created a substantive core curriculum, and it had a quality faculty to teach the courses. It simply had to apply techniques common to the private schools, e.g., creating sophisticated posters, including one "with nice looking students ... ivy and an oak door ... [and] a caption: 'A touch

---

[121]Morphew and Toma, "Becoming a Public Liberal Arts College: Two Case Studies of Bucking the Trend," paper presented at the European Association for Institutional Research, Barcelona, Spain, September 2004.

of New England in Western New York.'" In time, the perception became reality—Geneseo became selective—surprising even those close to the college, including alumni and emeriti whose efforts contributed to Geneseo's growing reputation. Also, for the most part, it has overcome opposition within and without to the equity issue—whether a public college should be selective.[122]

The issue of selectivity will remain, however. SUNY was created to provide access and we are still reminded of the mantra that SUNY is to complement, not compete with, the privates. And this may be reflected in Geneseo's faculty and emeriti (possibly alumni as well) who remain somewhat divided over the issue of selectivity. Geneseo had for years served those who were the first in their families to go to college, and the faculty for much of the college's history well understood and appreciated that. While a teaching career may not have been the goal (it wasn't for Oneonta graduate Robert W. MacVittie), the normal school, later teachers college, offered many students over the years a means to a higher socioeconomic status than their parents. So by touting its selectivity, Geneseo has earned its share of critics. However, the same charge could be mounted against sister schools New Paltz, which claims to accept 36 percent, (a lesser percentage than Geneseo), or Binghamton, which accepts 39 percent, or Cortland with just a 44 percent acceptance rate.[123]

3. Price

Certainly, SUNY's lower tuition, based largely on the state legislature's reluctance to raise it, has helped Geneseo and other SUNY schools. Geneseo sold itself as on a par with private colleges, but cheaper. In 2006, the *New York Times* listed Geneseo as one of only three colleges in the northeast "seen as a first choice for high achievers who cannot or won't do the financial aid dance with private colleges."[124]

4. A Clear Message

Getting the message out to college counselors was vital. One of presidential assistant Kemmerer's early acts was to meet with college counselors in public schools to obtain their perceptions of Geneseo. Profiting from what he learned, Geneseo's beefed-up admissions staff, assisted by volunteer administrators and faculty, traveled the state clutching colorful brochures prepared by a newly-hired public relations person. Also Geneseo gained notice by being identified as a "wired," i.e., Internet-connected, college, before most, if not all, of its sister

---

[122]Ibid., 17.

[123]*New York Times*, January 10, 1946; www.collegesearch.collegeboard.com.

[124]Randal C. Archibold, "Off the Beaten Path: Twenty Colleges Worth a Trip or at Least a Detour," *New York Times*, July 30, 2006, sec. 4/A, 22–25.

schools. Not surprisingly, students and recent alumni were telling the "Geneseo story" to friends and acquaintances back home. Favorable media coverage both locally and nationally over the years has reaffirmed Geneseo's reputation as one of the nation's better public colleges.[125]

5.   A Disciplined Approach

One of those administrators who headed up the transformation claimed that Geneseo faculty and staff worked hard to "look, sound and act" like the school it wanted to be. The Rensselaer Conference attended by forty-two faculty and the following extended on-campus meetings set the tone. The commitment by President MacVittie and the three persons on whom he placed primary responsibility illustrates what it takes for a transformation. Their plan required discipline, focus, and initiative. There was a bit of gambling, also. The college would remain small, countering the rush to grow. Instead, it touted its liberal arts programs, its professional programs, and the newly-developed "practical, vocational minors." Further, faculty and staff proved willing to "go on the road" to display their "wares," even on occasion teaching public school classes on their visits to advertise the college. Not even the little "touches" were forgotten. For example, the admissions office "was completely refurbished, changing from a 'bureau of motor vehicles' motif to … one that corresponded more closely to what one might expect to find [at] a private college …." And the director, a Cortland alumnus, was renamed "Dean," to offer "a more exclusive-sounding term."[126]

6.   Faculty Hiring

A conscious decision to hire faculty who could and would do research to strengthen their teaching paid off. Once hired, faculty were put on notice that they would, as would SUNY faculty generally, be evaluated based on clear criteria, fifty percent of which was teaching quality. Moreover, Vice President Colahan valued flexibility. For example, in the mid 1980s, just sixty percent of the faculty were tenured and less than thirty percent of the faculty were full professors. The goal was to assure high quality faculty appropriate to the college's changing mission. The number of Geneseo faculty recognized as distinguished teaching professors or chancellor's awardees for teaching helps justify the college's reputation.

As Morphew and Toma have written, Geneseo has demonstrated "that change is possible in higher education—even monumental change." The

---

[125]*Yahoo Internet Life*, May 1998, May 1999, May 2000, May 2001; News Release, "SUNY Geneseo Ranks Among Top 'Unwired' Colleges in the U.S.," April 22, 2004.

[126]Christopher C. Morphew and J. Douglas Toma, "Becoming a Public Liberal Arts College: Two Case Studies of Bucking the Trend," paper presented at the European Association for Institutional Research, Barcelona, Spain, September 2004, 19.

venerable school has remarkably transformed itself from a normal school to a teachers college to a nationally-recognized public liberal arts college—and hopes its best days are still ahead.[127]

IV. From Schools of Agriculture to Colleges of Technology: A Century of Evolution

Joseph Petrick, SUNY College of Technology at Alfred

> Editors' note: This paper is devoted to the original six Colleges of Agriculture and Technology of the State University of New York. Consequently, two other current members of the technology sector are not included: the SUNY Institute of Technology at Utica-Rome and the SUNY Maritime College located in the Bronx in New York City. The former institution was founded in 1966 as an upper-division college providing graduate education programs and in 1973 received the authority to offer bachelor's degrees. In 2003 after converting to a four-year institution, it admitted its first class of freshman, who graduated in May 2007. The latter institution is a specialized college. For a full discussion, see Maryellen Keefe's paper "SUNY Maritime College: A History" in chapter 3.

Like other units of the State University of New York, New York's six schools of agriculture, which have evolved into Colleges of Technology, have adapted to administrative actions coming from various branches of state government throughout their history. As a result, the colleges of technology located in Alfred, Canton, Cobleskill, Delhi, Farmingdale, and Morrisville have evolved into hybrid institutions, offering associate, certificate, and baccalaureate programs in the applied sciences and technologies, as well as limited liberal arts. In addition to the similarities of program offerings, these six colleges of technology share a common history, having started as publicly funded schools of agriculture in the first decades of the twentieth century. For over a hundred years each of these colleges has undergone changes, and their evolution can be seen as a case study of the relations of public postsecondary schools with New York State.

A. Contract Colleges

The schools of agriculture started as a response not only to conditions in rural areas of the state, but also to the development of statutory or contract colleges, which are schools at private institutions that receive state subsidies. The concept began at Cornell University, where in the last decades of the nineteenth century

---

[127]Ibid., 20.

successive presidents had a vision for the development of the school, but, in spite of capital acquired from the 1862 Morrill Land Grant Act, lacked the money to attain that vision. In petitioning the state for more money, Cornell created the first statutory college in New York State, the Veterinary College at Cornell, founded in 1894. The legislation was vague, as the legislature did not seem to regard creating a school as being any different than providing funding for a dairy husbandry building at Cornell. The New York State College of Forestry was established at Cornell in 1898 with similarly vague legislation, but was later closed because of perceived duplication with the forestry school in Syracuse.[128]

A few years after the creation of the veterinary and forestry schools at Cornell, the proprietor of the Celadon Terra Cotta Company in Alfred suggested establishing a college of ceramics, to be funded by New York State. Legislation forming the New York State School of Clay Working and Ceramics at Alfred University was approved and signed into law by Governor Theodore Roosevelt in 1900.[129] Meanwhile, the dean of the agricultural school at Cornell, Liberty Hyde Bailey, successfully lobbied for state funding for the existing New York State College of Agriculture at Cornell. The state-supported schools at Cornell and Alfred became models for other schools. Without the establishment of the contract colleges, it would not have occurred to anyone to introduce legislation creating schools of agriculture.

B.   Schools of Agriculture

With the establishment of state-funded veterinary, agricultural, and forestry colleges at Cornell, as well as the clay-working college at Alfred University, the president of St. Lawrence University petitioned the appropriate state senator and assemblyman for a school of agriculture to be located in Canton. Legislation to create a state school of agriculture at St. Lawrence University was passed in 1906, with the understanding that the governor might not sign the legislation. A letter-writing campaign was undertaken, and Governor Hughes later joked that he "did not know there were so many inhabitants in all the North Country."[130] The Board of Trustees at St. Lawrence University controlled the operations of the agricultural school, and the St. Lawrence University business office controlled the accounts.

---

[128]Frank C. Abbot, *Government Policy and Higher Education: A Study of the Regents of the University of the State of New York, 1784–1949*. Ithaca, N.Y.: Cornell University Press, 1958, 60, 140.

[129]State University of New York College of Ceramics at Alfred University, *50 Years of Ceramic Education*. Alfred, N.Y.: SUNY Ceramics College, 1950, 4–5.

[130]Camille Howland, *Seventy Years of Change: A History of the State University of New York Agricultural and Technical College at Canton*. Ogdensburg, N.Y.: Ryan Press, 1976, 1.

In 1907 Morrisville lost its position as county seat of Madison County, and there were fears that it would become a ghost town as a result. A businessman suggested the municipality petition the New York state legislature for an agricultural school to be located in vacant county offices.[131] Meanwhile, the administration at Alfred University, which had already gone through the legislative process to have created the College of Clay Working, also petitioned its state senator and assemblyman for an agricultural school. Legislation creating the New York State School of Agriculture at Alfred University was passed on May 6, 1908, and legislation creating the New York State School of Agriculture at Morrisville was passed two days later on May 8, 1908. Although Alfred began operations in 1908, Morrisville did not begin classes until 1910.

At Delhi, a concerned local woman advocated for an agricultural school to be located in the recently closed Delaware Academy. The legislation creating the school was passed in 1910, but was vetoed by Governor Hughes because four bills that would have established agricultural schools were introduced into the legislature in 1910, and he would not endorse them all. Only on the fourth attempt in 1913 was the legislation signed into law by Governor Dix. The State School for Agriculture and Domestic Science (now SUNY Delhi) was formed in 1913, and instruction began in 1915.[132] The Schoharie College of Agriculture (now SUNY Cobleskill) was founded in 1911, and first admitted students in 1914. Legislation creating the New York State School of Agriculture at Farmingdale was passed in 1912, and classes were first offered in 1916. In each case, concerned citizens, whether educators, businessmen, Grange members or other interested parties were instrumental in lobbying for the legislation. There was no strategic planning used to determining where the schools were to be located, a fact noted in 1946 by a Joint Committee appointed by New York Governor Thomas Dewey.[133]

Buildings were constructed for the schools of agriculture on the campuses of St. Lawrence and Alfred universities, and thus there were college environments there that were unavailable at the other four schools. At Cobleskill, for example, the campus consisted of four buildings constructed by the late 1920s, and during its early decades the school had no dormitories. There was

---

[131]William M. Houghton, *History and Development, 1908–1968: State University of New York, Agricultural and Technical College*, Morrisville: Donald G. Butcher Library, 1968, 5–6.

[132]Eleanor Hussey Smith, *Delhi Tech: The First Half Century*. Delhi, N.Y.: Alumni Council, 1970, 5–6.

[133]Joint Committee on Rural Educational Services, *Agricultural Education in the State of New York: A Report of the Joint Committee on Rural Educational Services*. Albany, N.Y.: The Committee, 1946.

little change in the campus until the late 1950s.[134] Enrollment at each school of agriculture was less than 100 per year from 1908 to the mid-1930s, with the exception of Farmingdale, which had around 200 students in the early 1930s, and Canton, whose home economics program, which admitted several times the number of agriculture students, allowed the school to grow to around 200 students.[135] Rural teacher training was offered at some of the schools of agriculture, but such training was discontinued at the six agricultural schools between 1927 and 1931 to bring them into line with State Department of Education policy restricting rural teacher training to the normal schools and colleges.[136]

While the schools at Cobleskill, Delhi, Farmingdale, and Morrisville were autonomous from supervision of private institutions from the time of their inception until 1927, the relations between the schools of agriculture at St. Lawrence University and Alfred University and their host institutions were much like those between the College of Ceramics and Alfred University, in that they were controlled by the respective university's Board of Trustees.[137] The Hughes Commission of 1926 proposed a number of changes to the structure of state government, and was the first commission or committee to propose that there be a single administrator for education responsible to the governor. Some of the commission's recommendations were put into effect by legislation passed in 1927.[138] As a result, the schools of agriculture came under the direct supervision of the State Education Department. The schools of agriculture at St. Lawrence University and Alfred University were taken out of the direct control of the campuses at which they were located, and, like the schools that had no host campus, were placed under boards of visitors to oversee the campus for the Education Department. As a consequence, the Alfred and Canton schools became state-operated campuses with the formation of SUNY in 1948, and did not become contract colleges like those at Cornell or the New York State College of Ceramics at Alfred University.

---

[134]Freeman Ashworth, *History of Cobleskill College*. Klamath Falls, OR: Free-Mark Co., 2004, 27.

[135]Association of Teachers of Agriculture of New York, *The Record of Vocational Education in Agriculture: 1911–1941*. The Association of Teachers of Agriculture of New York, 1941, 6.

[136]Louis H. Pink and Rutherford E. Delmage, *Candle in the Wilderness: A Centennial History of the St. Lawrence University, 1856–1956*. New York: Appleton-Century-Crofts, 1957, 250.

[137]David Henderson, "Public and Private Relations in the Educational Complex: A Case Study of Alfred, New York." Unpublished Herrick Library, Alfred University, 2.

[138]Association of Teachers of Agriculture of New York, *The Record of Twenty Years: Vocational Agriculture in New York 1911–1931*. The Association of Teachers of Agriculture of New York, 1931, 13.

The six schools of agriculture had much in common, including a lack of funding. In 1931, during the Great Depression, a Special Committee was convened by Governor Franklin Roosevelt to study the state schools of agriculture. Despite the difficult economic situation facing the country, the commission concluded funding for the schools was inadequate, and recommended increasing their budgets.[139] It would be some time before the state was able to more fully address the conditions at the schools of agriculture, but when it did so it forever changed the mission of the schools and enabled them to adopt other curricula, thus encouraging their expansion.

C. Agricultural and Technical Institutes

In 1935, Lewis A. Wilson, then assistant commissioner for vocational and extension education for the State of New York, authored a report on technical education in New York State, titled "A New York State Technical Institute." Wilson envisioned an institution that would train students for industry in a manner similar to the agricultural education available at the schools of agriculture.[140] Because there was a perceived need for technical education and federal funding became available, in 1937 the New York State Education Department asked the schools of agriculture at Alfred, Canton, Morrisville. and Delhi to offer industrial and technical courses. A two-year course of study in technical electricity was offered in Alfred. Canton offered technical electricity and industrial chemistry, Delhi offered architecture and building construction, and at Morrisville, a two-year course of study was offered in watch and clock repairing and another in automobile mechanics.[141] In 1941 each school was renamed a New York State Agricultural and Technical Institute, at their respective locations. The adoption of technical curricula in the late 1930s led to requiring graduation from high school as an admission requirement, which had not previously been mandatory. Tuition continued to be free, but nominal fees were charged for materials.

With the expansion of the scope of the agricultural schools came the possibility of increased enrollment, and the technical institutes continued

---

[139]C. R. White, et al., *Report of Special Committee of the Governor's Agricultural Advisory Commission to Governor Franklin D. Roosevelt Concerning the Functions, Services, and Needs of the State Schools of Agriculture.* Albany, N.Y.: The Special Committee, 1931, 1–2.

[140]Albert E. French, "Autobiographical Recollections." In *Seventy Years of Change: A History of the State University of New York Agricultural and Technical College at Canton,* ed. C. Howland. Ogdensburg, N.Y.: Ryan Press, 1976, 48.

[141]George A. Gilger, "A Comparative Study of the New York State Schools of Agriculture at Alfred, Canton, and Morrisville to Determine Whether or not the School Programs are Suited to the Abilities and Interests of the Students for Vocational Training." Doctoral dissertation, Syracuse University, 1941, 14.

to grow during World War II. One of the reasons for this growth was war-related instruction, such as a training program for nurses at Delhi that began in 1943.[142] Another example was civil aviation instruction at Alfred, in which students received classroom training in Alfred and flew airplanes at the Hornell Airport.

As the institutes trained students and participated in the war effort, the Board of Regents developed its 1944 report *Regents Plan for Postwar Education in the State of New York*. The Regents were interested in promoting vocational education in New York State and proposed the creation of twenty-two new publicly-funded institutes of applied arts and sciences. Had the plan been implemented, these would have been the only additional institutions of public higher education in New York State, because one objective of the Board of Regents was to further strengthen existing private colleges.[143]

As Governor Dewey contended with the Board of Regents about the future of public higher education during World War II and the years immediately after, in 1946 the governor's office commissioned the report *Agricultural Education in the State of New York: A Report of the Joint Committee on Rural Educational Services*. The report assessed the six schools of agriculture and examined their position between agricultural programs in high schools and the New York State College of Agriculture at Cornell University, concluding that because they lacked land, classrooms, funding for qualified teachers, library facilities, and student housing, they were effectively not in a position to teach vocational students. The report stated that they either become properly equipped or close. The Joint Committee concluded, "The rural people of New York will support the existing agricultural and technical institutes if the state makes them worthy of support."[144]

With an increase in interest in technical education, the State Education Department created the Division of Technical Institutes in 1948. Five institutes of applied arts and sciences had been created as a result of the Board of Regents wartime plan at Binghamton, Brooklyn, Buffalo, Utica, and White Plains which, combined with the six agricultural and technical institutes, meant eleven institutions were serving the post-secondary vocational education needs of the state. Because the institutes were subsidized by New York State, they were included in the SUNY system in 1948. The SUNY Master Plan of 1950 recognized the need for community colleges, and in 1953 the SUNY Board of

---

[142]Smith, *Delhi Tech*, 22.

[143]Abbot, *Government Policy*, 199.

[144]Joint Committee on Rural Educational Services, *Agricultural Education in the State of New York*, 10.

Trustees approved conversion of the five institutes of applied arts and sciences to community colleges.[145]

D.   SUNY Institutes of Agriculture and Technology

With the creation of the State University of New York, the agricultural and technical institutes could award associate degrees and be granted accreditation by the Middle States Association of Colleges and Secondary Schools, and students could its transfer to other units in the university. The stand-alone units could continue much as they had before, but the schools at St. Lawrence and Alfred created particular problems for their host institutions. Although the institutes at Canton and Alfred had become independent of St. Lawrence University and Alfred University, respectively, the main buildings of each school were surrounded by private college property at both locations. As both SUNY units grew in enrollment, they increasingly placed a burden on the private universities whose administrations had lobbied for them over forty years earlier. The primary problem was that the Alfred and Canton institutes reported to SUNY rather than to the Board of Trustees at their respective institutions, in contrast to the statutory or contract colleges that continued to be administered by private universities.

As the physical plants at Cobleskill, Delhi, Farmingdale, and Morrisville slowly developed in the 1950s, the situations at St. Lawrence and Alfred Universities did not improve. SUNY did not take action to resolve the problems created by having public institutes of agriculture and technology located on private university campuses. At Canton, the Agricultural and Technical Institute's (ATI) agricultural operations were transferred to a farm purchased away from the campus in 1946.[146] The Alfred ATI increased the size of its farm with the purchase of additional land in 1951. In neither case was there any movement towards relocating either campus to nearby land holdings. There was no incentive for SUNY to move the campuses, and for the next thirteen years the Canton ATI made no further progress in separating itself from St. Lawrence University. By the early 1960s St. Lawrence University threatened to sue the state to recover the costs of improvements to the campus, although the improvements had been undertaken at the expense of the state.[147] The situation was resolved when it was announced on March 28, 1962 that the Canton ATI

---

[145]State University of New York Board of Trustees, *Annual Report, 1953*. Albany, N.Y.: The University, 1953, 13.

[146]Edward J. Blankman, Thurlow O. Cannon, and Neal S. Burdick, *The Scarlet and the Brown: A History of St. Lawrence University, 1856-1981*. Canton, N.Y.: The University, 1987, 48.

[147]French, "Recollections," 63.

would move to a 620-acre campus whose land had been donated to the state by the person who had in 1948 sold the state the land for the Canton farm.[148]

The situation in Alfred was similar. No attempt was made to move the SUNY unit, much to the concern of the Alfred University administration. In fact, SUNY aggravated the situation through the construction of an industrial building on land gained through a concession from Alfred University. President J. Ellis Drake reported to his Board of Trustees in June of 1948 that the relocation of the Alfred ATI would be beneficial to Alfred University, because it would relieve the housing shortage in Alfred and would allow the university to expand its classroom and laboratory facilities.[149] By 1955 the enrollment at the ATI had surpassed that of Alfred University's by a few hundred students, even though they were located on the same grounds. The strategy of Alfred University, as President Drake told the Alfred University Board of Trustees in 1955, was to wait for the institute to move to another location. Eventually land was purchased across Main Street and through the mid- to late-1960s the Alfred ATI built its campus essentially across the street from Alfred University. As with the other existing SUNY units, the Canton ATI and Alfred ATI were able to develop their campuses as a result of the policies of Governor Nelson A. Rockefeller.

E. Rockefeller Years

Soon after election to his first term as governor, Nelson Rockefeller empanelled a Committee on Higher Education, which in November 1960 issued the Heald Report. In addition to its recommendation that SUNY be given greater freedom to carry out construction and charge tuition, one of the committee's proposals suggested "the agricultural and technical institutes be converted into community colleges."[150] The conversion would have had the advantage of having the counties in which ATIs were located support the schools. Not only did the affected counties lobby to keep the institutes as state-operated campuses, but St. Lawrence and Alfred universities also objected to such a change. The conversion of the ATIs to community colleges would have shifted their missions away from a predominantly vocational and technical curriculum towards a liberal arts curriculum in direct competition with nearby liberal arts institutions.

---

[148]Blankman, Cannon, and Burdick, *The Scarlet and the Brown*, 48–9.

[149]M. Ellis Drake, *Report to the Alfred University Board of Trustees*, 1948. Drake Papers, Herrick Library, Alfred University, 21.

[150]New York State Committee on Higher Education, *Meeting the Increasing Demand for Higher Education in New York State: A Report to the Governor and the Board of Regents*. Albany, N.Y.: State Education Department, 1960, 30.

In addition to the ongoing construction at the six ATI campuses, Alfred ATI created a vocational division by renovating and remodeling eight buildings at the deactivated Sinclair Oil Refinery in Wellsville, and classes began there in October of 1966.[151] Although the location of the vocational division had advantages such as the use of existing structures, its distance from the main campus in Alfred created transportation problems because dormitories were never built there. Although the Wellsville campus was intended as a model for other SUNY institutes of agriculture and technology, no campus emulated Alfred by creating a vocational division so far removed from its main campus.

F.   Baccalaureate Programs

The administrations of the agricultural and technical institutes have sometimes been interested in expanding their missions. One example is President David Huntington's 1972 "Proposal for a Polytechnic College at Alfred," which included bachelor of technology and bachelor of business administration degree programs.[152] The administration at Alfred University did not want bachelor's degrees to be offered at what President Huntington was already calling Alfred State College, and was relieved that the programs were not approved by SUNY. It was not until the mid-1980s that SUNY encouraged the agricultural and technical colleges to offer their first bachelor's degrees. After the building construction of the 1960s, the developing financial crisis in the State of New York in the mid-1970s prompted the *Second Report of the University Commission on Purposes and Priorities* to suggest increasing efficiency by deferring new activities, decreasing program diversity, reducing enrollments, and consolidating or closing campuses.[153] The *Second Report*, which intentionally concentrated on budget and administration, aimed to provide an approach for SUNY to use in considering difficult budget decisions. The *Final Report of the University Commission on Purposes and Priorities*, released six months later, instead focused on the educational mission of the campuses and the implementation of that mission. Regarding the institutes, the *Final Report* noted that although they offered associate degree and certificate programs, "In the future they may offer baccalaureate programs in a limited number of fields not readily available elsewhere within the university."[154]

---

[151]Elaine B. Hritz, *The First Sixty Years: A History of the State Agricultural and Technical College at Alfred*. Alfred, N.Y.: SUNY Agricultural and Technical College, 1971, 177–78.

[152]David Huntington, *Proposal for a Polytechnic College at Alfred*, Huntington Papers, Hinkle Memorial Library, Alfred State College.

[153]State University of New York, *Second Report of the University Commission on Purposes and Priorities*. Albany, N.Y.: State University of New York, 1975.

[154]State University of New York, *Final Report of the University Commission on Purposes and Priorities*. Albany, N.Y.: State University of New York, 1976, 41–42.

Five years later, the State Education Department report *Engineering Manpower and Engineering Education in New York State: A Report and Recommendations for Action* recommended increased capacity in undergraduate engineering. It also suggested the establishment of upper-division programs in engineering technologies, because of a perceived general need for more engineers.[155] One of the ways the SUNY Board of Trustees acted on the report was to encourage the institutes to offer a limited number of baccalaureate degrees in engineering technology. For example, in 1985 Alfred State College began offering a bachelor of technology in electrical engineering technology in conjunction with the State University of New York at Binghamton. Although there was interest in offering bachelor's programs at the agricultural and technical institutes, the primary impetus of such programs came from SUNY system administration's response to a report concerning a shortage of trained engineers. Once bachelor's degrees were offered in the sector, additional offerings became possible.

The institutes of agriculture and technology had already substituted the word "college" for "institute" in the names of their schools by the mid-1960s. Twenty years later, the Agricultural and Technology Colleges Presidents Association agreed to change the names of the colleges to "colleges of technology."[156] The campuses at Cobleskill and Morrisville retained agriculture in their names, becoming the State University of New York College of Agriculture and Technology at Cobleskill and the State University of New York College of Agriculture and Technology at Morrisville. The changes were approved by the SUNY Board of Trustees on February 25, 1987.

In the 1990s, there was an interest in cost savings resulting not only from financial problems, but also from political pressures. In 1995 the Board of Trustees of the State University of New York delivered to Governor Pataki the report *Rethinking SUNY*, which recommended a collaborative project among the colleges of technology. As a result of the report, the University Colleges of Technology Alliance was developed. In cooperation with a liaison from SUNY System Administration, the presidents at each of the five upstate colleges of technology (Alfred, Canton, Cobleskill, Delhi, and Morrisville) formed an executive team to find ways to facilitate institutional cooperation. There was a good faith effort to form a real alliance, as administrators and faculty from each institution worked together to solve the problems inherent in such a project. SUNY allocated millions of dollars for things such as video and computer equipment, and courses were made available via video as early as 1996. The videoconferencing and computer equipment did not prove to be an effective

---

[155]University of the State of New York, *Engineering Manpower and Engineering Education in New York State: A Report and Recommendations for Action*. Albany, N.Y.: University of the State of New York State Education Department, 1982, 112–14.

[156]Earl W. MacArthur, "Letter to State University of New York Board of Trustees, February 6, 1987," Alfred State College Council Minutes, Hinkle Memorial Library, Alfred State College.

solution to the problem of the geographic distance separating the individual schools, however, and by 2002 the project was quietly put aside.

G. Conclusion

The colleges at Alfred, Canton, Cobleskill, Delhi, Farmingdale, and Morrisville, having evolved from schools of agriculture, to agricultural and technical institutes, to colleges of technology, have long been responsive to pressures from various agencies and administrations in the State of New York. Their founding depended not only on the passage of legislation by the New York state legislature, but also on support from successive gubernatorial administrations. When the State Education Department suggested a change in mission, the schools changed their curricula. With their inclusion in the State University of New York, the schools continued to be responsive to the state over the course of the next six decades, either through cooperation in developing technical curricula, changing the mission to include baccalaureate programs, or experimenting with a collective administrative structure. The colleges of technology have accommodated successive New York administrations and will continue to do so. To paraphrase the report of the 1946 *Joint Committee on Rural Educational Services*, the people of New York will support the existing colleges of technology if the state continues to make them worthy of support.

Varied Missions in America's Largest "Comprehensive University"

Introduction

Christopher C. Dahl, President, SUNY Geneseo

In the house of SUNY are many mansions; the State University of New York is not only the largest comprehensive system of higher education in the United States, in many ways it is also the most complex and diverse. From this diversity comes great strengths. By the same token, however, the history of SUNY is complicated by the centrifugal and centripetal forces that such diversity within a single system entails. As a relatively young system of higher education composed of both new and previously existing institutions, moreover, SUNY has also been strongly affected by New York State's history of competition between public and private higher education and the extensive interpenetration between the two sectors, both before the establishment of SUNY and since. The histories of the campuses discussed in the first two papers in this section— SUNY College of Environmental Science and Forestry and SUNY Maritime College—bear out these generalizations repeatedly, reflecting the forces and counter-forces that have shaped the state university from its creation and still affect it today. The subject of the remaining paper, the SUNY Press, was founded almost two decades after SUNY, and is itself, a creature of the whole University as it reached maturity.

Hugh Canham's incisive article on the College of Environmental Science and Forestry (ESF) plainly shows the interpenetration of public and private in SUNY's history. In 1898, Governor Black called for a full four-year curriculum in forestry at Cornell—New York's (largely private) land-grant university, and Cornell continued to offer a degree in forestry until 1936. Syracuse University President James Roscoe Day wanted a state-funded school at his institution, and through his efforts, the College of Forestry was founded in 1911. Syracuse's strong Methodist control spurred opposition, however, and authority to appoint the college's Board of Trustees was transferred from Syracuse University to the governor of New York.

As Canham points out, ESF's history was shaped not only by the development of the profession of forestry, but also by changing attitudes to the environment and by federal legislation (notably the Multiple Use Sustained Yield
Act of 1960) as well as the original state law granting ESF's charter. Although
ESF was an original SUNY campus, its own development as a distinguished
professional school was in turn shaped by membership in the system, leading
to new curricula in 1958 and a change of name, from the College of Forestry to
the SUNY College of Environmental Science and Forestry in 1972—a transition that elevated the role of environmental sciences in its programs and clearly
marked the college as a fully independent unit of SUNY. As Canham ably
demonstrates, the college's "unique relationship" with the system has helped it
become "one of the true gems" in SUNY.

The historical roots of SUNY Maritime College go back even further,
to the 1860s. Its pre-SUNY history is, if anything, even more complicated
than that of ESF. It began, according to Maryellen Keefe, with the dream of
its "progenitor," Stephen B. Luce, commandant of midshipmen at the Naval
Academy: a vision of a nautical college where young men could be trained as
"officers of the commercial marine." Making shrewd use of the Morrill Act and
pulling strings in both Albany and Washington, Luce persuaded the New York
state legislature to establish a nautical academy and the federal government to
provide a training ship.

Two generations later, the institution, now called the New York State
Merchant Marine Academy, moved to Fort Schuyler (Thanks to the shrewd
political efforts of another graduate and faculty member). It received a permanent lease and WPA funding for buildings and a new pier. After the creation
of the U.S. Maritime Service in 1936, enrollment grew, and by 1942, as the
United States entered World War II, enrollment was so high that the maritime service cadets were moved to King's Point and the U.S. Merchant Marine
Academy was established. The institution at Fort Schuyler became the New
York State Maritime Academy and was authorized in 1946 to grant bachelor's
degrees. It became part of SUNY in 1949. Keefe argues that this was the real
turning point in Maritime's history. The pull of the university status conferred
by SUNY shaped the college into something much greater than the vocational
institute it had been: a nationally accredited college, "the premier maritime
education and training institution in the United States." The centrifugal tendencies of Maritime's specialized mission, having been brought into the orbit
of the SUNY system, led to a new level of excellence not possible before.

If Maritime and ESF represent centrifugal tendencies in SUNY, the State
University of New York Press is a unifying force. In "Why a University Press
Should Be and Must Be Relevant," Gary Dunham cogently addresses the
challenges and potential of a university press in the unique context of SUNY.
He hearkens back to Johns Hopkins President Daniel Coit Gilman's vision of
a great university press as a full partner in the advancement of knowledge and

the primary vehicle for its diffusion, "not merely among those who can attend the daily lectures—but far and wide." The SUNY Press is unique because it serves not a single campus, but a sixty-four-campus system. It can best partner with those campuses in advancing and disseminating knowledge by serving three audiences: "the community of scholars in a discipline, the university community, and the regional non-academic community." SUNY Press is well positioned to do this, but much of its potential—and thereby its claim to relevance—remains as yet unfulfilled. Looking to the future, the press could be one of the most effective means of leveraging the diversity of missions in SUNY to advance knowledge and to make more powerful the voice of the University as a whole.

The diversity of its missions and the breadth of its reach are two things that characterize/differentiate/distinguish SUNY. If it can achieve the proper balance between unity and diversity, between centripetal and centrifugal, SUNY will achieve its potential as a truly great system of higher education.

I. The College of Environmental Science and Forestry and SUNY: A Unique Relationship*

Hugh O. Canham, Emeritus Professor, SUNY College of Environmental Science and Forestry

The SUNY College of Environmental Science and Forestry (ESF), located adjacent to Syracuse University, will celebrate its 100-year anniversary in 2011. This unit of SUNY is one of the oldest continuous forestry schools in the country and more recently, a leader nationally and internationally in environmental sciences. The unique location at Syracuse is in no small part due to the strong advocacy of Syracuse University to have such a school a century ago. Forestry was the only program initially, but the evolution of the college and the changing political and social milieu not only changed the program, but led the addition of new ones. The formation of SUNY in 1948 added a new dimension to the operations of the college. Today ESF operates within a complex set of arrangements involving many audiences.

Professional forestry arose in early 1800s Europe, especially in England, France, and Germany. Foresters had been recognized as a part of the royal entourage since the Middle Ages, but a recognized profession with formal

---

*Author's note: For further reading and the source of the quotes please see: *Forestry College: Essays on the growth and development of New York State's College of Forestry 1911–1961*, Eds. G.R. Armstrong & M.W. Kranz. Buffalo: Wm. J. Keller Inc., 1961. For the last quarter century, please see Hugh O. Canham, *An Update on the History of the SUNY College of Environmental Science and Forestry: The Last 25 Years*, Syracuse: SUNY College of Environmental Science & Forestry, forthcoming, 2011.

education started in the 1800s. In 1873, Dr. Franklin B. Hough, a doctor from upstate New York, presented a paper at the American Academy for the Advancement of Science on the impending lack of productive forests in the United States. Other reports and studies followed and the need for professionally trained foresters was recognized.

By the 1870s several American universities, notably Cornell, were offering forestry lectures. Material was patterned largely after European practices, especially those in Germany. In 1898, New York's Governor Black requested a full four-year curriculum at Cornell University. Bernard Fernow, former chief of the U. S. Division of Forestry and a German forester, was selected to head the program. However, the fate of the Cornell forestry program got entangled in the ongoing controversy in the Adirondacks. Fernow, a strong advocate of European silviculture felt the best use of the Adirondack forest was to get rid of the native hardwoods where present, and replace them with planted softwood species (Norway Spruce, Red Pine, Scots Pine). His logging on the school forest in the region involved clearcutting and shipping hardwood to the Brooklyn Cooperage Company. Such unusual practices greatly upset the wealthy landowners of large tracts in the Adirondacks (Brandreth, Durant, Whitney, Huntington, Litchfield, etc.). They brought pressure on Governor Odell who vetoed the school's appropriation and effectively closed it in 1903. Fernow might have been justified on strict biological (i.e., silvicultural) grounds for his program but the events portended the strong social and political context in which U.S. forestry has always existed.

James Roscoe Day, chancellor of Syracuse University, wanted to have a state-supported school at Syracuse University and considered starting a forestry school as early as 1905, following the closure of the Cornell school. In 1907 Dr. William Bray was added to the Syracuse University faculty. Bray had experience in forestry and offered several courses in dendrology and forest ecology. Syracuse University also pushed for starting a state-supported College of Agriculture with two curriculums: agriculture and forestry. However, the creation of other agricultural education programs in the State led to modification and only the forestry program was carried forward. In 1911, the College of Forestry at Syracuse University officially opened with fifty-two students and two faculty members, along with the dean, Dr. Hugh P. Baker.

Opposition to the school was soon forthcoming from Cornellians who wanted to restart their own forestry program. In addition, there were arguments against having a state-supported school at a strongly religiously dominated university (Syracuse University was a Methodist-backed institution and its chancellors, until the middle of the 20th century, were ordained ministers). These arguments were quelled when a subsequent bill was passed in the state legislature transferring authority to appoint the college's Board of Trustees from Syracuse University to the New York governor.

Heated arguments persisted and several public hearings were held. A major point of contention was funding for a new building. Chancellor Day enlisted the help of Louis Marshall, president of the newly-formed Board of Trustees, to bring pressure on Governor Dix. Marshall was from Syracuse, the son of German immigrants, and a successful lawyer. He had a strong love of the outdoors, served on several state commissions, and influenced legislation. Well known in the state capital, Marshall single-handedly got the governor to sign the construction bill. The new building, Bray Hall, was first occupied in 1917 with 9 departments: Silviculture, Forest Technology, Forest Engineering, Forest Utilization, Forest Botany, Forest Entomology, Forest Zoology, City Forestry, and Forest Economics.

The college extended its programs in 1912 with the opening of the New York State Ranger School as a part of the College of Forestry, at Wanakena in the western Adirondacks. This technical program initially provided a certificate and now offers associate's degrees in forest technology and surveying.

The scope and content of a professional forestry program was debated at several national Conferences of Forestry Schools. There has always been a "healthy tension" between courses in necessary foundations (history, economics, mathematics, language, botany, geology, etc.) and applied or technical courses (such as surveying, timber measurements, forest roads and engineering, etc.). The general program adopted at Syracuse was for 135 to 140 credit hours with general education accounting for about 20 percent, and the remaining 80 percent divided equally among technical and science courses. The tension has resurfaced in recent years after the SUNY trustees sought to prescribe general education courses for all campuses.

A unique feature of the forestry program at the college from its inception was the inclusion of a required summer field session. In 1913, it was held in the Catskills at the 100 acre estate of John R. Strong, who generously offered his property for college use. In 1915 the summer camp was transferred to the Adirondacks with the acquisition of land at the eastern end of Cranberry Lake on Barber's Point. The forestry summer camp remained there until the mid 1960s, when it moved to college land at Warrensburg and subsequently moved in 1992 to its present location back on Cranberry Lake at the Ranger School facilities located at Wanakena. The original site of the forestry summer camp at Barber's Point is now used as a biological field station for students at the college majoring in biological sciences.

In 1910, Cornell University restarted a four-year forestry degree within the Department of Forestry in the New York State College of Agriculture. During the depression of the 1930s, Dr. Harlan H. Horner, the New York State Assistant Commissioner of Higher Education, was authorized to study the situation of two institutions within the state offering forestry education. As a result of his study, Cornell agreed to discontinue professional forestry education, with the last class graduating in June of 1936. Today Cornell still offers some courses in forestry and is the location of the federally-supported state extension program in forestry, since Cornell is the federal land-grant-supported college in New York.

The New York State College of Forestry at Syracuse grew and programs were added and changed. However, emphasis remained on a strong professional forestry program. Nationally there was considerable debate on what constituted appropriate education for foresters and in the 1920s and 1930s; this debate colored the college's academic programs. Foresters in the early part of the 20th century found employment mainly in public agencies, such as the U.S. Forest Service, Park Service, and state forestry agencies. Timber harvesting, fire protection, and providing access to remote areas were among the main activities of foresters.

By 1933, a new curriculum was approved at the college. This curriculum was, in part, a reaction to what was seen as too much specialization and a tendency towards a trade school orientation, rather than a professional program. As Dean Hugh Baker stated in 1931, "It seems desirable and necessary that the work of the college should be kept always within the broad field of forestry with the understanding that the objective in the training of men ... is a well rounded education and a sound foundation for the profession of forestry."

The new curriculum contained two divisions, general forestry and forest production, with a common freshman year. All students continued to attend a summer camp after their sophomore year, although different for the two divisions. For the senior year there were ten areas of specialization: forest management, forest pathology and entomology, forest zoology, forest botany, park engineering, forest recreation, arboriculture, wood technology, conversion and distribution, and pulp and paper. This curriculum design reflected the changing role of foresters. While still finding employment with public agencies, the scope of activities broadened. In New York State, replanting of abandoned farm lands was a major task. Farm forestry, wherein foresters employed by public agencies provided advice to private forest owners, was emerging. Private industry was recognizing the importance of sustained management of its lands and was hiring foresters to manage company lands.

Thus the college had expanded, but the central orientation was always on forestry. The definition of forestry had changed somewhat over the years, as had the social and political environment in which the profession of forestry found itself. Still, much of the European culture persisted, both in professional forestry and in the forestry curriculum. European public forest services were often similar to military organizations with uniforms, a strict code of conduct, very specific course content, and a lore of forestry that permeated the education.

After World War II, all colleges and universities saw tremendous growth in enrollment. Coincident with national and internal changes was the formation of the State University of New York in 1948; Forestry was one of its thirty-two founding institutions. Initially, this had little effect on the College of Forestry and its programs. The name of the college remained the same. New York State was in good fiscal shape and both operating and capital budgets were favorable. More important were the changing social and cultural environments in the country, at the college, and in the forestry profession.

The GI Bill enabled returning veterans to complete a college education. Syracuse shared in this growth. The veterans mingled with the more typical undergraduates, but tensions existed. The older veterans questioned some of the courses and procedures. Foresters' roles were also changing. Recreational use of forests exploded after World War II. Watershed protection as a use of forests rose in importance. Private forest ownership became more and more dominated by non-farm owners as farm abandonment continued in the Northeast. Finally, the public was becoming more vocal in what they wanted from forest lands. Foresters were becoming land managers. Change in the curriculum was inevitable. Immediate postwar Dean Joseph Illick issued a comprehensive report in 1948 stating:

> The growing independence of the different people of the world, the importance of fostering international understanding and cooperation, the need for training in responsible citizenship, the increasing emphasis on human relations in forestry, the broadening and deepening base upon which forestry is now operating, and the many new forestry functions and responsibilities that are required in an adequate program of forestry education require a rethinking of objectives in forestry education.

At that same time, the college's enrollment committee issued a report stating that the demand for specialists in forestry and forest industry would be high in the future and that the college should consider several new curricula or options including:

1. Recreation management
2. Forest extension
3. Forest education
4. Forest botany
5. Forest entomology
6. Forest zoology
7. Microbiology option in pulp and paper
8. Administration option in pulp and paper
9. Cellulose and plastics option in pulp and paper

Interestingly, some of these options, especially those in the biological sciences, were brought in with the new curriculum in 1958, but formal recognition of recreation management program had to wait for several decades and forest extension and forest education have yet to be fully implemented.

The new programs were viewed as compatible with retaining forestry as the centerpiece of the college. However, viewed from the vantage point fifty years later, those new programs marked a major turning point for the college. Only students in land management-oriented programs attended the summer camp. Within the broad land management category, students enrolled in the biological sciences took different courses from their sophomore year onward. Their orientation was toward a particular science and not to forestry as a professional area of study. Also, within what was still considered forestry, several areas of specialization appeared at the undergraduate level: world forestry, social sciences, forest measurements, and management.

By 1961 there were five broad curricula within the college: general forestry, pulp and paper technology, wood products engineering, wood chemistry, and landscape architecture. These academic programs were organized into three major divisions: biological sciences, resources management, and physical sciences. In addition, much effort was put into forest extension through outreach in public lectures, short courses, radio, film, newspaper releases, exhibits, brochures. Research and graduate study exploded with the infusion of federal grants and added state monies. The college became one of the major forest and natural resources research centers of the world. Many areas were explored, but all centered around forestry, the forest and its uses. The original Article 121 of the State Education Act of 1911 still held; the college was to educate people in the management and use of the forest resource for the benefit of humanity. Passage of the national Multiple Use-Sustained Yield Act in 1960 gave further impetus to equal consideration of outdoor recreation, fish and wildlife, water, range, and timber resources of the forest as national policy.

In 1964 the general forestry curriculum was abolished and replaced by four new curricula: forest biology, resources management, forest engineering, and landscape architecture. In the resources management curriculum, the summer camp, which had taken place after the freshman year since 1958, was shifted to follow the sophomore year and moved from Cranberry Lake to Pack Forest, Warrensburg. The field camp at the end of the junior year was eliminated. The program thus accommodated transfer students from two-year associate programs at other SUNY institutions, something that would greatly alter the forestry program for many years. Students in the forest biology program were given the option of attending a biological field session at Cranberry Lake at the site of the former forestry summer camp, operated by the college in conjunction with SUNY Albany or attending the forestry summer session at Pack Forest. Later all biological sciences majors were required to attend the biological summer session at Cranberry Lake.

Throughout the history of the college up to the 1960s, general forestry had dominated all curricula. In 1961 it accounted for 45 percent percent of undergraduate enrollment. However, by the fall of 1970, Resources Management (the new name for the general forestry program) accounted for only

26 percent. There were the strong beginnings of a major shift away from the core of forestry. This was predicated partly by a desire to show the public and potential students the breadth of natural resources management opportunities at the college and by the desire to have curricula which were not tied to professional forestry. The shift received further impetus from the expansion of research in areas related to forestry, but not usually thought of as forestry. Faculty and graduate students who studied in these areas sometimes knew little of, and did not relate to, forestry as a field of study. Instead they related to their basic science discipline.

Under the leadership of Dr. Edwin C. Jahn, dean of the college in the late 1960s, extensive academic planning took place. Among the questions raised by the planning committee was, "Is there a definable natural resource understanding, a central resource core that all graduates of a Forestry College should have?" The question would be answered in various ways throughout the next several decades.

In the late 1960s, the College Board of Trustees approved, in line with the SUNY policies, the change in name of the head of the college from "dean" to "president." Dr. Edward E. Palmer was appointed the first president in September 1969. He was also the first chief executive officer not to come from a natural resource background; instead, he was familiar with higher education and government. President Palmer's background included tenure as a faculty member in political science at Syracuse University and Director of Overseas Academic Programs for SUNY at Planting Fields Long Island.

Throughout much of U.S. history, forestry was a leader in conservation efforts. The early development of national forests, various programs of the Depression years such as the Civilian Conservation Corps and the Soil Conservation Service, and the immediate post-World War II era all saw forestry as a protector of the environment. However, during the 1960s, other calls for environmental protection were raised. Concerns arose over sewage disposal, air pollution, and the quality of life in inner cities. Books and other media portrayed the changing quality of the natural world. Other professions began taking up the same activities that foresters had previously performed.

Across the country, academic institutions were actively developing programs in environmental studies. Within New York State, units of SUNY and private colleges were moving to become centers of environmental education. In addition, the agricultural and technical colleges of SUNY—notably Morrisville and Cobleskill—developed forest technician programs. President Palmer and the college faculty became concerned that the college was not being recognized for its strong historical role in environmental issues. Accordingly, the president proposed renaming the New York State College of Forestry at Syracuse University to the State University of New York College of Environmental Science and Forestry and establishing four schools within the college: the School of Environmental and Resources Management; the School of Environmental and Resource Engineering; the School of Biology, Chemistry, and Ecology; and the School of Landscape Architecture. Faculty favored the name College of Forestry and Environmental Science, a reversal of the two components, but this was not done. The Syracuse University designation was dropped due to confusion over the college's identity and in recognition that it was a unit of SUNY.

In January of 1972, the name of the college was officially changed. Many faculty and alumni were unhappy with the change and especially the loss of forestry as the central focus of the college. They felt that if the public did not understand what the college was, it should be explained, rather than continue the misconception that forestry was a narrowly-defined technical area.

In 1978 the college moved to full upper division status, accepting only junior transfers from other colleges. This change hurt enrollment initially, but programs recovered. The strictly upper division status remained in place until the early 1990s, when freshmen were again accepted. The shift to upper division status was done to foster cooperation with other SUNY units, to combat what was seen as possible declines in enrollment, and to remove the pressure from lower division courses, many of which were taught at Syracuse University, requiring a large accessory tuition cost to the college. This arrangement with Syracuse University was always difficult for SUNY administration to fully understand.

Dr. Ross Whaley became president following the retirement of Dr. Palmer in April 1984. He began another extensive program review. The times had changed. Budgets were limited, the central administration of the State University and Board of Trustees were taking active roles in specifying enrollment targets and other procedures, and student enrollments were in decline from the heady days of overcrowded classrooms of the 1970s. Dr. Whaley eliminated the schools and replaced them with eight "faculties": chemistry, environmental and forest biology, forest engineering, forestry, landscape architecture, paper science and engineering, wood products engineering, and environmental studies. The move was designed to encourage cooperation and integration among units and to break down historic divisions that tend to surround a strong "department" designation. In 2000, following Dr. Whaley's retirement, Dr. Neil Murphy became the president of ESF. He has overseen incorporation of new technologies into existing programs, the change in unit designations back to departments, and the recognition of ESF as a doctoral conferring institution and one of the true gems of the SUNY system.

Several issues have arisen over the last sixty years as ESF tried to fit within the SUNY structure. First, the College Board of Trustees is appointed by the New York State governor; a unique arrangement within SUNY, leading to several instances where the ESF trustees disagreed with the SUNY trustees. Second, ESF is similar to the University Centers, or Doctoral Centers as they are now called. However, the college is much smaller than the centers, but has a disproportionally-large research program and funding. Third, the college operates no dormitories. Instead, students contract with Syracuse University for lodging or stay in private housing surrounding the campus, although for the future, specific housing for SUNY ESF students is planned.

Finally, ESF utilizes Syracuse University for teaching several general education courses and some specialized upper division and graduate courses. Although this has changed in recent years with the college teaching more general education courses, Syracuse University remains a vital partner to the college with the attendant benefits, yet significant differences from other SUNY units.

Several lessons can be learned from looking at the history of ESF. Similar issues and questions arose over the years. The question of how to balance technical or "skills" courses with basic science and humanities courses has been persistent. Another question has been the role and place of professional programs in the evolution of the college. A third question is how academics specializing in a particular area (which is the nature of academia) relate to their specialization while remaining attached to a broad professional area.

Another lesson is that curricula and courses are never static and academics will constantly work for some changes. However, those changes are often without major changes in actual course content. Each reiteration of curricula or administrative arrangement developed at the college was thought to be optimal. The college struggled to teach students things that it felt they should know, in a manner that would insure retention, integrate subject matter, concentrate on principles rather than specifics, and to stress team work, written and oral communications, problem analysis, and decision-making. Those things that were successful were so because of specific personalities and a strong commitment to teaching. Those that failed were due to lack of resources, conflicts among personalities, and the changing times.

History can be very useful in planning for the future. Professional forestry is still important in state and national resource management. The environmental programs at the college are growing and will be even more important in the future, and ESF is well-positioned to play an increasingly important role in SUNY and society as a whole.

II.   SUNY Maritime College: A History

Maryellen Keefe, OSU, Ph. D., Department of Humanities, SUNY Maritime College[1]

In 1837 the combined efforts of New York ship-broker Thomas Goin and the U.S. Navy succeeded in establishing a nautical school for American teenagers.

---

[1] Author's note: I wish to acknowledge my debt to Norman J. Brouwer's previous account for the College's Centennial in 1974; his fine work provides the context for my account of Maritime's succeeding thirty-four years—1974 to the present.

Anchored off the Battery, the USS *North Carolina* became the school's venue and among its crew in 1841 was fourteen-year-old midshipman—Stephen B. Luce—destined to become SUNY Maritime's progenitor. Luce's invaluable training aboard the USS *North Carolina* inspired a dream he nurtured for twenty years: to establish a "nautical college where young men [seeking] ... to become officers of the commercial marine ... [could learn] maritime law and the laws of marine insurance ..."[2]

In 1864, Luce prepared to implement his dream by researching British nautical education aboard the HMS *Conway* and the HMS *Worcester*, and in 1866, as commandant of midshipmen at the Naval Academy, he wrote a manual of seamanship that became the standard Navy textbook for forty years. Next, Luce turned to citizens in New York and Boston, urging them to rally behind his project and arguing that naval education would reduce marine disasters and provide an available cadre of trained sailors for the Navy in times of emergency.[3] Unexpectedly, an 1866 amendment to the 1862 Morrill Act provided Luce a further strategy.

Designed to establish land grant colleges, the amended Morrill Act authorized the hiring of Army officers to teach military science courses. Shouldn't it also contribute to the education of merchant mariners? With this end in mind, Luce sought to upgrade the quality of ships' officers; to obtain licenses, masters of merchant marine vessels would have to pass qualifying examinations. Aided by a letter of introduction from Captain Schufeldt of the USS *Wabash*, Luce met with Isaac Bell, Commissioner of Charities of New York City, on April 29, 1872, and demonstrated that America's loss of commerce to foreign ships correlated with the scarcity of both good sailors and good ships.[4] A year later, on April 24, 1873, when the New York state legislature authorized New York City's Board of Education to establish a nautical school, it provided $50,000 in state taxes, but asked that the Board apply to the federal government for vessels and supplies. Accordingly, on July 11, C.R.P. Rodgers, chief of the bureau of navigation, invited Luce to consult with the Board of Education, and

---

[2] J.D.H., "Stephen B. Luce, Class of 1846, Educator of the Navy, Founder of the Maritime Colleges," SHIPMATE Nov. 1856, p. 5.

[3] However, Luce's efforts met an unforeseen obstacle. In 1869 the Grand Jury of the District of Columbia had recommended creating a reformatory aboard a ship in the Potomac River. At the same time New York City, responding to a rapid growth in the number of delinquent and vagrant boys in its midst, created a similar reformatory aboard the USS *Mercury*, in conjunction with the Reform School on Hart's Island. The *Mercury* could accommodate 300 boys and its staff aimed to teach these boys "a sure and honest means of livelihood suited to their adventurous spirits." In its wake, this short-lived experiment tainted the fund-raising efforts of Luce and his fellow advocates for a New York Nautical School: citizens were reluctant to have their tax dollars spent on reformatories. See Cruise of the Schoolship MERCURY in Tropical Atlantic Ocean, 1870–1871. See also, American Heritage.com/Masters of the Merchant Marine.

[4] R.W. Schufeldt, letter to Isaac Bell, April 1872.

in August, the Nautical School Executive Committee asked that Luce prepare for Congress a bill for the encouragement of marine schools.

By September, Luce had sent Secretary of the Navy George M. Robeson a copy of the New York State bill and other materials to support his request that "the matter of nautical schools" be placed before Congress. Now a captain, Luce urged Congress to hold officers of the merchant marine to a "certain standard of proficiency" with penalties for substandard behavior.[5] Such a Congressional measure, he believed, would create a demand for nautical instruction. On November 13, Luce took several additional steps: he addressed the Naval Academy with his topic, "Manning the Navy"; he distributed copies of the Nautical School Bill, setting it in the context of an amendment to an 1871 law requiring certification of steam vessel officers; and he asked that a government-appointed agent inspect and report regularly on nautical schools. With support from legislators and commercial leaders in the port of New York, Congress passed Luce's proposed bill on June 20, 1874, and authorized the Secretary of the Navy to provide a suitable vessel "for the benefit of any nautical school or college."[6] Largely through Luce's persistent advocacy, federal assistance for maritime education had been realized, and by September 30, the sloop of war, USS *St. Mary* (now known as the New York Nautical School), had been assigned to Captain Luce's command and taken occupancy of her designated berth at 23rd Street and the East River. Seventeen men formed the crew and twenty-six cadets arrived on January 11, 1875, their number increasing to 123 by June 3. The first official inspection on September 15 found the school in excellent condition.[7]

For the next seventeen years—until 1893—the school continued, thanks to New York City Board of Education funding and the Navy's absorbing costs of ship repairs and replacement equipment. However, a roller-coaster pattern of insufficient funding and low enrollment would dog the school's operation for its first thirty-four years. Like the tide's ebb and flow, funds would be allocated and then withdrawn, larger ships would replace the USS *St. Mary* but enrollment would decline, and resignations and moves to abolish the school would stir the waters of alumni support and other initiatives that kept the

---

[5] Stephen B. Luce, "Nautical Schools in the U.S., a Historical Sketch," the NAUTICAL GAZETTE, Feb. 15, 1873.

[6] The Bill also stipulated that no person be admitted or sentenced to nautical schools as "punishment for crime." See Robert T. McLaren, *School Ships of the Maritime Academies, Sea Classics*, November 2005, (BNET website). Earlier incidents of nautical schools established as rehabilitation or punishment venues for delinquent boys had set precedents. See Brouwer, p. 6. Actually, no one who had been convicted of a crime could be admitted. See "The Nautical School St. Mary's" in *Harper's New Monthly Magazine*, Vol. LIX, No. 351, p. 343.

[7] *New York Times*, October 16, 1875. November 20, 1876, marked the U.S.S. *St. Mary*'s first commencement. Of the fifty-eight graduates, twenty-five had already been hired, and within a year, forty-one had gone to sea or served as third mates.

school afloat. Proponents targeted four major goals: state support, a larger ship, increased enrollment, and an on-shore base. All were achieved largely through Governor Sulzer's April 17, 1913 signing of the bill making the state responsible for New York's merchant marine school. Though the roller-coaster pattern continued through the Great War, the school survived. Superintendent and Captain J.H. Tomb's requested name change became official on July 1, 1929—the New York Nautical School(still located aboard a ship at a designated Manhattan pier) would become the New York State Merchant Marine Academy. President Franklin D. Roosevelt, meanwhile, had been asked for support and responded by requesting of the Navy a new training ship. In May, he also wrote to the Secretary of War for permission for the Academy to use a portion of the Fort Schuyler military reservation at the western end of Long Island Sound. The climate was ripe for expansion: a year earlier, Congress had passed the Jones-White Act which, with its $250,000.00 in ship construction loans, enabled the building of thirty-one passenger ships and the reconditioning of an equal number of cargo vessels.[8] Since New York was the busiest port in the world, Arthur M. Tode, a USS *St. Mary* alumnus, class of 1912, and a progressive head of the academy's Engineering Department, advocated that the New York State Merchant Marine Academy become a federal academy and that other states, rather than build separate schools, fund scholarships to the New York school.[9]

In 1931, when over 250 students applied for admission despite the program's increased requirements—a high school diploma and three years of study—Tode's dream of a merchant marine academy soon rivaling Annapolis seemed all but fulfilled. The Alumni Association, however, did not share Tode's vision. The Depression was affecting the maritime industry, job openings had declined, and fear of losing legislative support, coupled with opposition to sail training, grew daily. Nevertheless, in December 1932, Roosevelt signed a five-year lease for the Fort Schuyler property, providing the land base that Captain Tomb had been seeking for the New York Merchant Marine Academy, but the lease was subsequently voided because state law required that the

---

[8]Additionally, plans were in the making for nautical schools in California, Maine, Connecticut, and Maryland. In fact, a national merchant marine academy was under consideration. See *The American Merchant Marine*, April 1933, p. 13 ff.

[9]In March, 1931, however, when the USS *Procyon* was scheduled for decommissioning at Puget Sound Navy Yard, the Navy was reluctant to see her transformed into a training ship only for boys from New York. President Roosevelt, therefore, presented an emergency bill allowing enrollment of out-of-state residents, which became law on April 6. Next, Roosevelt had the *Newport* replaced by the *Procyon* and renamed the *Empire State*. In June, the *Empire State*, now transformed into a training ship, set sail for New York, arriving at Pier One on the Hudson on September 17th. After welcoming ceremonies, she proceeded to her winter berth in the Brooklyn Navy Yard. The name lives on—today's training ship is the *Empire State VI*.

101

school operate on-board ship. By May 5, 1933, new legislation had become law, but a new battle ensued.

Herbert H. Lehman, now governor, and related by marriage to Nathan Strauss, chairman of the Park Association of the City of New York, knew that the association wanted the Fort Schuyler land. Not until March 22, 1934, was a new lease signed, but though it involved only twenty-two acres, they included the Fort. More than one hundred years old, the Fort was dilapidated and the pier inadequate for mooring the training ship. Fortunately, the Temporary Relief Administration, having agreed to take on the necessary repairs as a relief project for the building trades, and, having initiated preliminary surveys and plans, requested and received a grant of $1,720,000. However, in 1936, just as the pier's restoration was nearly half complete, the Supreme Court ruled against Roosevelt's first National Recovery Act and abolished TERA (the Temporary Relief Administration).

All was not lost. In September of 1935, the Works Progress Administration (WPA) had been established and the New York State Commissioner of Education submitted a new request for the $1,720,000. As luck would have it, though approved by the WPA and forwarded to Washington, the paperwork was lost in bureaucratic channels for two months. When the New York secretary of state went personally to FDR for help, the president ordered the project expedited and increased the allocated funds to $2,900,000. Then, on June 29, 1936, Congress created the U.S. Maritime Commission and the U.S. Maritime Service to revitalize the shipping industry. On or before January 20, 1939, they were to establish a comprehensive system for the training of U.S. citizens to "serve as licensed or unlicensed personnel of American merchant vessels."[10]

By 1937 the new pier at Fort Schuyler had been completed and on January 19, the USS *Empire State* and the USS *Annex* arrived from the Brooklyn Navy Yard. The fort was dedicated as the New York State Merchant Marine Academy on May 21, 1938. By November 1, the U.S. Maritime Service had received applications from 3,275 prospective cadets, and by July 1940 the governor had directed the school to share its facilities with a limited number of maritime service cadets and a Naval Reserve School of Indoctrination. A year later, the naval reservists at Fort Schuyler numbered 150 and the maritime service cadets 100, in addition to the 171 already enrolled, for a total population of 421 in a facility designed for 300. Though maximum enrollment for the school had been set at 200, the Maritime Commission agreed in 1942 to raise it to 400. To avoid overcrowding, it moved 200 maritime service cadets across Long Island Sound to the former Chrysler Estate at King's Point in Great Neck, forming the U.S. Merchant Marine Academy. Naval reservists moved into the cadets' vacated

---

[10]U.S. Maritime Commission, Report to Congress on Training Merchant Marine Personnel, January 1, 1939, p. 181.

quarters and Captain Tomb went to King's Point to supervise the establishment of the new federal academy. Admiral Craven, a fellow Annapolis graduate and former navigation instructor on the USS *St. Mary*, assumed responsibility for Fort Schuyler and, that same year, the state legislature approved designation of the New York State Maritime Academy.

By the end of 1942, enrollment had grown to 310, and in 1943 it reached 415. The campus also grew—a new athletic field in 1941; a machinery hall in 1943; a boat shed in 1944; physics, chemistry, radio, and gyro laboratories by 1945; and, in 1946, a new training ship—the USS *Hydrus*, re-christened the USS *Empire State*—with a new superintendent, retired U.S.N. Admiral Herbert F. Leary. Then, on April 6, 1946, Governor Thomas E. Dewey signed a bill authorizing the New York State Maritime Academy to grant the degree of Bachelor of Maritime Science. To qualify as a degree-granting institution, however, the academy had to make some administrative changes. Admiral Leary would no longer serve as captain of the school ship, but become instead Maritime's first "president." An appointed dean would supervise all academic matters, assisted by newly-designated heads of departments possessing academic degrees, as well as merchant marine licenses. Dean Porter, himself a Harvard graduate, would encourage other faculty to earn appropriate degrees at nearby Fordham University and New York University. Lastly, a commandant of cadets would oversee discipline and all internal administrative matters.

Prior to 1948, the New York State Board of Regents had controlled all higher educational programs, public and private. Before the Board of Regents surrendered control of these colleges, it attained an agreement with Governor Thomas Dewey—no program in the state university system would compete with existing programs in the state's private colleges and universities. The Regents, largely alumni of private eastern universities and loath to compete with the private sector, agreed that there would be no "civil, electrical, or mechanical engineering curriculum in any state college."[11] Exceptions, however, were made for Maritime; it would have a marine engineering program and a marine transportation course.

The new university status conferred on Maritime College raised perplexing concerns for both Albany academics and the Maritime faculty. Could a Maritime education really be considered "collegiate?" Would its vocational tradition submerge the college's broadening academic goals? Despite such questions, in April 1949, the New York State Maritime College officially became part of the State University of New York—with the privilege of granting the Bachelor of Science degree in four areas: marine transportation, marine engineering, science, and humanities. In 1950 President Truman signed into law

---

[11] The New York colleges destined to become part of the state university system included eleven State Teachers Colleges, the College of Forestry at Syracuse, the Agriculture and Veterinary College at Cornell, the College of Ceramics at Alfred, Maritime College in the Bronx, and several two-year agricultural and technical institutions.

the Congressional bill that transferred Maritime's ownership from the Army to New York State and set the stage for further growth.

During Vice Admiral Durgin's administration, academics began to flourish. Whereas in 1947, for example, the library boasted slightly fewer than 4,000 volumes, by the end of 1948, its holdings had nearly doubled, and by 1950, numbered over 12,000 volumes. Extra-maritime curriculum likewise developed. Dr. George Gregory, chair of the Humanities Department, implemented courses in history, French, Spanish, English composition, literature, philosophy, and psychology. More instructors with degrees and Coast Guard licenses were hired. In 1952, with these improvements in place, Maritime welcomed its first visit from the Middle States Association of Colleges and Schools. After hours meeting with faculty, administrators and students and visiting classes and labs, the team gave Maritime College excellent ratings and praised many faculty members' superior performances. The Commission on Higher Education of the Middle States Association of Colleges and Secondary Schools readily granted full accreditation to Maritime College.

In 1952 the freshman class was split between deck and engine cadets and over the next five years, both programs expanded so that by 1957, a report recommended establishing three distinct curricula: operation of ships, marine engineering design and construction (including naval architecture), and marine business administration. Besides academic growth, Vice Admiral Durgin also attended to facilities expansion. He initiated several projects: a towing tank to study ships' hulls, installations for operating boilers and internal combustion engines, a sub-critical nuclear reactor, machine shops, computer labs, a meteorological station, and an oceanography lab. Then a 1954 fire destroyed one of the wooden dorms, necessitating the use of the training ship for sleeping and living quarters and sparking plans for new construction.

In 1958, the long-awaited building program began with a planetarium atop one bastion of the Fort (funded with $20,000 from R.J. Reynolds) and a nuclear science lab funded by the Atomic Energy Commission. In June of 1961, construction started on two three-story dormitories and a two-story mess hall. The new complex cost $3.4 million and was named after Vander Clute, class of 1921, former chairman of the Maritime College Council. The Fort, after a $375,000 renovation, housed a new, larger library with shelving for 80,000 books, and a spacious, carpeted reading room. One of four libraries to earn an annual award for design from the American Library Association and the American Institute of Architects, its collection numbered 45,000 volumes when it opened on December 27, 1964, but not until ten years later, on December 10, 1974—one hundred years from the day the USS *St. Mary* arrived in New York with Captain Luce at the helm—was the new Stephen B. Luce Library formally dedicated.

During 1964 the new physical education building, complete with an Olympic-size swimming pool, was named after former Superintendent Felix

Riesenberg. A waterfront building for storage, space for working on boats, and expanded recreational facilities came next. In 1967, the newly-constructed boathouse and student activities building over the water and north of the training ship's pier was named for former Superintendent Frederick S. McMurray, class of 1896. In May 1968, Maritime College dedicated its new science and engineering buildings to Arthur M. Tode, class of 1912, and Ross G. Marvin, who died on Admiral Perry's expedition to the North Pole in 1909.

Since wartime spurs all activity connected to transportation or national defense, the Vietnam War made the mid-and-late sixties a prosperous era for maritime education. One-hundred-sixty-seven cargo ships removed from the reserve fleet were reactivated, and in 1967, the shortage of personnel was so acute that Maritime's 107 graduating seniors had to rush through their program and deploy weeks earlier than scheduled. By 1969 enrollment at Maritime had reached capacity—725 cadets—and plans were in the works for an additional 300 cadets, another dormitory, and an expanded mess hall. Completed in 1972, Maritime's third new dormitory was dedicated to Commodore John S. Baylis, USS *St. Mary* class of 1903.

As early as 1964, Admiral Moore had appointed a Long Range Curriculum Study Group composed of staff and consultants to research and make recommendations regarding the academic program. After three years of study, discussion, and debate, the group submitted a comprehensive, revised report in December 1967. Its strong recommendations fell into two categories: academic and student life. The first included:

1. Adding new majors in: computer science, electrical engineering, modern languages, comparative civilizations, world trade, oceanography, meteorology, and ocean engineering
2. Initiating a summer session for Maritime students and the surrounding community
3. Establishing two new departments—economics and business administration
4. Demoting from required to optional the courses leading to licensing[12]

Recommendations in the second category—student life—were, perhaps, somewhat startling, since they presented serious doubts about the value of Maritime's strict military structure. The sixties witnessed demands for civil rights for the segregated South, rejected oppression in any form, and called for an end to the Vietnam War. "All we are saying is 'Give peace a chance'" filled the airwaves and anything smacking of militarism appeared offensive. School newspapers were often the venue for these protests, and even at Maritime, students staged anti-war demonstrations, but little change in student life

---

[12]Long Range Curriculum Study Group, Comprehensive Report, December 1967, p. 52.

resulted. Exit surveys of Maritime graduates reflect the mood shift in American culture at large. Whereas the class of 1952 strongly believed that Maritime instilled moral and ethical values, the class of 1964 urged that since so many graduates "find the military [structure] distasteful, to say nothing of those who [earlier] dropped out because of it," the military program should be de-emphasized. Maritime's Curriculum Group concurred, recommending, among other things, a relaxation of the student's military obligation during the academic week.[13] Although the college subsequently adopted some of the committee's recommendations, it bowed to strong voices defending the traditional military structure as a necessary prerequisite for future shipyard discipline and possible appointment of cadets to reserve commissions in the Navy.[14]

Implementation of the Study Group's academic recommendations, on the other hand, was more successful. On September 1, 1967, the new title "vice president for academic affairs" was conferred upon Dr. Alfred Lawrence, dean, and under his leadership, a program of continuing education supervised by the Marine Transportation and Marine Engineering departments, was endorsed in 1968 and grew to 721 cadets. On February 17, 1969, a new graduate program—the first of its kind in the United States, leading to a Master's of Science in Marine Transportation Management—met with final approval as did two new courses: Analysis of Ocean Transportation and Management, Statistics, and Finance: Money and the Capital Market. That same spring, Maritime offered a day-student program for older merchant mariners who wished to complete college degrees. In the summer, Maritime hosted two National Science Foundation institutes for middle and high school teachers of math and earth sciences. These programs further advanced Maritime's reputation as an important educational resource for the local community.[15]

1969 also saw Maritime's Humanities Department hosting a conference called "Conversations in the Disciplines." Directed by department chair

---

[13]Ibid., p.54 The other recommendations were: 1) A study of the reasons students dropped out or transferred; 2) Modification of dormitory rules, removing some restrictions; 3) "Open gangway" with curfews according to class; 4) Elimination of the use of student waiters in the mess hall; 5) Elimination of mandatory recreation periods.

[14]"A military atmosphere may create conditions ... in conflict with the academic atmosphere so necessary for the development of intellectual curiosity ... for a mind capable of imaginative thought," Ibid, p. 12. Similarly, the King's Point report stated: "Underneath the official time demands of the military structure is a whole substructure devoted to evading, avoiding, and escaping detection. These things ... consume an enormous amount of cadet time and creative energy." Ibid. p. 12. An earlier 1961 report on Kings Point had noted: "the cadets do not feel a strong moral or ethical relationship to the disciplinary procedure, but rather regard it as a system to be beaten." Kings Point cadets also found Maritime's summer cruise discipline less harsh than their Academy's. Ibid, p. 13.

[15]See the *Bulletin of the Alumni Association*, Volume 15, no. 2, April 1969, p. 2 and Vol. 17, February 1971, p. 8.

Dr. Joel Jay Belson, the conference emphasized scholarly development. In 1970, with $15,000 from the Equal Opportunity Program, Maritime sought to diversify its student population. In response to recruitment efforts, fourteen students (among them, three blacks and two Puerto Ricans—all culturally disadvantaged and needing financial support—were admitted and the next year, eleven more— among them two blacks, one Chinese, one Mexican, and one Puerto Rican).

Perhaps the most significant change in the college's history, however, occurred in 1972 when the first female, Marjorie M. Murtagh, applied for admission as a Naval Architecture major. She was rejected. Subsequently, the American Civil Liberties Union sued the state university, charging illegal gender discrimination, and when Maritime admitted her to the program, Murtagh became the first woman enrolled in a U.S. merchant marine institution.[16] By 1973, Maritime College had changed its regulations. Six women were admitted—including two daughters of alumni—and quickly proved capable of dealing with life at sea. Marjorie Murtagh, having proven both her competence and the rightness of Maritime's accepting her, assumed upon graduating in 1974 the position of Dean of Women, a role she held until she received her license as 3rd assistant engineer.[17] 1974 also witnessed the arrival of Maritime's first female professors, Janet Pomerantz (mathematics) and Karen Markoe (humanities).

As matters related to academic and student life continued to expand, new developments emerged, particularly in the Humanities Department. *Scrimshaw*, Maritime's first literary magazine, appeared in 1979, followed in 1980 by the *Humanities Newsletter*. That same year, the first humanities majors graduated. On April 3, 1981, Maritime's Humanities Department hosted the first annual Lawrence Durrell Conference with Dr. Julie Wosk delivering a paper titled, "Humanities and the Machine: Responses to Technology." In September, Professors Arnold and Karen Markoe directed and hosted "To the Sea in Ships—a Conference on Maritime History." Later, Dr. Markoe became president of SUNY's University Faculty Senate and served from 1987–92.

Throughout the late eighties and nineties, increased funding allowed enrollment to continue to grow and diversify. Increasing numbers of nonregimental or "regular" students applied and were admitted, as was an annual complement of international students, notably from Turkey. Another new dorm opened and more women joined the faculty. Humanities professors increasingly sponsored field trips so that New York City's museums and theaters might enrich course content. Today, Maritime College numbers almost 1,600

---

[16]See the *New York Times*, 29 June 1972, p. 43. Women constitute nearly ten percent of Maritime's student body, excelling in academics, intercollegiate programs, and receiving job offers from leading shipping and maritime companies well before graduation.

[17]*Bulletin of the Alumni Association*, Vol. 24, p. 4.

students and has doubled its applications for the 2009/10 academic year—this even before the current fiscal crisis.

How would Maritime College be different had it not become part of the SUNY system? Most likely it would have become the New York Maritime Academy and continued its tradition of maritime education and training. However, its thrust would have been directed toward vocational training, rather than a broader educational scope. It would never have gained ABET accreditation for its marine engineering and naval architecture programs. Already the oldest and largest, the SUNY affiliation has made Maritime the premier maritime education and training institution in the United States. Its Naval Architecture degree program, one of six in the United States, is the largest undergraduate program in the country. Its MS in International Transportation Management is unique (and celebrating its fortieth year), as are its degree programs in marine environmental science and maritime studies. Lastly, the size of Maritime's undergraduate engineering programs is most impressive—537 undergraduate engineers.

When Maritime College celebrated its centennial on December 10, 1974, many graduates could still remember those early years of sleeping in hammocks aboard small sailing ships and being called out at all hours to handle sail. The once 100-cadet school ship had evolved into a four-year college based ashore. As part of SUNY, Maritime College's facilities and programs have become an educational enterprise worthy of the Empire State and the greatest seaport in the Western Hemisphere. Though the current financial picture for New York State is dim, Maritime has a strong record of weathering financial storms. Administration and faculty look forward to continuing excellence as they strive to fulfill the college's mission for its students, the local community, the nation, and the world. "Fair winds and following seas!"

References

American Bureau of Shipping. *The American Merchant Marine*. New York: 1933, p. 13 ff.

Annual Report, New York City Board of Education, 1905, p. 405.

Annual Report of the Corporation, N.Y. Chamber of Commerce, 1883.

Brouwer, Norman J. *Centennial History of the S.U.N.Y. Maritime College at Fort Schuyler, 1874–1974*, SUNY Oneonta at Cooperstown, master's thesis, 1977.

Bulletin of the Alumnae Association, SUNY Maritime College, Vol. 15, no. 2, April 1969, p. 2 ; Vol. 17, Feb. 1971, p. 8; Vol. 24, p. 4.

Hess, Fred C. *Fort Schuyler and Me.* New York: City Island, 1996.

Harper's New Monthly Magazine, Vol. 59, No. 351, Aug. 1879, pp. 340–349.

Long Range Curriculum Study Group, Comprehensive Report, Dec. 1967, p. 52.

Marine Journal, Jan. 11, 1913.

McLaren, Robert T., *School Ships of the Maritime Academies, Sea Classics,* Nov. 2005, on BNET website.

National Gazette, Feb. 15, 1873.

New York City Department of Public Charities and Corrections. *Cruise of the School Ship MERCURY in Tropical Atlantic Ocean, 1870–1871.* New York: New York Printing, 1871.

New York Sun, Jan. 5, 1916.

New York Times, June 29, 1972.

Quinn, Brother Charles. *Iona College, Golden Jubilee: 1940–1990.* New Rochelle, N.Y.: Iona College, 1991, p. 67.

U.S. Maritime Commission, Report to Congress on "Training Merchant Marine Personnel," Jan. 1, 1939, p. 181.

III. Why a University Press Should Be and Must Be Relevant

Gary Dunham, Executive Director, SUNY Press

Let's go back 140 years and watch the dance of dissemination begin in earnest. It's 1869, and New York State bears witness to the opening of the first university press in the United States to operate in the name of the university itself. Although the first incarnation of Cornell University Press was short-lived, nine years later, in 1878, Johns Hopkins University Press opened its doors and has never closed them. The founder of Johns Hopkins University Press, Daniel Coit Gilman, felt clearly that his press played a vital role in carrying out the mission of the university: "It is one of the noblest duties of a university," Gilman announced, "to advance knowledge and to diffuse it not merely among those who can attend the daily lectures—but far and wide."[18]

Four key, interrelated truths tumble forth from Gilman's strategic vision and resonate across 131 years, truths that are crucial to the continuing relevance of university presses in the twenty-first century. There is much promise in the vision that led to the founding of Johns Hopkins University Press. A promise, I would argue, that unfortunately has not been fully realized or appreciated at institutions of higher learning today.

The first essential truth? *Dissemination matters.* Dissemination matters for institutions of higher learning. Universities have a "duty"—a mandate, a mission—to share, to publicize, to communicate the knowledge acquired by faculty and through research initiatives. Scholarship is not an isolated exercise; research is not an end in itself—in lock-step with researchers is the audience with whom they must share what they are learning, what they are finding.

The second truth? *Dissemination must be "far and wide" in intent and effect,* reaching and affecting scholars and students and those beyond the walls of academia. Not all knowledge, not all research, is aimed for and will appeal

---

[18]Lewis, Lionel S., *Scaling the Ivory Tower: Merit and Its Limits in Academic Careers.* New Brunswick: Transaction Publishers, 1998, p. 5.

to a wide-ranging audience—some remains rightfully within the classroom or scholarly vehicle of communication—but the mechanisms to disseminate relevant and useful information to benefit the regional community must be one of a university's priorities. In this way, a university press helps to bridge town and gown.

And the third truth? *An effective mechanism for concerted, ongoing dissemination of knowledge by a university is its press.* In 1878, Gilman saw clearly the vital role that a press could and should play at a university. It can become an encompassing mechanism for dissemination of knowledge and research; an opportunity to funnel and thus brand a university's knowledge and research as its own. As such, a university press is a unique entity on a campus because it and it alone possesses the specialized, transformative skills crucial for disseminating and publishing knowledge. These skills include developmental editing with a specific audience and form of presentation in mind, vetting and thus legitimizing through the peer review process, copyediting, typesetting and design, marketing, and sales.

The final truth springing from Gilman's long-ago vision is a logical consequence of the first three: *A university press can best achieve its totalizing promise, and a university itself can best fulfill its mandate of dissemination within and without its walls, when there is a close interconnection, an ongoing synergy, between the operations and mission of a university and its press.*

And so the dance of dissemination between a university and its press began, and we all are still learning the steps today.

So much and so little has changed during the 131 years since the founding of Johns Hopkins University Press. For-profit publishers with investment in disseminating research, proliferate across the landscape, offering good choices, but expensive publications to scholars and university officials. The vehicles and possibilities of dissemination in the digital age are increasingly complex, yet they are also exhilarating and so full of promise for content-providers and readers alike.

Yet, despite the obvious dramatic shifts in the forms and business of scholarly communication, the dance remains. Answering Daniel Gilman's call, some 125 university presses have sprung up at campuses across North America and beyond.

One of those presses is our very own State University of New York Press. SUNY Press has sponsored nearly 5000 publications since it was founded in 1966, publications that speak effectively to SUNY Press's three crucial roles in 2009: (1) an international publisher of distinguished scholarship in several fields; (2) through its Excelsior Editions imprint, an energetic regional publisher of books of general interest on New York State history, culture, and lives; and (3) the disseminator of research and knowledge when needed on the sixty-four SUNY campuses. And SUNY Press is unique among its sister university presses, as it answers not to a single campus, not to a consortium of a few campuses, but to an entire state's integrated educational system of higher learning.

That unique relationship is powerful and full of promise for both the SUNY system as a whole and its press. That collaboration over the past year has been reforged and we are, together, rapidly moving forward in the same direction toward mutually defined, mutually shared goals. Through digital and print media, SUNY Press continues to make an important difference in several scholarly disciplines. At the same time, through digital and print media, SUNY Press has renewed its commitment to disseminating research when needed on the sixty-four campuses—publishing scholarly research, as well as works of cross-over and general interest written by SUNY faculty; vetting and disseminating in timely fashion the proceedings of research conferences and symposia held at the campuses; offering free workshops on publishing to faculty and graduate students; and partnering with museums and research institutes to not only market and sell what they have already published, but also to serve as a full-fledged publishing partner from inception on future projects. As needed, we are there, including disseminating papers emanating from SUNY's 60th anniversary conference.

But when one looks at the landscape from above, gazes at the entire sweep of all university presses, far less satisfying and much less interesting scenarios abound. In my view, Gilman's vision of university dissemination, his dream of the promise of a university press, has not been fully appreciated or realized in the twenty-first century. This is a dangerous time for university presses as their relevance, their centrality to the university's mission, is called into question by their universities. Even before the current economic crisis and now, especially, university presses on several campuses are under siege. Budgetary pressures force previously latent attitudes of indifference and irrelevance to the surface and university presses are now suffering for it. Some will undoubtedly disappear this year or next; some will be absorbed by the university's library system, a process that has escalated in recent years; and many press's budgets will lose a sizeable amount of funding from their host institutions.

Yes, university presses are in many places under siege and are losing battles in the war for relevance. In most cases, both universities and university presses are to blame.

Let's look at it from the university's side first. Over the last century, over 120 universities decided at some point to support a press in their midst. Over 120 universities at some point saw the investment in their press as closely tied to their mission. But over the years, for various reasons, tectonic plates began shifting and a number of universities and their presses have begun drifting apart.

In my view, a university's lack of appreciation of the promise of its press today speaks to a much greater problem: that universities do not appreciate and embrace dissemination in the holistic, mission-driven manner that inspired Daniel Gilman. These challenges include:

- There are few systematic programs to train doctoral students and junior faculty how to present and publish their research.
- Although campus-based conferences and symposia offer a wonderful opportunity to brand and make quickly-accessible a university's research initiatives, there are few systematic programs to process and publish such research conferences—organizers are left to scramble on their own to find a way to publish the proceedings and findings.
- Although different sectors of a university community—museums, academic departments, research institutes—are engaged in separate publishing initiatives, there's usually precious little effort by the university to integrate them organizationally or even conceptually in a way that could brand, and thus support, the university system as a whole.
- There is often insufficient real discussion, let alone systematic programs, to disseminate university-based research to the non-academic community.
- Tenure committees frequently discourage faculty publishing through their own university press because it is bewilderingly seen as less rigorous, less high profile.

How ironic that the same universities that mandate continual dissemination by faculty for advancement often do little programmatically themselves to disseminate for the university system as a whole. What about outsourcing? Outsourcing such integrated and concerted dissemination is not an ideal solution, as it reduces the potential of branding for a university, usually makes the final publication more expensive than if published by the university's non-profit press, and unnecessarily pulls publication funds out of the university system.

What a lost opportunity for a university to capitalize on the promise of its press. What a lost opportunity for all of us.

By the same token, university presses, especially their directors, are equally, if not more, to blame for the precarious positions that many now find themselves. Directors fold their arms and insist on being considered relevant by their universities, while at the same time doing precious little through their actions and their publications to demonstrate that relevance on an ongoing basis.

Ideally, a university press serves three communities equally, and in different ways: the community of scholars in a discipline, the university community, and the regional non-academic community. That balance has been upset over the years as many university presses shifted their attention more towards academic fields at the expense of their university's research initiatives. So many presses promote greatly through their catalogs and online presence their service to an international community of scholars; much less publicity is given to demonstrating their promise, and thus, relevance, as a disseminator of their university's mission to share knowledge and research. As a result, a number of university presses are little known and little visible on their campuses; they don't track and connect deeply enough with research initiatives and signature events, and so are not seen as players and contributors to the environment and mission of their campuses.

Relevance for a university press cannot be assumed by the press. That relevance must be earned and it must be demonstrated through synergistic strategic planning, continual action, and an indefatigable willingness to become intimately familiar with and embrace university research initiatives.

On many campuses today, bringing to fruition Daniel Gilman's inspired vision for a university and its closely collaborative press requires a great deal of strategic rethinking by university administrators and the press, alike. Clearly, a university press cannot function as simply a mirror of *all* research initiatives on a given campus—it's logistically impossible for most presses to do it all; publishing competition and choice for faculty members are healthy; and presses sometimes in their own right bring academic luster to campuses by showcasing academic areas not found at their host institutions.

Nonetheless, there are many, many unrealized opportunities for productive collaboration; as a university fully appreciates and exploits the specialized publishing entity within its midst, and as a university press works harder and more holistically to serve as a research portal and disseminator for its campus.

Such collaboration and energetic, encompassing vision are what the new SUNY Press is all about. As a unit of SUNY Central Administration, the press is uniquely positioned among university presses to address the dissemination and branding needs simultaneously of the state's largest system of higher education, each campus, and the particular research organizations at those universities and colleges. We are there to help when needed, to carry SUNY research and its distinguished brand into the world. A university press thus fully realized—a press making available its distinct skill set to further the strategic objectives of campuses and system, a press pivotally bridging campus, community, and scholars—becomes indisputably indispensable and relevant.

Community Colleges: Emergence of an Educational Giant

Introduction

Dennis Golladay, Vice Chancellor for Community Colleges, State University of New York

It was a small beginning, but one with great promise and a potential for explosive growth.

At the conclusion of the Second World War, national interest dictated access to higher education for thousands of returning veterans and a new emphasis on technical programs. As the paper by Marjorie Glusker details, New York's initial response in 1946 was the establishment on a five-year experimental basis of five Institutes of Applied Arts and Sciences, spread across the state and featuring two-year programs of study.

Fast upon the heels of the historic 1947 Truman Commission Report, Higher Education for American Democracy, New York's own Temporary Commission on the Need for a State University issued its 1948 report calling for the establishment of a state university system based on "a broadening of the public provisions for higher education on all fronts." One front was that of two-year community colleges, with the state institutes cited above converting to that status "where feasible." With enabling legislation later that year, the path was established for the creation of community colleges across the state as an integral sector of the State University of New York (SUNY). As envisioned, the community colleges would do more than focus on technical education, they would also offer general education curricula leading to transfer to a four-year institution, as well as specialized courses and education for part-time students. Thus was born the framework for the state's constellation of broad-based community colleges.[1]

The number of community colleges—and the number of students attending them—expanded rapidly in the following two decades. By 1967 the State

---

[1] Freda R. H. Martens. "The Historical Development of the Community Colleges of the State University of New York." SUNY Community College Topical Paper Number 1. (SUNY Office of Community Colleges: September, 1985), pp. 2–5.

114

University included thirty-six two-year community colleges, serving almost 80,000 full and part-time credit students. In 1975, six community colleges located in New York City were joined to the City University of New York system (CUNY), leaving the Fashion Institute of Technology as the only two-year SUNY institution in the city. Enrollments at SUNY's remaining thirty community colleges, however, continued to escalate dramatically, climbing to a headcount of more than 221,000 credit students in the fall of 2008, or over 50 percent of all SUNY enrollments.[2]

The dramatic increase in the number of community college students enrolled in college credit courses is only one chapter in the story of growth. A like number of students enrolled in non-credit instruction adds to the number of state residents served. Other chapters of that story deal less with numbers than with the growth of other important roles community colleges play, ranging from economic and workforce development, to community cultural activities, to remediation for under-prepared students. In other words, SUNY's community colleges have become essential players in the structure and future of the communities they serve.

All these aspects of growth are reflected in Marjorie Glusker's study of Westchester Community College. From very humble beginnings, Westchester has evolved into the fifth-largest community college in the state and one of the premier community colleges of the nation. Its participation in an inter-state WIRED grant and its pioneering construction of the Gateway Center for the area's immigrant population are only two of the noteworthy activities that have moved the college well beyond the traditional concept of a community college. In this fashion, Glusker's paper serves as a fitting "micro" study of the evolution of the state's community colleges in general.

If growth alone were the measure of success, SUNY's community colleges have been spectacularly successful. The constructs for the funding and governance of the community colleges, however, have been recurring problems throughout SUNY's history and have presented issues that have yet to be totally resolved. Both the original public funding formula of community college operating budgets (1/3 funding from the state, 1/3 from the local sponsor, and 1/3 from student tuition and fees) and the amended statutory provision for 40 percent funding from the state have traditionally been met on a statewide average only sporadically. The statutory provision for capital projects on a fifty-fifty matching basis of state and local sponsor funding has led to a system of "have" and "have-not" community colleges, depending upon whether the local sponsor is willing or able to provide its half of the capital funding.

---

[2]Denise Bukovan. "The Community Colleges of the State University of New York: An Overview." SUNY Office of Community Colleges: June, 2007; p. 9; "Official 2008 Fall Headcount." Department of Institutional Research, State University of New York: 2009.

Governance of the community colleges can also be an issue leading to various interpretations of authority. While SUNY's state-operated campuses are governed by a single Board of Trustees, each community college also has its own local board of trustees with statutorily assigned authority. This arrangement has occasionally resulted in differing views on the relationship of community colleges to the state university system. This college-system issue is the subject of the chapter's second paper on SUNY's community colleges by Cornelius Robbins and Benjamin Weaver. Fortunately, they realized in time that many of the key persons who played a major part in the development of SUNY's community colleges were still available and must be contacted and interviewed if an oral history was to be recorded, or the opportunity would be soon lost. In 2005 and 2006, the team conducted over one hundred interviews of major figures of all thirty SUNY community colleges, including presidents, trustees, deans, administrative staff, faculty, foundation board members, and alumni. Relying on the techniques of oral history in a "macro" examination of SUNY's community colleges, the study reveals that more often than not, the relationship between the colleges and System Administration has been smooth and mutually advantageous. Importantly, the interviewees felt proud to be part of a comprehensive system of higher education that could further benefit their students as they advanced to study at SUNY's baccalaureate-granting institutions.

These two papers—one a case study of the history of a single college, the other an examination of the early years of all thirty—chronicle an amazing transformation of SUNY's community colleges from the humblest of origins to the eminent position they occupy today. In the span of sixty short years, community colleges have emerged as a vital sector of higher education not only within SUNY, but also across the nation. That value was reinforced recently when the president of the United States cited community colleges as a key factor in the nation's economic recovery and vitality.

The promise has been realized.

I.   A Retrospective View of the Westchester Community College Experience

Marjorie Glusker, Westchester Community College

Westchester Community College (WCC) is a fitting case study for understanding the past development and future aspirations of SUNY's community colleges. WCC exemplifies the community college philosophy of responding to the needs of various constituencies and of adapting to their changing demographics, albeit with its own character.

WCC's uniqueness manifested in several ways. First, since the day it opened in September 1947, the college has had only two presidents. The first was Mr. Philip Martin, who served until 1971, and the second is Dr. Joseph N. Hankin, who has served since September 1971. Secondly, the WCC campus was the estate of John Hartford, an heir to the A&P supermarket fortune, and therefore, is a beautiful country campus in the midst of urban and suburban development. Thirdly, Westchester serves an extremely diverse county that has some of the poorest cities in the state—Yonkers, Mount Vernon, New Rochelle, Peekskill; some of the wealthiest villages—Chappaqua, Scarsdale, Briarcliff; and everything in between. The college also has a racially and ethnically diverse population. Fourth, WCC has the largest continuing education unit in the state and one that is fully integrated into the life of the college through the "one college concept." The non-credit offerings require approval from credit departments, the continuing education division administers some credit programs where appropriate, and some programs that start as non-credit offerings may transition to credit offerings, as the EMT/paramedic program did. Despite these and other unique features, in most ways, WCC's history and vision echo those of other SUNY community colleges.

A.   History

WCC began life as the Institute of Applied Arts and Sciences at White Plains, one of five such institutes established by the legislature of the State of New York on April 4, 1946. The institutes were established on an experimental basis after years of planning. World War II technology emphasized the urgency for the establishment of such educational institutions to train technicians. The Dewey administration established committees to survey occupational trends and to recommend a pattern of training for youth. These committees recommended that the legislature establish tuition-free, community-centered Institutes of Applied Arts and Sciences to extend educational opportunity for training at the semi-professional level to the youths and adults of the state.[3]

The Institute opened in White Plains on Sept. 29th, 1947, one result of New York's educators and legislators planning for the tidal wave of troops returning from World War II in need of training in new technologies that developed during the war. The institutes also were sensitive to the kinds of jobs that would be available in the communities. So for example, one of the first academic programs at WCC was building construction technology, in response to the impending residential and commercial building boom.

So it was that the workforce development focus of community colleges was already embedded in the institutes' DNA. Interestingly, more than sixty years later, responding to economic and environmental concerns, community colleges are returning to a variant of building construction technology with the new emphasis on green technologies.

---

[3]1951,'52,'53 *Institute of Applied Arts and Sciences Bulletin*, p. 11.

The five institutes (the other four were in Brooklyn, Buffalo, Binghamton, and Utica) that opened in September, 1947 were established by the legislature on a five-year experimental basis to see whether they succeeded and whether permanent quarters and additional institutes would be necessary. Five years later, all five of the original institutes were incorporated into the SUNY system as community colleges. To launch the Institute in White Plains, the state provided $75,000 for the acquisition of equipment and $73,000 for the first year's operation, a significant sum in 1947 that demonstrated the state's commitment to the project.[4]

The chair of Westchester's Board of Trustees in 1947 foresaw the Institute as "a school of technology and not trades ultimately might embrace the teaching of general college subjects."[5] So the seed of the comprehensive community college was planted in the development of New York State's system by the very early leaders of the institutes.

The first academic programs offered by the Institute were building construction technology, electrical technology, mechanical technology, and food service administration technology, and the first students were overwhelmingly male. When a medical and dental office assistant technology program began in the second year, more women enrolled. In June 1949, the first graduating class was composed of 183 males and 23 females in seven programs:

Building Construction Tech	31 males/0 females
Building Construction	33 males/0 females
Electrical Tech	53 males/0 females
Mechanical Tech	42 males/0 females
Industrial Chemistry	11 males/1 female
Food Administration	10 males/4 females
Medical and Dental Tech	3 males/18 females[6]

There was a work experience incorporated into each of these programs, whereby students studied for nine months and worked in industry for three months. This strong link between the Institute and business and industry is a legacy the community colleges have followed. The Institute responded to the training needs of mainly young men who needed more sophisticated technological skills and knowledge for a post-war job market than a high school

[4]*New York Times*, March 26, 1947, p. 30.

[5]*New York Times*, September 30, 1947, p. 23.

[6] The Techannual 1949, First Edition, pp. 27–33, (WCC's first yearbook).

education could provide. Women were largely absent in these work places after the war ended, as many left the workforce to begin families.

A poem from one of the 1949 graduates in mechanical technology gives a human face to that group of pioneers. Although presumably the work of a twenty-year old six decades ago, it sounds as if it might have been written on a different planet; however, it shows the same striving, grit, and determination, as well as humor, that can be seen in today's students.

Mechanical Technology Blues
Each Monday to Friday, from nine to four,
We do as we're told, their word is law.
What did you say? Another test?
But surely you jest, we're doing our best
Be sturdy and bold
So your mind will hold, remember
There's no greater pain
Than stress over strain.
Our friend, he says, "Test marks don't count,"
Listen, but watch the failures mount.
Don't you study? Why do you cram? Why use caution,
When someone might die and leave you a fortune.
Draw in drafting, work in shop,
Then across to the lounge for a soda-pop.
Supervisors, Executives, Designers and Draftsman,
One or the other we're planning to be,
But how many will make it, we soon shall see.
My advice to you all is,
"This can't keep up long"
As our instructor would say,
"Just push right along."
By Stumpy[7]

As Stumpy presumably said sixty years ago, "Just push right along." And today our community college students, who have multiple responsibilities, are pushing harder than ever to complete their studies and forge a better life for themselves, and in many cases, for their families, as well.

Since the Institute was a five year experiment, it had no permanent campus. The Institute was housed in a remodeled wing of the Battle Hill School, a public junior high school in White Plains. "It occupied three floors of a modern construction fireproof school building which was extensively remodeled to meet the particular needs of a technical education program. In addition to

---

[7] Ibid., p. 34.

cafeteria, auditorium, and gymnasium facilities, there were 38,000 sq. feet of floor space."[8] Within a few years, the library housed 3,500 volumes and subscribed to eighty periodicals, and the laboratories had the most modern equipment available. The Institute was an eight minute walk from the White Plains bus and train terminals, which was important, since the first class came from sixty-seven different communities. Thus, a cardinal principle of community colleges was established early—that of access.

While the Institute in White Plains was being established, the battle over the creation of a state university was being fought. By January 12, 1948, the *New York Times* reported that "both major parties (had committed) to the establishment of such an institution."[9] The details of the controversies and how they were resolved are not the subject of this presentation. From the point of view of the community colleges, the important fact is that all of the conflicting proposals included two two-year institutes with both terminal programs and transfer privileges. Studies had indicated that an overwhelming number of students did not get college training because of cost, rather than because of racial or religious discrimination. It was envisioned that no student in New York State would have to travel more than 25 miles from his home to reach a constituent college.[10]

Two months later, the *New York Times* reported that the establishment of a state university had bipartisan sponsorship. "Three separate measures were involved: One would set up a state university to consist of existing higher educational institutions supported by the State and such additions and extensions as might be authorized. The second would provide for the establishment and government of community colleges and the third for the outlawing of racial and religious discrimination."[11] Governor Dewey endorsed the proposals, saying that, "The barriers imposed by economic needs and those imposed by restrictions on members of minority groups will be overcome."[12]

The legislation specified the types of units to be included in the state university, specifically citing community colleges and setting up a temporary 15-member Board of Trustees. Senator Irwin Pakula, a Queens Republican, and Assemblyman Bernard Austin, a Brooklyn Democrat, were co-sponsors of the legislation that authorized counties to establish two-year community

---

[8]1951, 2, 3, Bulletin, p. 14.

[9]*New York Times*, NY Times, January 12, 1948, p. 21.

[10]Ibid., p. 21.

[11]The *New York Times*, March, 6, 1948, p. 15.

[12]Ibid., p. 15.

colleges.[13] And so SUNY was conceived with community colleges as a prominent component of its structural body.

SUNY's philosophy was clear from the very beginning. A few months after signing the legislation, Governor Dewey reiterated that "in the field of higher education we have also made advances (to make sure) .... that no youth, veteran or non-veteran, should fail of opportunity for higher education."[14] This philosophy has reverberated down the years through the halls of every SUNY community college.

On September 29, 1948, just one month after Dewey appointed the SUNY trustees, the White Plains Institute opened for its second year with three new features. First was the addition of medical and dental office technology. Second, a *New York Times* article stating that the Institute's purpose is "designed to train young men and women who cannot attend regular colleges because of time and finance, and other reasons" has significance.[15] Its reference to the students as young "men and women," as opposed to boys and girls, as in the announcement of the original opening a year earlier, probably meant the inclusion of older students into the day program. And thirdly, the Institute was opening evening courses for a minimum of 300 adults. Thus, very early in their history, community colleges were becoming diverse and inclusive institutions. Women were now mentioned and the opening of an evening program welcomed part-time students, as well. The Institute had come a long way in just one year. Its mission was taking form, one that would later be central to WCC and other community colleges.

The second year began well. Of the 225 first year students, 160 (approximately 70 percent) returned in 1948 for their second year. In addition, 270 new pupils entered the Institute, and 300 enrolled in the evening courses. A *New York Times* article declared the first year of the Institute experiment a success.[16]

It took nearly five years (and one extension) of the Institutes' five-year charter from the time Governor Dewey appointed SUNY's first trustees in August 1948 until the five Institutes of Applied Arts and Sciences became SUNY community colleges. It was a story filled with controversy over funding, location, and purpose. The transition began with a report in 1950 by the Temporary State Technical Institute Board recommending that the legislature study the possibility of converting the Institutes into community colleges.[17]

---

[13]Ibid., p. 15.

[14]*New York Times*, Aug. 26th, 1948, p. 1.

[15]*New York Times*, Sept. 28, 1948, p. 24.

[16]Ibid., p. 24.

[17]*New York Times*, March 10, 1950, p. 29.

A battle over funding then followed. The next year, Westchester's Board of Supervisors commended the Institute and asked for a one-year extension of the Institute's life, but protested against shifting any part of the cost to the county. In 1953 Governor Dewey proposed to the legislature that the state-operated Institutes of Applied Arts and Sciences be turned over to the cities in which they were located to be operated as community colleges under the state university program. This bill also laid out the funding formulas for both capital and operating expenses. The Governor asked for legislative action by August 31st of 1953. A few days later, the *New York Times* reported that if the cities where the Institutes were located refused to take them over with the proposed funding formula, they would be discontinued or go to cities that were willing to fund them. The Republican leaders of the Westchester Board then reversed their opposition to the conversion of the State Institute in White Plains into a SUNY community college and accepted Republican Governor Dewey's plan, claiming they had received concessions. The state legislature approved Governor Dewey's proposal to discontinue the Institutes and convert them into community colleges. Dewey signed the legislation on March 28, and on May 21, the Westchester Board of Supervisors voted in favor of operating the school after the state ended its control on Sept 1. Finally, on September 1, 1953, the Institute at White Plains became Westchester Community College.[18]

Next, WCC needed to find a campus, since the city of White Plains needed the Battle Hill School for the growing school-age population, and WCC had outgrown the space. After several false starts, the estate of John and Pauline Hartford, heirs to the A&P fortune, became available. The Hartfords willed the estate to Yale University, which used it for environmental and other research. Yale built one academic building, but the mansion, farm buildings, riding stables, and other amenities from the Hartfords remained. Since it was not cost-effective for Yale to maintain the property for so few students, it moved the program and the county approached Yale. Yale agreed to sell the 368 acres to Westchester County, which gave 218 acres and all the buildings to WCC and kept 150 acres. The price tag was $750,000, although the property was appraised at $1.5 million. The state university reimbursed the community college for 50 percent of their capital investments, as required by State law. The County received the $750,000 from Albany, and so the lovely pastoral campus with rolling hills, ponds, and all its buildings, cost the county nothing.

The students arrived on the new campus in 1958. Initially, classes were conducted in the greenhouses of the estate, in converted farm buildings, and in several rooms of the Hartford mansion itself. The first library was a stone garage. During the 1960s, an expansive building program began at the same

---

[18]Ibid., March 6, 1951, p. 29; Jan. 27, 1953, p. 27; Feb. 1, p. 76; March 10, p. 22; March 23, p. 18; March 28, p. 15; May 5, p. 21; and May 21, p. 33.

time that social, political, and economic currents were changing the world, including community colleges with their commitment to broad access.

In 1971, in the midst of this critical time, Phil Martin, the first president of WCC, retired. Dr. Joseph N. Hankin was hired as the new President, starting his tenure in September of 1971. Today, he is the longest-serving president in the SUNY system, completing his 38th year as president in 2009. His philosophy has always stressed expanding educational opportunities. Symbolically, one of the first things that Dr. Hankin did was to take down the barbed wire fencing that surrounded the campus and opened up the campus to the community. By 1972, the first off-campus and non-credit courses had been offered and open admissions was introduced.

B. Programs and Services for Special Populations

Just as the Institute was first established to serve the needs of the returning GIs from World War II, WCC saw the need to serve Vietnam veterans and women in the early 1970s. In 1972, GOAL (Growing Options for Adults through Learning) was established to support veterans returning from Vietnam and the many women who were returning to school after an absence from formal education to raise their families. Two WCC counselors ran the program and as the veterans assimilated into the college, it was decided that the women needed their own program of support that targeted their experience. So in 1975, the women's forum was created to help returning women negotiate the complexities of pre-computer registration, create a special orientation day, provide weekly counseling support groups, publish a newsletter, and have an open door counseling policy. At a time when many women—especially working-class women—were struggling to have their voices heard, the women's forum helped them achieve their goals. The program still exists, but with a more academic focus. It has served literally thousands of returning women for more than thirty years.[19]

This pattern of serving the needs of special populations continued throughout the 1970s, 1980s, and 1990s. For instance, in 1973 SUNY merged the more comprehensive Educational Opportunity Centers (EOCs). The centers had been created to serve what was then called the "educationally disadvantaged" (now commonly called the "underserved") in response to the flight of the middle class, the loss of manufacturing jobs, and declining schools and tax revenues in some neighborhoods of many cities. The new centers emphasized general/basic education, college preparation, and vocational and technical preparation, and offered counseling and specialized referral services for residents in the communities served. The EOCs were one of SUNY's main efforts to assist the underserved and WCC assumed the responsibility for administering

---

[19]Interview with Sue Shumejda, Founding Counselor of the Women's Forum, March 18, 2009.

the EOC-W, located in downtown Yonkers. Today it serves approximately 800 students annually, in a variety of developmental, academic, and vocational programs.[20]

In 1971, the introduction of non-credit courses opened up new possibilities for serving a myriad of constituencies. The Community Services Department, housed within the Division of Continuing Education, provides non-credit programs through innovative delivery systems. Starting with ninety-two students in 1971, it now serves more than 7,000 students per year. Originally, Community Services offered programs relevant to the economy such as travel agent, bank teller training, and shorthand. With technology and jobs changing, modern offerings include green technology and sustainable living courses, courses to enhance our connection with the environment, courses in new media, and sophisticated computer programs.[21]

Other special constituencies for which programs were established include older adults, businesses and career changers, displaced homemakers, and both unemployed and incumbent workers. For example, the mainstream program for older adults, which began as a student club in 1976, became the Retirement Institute in 1982 and established the Center for the Mature Workforce in 1984. Today, the mainstream program serves the occupational, recreational, and intellectual needs of older adults through programs such as the Collegium, which offers rigorous intellectual stimulation and social networking for older seniors. Other examples include Project Transition, a program with more than a twenty-year history that provides workforce training for widowed or divorced women who are now the sole wage earners for themselves and their families. The Professional Development Center (PDC) offers training and development strategies for large and small businesses, government entities, labor, and the not-for-profits. The PDC also focuses on entrepreneurship for aspiring as well as established business owners.

Through the years, the college created additional programs to serve the many underprepared students, low income students, students of color, and students with special needs who began attending the college. An Academic Support Center was created in 1984, the primary purpose of which was to assist students having difficulties in reading, writing, and mathematics. The college has an EOP program and a TRIO program, a federally-funded program for low income, first generation college students, and disabled students. At WCC, TRIO provides one-on-one tutoring, advisement, financial aid assistance, career counseling, and other services to help students become successful. WCC has a Black Male Retention Initiative, and took part in a Year of Diversity from 2008–2009, featuring speakers, activities, and recruitment initiatives all geared

---

[20]Information prepared Renee Guy, EOC-W Director and Associate Dean at WCC.

[21]Information provided by Sarah Fowler-Rogers, Director of Community Services at WCC.

to appreciating the diversity of our student population and further diversifying our faculty.

In the late 1980s, WCC began serving students with disabilities by hiring a learning disabilities specialist. Today the Office of Disabilities Services provides services to over 1,100 students with a full spectrum of disabilities, including learning disabilities, psychiatric disabilities, and other health impairments (health, visual, traumatic brain, Aspergers, etc.).

C. Three Major Efforts to Serve Our Changing Community: Extension 'Hubs,' W.I.R.E.D., and the Gateway Center

Over the last fifteen years, the college became a lynch pin in the economic development strategies of some of the economically abandoned downtown areas in some Westchester cities. The first extension "hub" center opened in Peekskill in 1994 in an abandoned Woolworth's building. An old Hudson River mill town that had fallen on hard times, Peekskill's once vibrant downtown was a shell with boarded-up businesses, very little activity, and a low income population. The city hoped to turn the downtown into a haven for artists fleeing the high rents of Manhattan by turning abandoned warehouses into artists' lofts. It also refurbished an old Paramount Theater into a rich cultural resource and asked WCC to open an education center to complement these efforts to revive the downtown. The college set up a new media center that focused on the digital arts, with cutting edge equipment and specialized staff, and offered liberal arts, ESL, and non-credit activities for the community and school district. It was an immediate success. Businesses went where they could get a trained workforce, student/artists went to where they could get skills and training on the latest equipment and have access to gallery space, and community groups and educational institutions used the facilities after school and in the summers. In 2007–2008, Peekskill had a credit enrollment of 2,243 and a non-credit enrollment of 690; its center has been a key to the ongoing recovery of Peekskill's downtown.

Peekskill's success drew the attention of county legislators representing several other cities, and the college was encouraged to build other extension hubs where it could contribute to renewal and economic development. The college was responding not only to different demographic populations on campus, but also to the needs of cities throughout the county, with new program ideas and new facilities. Each facility was developed with county, city, and a broad spectrum of stakeholder collaboration and input. Each facility had planning committees and advisory boards from the community, and each was developed with a particular focus. In 2001, new hub sites opened in Ossining and Yonkers. The Ossining Center, located in a former beer distributorship, offers courses in the life sciences and health care, with an active Summer Science Academy for kids and teens. Yonkers is located in one of the oldest open air shopping malls in the country and focuses on computers and information technology. Its enrollments have grown rapidly.

The Mount Vernon Extension Center opened in the heart of the city's Empire Development Zone in 2003. The center focuses on small business development, offers credit courses in culinary arts with a state of the art instructional kitchen, and provides the college's only off-campus academic support center for students. It is about to become a part of a new wave of development in Mount Vernon's downtown in expanded quarters, offering new technologies in addition to established programs.

Another large effort to extend the college's reach is participation in the WIRED (Workforce Innovation in Regional Economic Development) initiative of the U.S. Department of Labor for Westchester and Putnam Counties in New York and Southeastern Connecticut. The purpose of WIRED funding is to prepare American workers to compete for high-skilled high-wage job opportunities by coordinating business, education, economic development, workforce development, and community leaders to develop innovative, transformational changes to the workforce system.

The college's WIRED initiative, WIRED's Health Careers without Borders, is being conducted in partnership with Norwalk and Housatonic Community Colleges (CT) and enables Certified Nursing Assistants to become Patient Care Technicians. With the economic downturn, the regional workforce development infrastructure is being used to access federal aid for the region. The emphasis is training people for jobs that actually exist.

WCC also serves the influx of immigrants into Westchester's communities. The English Language Institute began to have long waiting lists for its ESL programs. Additionally, in 1999, the Westchester Community College Foundation received a grant from the Hitachi Foundation to assess the services and programs available to help foreign-born workers succeed in the Westchester workforce. The study showed that more than 63,000 immigrants had come to the Lower Hudson Valley between 2000 and 2007 and that 25 percent of Westchester County residents were born in another country. In Westchester County, 30.4 percent of the population speaks a language other than English at home. Westchester residents who do not speak English and have not attended college earn an average of $15,345 per year.

In response to the study, waiting lists for entrance into ESL classes, and other factors, WCC decided to build the Gateway Center, a 70,000 square-foot environmentally-green building that will provide programs targeted to the needs of new Americans.[22] Scheduled to open in summer 2010, the Gateway

---

[22]Information provided by Mia Fienemann, Director. Preparing Tomorrow's Workforce; The Gateway Center. Westchester Community College, 2007.

Center will house innovative credit and non-credit programs and activities, already-established college programs, and have a café, conference space, and a performance space. The center is the largest partnership of public and private funding ever undertaken by the college. The foundation not only raised money for the building, but also for programming. More than a full year before the building is scheduled to open for students, the college already has funding for an Institute for Entrepreneurial Studies to support and coordinate entrepreneurship education in Westchester County. It also has funding for the Community College Consortium for Immigrant Education (CCCIE), which raises awareness of the role community colleges play in immigrant education and integration nationally and promotes programs for immigrant students in the 1,200 U. S. community colleges.

Thus, WCC has stepped onto the national stage to be a leader in this issue because new Americans will be an important part of the solution to the problems that our country faces today, just as many of our forebears were part of the solution to our country's problems in their time. WCC accepted this challenge as a natural evolution given the college's tradition of serving—in every period—the populations that walk through its doors.

D. Conclusion

In the first edition of the Institute of Applied Arts and Sciences' yearbook, *The 1949 Techannual*, the president, faculty, and students called themselves pioneers. They knew that they were the first in a great new enterprise that would provide working people with access to education and training that they did not have, nor could they get elsewhere. In many respects, the experience of Westchester Community College in providing broader access to higher education to those who live and work in its service area, parallels the experience of the State University of New York. Westchester Community College is dedicated to the belief that growth and adaptation through educational experience are possible for individuals, organizations, and even whole communities at all stages of development. Over the past sixty years, the college has served students, organizations, and communities reflected in the ever-changing demographic composition of its service area. The ability of the college to change over the years to include first women; then all races, ethnicities, and ages; then all income levels; then business, government, and labor; then different special needs populations; and now recent immigrants, reflects public higher education's commitment to provide broad access and speedy responses to emerging community problems.

WCC's mission sometimes leads it to play roles that are not always comfortable for the college or its sponsors. Just as students are expected to stretch themselves, SUNY's community colleges have to continue to stretch themselves to fulfill the vision that the founders laid out more than sixty years ago.

They must continually take advantage of opportunities as they present themselves to broaden their reach and contributions. WCC makes decisions based on what the data demonstrates, but it also make decisions based on its values. As the college celebrates sixty-two years of service to Westchester County and the surrounding communities, it is also preparing to meet the challenges of the next six decades.

II. The Pioneers Speak: Voices from the Early Years of the SUNY Community Colleges

Benjamin J. Weaver, University at Albany

Cornelius Robbins' "SUNY Community Colleges: an Oral History of the First 30 Years" project produced an invaluable compilation of more than one hundred interviews conducted between 2005–2006 designed to preserve the memories and histories of the early years of the SUNY's community colleges. The foreword to the project's final report, written by Neal Robbins, the project director and editor, explains the study's purpose:

> Why have we undertaken this oral history project, producing a collection of some 109 interviews, with "veterans" of State University of New York Community Colleges? I, for one, have long been interested in hearing the stories of many of the leaders of these institutions, and have reached the conclusion that if we don't record them now, they may never be gathered. And I noticed with regret that we were losing those excellent founders who have passed on—so I made a proposal to some SUNY leaders and they offered the support needed. (Robbins 2006).

We interviewed those who were involved in the community colleges' early years (defined as from 1950 to 1980) and have intimate knowledge of the challenges initially faced and methods used in establishing and developing these institutions. Only the thirty community colleges that are presently part of SUNY were included, thus excluding the City University of New York's community colleges. This article provides an overview of the oral history project, some of the resulting findings about the relationship between SUNY and its community colleges, and the study's afterlife since its dissemination in 2007.

A. Methodology and Process

1. Funding and Support

The broad scope of this project, coupled with the sheer number of institutions included in the study and the expansive geography of New York State, required significant human and financial resources. The researchers were fortunate to have been supported by four main entities: the New York Community College Association of Presidents, the New York Community College Trustees, the Department of Educational Administration and Policy Studies in the School of Education at the University at Albany, and the Office of the Vice Chancellor for Community Colleges at SUNY System Administration. The funds permitted the researchers to travel across New York State to conduct the interviews face-to-face, a highly-recommended method for oral histories (Harris et al. 1975; Shafer 1980).

2. *Interviewing*

Keeping with the goal of creating a record of the early years of SUNY's community colleges, the researchers developed a series of nineteen questions that the interviewers would ask each interviewee, as applicable. The set of questions was designed to extract information on the interviewees' involvement in SUNY community colleges and the key issues involved in establishing and developing the colleges. The questions addressed the following:

- How the interviewee became associated with the college;
- Who were some of the interviewee's colleagues;
- What were some of the town-gown problems, if any;
- How the campus community reacted to the Taylor Law and collective bargaining;
- How the college worked to develop the campus;
- How and when the college established its foundation;
- What were some of the most interesting/exciting times for the interviewee;
- What the interviewee believes the impact of the college has been on the community;
- What the interviewee wishes had been achieved at the college;
- What were some of the difficult problems during the interviewee's time at the college;
- What were some of the top programs or services at the college;
- What was the relationship between the college and SUNY, and how did it evolve;
- How did the need for the college arise;
- Who were some of the opponents to the development of the college;
- How they selected their first president;
- What attracted the interviewee to the college; and
- Did the interviewee have any suggestions of others to interview (Robbins 2006).

To address these questions, it was important to have diverse interviewees. They were selected through the snowball sampling technique, which utilizes an interconnected network of people and groups (Neuman 2006). In this case, we began by reaching out to a list of contacts known to the researchers, as well as to individuals identified by staff at the Office of the Vice Chancellor for Community Colleges at SUNY System Administration. At the end of the interviews, these individuals were asked to identify others who might qualify for inclusion in the study. The expansion of the list of interviewees continued until each institution's list contained individuals with varying connections to the college (i.e. faculty, staff, trustee, administrator, student, etc.). The minimum number of interviews for each community college was set at three. However, when more than the required minimum number of interviewees were identified, these additional individuals were also included (Weaver 2008). To qualify as an interviewee for this project, the individuals must have been involved in the community colleges before 1980. A complete list of interviewees is included at the end of this chapter.

We initially conducted all of the interviews, however, as the project grew, additional interviewers were recruited. SUNY System Administration recommended two additional interviewers, Ronalyn Wilson, formerly of the Office of the Vice Chancellor for Community Colleges, and Jane Graham, former assistant to the executive vice chancellor and director of archives and records management. Additionally, as word spread across the state about this project, several individuals from SUNY community colleges volunteered to conduct interviews at their respective institutions.

The majority of the interviews were conducted in 2005 and 2006, although a few were conducted outside of this timeframe. Whenever practical, the interviews were conducted face-to-face. There were, however, cases in which face-to-face interviews were not practical. In these cases, interviews were conducted via telephone. All interviews, both those conducted face-to-face and those conducted via telephone, were recorded. The recordings were then transcribed and edited as needed, for inclusion in the final compilation.

B.   Final Product and Dissemination

The final product is a CD that contains at least three interviews from each community college. In addition to the interviews that were conducted in person, a small number of the interviews of individuals who passed away prior to 2005 are included in this collection. These were interviews provided to us for inclusion in the final product. The introduction includes a foreword by Neal Robbins, a greeting from Chancellor John Ryan, and a table of contents. The 109 interviews are organized into 30 separate folders, one for each community college.

The CD also includes a sizable appendix. It brings together six invaluable papers, four by Freda Martens and one each by Sanford Levine and George Anker (see Bibliography "The History of SUNY & of Higher Education in

New York State" for full citations.). It also includes later interviews with project director Neal Robbins and former FIT President Marvin Feldman, as well as lists of institutional founding dates and of system and institutional leaders from 1944 to 2005.

Over one hundred copies of the compact disc were created and disseminated across SUNY and beyond. Each community college received a copy of the final product and most placed the discs in circulation at their college libraries. The complete collection is also available on the SUNY digital repository website (please see the link at the end of this chapter).

C. Excerpts and Findings

This study successfully recorded the memories of more than one-hundred pioneers and extracted very important information on the thirty institutions. Since this book focuses on the history of SUNY as a system, however, the rest of this article highlights the findings related to the perceptions of the relationship between the community colleges and SUNY System Administration, or "SUNY Central," as it is commonly referred to in the interviews.

The State University of New York was founded at the peak of the "community college movement," and at a time when the systemization and coordination of community colleges was recommended by scholars in the field (Hillway 1958; Seashore 1940; Starrak and Hughes 1948; Stoddard 1944; Witt et al. 1994). While a number of states had taken the initial steps to crate a statewide system of community colleges, California, Florida, and Mississippi, in particular, "no state had been successful in creating a complete system of community colleges that covered the state geographically" (Weaver 2008). New York State was the first to plan and implement a comprehensive system of higher education that included community colleges, as well as four-year institutions and research centers.

The interviews suggest that the newness of this type of institution, the community college, affected the relationship between the community colleges and SUNY System Administration. During the early years of SUNY, administrators and members of the Board of Trustees were not completely familiar with community colleges' missions, nor how valuable they could be. Darwin Wales of Broome Community College recalled his early experiences with SUNY System Administration:

> SUNY Central had a Board of Trustees of which I eventually became a member that did not really believe in the greatness of community colleges. I can tell you that when I was first appointed, I was about the only person on that board who knew what a community college was or how it operated. And that is actually the reason I was appointed. But the chairwoman, who was a Rockefeller appointee, she had a recognition that the community

colleges were more important than the rest of the board thought they were. (Wales 2006).

Other interviewees echoed Wales's recollection that the community colleges were not completely understood during the early years. John Deans of Jefferson Community College explains:

> I think that for a long time the community colleges were not par-
> ticularly well-understood and certainly did not receive the focus or
> the attention that the four-year institutions did. Again, a function
> of the newness. I could remember many times going to meetings
> with whoever happened to be chancellor. We would get a little
> rowdy trying to get across the message that look at the number of
> students that are beginning their education at community colleges.
> It was quite clear that we were educating, to some degree, those
> who themselves might be leading the system but had never had
> any contact with a community college. So for a long time people
> would slip and refer to us as junior colleges. Then when you grew
> up you would be a real college, a senior college. That has changed
> today (Deans 2006).

This sentiment, that the relatively sudden arrival of the community college as a sector of the system of higher education caused uncertainty among administrators, is echoed by John Vadney of Fulton-Montgomery Community College:

> Historically, you've got to realize that community colleges were
> the slightly illegitimate children of the State University of
> New York. They existed, somebody passed a law and, all of a sud-
> den, we got these things. What to do with them was a real question.
> The entire community college law, which now runs at least two, if
> not three volumes, being constantly updated (I had a copy of the
> first two volumes), was about 12 pages long. Those are regular 8½
> folded-in-half pages. This was all there was to the community col-
> lege law. There was no Vice Chancellor for Community College
> Services or community colleges. We were tolerated. The concept
> of an open-door policy, which got its start, I believe, at the com-
> munity colleges, was very shocking at those times (Vadney 2006).

Some early administrators of the community colleges reported initially struggling with a perception that SUNY System Administration was "only interested in the research universities" and that they focused their efforts on "the four-year, state-operated campuses" (Katt 2006; Fatato 2006). The SUNY community colleges were viewed as being "treated as second class" early in the history of SUNY (Schafer 2007). Kim Martusewicz of Jefferson Community College suggested that in the past, it was perceived that "the four-year institutions got more attention at the SUNY Central level than the two-year institutions" (Martusewicz 2006). It was just a matter of time, though, before the situation improved. John Deans credits the rough beginning to the fact that the community colleges "were so new and it took a while for people to understand" (Deans 2006).

Aside from the newness of the community colleges, Carl Haynes of Tompkins-Cortland Community College suggested that the community colleges' unique funding structure, with funds coming from state sources, local sponsors, and student tuition, contributed to a relationship that was different from that of the state-operated campuses. Haynes explains that "the SUNY community college office had a staff but we weren't plugged in directly to the chancellor and I don't think we were seen as one of the sectors. We were seen as a product of the legislature because we were the local communities and that's where we were going to get our attention" (Haynes and Poland 2006).

Despite the rocky beginning to the relationship between the state university and its community colleges, this oral history indicates that the relationship evolved and quickly flourished over the first thirty years, as the community college began to earn its rightful place as an integral part to the American higher education system and indeed, the State University of New York's comprehensive system. This was essential because, as Orange County Community College trustee Jack McMahon stated, the administrators at SUNY Central "were holding the fate of the community colleges in their hands" (McMahon 2006).

Genesee Community College President Stuart Steiner recalls that during his "first 20 years or so in the system, there might be a member of the board who had an interest in community colleges, but they're very aware of community colleges now" (Steiner 2006). John Deans, former president of Jefferson Community College, agrees, stating that "you only need to attend a SUNY board meeting and you can begin to pick up that they recognize full well the role that community colleges play and their value to the system" (Deans 2006).

New York's community colleges' relationship with its system was considered by one interviewee to be much stronger than those of public community colleges in other states. Hadley DePuy, of Fulton-Montgomery Community College, recalls having a very positive relationship "at a time when, clearly, in many states the community college presidents would sit in the back of any meeting because with university and college presidents they were regarded as inferiors." He continued, saying that he "never once felt that at SUNY" (DePuy 2006).

Indeed, as the SUNY system matured, the relationship between the System and the community colleges also appears to have strengthened. James Hall of Dutchess Community College observes that "the relationship with SUNY is stronger now than when it first started because it was so new. I think SUNY is involved. You have a great deal of support and help from SUNY. Their interest, for example, in this history of the community colleges, is an indication of that." He continues, "there is a stronger relationship now than there was before.

I think the state university is very much closely tied together as a public institution in its totality" (Hall 2006).

In the aggregate, of interviewees who commented on the relationship between the community colleges and SUNY System Administration, the great majority (70 percent) reported a strong, positive relationship. Words used to describe the relationship include "wonderful" (McLean 2006; Locastro 2006), "supportive" (Coolidge 2006; McLaughlin 2006; Barber 2006; Martusewicz 2006; Chambers 2006; Hankin 2006; Fatato 2006; Miller 2006), "excellent" (Shattenkirk 2006; Jiudice 2006; Connors 2006), "cooperative" (Famellette 2006; Larsson 2006), and "positive" (Giblin 2006; DePuy 2006; Kochersberger 2006; Rogers-Rice 2006; Larsson 2006), among others.

Most of the remaining interviewees who commented on the relationship indicated that it was somewhere in between positive and negative (26 percent) or more negative (4 percent). The main criticisms relate to the perception that SUNY System Administration was distant or overly bureaucratic. Professor John Murray of Hudson Valley Community College described the relationship as "ebb and flow," explaining that the "relationship with SUNY is back and forth, ebb and flow. Never terrible. We've never been in real bad shape. We always come back to SUNY. No matter what I say, we pay attention to SUNY. We value our relationship with SUNY." (Murray 2006).

Robert Barber, vice president for administration and continuing education at Jamestown Community College, describes its relationship with SUNY as "good but distant," continuing that Jamestown Community College has "had, if you asked a lot of SUNY administration, a long reputation as being innovative and independent as a community college. Maybe the distance has played some kind of a role in that. So we've certainly felt, generally, supported by SUNY but we have also felt distant and that's not necessarily a bad thing." He continues, "it's been an interesting relationship and I can't remember a lot of tension ever between the SUNY leadership and the college. On the other hand, we've kind of done our own thing out here and that's probably not all bad" (Barber 2006). Robert Kochersberger of Jamestown Community College described the relationship between SUNY and the colleges as a "mixed bag" and that it varied depending on the individuals involved, both at the college and at System Administration (Kochersberger 2006).

The view of the SUNY System as overly bureaucratic was raised in a few interviews. Rogers-Rice of North County Community College suggested that this minor irritation likely went both ways, and was simply part of being a system:

> We have found generally that while we have our moments of irritation with bureaucracy as anyone and everyone does—and I am sure they have had their moments of irritation with us because we

aren't quite as simple or as quickly compliant as they would have liked us to be—because we're so unique, it's sometimes hard to do some of the things way the larger schools do. We've had, what has been, I think, at least in terms of talking to other folks from community colleges, we've had a very cordial relationship with SUNY (Rogers-Rice 2006).

Despite the occasional account of a difficult or unpleasant situation involving SUNY System Administration, the great majority of the interviewees report having a very positive and strong relationship with SUNY. In fact, at least six interviewees assert that the community colleges' affiliation with the State University of New York is a tremendous asset. The benefit for the students of the community colleges was identified as a substantial benefit of being part of a larger, comprehensive system. Robert Novak of Orange County Community College explained: "I can't remember a time when we had a student call me or talk to me and tell me that they can't get into New Paltz or they can't get in here or they can't get in there" (Novak 2006). Without a doubt, being part of the SUNY System allows virtually unrestricted possibilities for students to design a relatively seamless academic path that suits them. Professor Henry French of Monroe Community College agrees that the diverse system of sixty-four campuses is a strength: "I think it's been good that we have been under that umbrella [SUNY]. I like the concept of the 64 campuses." He continues, "I've been very, very pleased with the association that we've had and, when possible, either as transfer students or taking classes at other campuses because we don't offer them, I find the relationship with SUNY has been quite outstanding … We're the largest university in the country. Even though we're at somewhat disparate campuses, I think it's been very, very beneficial. I think SUNY was a great idea" (French 2006).

Interviewees also find their affiliation with SUNY to be a great advantage in terms of the support offered by the System. It benefits the community colleges to have the support and backing of a larger institution, with a team of knowledgeable individuals who can assist in any situation that arises at the campus level. Jean-Ellen Giblin of Fashion Institute of Technology claims that:

SUNY has a lot to offer the colleges that are part of the network. There's a lot of support that comes from SUNY and we need to remember that. Sometimes when we're filling out the ninety-ninth form that has to go in with something, we get a little frustrated but the reality is they play a very important role and can be very supportive. I think those relations have really strengthened. I think they were strong in the early days and the days of President Feldman and I think they are again strengthened under Dr. Brown (Giblin 2006).

Tom Murphy of Tompkins Cortland Community College agrees that the organizational structure and the administrative support of the state university were tremendous assets to the community colleges:

> I thought we got tremendous service from SUNY just because of, like everything else, the people. I liked the structure. At most of that time, you were the Associate Chancellor for CC's, who had three people reporting. My contact person was David Van Nordwick, who was unbelievable-good [sic]. I always worked with George Anker in the budget office, John Murphy in audit, Rich Rohstead in legal. If I had a problem, I knew where to go and I knew these guys were real good and they were going to help with any problems, and the budget situation and everything else. I don't have any complaints in my 15 years there and 11 years later at Monroe. I liked the structure (Murphy 2006).

John Deans of Jefferson Community College recalls conversations among community college presidents about whether the community colleges would be better served if they were not part of a larger system, something that he opposes:

> I think it's just that we were so new and it took a while for people to understand. I was asked a question in my last interview here with the board of trustees, what did I think community colleges tend to be with SUNY? So I said that from everything I can see we're really pleased to be part of the system and I really do believe that. Apparently there has been some discussion over the years by some community college presidents that maybe the community colleges might be better as some kind of a separate system. I don't endorse that. I didn't then and I don't now. We're far stronger, the more seamless we can make the system (Deans 2006).

The affiliation with the State University of New York is, for some community colleges, more than a means of support; it is also a source of pride. Joseph Hankin of Westchester Community College suggests that, while some of the four-year institutions try to disassociate themselves from the SUNY name, the community colleges celebrate their affiliation. He explains that "SUNY has always been supportive of us and I'm looking right now at my wristwatch, which says 'SUNY Westchester Community College.'" While he suggests that some SUNY institutions "try to avoid the use of the word 'SUNY,'" Westchester Community College is not one of them. He continues to say that at Westchester, "we're proud of it" (Hankin 2006).

In sum, the interviews in this oral history illustrate an early view of the community colleges in New York State that was consistent with the era—a period in which these new institutions were just beginning to occupy a significant portion of the American system of higher education. While the early years of the relationship between SUNY and the community colleges were filled with uncertainty about these institutions, the interviews clearly point to a positive trajectory in the relationship from 1950 through 1980.

Again, these findings on the relationship between SUNY System Administration and the community colleges emerged from just one of nineteen questions included in the 109 interviews of this study. The interviews, as a whole, paint a complete picture of the beginnings and development of SUNY's thirty community colleges and communicate the experiences of the leaders of this very important component of America's largest public comprehensive system of higher education.

D. Developments and Continuation of the Study

Since the duplication and dissemination of the final oral history project on CDs, we have been working with SUNY system administration's Office of Library and Information Services to make the compilation more accessible to the public. As an alternative to accessing the project at SUNY community college libraries, it is now available online through the State University of New York's digital repository.

There have since been two follow-ups of the study. First, we conducted an additional interview with Clifton R. Wharton Jr., former chancellor of the State University of New York on May 4, 2009, available on the project website. Second, this oral history project (in particular the responses to the question that asked how the colleges developed their campuses) served as the main data set for Benjamin Weaver's dissertation, entitled "Bringing the Colleges to the Communities: An Historical Analysis of the Siting of the State University of New York Community Colleges." The dissertation identifies and discusses the influences involved in the decisions of where to site the SUNY community college campuses across the state, from the viewpoint of New York State, the State University of New York, and the local sponsors. The data collected from the oral history project suggested that the influences on the siting decisions at the local level include: availability of services, buildings available, business/industry influences, community enthusiasm, donated property, financial influences, geography, influence of other colleges/universities, land available, legal issues, political influences, property already owned, suitability of land, system influences, and transportation connections (Weaver 2008).

The dissertation suggests that the influences involved in the siting decisions of the community colleges in New York align with those in other coordinated systems of the time, as well as the recommendations put forward by scholars prior to SUNY's founding. However, several influences involved in the siting decisions were unique to the SUNY community colleges.

This oral history project has preserved very important information on the origins of our community colleges, has contributed to further scholarship on this topic, and will continue to inspire researchers in the areas of public history and higher education. While no known plans have been made to continue this study beyond the first thirty years, 2010 will mark the end of the *second* thirty years of SUNY's community colleges. An oral history of the developments and successes of our community colleges between 1980–2010 would be an ideal second volume documenting the continuing history of this thriving and indispensable system.

References

Harris, Ramon I., Joseph H. Cash, Herbert T. Hoover, and Stephen R. Ward. 1975. *The Practice of Oral History*. Glen Rock, NJ: Microfilming Corporation of America.

Hillway, Tyrus. 1958. *The American Two-Year College*. New York: Harper.

Neuman, W. Lawrence. 2006. *Social Research Methods: Quantitative and Qualitative Approaches*. Boston: Pearson Education, Inc.

Robbins, Cornelius V. 2006. *SUNY Community Colleges: an Oral History of the First 30 Years*. Albany, NY: State University of New York.

Seashore, Carl E. 1940. *The Junior College Movement*. New York: Holt, Rinehart and Winston.

Shafer, Robert Jones. 1980. *A Guide to Historical Method*. Homewood, IL: The Dorsey Press.

Starrak, James A., and Raymond M. Hughes. 1948. *The New Junior College: the Next Step in Free Public Education*. Ames, IA: The Iowa State College Press.

Stoddard, George D. 1944. *Tertiary Education*. Cambridge, MA: Harvard University Press.

Weaver, Benjamin J. 2008. "Bringing the Colleges to the Communities: an Historical Analysis of the Siting of the State University of New York Community Colleges." PhD diss.: State University of New York at Albany.

Witt, Allen A., James L. Wattenbarger, James F. Gollattscheck, and Joseph E. Suppiger. 1994. *America's Community Colleges: the First Century*. Washington: Community College Press, a division of the American Association of Community Colleges.

The interviewees in this oral history include: Adirondack Community College: Gordon Blank, Norman Enhorning, Merritt Scoville; Broome Community College: George Higginbottom, Richard

Romano, Darwin Wales; Cayuga Community College: Donald Fama, Harold Leonard, Anthony Locastro; Clinton Community College: Karen Burnam, Nina Coolidge, Michael Helinger, Albert B. Light; Columbia-Greene Community College: James Campion, Charles Shattenkirk, Martin Smith; Corning Community College: Neil Buckley, Vernon Patterson, William Perry, William Thompson; Dutchess Community College: James Hall, Joseph Jiudice, Edna Silber; Erie Community College: Cosmo Fratello, Greg Gillis, John Rydzik; Fashion Institute of Technology: Jean-Ellen Giblin, Peter Scotese, Elaine Stone, Marvin Feldman; Finger Lakes Community College: Collins Carpenter, Henry Maus, Charles Meder; Fulton-Montgomery Community College: Rita Mary Burke, Hadley DePuy, Helen Mandato, George Pilkey, John D. Vadney; Genesee Community College: Eva Bohn, Neil Burns, Bernie Hoerbelt, Stuart Steiner, Tony Zambito; Herkimer County Community College: James Anderson, Robert McLaughlin, David Trautlein; Hudson Valley Community College: Conrad Lang, John Murray, Don Schmidt; Jamestown Community College: Robert Barber, George Bataitis, Robert Kochersberger; Jefferson Community College: John Deans, John Henderson, Kim Martusewicz, Thomas Myers, Richard Parker; Mohawk Valley Community College: Jack Dizer, Jim Dyer, Bruce McLean, Michael Schafer; Monroe Community College: Thomas R. Flynn, Henry French, Alice Holloway-Young; Nassau Community College: George Chambers, Al Donor, Terry O'Dwyer; Niagara County Community College: Graham Millar, Jerry Miller, Edward Pawenski; North Country Community College: Ralph Cardinal, Howard Maat, Gail Rogers-Rice, Kenneth Wiley; Onondaga Community College: Barbara Davis, Jane Donegan, Don Mawhinney, Andreas Paloumpis; Orange County Community College: Ada DeGeus, John McMahon, Robert Novak; Rockland Community College: Steve Eskow, Joseph Famellette, Dan Masterson, Joan Silberman; Schenectady County Community College: Tom Baker, Vladia Boniewski, Carol Fatato, Robert Larsson, Richard Leveroni; Suffolk County Community College: Alan Ammerman, William Connors, LeRoy Van Nostrand; Sullivan County Community College: Harold Gold, Richard Greenfield, Wendy Grossman, Joel Lerner; Tompkins-Cortland Community College: Carl Haynes, Tom Murphy, Walter Poland, Ron Space; Ulster County Community College: Bob Brown, Don Katt, Dale Lake, Chris Larios; Westchester Community College: Arthur Hackett, Joseph Hankin, Harry Phillips.

Author's note: The full citations for all interviews are available at the SUNY digital repository Web site: http://dspace.sunyconnect.suny.edu/handle/1951/41212 and on a CD: Robbins, Cornelius V. 2006. *SUNY Community Colleges: an Oral History of the First 30 Years*. Albany, NY: State University of New York.

SUNY Strides onto the National Research Stage

Introduction

John W. Kalas, University at Albany

The studies in this section describe the transition of SUNY campuses from an early preoccupation with undergraduate education to their current position as a research force. In the early 1960s, following the 1957 *Sputnik* launch, when the federal government rapidly expanded support of basic research, many universities across the country were poised to take advantage of the growth. At that time, however, SUNY campuses were ill prepared to become serious participants in these efforts. All four doctoral centers were in the process of either creation or transformation and each was engaged in fundamental campus construction. Stony Brook was emerging as a new institution and occupied its first building in 1962. Buffalo became part of SUNY from its previous existence as a private institution, also in 1962, and, as Patricia Maloney describes in her study, was involved in the construction of a major new campus in Amherst under the direction of Presidents Martin Meyerson and Robert Ketter. Binghamton was undergoing its second transformation, first from the private Tri-cities College to Harpur College, and then in 1965 to the University at Binghamton with its own major campus construction. Albany, once the New York State College for Teachers, moved to its new campus in 1966, concurrent with becoming the comprehensive University at Albany.

SUNY had (and has) no "flagship" campus, despite some public relations claims to the contrary and its decentralized distribution of campuses across the state has complicated the coalescence of research resources. In addition, overly rigid control of SUNY's life from several state agencies, which has been described as more appropriate to a Department of Motor Vehicles than to a university, has inhibited the entrepreneurial spirit so vital to the research enterprise.

So how did SUNY become a significant research force in both the state and the nation? The papers in this section tell us much about that emergence.

As Roger Geiger points out, Governor Nelson Rockefeller, working with then-Chancellor Samuel Gould, resolved to move the university to more prominent status from the position that had been assigned to it in its 1948 creation to "supplement but not supplant" the private universities which dominated higher education in New York State. Rockefeller established the Heald Commission, whose 1960 report called for the development of major graduate education and research centers within SUNY, the very centers described above that emerged during the 1960s.

Some years later, as Geiger also reports, the Commission on the Future of State University, established by Governor Mario Cuomo working with Chancellor Clifton Wharton, issued a 1985 report which called for the emancipation of SUNY from massive state control. The recommendations in this report met with resistance from the controlling state agencies and the report has achieved only some of its aims. Some research flexibility has, nevertheless, been achieved through the existence of the SUNY Research Foundation, a separate non-profit corporation which administers the grants and contracts for all of SUNY's state operated campuses.

However, it is mainly the initiative from within that has led to the emergence of SUNY as a research force. As Nancy Diamond points out in her paper, when one moves away from assessment instruments that are based primarily on institutional reputation, and looks instead at current data on publications, citations, and books provided in the Faculty Scholarly Productivity (FSP) survey of the Academic Analysis Organization, SUNY faculty more than hold their own when compared with faculty from other institutions nationally.

In some instances SUNY faculty have overcome the barrier of decentralization through research collaboration. A notable example is the Great Lakes Research Consortium, which coordinates the efforts of faculty on eighteen campuses (twelve SUNY and six independent). The effort was begun as a simple collaboration on three campuses—the College of Environmental Sciences and Forestry and the colleges at Oswego and Brockport—which grew because of the need to understand and support positive environmental efforts on Lake Ontario and the St. Lawrence Seaway comparable to the efforts on the western Great Lakes undertaken in the states of Michigan, Wisconsin, and Minnesota.

Much of SUNY's research is conducted with the end-view of transforming New York's (particularly upstate New York's) status as a Rust Belt state through advanced technology. In the mid-1980s, the state's Office of Science and Technology provided funds on a competitive basis to develop Centers of Advanced Technology that would attract both federal dollars and corporate partners. The most successful of these has been Albany's Nanotech Center, which has studied advances in computer chip technology and their applications in a broad range of fields. The center has attracted not only major federal support, but close industrial partnerships, as well, with both single corporations like IBM and industrial consortia like Sematech. The presence of the center has resulted in one major corporation deciding to build a computer chip fabrication facility which, when completed, will provide more than one thousand new jobs.

Similarly, Buffalo has worked closely to sustain Western New York through research industrial initiatives. Collaboration with the Calspan Corporation through the formation of a separate corporation known as the Calspan/University at Buffalo Research Corporation (CUBRC) has revived research in a wind tunnel facility in the field of aeronautics and expanded additional efforts through the construction of a transportation facility and other engineering-related activities. In medicine, the university has also worked closely with local research hospitals, such as the Roswell Park Cancer Research Institute, in emerging fields such as medical instrumentation.

Binghamton, too, has worked with industrial partners—notably IBM—in a broad range of computer-oriented technologies. With IBM's decision to greatly reduce its presence in nearby Endicott, Binghamton has worked successfully with many of the small regional IBM suppliers to transfer and extend their technology to other markets. Much of this work is conducted through the Small Scale Systems Integration and Packaging Center (S3IP), a state center of excellence, which collaborates on studies to design nanoscale devices and use specialized materials in microelectronic systems that accomplish goals such as temperature control.

As is often the case, some of SUNY research growth has been simply fortuitous. For many years, Stony Brook physics faculty had worked closely with nearby Brookhaven National Laboratory. It had been instrumental in the development of the Synchrotron Light Source, a major research facility for photonics research. The laboratory had been operated by a consortium led by Yale, with Stony Brook as a minor partner. But in the early 1990s, Long Island residents became concerned that the laboratory was leaking radioactive materials into the aquifer that provides much of Long Island's fresh water. Former Stony Brook President John Marberger, a physicist, stepped forward and brought closure to the leakage fear, leading the U.S. Department of Energy to replace the former "absentee landlords" with a new management group headed by Stony Brook and the Battelle National Laboratories.

These anecdotes only hint at the reasons for research growth of SUNY campuses over the past three decades, not only in the hard sciences, but in the social sciences and humanities as well. The growth in grant and contract funding does not tell the full story either, but it is useful to note that in the year ending June 30, 2008, the SUNY Research Foundation had research expenditures from external sources in the amount of $784,324,279.

Research on SUNY campuses has come of age. Earlier struggles that led to structured research collaboration among campuses and the successful application of basic research findings to the economic, social, and environmental needs of the region have led to recognition of the importance of SUNY's work. The contributions of SUNY in many areas of research continue and because of its early struggles, it is well prepared to grow even in difficult times such as our own.

I. Presidential Leadership, Change, and Community: SUNY Buffalo from 1966 to 1981

Patricia A. Maloney, PhD

The rapid growth of the State University of New York had a major impact upon communities, institutions, and individuals. In 1962, the private University of Buffalo joined the system as the State University of New York at Buffalo, becoming one of four research centers in the SUNY system. The university's transformation from "of" Buffalo to "at" Buffalo symbolizes major societal and political change that strongly affected the local and regional communities, as well as the university.

This study analyzes the leadership of Martin Myerson and Robert Ketter, the first two presidents to lead SUNY Buffalo. As the university changed from a private institution under local control to one made up of many institutions governed by a central board and chancellor, these presidents created and reacted to varying perceptions and expectations of the university. The communities that they engaged with included the campus, the local community, media, political leadership, SUNY System Administration, and numerous executive offices of the state. As state resources brought increased faculty hiring, enrollment, and program development, SUNY embarked on an extremely lengthy development of a new campus for its largest university.

SUNY Buffalo's most dramatic growth occurred during the late 1960s and early 1970s, a period of intense national, political, and civic engagement, and cultural exploration. The university's transformation from a service university to a potential "Berkeley of the East" led to major conflict between the local and campus communities.

Change at the University at Buffalo occurred on multiple levels, involving deep changes in structure, governance, culture, and identity. These ranged from the concrete to the symbolic, including adoption of a new name and symbols, to new forms of academic organization and governance structures.

Martin Meyerson was selected after serving as acting chancellor at the University of California Berkeley and brought a cosmopolitan worldview to his role. He served from 1966 to 1970. His successor, Robert Ketter, was a faculty member and administrator who began his career in Buffalo before the merger with SUNY and provided a local, institutional focus to his presidency, which spanned 1970 to 1981.

Meyerson's and Ketter's presidencies contrasted dramatically. Their leadership of the new public university in Buffalo began in a decade of fiscal

144

abundance and social upheaval, and concluded in a time of economic and institutional constraint.

Both presidents faced the challenge of dealing with a highly centralized bureaucracy and satisfying the expectations of a local community that was accustomed to the university being "of" Buffalo, while attempting to bring a new campus on-line, develop and oversee programs, and respond to faculty and student interests. But the context of these challenges and the manner in which each faced them contrasted starkly.

A.   Buffalo

Buffalo was incorporated in 1820, carved from Holland Land Company parcels surveyed by Joseph Ellicott. Its location at the eastern end of Lake Erie and its proximity to Canada were key factors in the city's growth. Buffalo is over 400 miles from New York City, while midwestern cities such as Pittsburgh and Cleveland are much closer than eastern metropolises.

The construction of the Erie Canal and development of rail transportation fueled Buffalo's growth. By the end of the 19th century, Buffalo was one of the largest and most prosperous cities in the nation, an industrial center that had sent two civic leaders—Millard Fillmore and Grover Cleveland—to the White House and staged the 1901 Pan-American Exposition.

Heavy industry dominated the Buffalo economy in the 20th century. Large steel mills and manufacturing plants were built in Buffalo and surrounding communities, providing thousands of well-paying jobs. In 1960, Buffalo had a population of 540,000 and was the twentieth largest city in the nation. The community's population included a sizeable number of African-Americans who had migrated north for industrial jobs (Porter, 1991). Buffalo's strong white ethnic composition, neighborhood orientation, and identification as the "City of Good Neighbors" gave the community a working-class image (Dudzick, undated).

B.   Buffalo's University

In 1846, a group of community leaders sold shares to establish the University of Buffalo, a medical school with Millard Fillmore as its first chancellor. Over the next five decades, the university established schools of pharmacy, dentistry, law, and pedagogy. In the first half of the twentieth century, divisions of arts and sciences, business and journalism, evening sessions, education, social work, graduate education, and engineering were added. The final academic unit established at the university was the former Albright Art School, which became part of the university in 1954.

The university had no central campus until 1922, when it moved to the former Erie County Almshouse bordering the town of Amherst. The "Main Street campus" became home to all divisions except the law school, which was located downtown near the courts.

Oversight was provided by the University Council, which selected the chancellor. In 1922, it appointed Samuel P. Capen, a role he filled until 1950. Capen was responsible for changing the university from a decentralized institution focused on technical disciplines, into a coherent academic institution (Capen, 1953). He was succeeded by T. R. McConnell, a well-known higher education scholar who served four years.

The final chancellor of the University of Buffalo and the first president of SUNY Buffalo was Clifford Furnas, chancellor from 1954 to 1962 and president from 1962 to 1966, who paved the way for the university's transition from private to public institution. His leadership combined Samuel Capen's strong academic focus with close ties to the local community.

C. Buffalo's University, New York's Needs, and the State University

Furnas led the university in a period marked by expanding enrollments and physical constraint. The university's physical plant was at capacity, due to increasing enrollment and a growing resident population, and the university instituted a successful capital campaign (Furnas, undated, pp. 57–64). The Main Street campus was only 178 acres. To gain space, the university purchased the Audubon Golf Course, a public course several miles away in Amherst, in 1958. The university sold the property back to the town in return for 264 acres of undeveloped land two years later.

In 1960, the university enrolled 14,700 students and the faculty included 450 full-time and 908 part-time members (university fact sheet, 1960). Sponsored research expenditures that year totaled $1,900,000 (annual report, 1960). The estimated value of the physical plant (including the golf course) was over $31 million, and the university's total assets were valued at over $85 million. The private university at the western end of the state was a major source of degrees. In 1960, Buffalo granted 1129 degrees, while the entire SUNY system enrolled only 67,000 students and awarded 10,000 degrees (University of Buffalo, 1960; SUNY, 1995).

The university in Buffalo and its leadership were noticed by state decision-makers. Furnas became familiar with James Allen, the state commissioner of education. Allen had persuaded the state's new governor, Nelson Rockefeller, to support a statewide commission on the future of higher education. The commission was led by Henry Heald, president of the Ford Foundation, and operated under the authority of the State Education Department, the only state agency not under the direct control of the governor. Furnas became a member of an informal group that advised the commission.

At the same time the university was charting its future, Furnas and his leadership team worked with the University Council to position the university in a positive light in the event of a merger or establishment of a nearby public university. In a 1960 report to the council, Furnas outlined plans for future academic growth and a confidential report written by one of his senior staff noted that "[t]he University of Buffalo is, in its own eyes and in the eyes of many persons, a private institution performing a public service" (University of Buffalo, 1960, pp. 4–5).

Furnas and the council were concerned that the State Education Department and SUNY might recommend funding formulas that would hurt private institutions, or establish a public university that would compete with University of Buffalo. In 1960, Furnas and several council members began merger discussions with the State University of New York. He insisted that the university maintain a strong position through the process, which led to an announcement of Buffalo being selected as the fourth "research center" recommended by the Heald Commission in late 1960. The university agreed to join SUNY and became the State University of New York at Buffalo on August 31, 1962 (Furnas, p. 88).

Joining SUNY presented many benefits to the university and the Buffalo community. The university would no longer be tuition-dependent, and tuition and fees would decrease. State resources would provide more generous salaries and benefits for faculty and staff, and spur facilities expansion. The benefits came with numerous challenges. The institution, self-governing for over a century, became part of a complex state bureaucracy (Gross and Murphy, 1966). The role of the University Council changed from governance to advisory and the university presidents' role within the expanded state system was still developing. Plus, the expansion and location of the Buffalo campus remained a major concern.

Buffalo joined SUNY when the system lacked a president. In the interim, Governor Rockefeller and the SUNY Board were directly involved in making major decisions. The State University Construction Fund, the independent agency overseeing campus development, commissioned a study on campus expansion in Buffalo, including development of land in Amherst and redevelopment of the Main Street campus as a health sciences center (Furnas, pp. 117–118). The university's growing need for space led it to lease property in Amherst, over the objections of town leaders.

Furnas, who remained president past the state mandatory retirement age of sixty-five until a successor was named, expressed increasing frustration with the centralized control that was delaying expansion. When he announced his resignation, SUNY began a national search for the first president to lead the public research university in Buffalo.

D. Martin Meyerson and the Challenges of Change

Meyerson was acting chancellor at the University of California Berkeley when he was selected to be president of the State University of New York at Buffalo (and tenth president of the university founded in 1846) by the SUNY Board of Trustees on April 15, 1966.

> Meyerson was a departure for Buffalo in many ways. Unlike most of his colleagues in higher education, he did not possess a PhD, although he had been a professor and administrator at several leading universities. His field of urban planning was so new that a doctorate had not yet been established, and the master's degree was considered the terminal degree in the discipline. He was well-known in the world of urban planning and had not published widely on higher education issues, but his writings and speeches on both urban communities and innovation in the modern university were hailed by higher education reformers (Meyerson, 1966a).

Meyerson accepted the presidency because he felt that

> [Buffalo] was just right for the kinds of improvement that would have been a lot harder to achieve in places that had ... more *pride* than Buffalo had at that time. And I felt part of my task was to instill pride in it, for good reasons from the past, and even what I hoped would be better reasons for things that we were going to do (Meyerson interview, 1997).

Meyerson was Jewish, coming to a community dominated by ethnic and largely Roman Catholic politicians, and would be working with an advisory University Council composed mostly of upper-class white Protestants. Meyerson presented a cosmopolitan image and was profiled in glowing terms in the Buffalo newspapers and soon was welcomed into the elite Thursday Club and onto several boards. His success in calming student unrest at Berkeley helped to present him as a hero and provided a sense that Buffalo and SUNY had chosen a dynamic young president with ideas and energy that matched their ambitions.

E.   Planned and Unplanned Change

Meyerson's challenges as president of SUNY Buffalo were numerous: to create programs of high academic quality; to recruit and retain talented faculty, staff, and students; to convince campus and external constituencies that a restructured university could serve both geographic and disciplinary communities; and to oversee construction of a large new campus located in suburban Amherst. Meyerson had many tools available for these tasks, but he also encountered political challenges and unexpected constraints. Meyerson inherited strategic plans developed under Furnas and arrived in Buffalo in the midst of construction delays for the new campus.

When Meyerson's presidency began, the structure of SUNY Buffalo as a large public research university was becoming apparent. Enrollment, funding,

148

and hiring had expanded exponentially since the merger. Plans for the new campus had been approved, but had encountered strong opposition from certain elements of the community, particularly business leaders in Amherst. Another group wanted the university to remain within the city and move the campus to the waterfront (Levine, 1980, p. 34; McAloon, 1994).

Changes and challenges were occurring within the campus, as well. Furnas's 1960 academic plan calling for sweeping changes in governance structure had not been adopted. In 1966, Meyerson appointed a committee of faculty and senior administrators to review the plan. Robert Ketter, a longtime engineering professor and dean of the graduate school, served as chair. Its findings, presented at the beginning of the fall 1966 semester, offered an innovative vision of a research university.

The committee endorsed a "college concept" to govern the institution. The committee called this structure "the horizontal and vertical involvement of the student, the faculty member, the administrator, and the community at large" (Levine, 1986, p. 37). The colleges were conceptualized as self-contained units with residential and learning space for faculty and students, including libraries and laboratories.

Meyerson and the committee met throughout the fall 1966 semester and convened a retreat facilitated by alumnus and scholar David Riesman. Meyerson made his own proposal to the Faculty Senate in November, based in part upon the Furnas recommendations (Razik, 1975, p. 122–123).

Meyerson emphasized that the university become a preeminent graduate center and a "great undergraduate center." He also noted that the university "must have a close and dynamic relationship with the community while recognizing our national and international ties" and be led "with a style which encourages the greatest degree of freedom for students and faculty to study and do other creative work not only in conventional, but also in new fields and through new ways of learning" (Meyerson, 1966b). The Faculty Senate adopted his proposal and the university established a non-traditional structure, including seven faculties (divisions) combining pure and applied research, as well as a collegiate structure for new and experimental units.

Meyerson's first year was very productive. His high-level committee recommended drastic changes to the structure and governance of the university and modified those into a complex but more palatable form. He recruited a flamboyant management scholar, Warren Bennis from the Sloan School at MIT, as academic vice president.

Several months before Meyerson's appointment, SUNY appointed an external committee headed by his former Columbia professor, Mason Gross, to review the plans for the new campus. The committee recommended that SUNY affirm the decision to place the campus in Amherst and the Board accepted the recommendation. The decision was based, in part, on enrollment projections predicting enrollment in Buffalo would reach 40,000 or greater.

F. High Hopes and High Achievements

Meyerson had connections in many fields and he utilized them well during his presidency. In addition to Bennis, he recruited Carl Willenbrock from Harvard to run the engineering faculty, and leading scholars Eric Larabee and James Danielli. Nobel laureate Sir John Eccles joined the faculty. Overall, faculty hiring accelerated. Some professors commuted from their homes elsewhere; poet Barbara Probst Solomon described her flights from New York to teach at the university she called "the yellow submarine" (1969). A young urban historian hired in 1969 described his first impression of the university's administration that it:

> ... was *about* something. It had a vision ... it was clear that these were thinking people who were going someplace, as opposed to caretakers, bureaucrats, functionaries or anything else. And that certainly meant a great deal to me. I think it had a lot to do with encouraging and inspiring part of this sense of citizenship (personal communication, 1996).

That perception was not universal. Another new faculty member noted that "[t]he senior faculty felt threatened by their younger colleagues and, in turn, the younger faculty felt threatened by the entrenched older faculty. There was no clear direction to the university" (Anonymous Interview, 1996).

Despite these conflicting views, the university's reputation and disciplinary strength were growing. In the 1960s, the American Council on Education (ACE) ranked American graduate program departments as distinguished, strong, good, or adequate. In 1964, Buffalo had three disciplines ranked by ACE: physiology, microbiology, and psychology. None were ranked strong and the report noted that "all other disciplines rated less than adequate." In 1969, twenty-two disciplines were ranked, with three (physiology, English, and pharmacology) ranked strong, ten ranked good, and nine adequate (American Council on Education, 1964, 1969). The growth and visibility of the English Department, in particular, has been recounted by Jackson, (1999) Probst-Solomon, (1969), and others.

Extramural support grew rapidly. In 1961–62, the university received $5.1 million in external support. In 1966–67, the amount grew to $10.7 million. The amounts continued to grow: two years later, external support was $13.5 million, and it reached $18.1 million in 1970–71 (National Science Foundation, 1996).

Enrollment and degree production reflected the university's dramatic growth and importance to SUNY. In 1962, its final year as an independent institution, Buffalo had 1166 graduates, including thirty-six PhDs. In contrast, SUNY (which did not yet include Buffalo), had 13,530 graduates and granted 124 doctorates. Four years later, Buffalo contributed 2380 degrees, including ninety-seven doctorates, to SUNY's totals of 28,693 degrees and 252 doctorates. In 1970, the last year of Meyerson's presidency, Buffalo had 3248 graduates and awarded 216 doctorates, among SUNY's 47,251 graduates and 542 doctorates (SUNY, 1995).

G.　"Albany"

Like Furnas, Meyerson found relations with SUNY and the rest of state government confounding. Meyerson had significant experience leading a public research institution, as did the SUNY Chancellor, Samuel Gould, a former chancellor at the University of California-Santa Barbara. Meyerson remarked that

> [T]he thing that shocked me the most in relations with Albany [was that] I just took it for granted that as president of one of these four university centers I would be meeting regularly with the board …. And I discovered—in Berkeley, the chancellors, they all met with the regents, and the regents met often—[that] this didn't happen [in SUNY] (Meyerson interview, 1996).

Furnas's and Meyerson's frustrations were not limited to SUNY itself; several entities within state government challenged university administrators. Although Meyerson was disappointed that he had little direct contact with SUNY trustees, he also learned that SUNY had no control in several areas, including employee relations, which was handled by the governor's office; construction, which was governed by a separate authority; and overall fiscal matters.

Meyerson and the other research center presidents may not have had direct contact with the SUNY trustees, but Meyerson had frequent contact with the governor. Meyerson first met Rockefeller several years earlier when Meyerson ran a national group called Action and wrote a speech for the governor. When Meyerson's name was forwarded to Rockefeller as a finalist for the Buffalo presidency, Rockefeller reacted enthusiastically, announcing that Buffalo "could become a Berkeley of the east" (Meyerson interview, 1997).

Rockefeller frequently ignored administrative practices when he wanted to acquire information, and that included going directly to the source (Glaser, 1989). Rockefeller often contacted Meyerson directly. Meyerson recalled that "he would call to invite me to meetings, and send his private plane. It was embarrassing to go to the airport, to be the president of a public university, and then take a private plane to see the governor" (Meyerson interview, 1997).

H.　Managing Innovation and Change

Meyerson's greatest challenges involved major academic restructuring and the development of the new campus. The academic reorganization resulted in the combining of many disciplinary areas into "faculties" that had not previously collaborated. The establishment of several innovative "colleges," some of which moved off-campus, brought criticism from both members of the university and local communities. Faculty governance changed from traditional Faculty Senate representation to "polity" governance, with more routine decisions made by professors within the seven divisional faculties. Warren Bennis oversaw the colleges, each of which was headed by a master, but oversight was highly dispersed (Levine, 1980).

Construction of the new campus became an extremely contentious issue. SUNY's Master Plan called for a bifurcated campus, with the Main Street campus becoming the health science facility, and the new Amherst campus housing all other university programs. Construction was scheduled to begin in 1966, following the SUNY Board's reaffirmation of the plan. Although Meyerson was a renowned urban planner and was selected to be president while protests and follow-up studies were taking place, he was selected after SUNY reaffirmed the plan. In 1967, the construction plan was altered to include the colleges, to be located in a large complex at the northern edge of the Amherst site.

Although it appeared that construction would commence soon, two factors impeded the project. First was a condition that no one could affect—the climate. The long winters in Buffalo made for short construction schedules. The second was incendiary and political. Numerous community organizations protested the lack of minority workers hired to build the new campus. Meyerson agreed with the concerns, and placed a moratorium on construction until the construction trade unions and community organizations could resolve their differences. This decision was tremendously unpopular in the Buffalo community, a majority-white community with many union members.

During the 1969 spring semester, the moratorium was rescinded and lifted several times by both Meyerson and the head of the State University Construction Fund (SUCF), the general contractor (personal communication, 1997).

By the fall of 1969, the community and university appeared to be in ongoing conflict. Controversy caused by two of the experimental off-campus colleges, A and F, roiled the neighborhood near the campus, and the frayed relations were reported in the national press (Bennis, 1972).

I. Departure

By the beginning of the 1969–70 academic year, the university and its related communities were at odds. The cycle of construction moratorium and resumption, the outrage by some in the community and media about the off-campus colleges and student activism, and lack of support from either the governor's office or SUNY isolated Meyerson. His stand on the moratorium led to threats on his life and to an FBI investigation and protection. For a period in the spring

1969 semester, the campus was closed due to demonstrations against Defense Department research on campus.

In fall 1969, Meyerson was appointed co-chair of the American Assembly on University Goals and Governance, which was established by the American Association for the Advancement of Science (AAAS) to develop frameworks for dealing with change on America's campuses. He took a leave from the presidency after only three years in office and ran the project from an off-campus office in Buffalo.

In the midst of Meyerson's leave, he made an announcement that startled the community. At the end of January 1970, he sent a letter announcing his resignation from Buffalo to assume the presidency of the University of Pennsylvania. He addressed the construction issue in the letter:

> Lest there be a misconception of the factors that led to my decision, let me emphasize that I remain fully confident about the building of our long-awaited, well-planned, new campus. Obviously I am frustrated by the delays, but I am convinced that it and the new community projected near it will proceed. Since last Spring those of us at the University have not been directly involved in resolving the conflicts concerning the new campus (Meyerson letter, 1970).

In the spring of 1970, the university was in turmoil. Numerous protests disrupted regular campus operations. In March, forty-five faculty members, many untenured, were arrested for staging a sit-in at the main administration building, an unprecedented action against college faculty. The "Faculty 45" arrests made national headlines. Later in March, the campus awoke one Sunday morning to find hundreds of police occupying the campus, and a headline in the morning newspaper declaring "VFW Demands Rocky Crush Sedition at UB" (Maloney, 1975).

During this period, Meyerson refrained from making public comments regarding the chaos on campus. Faculty and students described a sense of abandonment. One close observer confided to Bennis that "in every other university I've been to, the faculty hated the administration. Here they worry about desertion" (Bennis, 1973, p. 120).

Meyerson's official silence about events at the university continued until his return to campus for commencement. His speech was delivered a few weeks after American college students were murdered by National Guard troops at two campuses, following protests against America's invasion of Cambodia. Meyerson's arrival at and departure from Buffalo coincided with the class of 1970, and he told them:

> we have known turbulence, partly because of events on our own campus and other campuses, partly because of the way that you and other university students and teachers have interpreted national and world events and reacted to them, and partly because

of the way in which the citizens of surrounding communities have reacted to our reaction. (Meyerson, 1970).

Martin Meyerson officially left Buffalo at the end of June. His successor, announced at the beginning of July, was Robert Ketter, a longtime faculty member and administrator whose entire career had been at Buffalo.

J.   Robert Ketter and the Time of Constraint

Robert Ketter was selected to become the next President of SUNY Buffalo by the SUNY Trustees, strongly supported by the advisory university council. Ketter, 41, joined the faculty of the University of Buffalo in the early 1960s after graduating from Lehigh University with a doctorate in civil engineering. He was dean of the graduate school when Meyerson arrived in Buffalo, and chaired the committee whose drastic recommendations for academic reorganization Meyerson had modified. Ketter was regarded as part of the "old B," the community that existed before the merger with SUNY, and held numerous positions in the Meyerson administration.

Ketter acted quickly to distinguish himself from Meyerson and to re-establish cordial relations with parts of the local community. In his initial meetings with community leaders and area politicians, he made assurances that "stability" would return to campus. Symbolically, Ketter chose not to use the Darwin Martin House, a Frank Lloyd Wright architectural gem about two miles from the Main Street campus that Meyerson had chosen for the president's residence. (Quinlan, 1990) Instead, Ketter eventually moved to suburban Amherst, near the Main Street campus.

Ketter made his mark on campus immediately. Warren Bennis, one of Meyerson's leading administrators, was a candidate for the presidency and left Buffalo when he was not selected. Ketter chose a political scientist, Albert Somit, as executive vice-president. Somit was as colorful in his own way as Bennis had been, described by the head of a social science program as the "Rasputin of the organization" (personal communication, 1996). Ketter replaced the dean of undergraduate education, political scientist Claude Welch, with a colleague from the "old B," Vincent Ebert.

Ketter and Somit confronted many challenges left over from the Meyerson administration. One of the most perplexing was the role of the colleges. In 1970, there were nearly a score of colleges. Some provided an opportunity for faculty and students to work together in ways that were not innovative and not controversial. Some, such as Colleges A and F and Rosa Luxemburg, were run by faculty and students with radical views. During the Meyerson years, the colleges were largely unsupervised and were governed through a raucous body called the Collegiate Assembly.

Ketter's early goal was to restore "order" to the university, and his initial appointments and actions revealed more conventional choices than

Meyerson's. In the early 1970s, the university underwent both internal and external accountability measures. These included the decennial accreditation visit from the Middle States Association for Schools and Colleges, as well as an elaborate "chartering" process for the colleges.

Like Furnas and Meyerson, Ketter articulated goals for his vision of the university. Most echoed his predecessors', but one underscored his view of the university in the community: "The University will continue to recognize a special relationship with the community and region, and it will serve in this relationship according to its academic interests and abilities" (Levine, 1980, pp. 60–61).

Campus construction resumed and the first buildings on the Amherst campus opened in the fall of 1972. In the meantime, other community leaders (including presidents of private institutions) began to speak out publicly about the costs incurred to transport the university's students to numerous temporary campus locations while construction lagged. Ketter counterattacked publicly and vociferously (former department chair, personal correspondence, 1995).

Another issue that challenged Ketter was faculty unionization, a development that he vehemently opposed (Barba, 1979; Duryea and Fisk, 1975). He also expressed his frustrations with Albany in a more public manner than his predecessors. In the self-study prepared for the 1972 accreditation visit, the administration's resentment of state control is expressed bluntly:

> [m]embership in the State hierarchy, with all its benefits, also exacts a notable price. ... The very multiplicity of State agencies and of officials increase possibilities and misunderstanding, variances in interpretation of regulations and policies, and consequent administrative confusion, delay, and indeed error (SUNY Buffalo, 1972, p. 158).

Although Ketter's stated intentions were to bring stability to the university, there was considerable turnover in senior administrative positions, as well as practices that some faculty and program heads found threatening. During the 1970s, the office of vice-president for academic affairs (the job that Warren Bennis had held from 1966 to 1970), was occupied by five different individuals. Ketter and Somit paid very close attention to departmental activities. A scholar brought in from outside to serve as dean of the colleges noted that "Al Somit was [the head of] ... all the social sciences and humanities ... and Ketter took care of engineers and the scientists" (personal communication, 1995).

Ketter used program review to punish or eliminate programs he found objectionable or unnecessary, including American studies and performing arts. Ketter instituted a "chartering process" that involved review and recommendations regarding closure, continuation, or consolidation. The action was timely, since the university had finally hired an administrator whose sole responsibility was oversight of the units, and because construction of the Ellicott Complex, the residential and learning facility built for the colleges, was nearly complete. The chartering committee reviewed each of the fourteen colleges, followed by Ketter's own review of each unit (Levine, 1980; Shircliffe, 1996).

Along with the constraints and challenges, Ketter and Somit created an atmosphere than many found disquieting. A former staff member to both men described the atmosphere as

> all back door. Because people wanted to get things done, but they had to find another mechanism to do it. And so you kind of had ... not *shadow meetings*, but you had people working together in ways that you wouldn't expect an organization normally to do it (personal communication, 1996).

Ketter's presidency coincided with enrollment declines. In 1970, the final year of Meyerson's presidency, the University awarded nearly half of the doctorates awarded in the SUNY system and nearly one-twelfth of all degrees. Five years later, it awarded less than a third of the total doctorates and one-fourteenth of all degrees. By 1982, the year after Ketter left office, Buffalo's share was fewer than one-quarter of total doctorates and only six percent of all degrees awarded.

Ketter retired as president in 1981. His bitter farewell speech at commencement called "Dealing from Strength" decried the rise of unionization, condemned faculty for selfishly focusing on "economic self-interests" (Ketter, 1981), and gave an overall negative view of the higher education landscape.

K.   Conclusion

The Meyerson and Ketter presidencies spanned fifteen critical years for the young public university. Although Martin Meyerson was in Buffalo for only four years, his presidency and the events that took place on and off campus in the late 1960s were far more dramatic than the decade in which Ketter led the university. Meyerson and his leadership team embarked on planned changes that faced inevitable resistance, delay, and challenge. His leave to head the AAAS project and his silence during the campus unrest in spring 1970 disenchanted his supporters. His support of the construction moratorium alienated many segments of the Buffalo community, which was already offended by "outsiders" and radical political activism on and near campus. Meyerson's stand regarding the moratorium was highly principled, but his ability to influence construction was limited by SUNY and SUCF control. His resignation to head the University of Pennsylvania was denounced angrily by many faculty and administrators, who believed that he had violated his commitment to oversee the massive curricular and structural changes he had begun.

Robert Ketter felt a strong sense of responsibility to the university where he had spent his entire career. He was burdened with the tasks of reviving the construction project, mollifying segments of the Buffalo community, and making sense of curricular changes that were in flux. Ketter's commitment to the university and his vision of higher education were sincere, but his methods and actions were often counter-productive. His strong objection to faculty unionization created hostility between administration and faculty and professional staff. Although he found SUNY and state oversight hobbling, he and Somit micromanaged programs and departments.

Meyerson's strength was his ability to conceptualize a sophisticated vision of the university and to evangelize talented faculty and administrators to support it. Ketter had more traditional administrative leadership skills, and used these to help settle the university after the disorder at the end of the 1960s, but he used these skills in a manner that one professional staff member described as a "siege mentality" (personal communication, 1996).

Martin Meyerson was a president of innovation. Robert Ketter was a president of consolidation. Their actions and accomplishments must be viewed in light of their role as presidents of a university that was part of the largest state system of higher education in the United States, in a community that believed that the university was *of* Buffalo, not merely *at* Buffalo.

References

American Council on Education. *An Assessment of Quality in Graduate Education.* Washington, DC, 1964.

American Council on Education. *A Rating of Graduate Programs.* Washington, DC, 1969.

Barba, William C. "Academic Collective Bargaining: Unit determination factors in higher education, the NLRB, and the states." State University of New York at Buffalo, Buffalo, NY, PhD diss., 1979.

Bennis, Warren. "The Sociology of Institutions or Who Sank the Yellow Submarine?" *Psychology Today* 14, November 1972, 112–120.

Bennis, Warren. *The Leaning Ivory Tower.* San Francisco: Jossey-Bass, 1973.

Capen, Samuel P. *On the Management of Universities.* Buffalo, NY: Foster and Stewart, 1953.

Dudzick, Tom. *Over the Tavern.* Unpublished produced drama, undated.

Duryea, Edward D. and Fisk, Robert S. *Collective Bargaining: The State University of New York and State Government in New York.* Buffalo, NY: SUNY Buffalo Department of Higher Education, 1975.

Furnas, Clifford C. "Inputs and Overtones." Unpublished manuscript, undated.

Glaser, Judith. "Nelson Rockefeller and the Politics of Higher Education." *History of Higher Education Annual*, 1989, 87–114.

Gross, Ronald and Murphy, Judith. "New York's Late-Blooming State University." *Harper's*, December 1966, 87–95.

Jackson, Bruce. "Buffalo English: Literary Glory Days at UB." *Buffalo Beat*, February 26, 1999.

Ketter, Robert. "Dealing from Strength." Commencement Address. SUNY Buffalo. 1981.

Levine, Arthur. *Why Innovation Fails*. Albany, NY: State University of New York, 1980.

Maloney, Patricia A. "Vicious Vandals and Broken Windows: Press Coverage of Campus Unrest." Boston University, Boston, MA, master's thesis, 1975.

McAloon, Pierre. *Corridors*. Media Study, State University of New York at Buffalo, 1994. Videocassette.

Meyerson, Martin. "The Ethos of the American College Student: Beyond the Protests." *Daedalus* 95, no. 3 (1966a), 713–739.

Meyerson, Martin. Speech. University-wide convocation. State University of New York at Buffalo. Buffalo, NY, 1966.

Meyerson, Martin. "Justice." Commencement Address. State University of New York at Buffalo. Buffalo, NY, June 1970.

Porter, Connie. *All-Bright Court*. Boston: Houghton-Mifflin, 1991.

Probst Solomon, Barbara. "Life in the Yellow Submarine: Buffalo's SUNY." *Harper's*, October 1968, 96–102.

Quinlan, Marjorie L. *Rescue of a Landmark*. Buffalo, NY: Western New York Wares, 1990.

Razik, Taher A. "State University of New York at Buffalo: Case Study of Teaching and Research." In Victor G. Onoushkin (Ed.), *Planning in the Development of Universities—IV* (103–212). Paris: UNESCO, 1975.

Select Commission on the Future of Private and Independent Higher Education in New York State (Bundy Commission). Albany, NY, 1967.

Shircliffe, Barbara J. "History of a Student-Run Women's Studies Program." State University of New York at Buffalo, Buffalo, NY, PhD diss., 1996.

Smelser, Neil J. "Berkeley in Crisis and Change." In David Riesman and Verne A Stadtman (eds.), *Academic Transformation*, 51–69. New York: McGraw-Hill, 1973.

State University of New York at Buffalo, *Annual Report*, 1960.

State University of New York at Buffalo, *University Fact Sheet*, 1960.

State University of New York at Buffalo. *Portrait of a Decade: The University at Buffalo as a State University 1962–1972 and the 1971–72 Annual Report*. Buffalo, NY: State University of New York, 1972.

State University of New York at Buffalo. *Self-Study*. Buffalo, NY: State University of New York, 1972.

State University of New York. *Challenge and the Choice: Investing in Graduate Education and Research*. Albany, NY: State University of New York, 1986.

State University of New York. *Trends in Enrollment and Degrees Awarded*. Albany, NY: State University of New York, 1995.

University of Buffalo. *Roots Both Wide and Deep*. Buffalo, NY: State University of New York, 1960.

II. Documenting Research at SUNY University Centers: A Comparative Approach

Nancy Diamond, University of Vermont

Throughout much of its history, the State University of New York has been perceived as the "late blooming university."[1] Due in part to its founding in 1948 as the very last state public university system in the nation, SUNY and its university center campuses have been routinely criticized for lagging behind the top-tier universities in the research achievements of faculty.[2] During the late 1970s and early 1980s, nationwide studies of academic reputation fueled and codified this perception. In continuing comparisons with public universities in California, Michigan, Wisconsin, Illinois, and North Carolina, among others, New York's public research universities consistently appeared inferior.

Respondents to Ladd and Lipset's mid-1970s survey, for example, did not include a single academic department from SUNY university centers among the top five in their fields. In its extensive national study of academic reputation conducted in 1982 by the Conference Board of Associated Research Council, more than half of SUNY's doctoral programs scored below the nationwide average, and only seven out of eighty-one were among the top twenty in their fields. Continuing this disturbing (and possibly inaccurate) trend, no SUNY campus was among the nation's top twenty according to the National Research Council's 1993 rankings, also reputational.[3] Since that time, the SUNY university centers have made great strides in faculty research achievement, yet the expansion and development of research achievement remains a critical challenge.

---

[1] Ronald Gross and Judith Murphy, "New York's Late-Blooming State University." *Harper's* (December 1966), 87–95.

[2] The state of Vermont established the Vermont State Colleges in 1961, but this organization, confined to previously existing state colleges, did not include the University of Vermont. For planning the new public system in New York, see Carmichael, Abbott, and Gelder in the "Histories of SUNY and Higher Education in New York State" bibliography.

[3] Ladd and Lipset's study and the Conference Board assessment are cited in "State University of New York, The Challenge and the Choice;" Report of the Independent Commission on the Future of the State University. Albany: January 16, 1985, Retrieved from http://www.suny. edu/SUNYNews/pdf/ChallengeChoice.pdf For the Conference Board study, see Lyle V. Jones, Gardner Linzey, and Porter E. Coggeshall, eds. *An Assessment of Research-Doctorate Programs in the United States.* Washington, D.C.: National Academy Press, 1982; National Research Council, Research Doctorate Programs in the United States. Washington, D.C.: National Academy Press, 1995. The National Research Council's long-awaited follow-up study should be published soon.

A. Historical Impediments to Research Achievement in the SUNY University Centers

Over the course of SUNY's sixty-year history, many blue ribbon commissions, independent consultants, and state planners routinely have identified impediments to advancing research and graduate education at the SUNY campuses. Explanations of SUNY's "unfulfilled promise" have included New York's lateness in forming a state public research university; over-regulation of the university system; substantial state spending on welfare, the penal system, and state government; New York's shared public and private university mission; and rejection of the flagship model to support four university centers serving different regions.

During SUNY's first decade, consultant Thomas Blegen, graduate dean from the University of Minnesota, conducted a study to assess the research potential of the state's new public university. Opening his report by observing that SUNY was "an academic animal without a head," Blegen argued that New York needed to establish "a single public education and research center on a single campus ... with the accompanying power of reaching out its influence and aspirations." In addition to the lack of centralization, Blegen identified other inhibiting factors: heavy teaching loads, lack of flexibility in scheduling, lack of sabbatical leaves, the burden of excessive committee assignments, absence of graduate students, and added pressures due to extension teaching.[4] Perceived as a threat to New York's private institutions, Blegen's recommendation for a single university was rejected by the trustees and the barriers to research advancement that he identified remained.

As reflected in subsequent commission reports and consultant studies, these inhibiting factors continued to characterize and inform SUNY's development. The blue ribbon Committee on Higher Education (the Heald Committee) appointed by Governor Nelson Rockefeller "to consider how New York can meet on a Statewide basis the increasing demand for higher education, utilizing to the fullest extent the total higher education resources in the state" provided the justification to support Rockefeller's expansionist intentions.[5] Recommending that SUNY develop two major university centers offering comprehensive doctoral programs, the Heald report nevertheless emphasized "the

---

[4]Theodore C. Blegen. *The Harvest of Knowledge; A Report on the Research Problems and Potentials in the State University of New York.* Albany: The Research Foundation of the State University of New York, 1957.

[5]Karen Krischan Noonan. "New York State Higher Education Public Policy System, 1940 to 1980." PhD diss. State University of New York at Buffalo, 1986, citing New York State Public Papers 1959, p. 21. Noonan describes the major reports and planning documents that informed state planning during these years.

handicapping procedural requirements which now limit [SUNY's] capacity to act decisively ...."[6]

To promote SUNY's need for "freedom from budgetary requirements [and] ... the freedom to determine educational related positions ... necessary to attain the stature of a great institution," the Heald Committee called for a new alignment of responsibilities among the Regents, SUNY, and the Board of Higher Education of the City of New York, among others.[7] The Regents Master Plan of 1960 formally recognized the need to expand graduate education by increasing the number of graduate university centers to four (rather than the two recommended by the Heald Committee).[8] The result was the designation of university centers at Albany, Binghamton, and Buffalo, a decision that meant political maneuvering over institutional status and resources on an intra-system level.[9] Reviewing SUNY's new direction, another independent consultant, Chancellor Herman B. Wells of Indiana University, called similar attention to SUNY's continuing bureaucratic constraints and the lack of autonomy necessary to improve graduate education and research.[10]

SUNY officials' response to evaluations and recommendations of external commissions and consultants accelerated system expansion, and yet, strikingly similar impediments identified during early years continued to perpetuate a tradition of obstacles to advancement. Indeed, as one former state university campus president remembered, "the controls were quite outrageous."[11] Some twenty-five years after the Heald Committee called for regulatory reform, the influential report of the Independent Commission on the Future of the State University highlighted a consistent theme. SUNY was the most over-regulated university in the nation, with "over-regulation pervade[ing] every aspect of SUNY's operation." The report provided a clear statement of the commission's concern: "SUNY is a university where trustees, central administration, campus

---

[6]Committee on Higher Education, Meeting the Increased Demand for Higher Education in New York State; A Report to the Governor and the Board of Trustees. Albany: 1960, pp. 19–20. The Heald Committee recommendation led to the merger of the University of Buffalo into the SUNY system. See also Freda Martens. "Decision Making for Higher Education in New York State," PhD diss., Harvard University, 1966, traces the implementation of the committee's recommendations.

[7]Committee on Higher Education, Meeting the Increased Demand, pp. 17–18

[8]University of the State of New York. Board of Regents. *Investments for the Future. The Regents Proposal for Expansion and Improvement of Education in New York State.* Albany: 1960.

[9]For SUNY's expansion under the Rockefeller administration, see Judith S. Glazer, "Nelson Rockefeller and the Politics of Higher Education in New York State," *History of Higher Education Annual* Vol. 9. 1989: 87–114.

[10]Herman B. Wells. "The Legislature and Higher Education in New York State; A Report by the Legislature's consultant on higher education." New York: Academy for Educational Development, 1964.

[11]Martin Fausold, Interview with Bruce D. Johnson, December 18, 1997. Typescript, p. 17.

presidents and faculty lack much of the essential authority that they need to fulfill their responsibilities in teaching, research, and public service."[12] The commission concluded that "SUNY's achievement is well behind that of the leading public universities in other states and leading independent universities in New York." Their report argued that only a basic change in structure "would allow the university to carry out a function for which it was created."[13]

In response to this scathing assessment, SUNY proposed a major graduate education and research initiative designed to "permit [the state university] to carry out its mission more effectively and to realize more fully its potential." The strategy established four goals: the development of multi-disciplinary centers of excellence; the doubling of the number of SUNY PhD programs rated in the top 10 percent in their disciplines, and the number of other programs rated in the top third; doubling of real-dollar volume of sponsored research; and increasing the enrollment of under-represented groups in graduate and professional programs.[14] Each of the university centers crafted plans "to strengthen their graduate and research programs while maintaining their commitment to high-quality undergraduate education."[15] This university-wide initiative, endorsed by Governor Cuomo and the legislature, gave SUNY trustees and the campuses greater authority to develop plans that would strengthen their graduate and research programs.

The recommendations of the Independent Commission were instrumental in identifying the need for management flexibility, in securing legislation that significantly improved SUNY's regulatory environment, and in calling attention to the need for greater investment in graduate education and research. However, many of the same disabling circumstances addressed by their report continued to hamper the expansion of graduate education and research. The recent Commission on Higher Education in New York State still found evidence of SUNY's over-regulation and a detrimental lack of campus autonomy. Echoing the findings of previous commissions, their June 2008 report emphasized "SUNY's classification as a state agency ... extremely unusual" in comparison with arrangements in other states.[16]

---

[12]State University of New York, "The Challenge and the Choice; Report of the Independent Commission on the Future of the State University." Albany: January 16, 1985, p. 43.

[13]State University of New York. "The Challenge and the Choice: Investing in Graduate Education and Research in the State University of New York." October, 1986, p. 81. This report includes the campus plans for advancing research at Albany, Binghamton, Buffalo, and Stony Brook.

[14]Ibid., p. 2.

[15]Ibid., pp. 3–4.

[16]SUNY 2000. SUNY: A Planned System. A SUNY 2000 Occasional Paper, October 1992, p. 10. ERIC Document ED357725. Retrieved from http://www.eric.ed.gov/ERICWebPortal/custom/portlets/recordDetails/detailmini.jsp?_nfpb=true&_&ERICExtSe

These circumstances, the commission noted, continued to have particularly negative consequences for the university centers. Despite their critical importance to the state's research capacity and economic development, the four university centers' "autonomy in making decisions is severely limited, as they must seek approval ... from the Board of Trustees and the Legislature, waiting, when they should be instead, acting."[17] Recognizing New York's decline in national research share since the 1980s, the report concluded that it is "essential that SUNY's research universities receive focused attention and support." At long last, the commission report emphasized the "key role of New York's public institutions for attracting world class research and building public research capacity."[18]

B.   Assessing Research at SUNY University Centers

This paper tests those perceptions with quantitative data from the Academic Analytics Faculty Scholarly Productivity (FSP) database to provide a snapshot that documents and compares faculty research performance at the SUNY university centers with results from other research universities across the nation. Academic Analytics is a privately-owned for-profit company that has developed procedures and tools for rating annual scholarly output at nearly 7,300 PhD programs at 354 American universities. The FSP compiles for each PhD program, among other measures, the number and dollar award of selected federal grants, journal articles, journal citations, books, and awards and honors received.[19] Academic Analytics then normalizes the results in terms of the number of full-time, tenure, and tenure-track faculty engaged in doctoral education at each university.[20] The data for this analysis is drawn

---

[17]New York State Commission on Higher Education. Final Report of Findings and Recommendations (Albany: June 2008), p. 45. http://www.hecommission.state.ny.us/report/CHE_Final-Report_200806.pdf

[18]Ibid., pp. 18–19.

[19]Academic Analytics grant calculations reflect funding the following agencies: Department of Education ($18,000+ grants); Department of Energy (357 grants); Federal Aviation Administration (25 grants); National Institutes of Health ($170,000+ grants); National Science Foundation) $39,000+ grants); and the U.S. Department of Agriculture ($2,100+ grants).

[20]Academic Analytics obtains the number of faculty from each PhD-granting department's website and in most cases, reviews and then seeks confirmation from the institution. For more information about Academic Analytics and the Faculty Scholarly Productivity (FSP) Index and Data Base, see http://www.academicanalytics.com/ I am indebted to Lawrence Martin, President, for sharing data from the FSP Data Base for the purpose of this research. Dr. Martin developed the FSP index and serves as the president of Academic Analytics. Special thanks go to Maria Andersen, Chief Operating Officer, Academic Analytics, who provided important guidance, and to Kristin Camp, Executive Assistant to the Vice President for Research and Graduate Studies, University of Vermont, who compiled data and prepared tables and charts for this presentation.

from the 2007–2008 database, which reflects three-to-five year averages for a variety of measures. Externally sponsored funding from private foundations or industry are not included in the database or in this analysis.[21]

C. Why a Per-Capita Assessment of Research Achievement?

Historically, many previous studies of scholarly achievement have relied on reputational assessments. The Ladd and Lipset survey of the mid-1970s, the Conference Board 1982 study, and the National Research Council's assessment in 1993 all used measures that documented faculty and campus reputation to rank institutions and programs. More recently, however, the flaws inherent in such an approach have been identified and acknowledged. Reputational assessments tend to favor older institutions with enduring traditions of excellence. Generally, these studies are biased in favor of larger programs, which have more publishing faculty for raters to recognize and tend to conflate quality and quantity. Even more troubling, reputational studies have a tendency to obscure the achievements of faculty at newer or smaller campuses in favor of those of respected institutional leaders; perhaps inadvertently, these rankings can discourage talented faculty at aspiring departments, programs, and institutions.[22] The liabilities of such studies and their inevitable rankings might help to explain the SUNY university center's disappointing performance in comparison with the great midwestern flagships or the University of California campuses. At the time of the national reputational surveys mentioned above, the SUNY university centers, as newer and in some cases smaller campuses, had not yet established the reputations of their campuses or academic departments.

In contrast to reputational assessments, a per-capita approach helps to level the playing field of academic prestige. Controlling for institutional size permits comparisons that illuminate differences and similarities without conflating quality and quantity. Of particular importance to an assessment of research at SUNY university centers, per capita measures of research can provide a basis for identifying and comparing SUNY faculty achievements with faculty at larger, older institutions. As an example, using per capita assessments in our 1997 study of scholarly achievement across the academic spectrum, Hugh Graham and I found that among public universities, three SUNY university

---

[21]The 2007–08 data is based on the following averages: Books—five years; Journals—three years; Citations—four years of papers; Grants—three years (new, competitive awards only)—normalized on an annual basis. The Awards category is based on some 530 awards, ranging from book awards and distinguished achievement awards from professional associations to the National Medal of Science. A weighting system reconciles the differences in significance among awards.

[22]For a more detailed exposition of this position, see Hugh Davis Graham and Nancy Diamond, *The Rise of American Research Universities: Elites and Challengers in the Postwar Era*. Baltimore: Johns Hopkins University Press, 1997.

centers were among the top thirty. Stony Brook ranked third, just behind UC Berkeley and UC Santa Barbara, Albany was seventeenth, and Buffalo was twenty-ninth.[23] In previous national assessments, no SUNY campus had been included in a top-thirty.

In the discussion below, the research achievements of doctoral faculty at Albany, Binghamton, Buffalo, and Stony Brook are compared with other public research universities according six per capita measures drawn from the Academic Analytics Faculty Scholarly Productivity database (2007–08), and normalized according to the number of PhD program faculty at each campus. The indicators are: the number of grants and grant dollars received, the number of journal publications and citations, the number of books, and the number of awards and honors.

D. Research Comparisons for the SUNY University Centers

The first analysis compares faculty research at the SUNY university centers with research at other public universities classified by the most recent (2006) Carnegie Foundation for Advancement of Teaching as research universities with very high (RU/VH) research activity, or research universities with high (RU/H) research activity.[24] SUNY university centers at Albany, Buffalo, and Stony Brook are among the sixty-three public universities in the "very high" research category. Binghamton is one of seventy-six public campuses in the "high" research category.[25]

E. Public Research Universities with Very High Research Activity

As would be expected, the RU/VH list includes the nation's most distinguished public universities. The group features eight of the general campuses of the

---

[23]Ibid., Table 6.7, p. 167.

[24]Carnegie Foundation for the Advancement of Teaching 2006 classification can be found at http://www.carnegiefoundation.org/index.asp

[25]The Carnegie RU/VH and RU/H categories also include private universities, but those institutions are not used in this comparison. When the Carnegie Foundation classifications were first published in 1973, the top research category included six of New York's private universities, but none of the state's public institutions. Carnegie classifications have changed since 1973, with subsequent classifications offered in 1976, 1987, 1994, 2000, and 2008. New categories and names reflecting changing criteria make it difficult to identify campus movement from one classification to another. Nevertheless, SUNY university centers have advanced to higher research university classifications. In 1994, Albany and Buffalo (Research University/Very High in 2008) were classified as Research II. Binghamton (Research University/High in 2008) was in the Doctoral I category. Stony Brook was classified as Research I in 1994 and remains in the highest research university category.

University of California, the ten public campuses of the Big 10, and the Universities of North Carolina and Washington, among others. The average number of faculty engaged in doctoral education on these campuses is about 1,340, and almost half (45 percent) have medical schools.

In comparison with other public universities in the RU/VH category, Albany, Buffalo, and Stony Brook fared well on the publications measures and demonstrated room for improvement in grants categories (which are confined to a specific set of federal agencies). The number of books written by Albany faculty outdistanced the group's average. Buffalo's average publications per faculty approximated the RU/VH group mean, and average number of books was higher. Albany, Buffalo, and Stony Brook won a higher number of awards than by faculty at the RU/VH group. Stony Brook faculty demonstrated higher per capita scores than the RU/VH group in the number and dollar amount of grants and the number of publications and citations, with a considerably higher citation score (Table 5.1).

F. Public Research Universities with High Research Activity

The public universities classified by the Carnegie Foundation as RU/H represent a wide variety of institutional types and locations. The group includes the Universities of Oregon, Vermont, West Virginia, as well the City University of New York. Five have medical schools and an average of some 432 faculty in PhD programs (Table 5.1).

In several categories, RU/H group member SUNY Binghamton demonstrated higher per capita scores than the overall group, specifically in citations, publications, and the number of books; furthermore, Binghamton faculty demonstrated more books per capita than the RU/VH or RU/H average scores for that category. The number of per capita awards received at Binghamton was equal to the RU/H group average. When compared according to the Academic Analytics per capita grants measures from a specific set of agencies, Binghamton's number of grants and amount of grant dollars were lower than the RU/H group mean (Table 5.1).

G. Public Research Universities with and without Medical Schools

Research universities with medical schools (in both RU/VH and RU/H classifications) range from very large institutions like Michigan and Ohio State to the smaller Universities of Vermont and North Dakota. The faculty in this category average 1236. SUNY Stony Brook PhD faculty demonstrated higher scores in the per capita journal publication and citation categories, and slightly higher in the number of grants, but lower in grant dollars. Buffalo per capita scores were somewhat lower than the medical school averages (Table 5.2).

TABLE 5.1

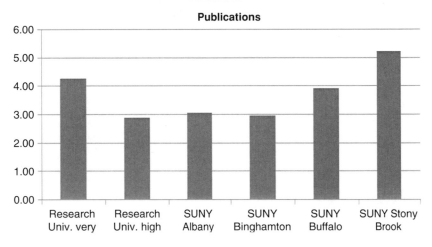

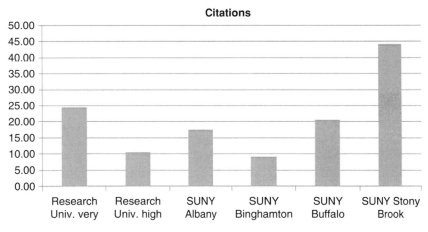

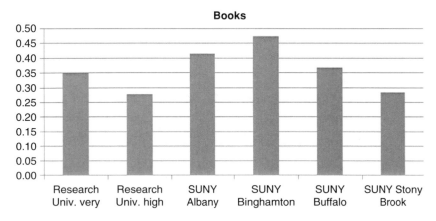

TABLE 5.2

Publications

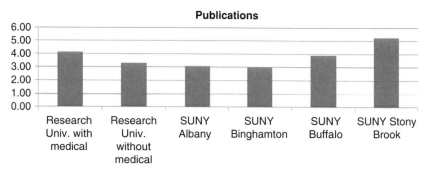

Citations

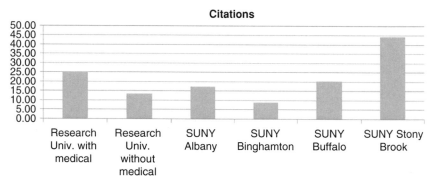

Books

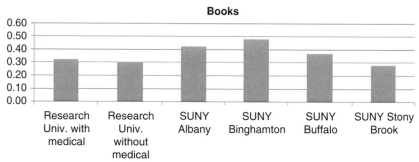

Research universities without medical schools (both RH/VH and RU/H) reflect a significant variety of institutional types and sizes, including UC Berkeley, and the Universities of Nebraska-Lincoln, Tennessee, and Oregon, but also the College of William and Mary. Doctoral faculty for these universities average 700. Due to the varied nature of campuses in the non-medical university group, comparisons may be of less comparative utility. Nevertheless, both SUNY campuses at Albany and Binghamton demonstrated higher per capita book scores than universities with or without medical schools, and Albany's scores were higher in the citation category than scores at other universities in the non-medical school group (Table 5.2).

H.   Public Research Universities in Peer States

To avoid the myopia "that sets in when we believe that the only good ideas are ideas that emanate here," the New York State Commission on Higher Education report (June 2008) identified seven peer states considered comparable to New York in terms of size, complexity, and diversity. These are California, Florida, Illinois, Massachusetts, Ohio, Pennsylvania, and Texas.[26] The analysis below compares the per capita performance of SUNY University Centers with per capita scores of PhD faculty at research universities in peer states. The RU/VH category includes Ohio State, Penn State, Illinois, and Florida State, among others. The RU/H category includes Temple, San Diego State, and Southern Illinois Universities, among others. Stony Brook faculty per capita publication scores were the highest—higher than the comparison RU/VH peers. When compared with faculty at institutions in peer states, Albany and Buffalo again demonstrate superior scores in the per capita book category, and Binghamton received the highest per capita book score among both RU/VH and RU/H universities in peer states (Table 5.3).

I.   Concluding Observation

While broad in scope, comparisons of per capita research achievement at the SUNY university centers with scores at other research universities nationwide highlight distinctive strengths and accomplishments, as well as areas for improvement. All the same, these measures must be used in the context of other indicators. Other important measures, especially research expenditures, contribute to the campus research profile. For example, of nineteen New York private and public research universities with more than $20 million in research expenditures ($ in thousands) in fiscal year 2005, Buffalo ($267.3) ranked fifth, Albany ($259.7) sixth, Stony Brook ($213.3) eighth, and Binghamton ($25.8) eighteenth.[27]

Whatever the indicator, and in light of the well-documented and continuing impediments to research achievement that have characterized SUNY's sixty-year history, the research accomplishments of faculty at the university centers are considerable. Commission after commission, consultant after consultant, identified a New York public higher education system plagued by

---

[26]New York State Commission on Higher Education, Final Report of Findings and Recommendations, pp. 1–2.

[27]Ibid.

TABLE 5.3

Publications

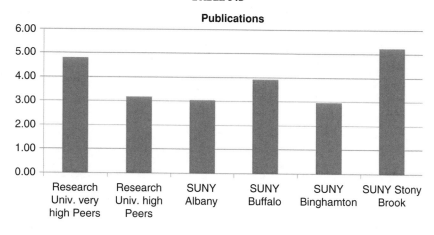

Citations

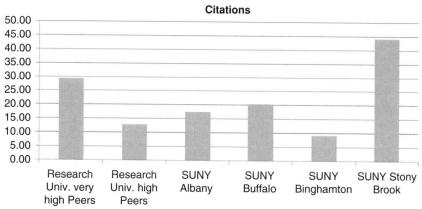

Books

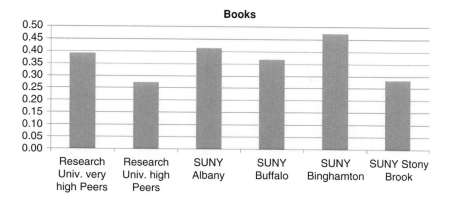

over-regulation and relationships more appropriate to the state Department of Motor Vehicles than the state university. Most commission studies and reports recognized and lamented structural impediments to achievement, ranging from Blegen's "headless animal," to the persisting lack of campus autonomy and under investment. Despite enduring constraints, SUNY faculty and researchers have been able to generate remarkable records of research achievement, and the system's potential can no longer be characterized as "unfulfilled." The advice offered in the *Challenge and Choice* 1987 report may provide useful guidance for understanding SUNY's current circumstances. In that report, the Independent Commission argued that "SUNY must be judged by the contribution it can make today, and for future needs, rather than by special circumstances of its past."[28] Above all, as former SUNY Chancellor Bruce Johnstone has noted, "It is important to tell the SUNY story better."[29]

III. Better Late Than Never: Intentions, Timing, and Results in Creating SUNY Research Universities

Roger L. Geiger, Penn State University

The American states have been called laboratories of democracy because they exhibit so many different permutations of public policies. For higher education, New York State presents a unique experiment; the first state to create a comprehensive organization to oversee education, the University of the State of New York (1787), it was the last state to create a public university. When it finally did so, it designed the most inclusive of all state universities in the variety of institutions it annexed into its bureaucratic domain. Belatedly, it resolved to establish public research universities that were not merely comparable to those in other states, but whose academic excellence would be a credit to what was then the largest and wealthiest state. This paper provides an historical assessment of this effort. It specifically asks whether or to what extent SUNY's late start compromised these efforts. Doctoral education will be examined here as a barometer of relative performance, in order to compare SUNY's growth and development with that of other public research universities. This data provides some basis for determining when the SUNY graduate centers achieved maturity as research universities, and how they then compared with public research universities in other states.

---

[28]Independent Commission on the Future of the State University, Challenge and Choice, p. 20.

[29]Martin S. Fausold, Interview with Bruce Johnstone, p. 28.

A. SUNY's Lost Decade

The launching of the State University of New York began with an abject surrender to the interests of private higher education. It was agreed that SUNY teachers colleges would teach no liberal arts subjects for at least ten years. Moreover, the understanding was that SUNY could only "supplement" the activities of private colleges and universities. Thus, the state university would have no teaching in the arts and sciences, no graduate education in those fields, and no research. A symposium held in 1950 on the "Functions of a Modern University" seemed designed to deflate any pretentions the fledgling institution might have harbored. Harvard President James Conant asserted that, "Certainly, we need no more four-year colleges in the northeast part of the United States" and Governor Thomas Dewey opined that "to regard a college degree as a guaranteed ticket to securing earnings is an illusion." Both men encouraged the state "university" to focus its energies on vocational community colleges. The 1950 "Master Plan" took its cue from these sentiments, subordinating the university to private sector interests and choosing to emphasize general and technical education in two-year institutions.[30]

Progress in the 1950s toward anything resembling a university was virtually non-existent. SUNY acquired two failing medical schools, three extension campuses in the Binghamton area were combined as Harpur College, and a research foundation offered small seed grants to faculty. In 1957 the State University College of Long Island opened as a teachers college on a temporary campus at Oyster Bay. The same year the Blegen Report described the university as "an academic animal without a head." The very idea that it should contemplate a central, campus-based university was anathema to the trustees and the rest of the state educational establishment.[31] Apparently SUNY president William Carlson was exploring the possibility of purchasing Syracuse University for this purpose. Instead, he was sacked.

However, 1957 was also the year of Sputnik, and the beginning of a decisive change in public opinion in favor of the expansion of universities and academic research. The bulk of federal support for university research shifted from the defense establishment to civilian agencies—the National Institutes of Health (NIH), National Science Foundation (NSF), and National Aeronautics and Space Administration (NASA). Appropriations for university research doubled in the next three years, and doubled again in just four more years. A succession of reports from the President's Science Advisory Council advocated the expansion of basic research and culminated in a 1960 recommendation to double the number

---

[30]Sidney Gelber. *Politics and Public Higher Education in New York State: Stony Brook—a Case History.* New York: Peter Lang, 2001, quotes, pp. 70, 71.

[31]Martin S. Fausold. "A Draft History of the State University of New York." ms., SUNY, Genesco, 1988: 30–33.

of American research universities.[32] With the "baby-boomers" advancing toward higher education and the federal government committed to a vast expansion of university research, the former views of Conant, Dewey, and the Albany educational establishment soon appeared antediluvian. The state university began to move ponderously toward establishing real universities. This movement occurred in two stages: from 1960 to 1964 the foundation was laid for establishing true universities; then from 1964 to 1970, under the chancellorship of Samuel Gould, the promise was realized in bricks, mortar, faculty, and students.

Besides the changing national mood, New York politics were forever altered by the election of Nelson Rockefeller as governor in 1958. He believed that government could solve all problems, and he had no qualms about spending the sum required. Rockefeller also had a personal concern for higher education and sought to restructure the state university early in his term.[33] In 1960 he appointed a blue-ribbon committee headed by the Ford Foundation's President, Henry Heald. The resulting Heald Report (November 1960) altered the role of SUNY in the state as its authoritative recommendations were swiftly adopted. Using demographic data, it forecast that public higher education would have to assume responsibility for educating the majority of New York's college students. No longer would SUNY merely supplement the private sector; instead it would be a partner that defined its own role. One helpful step was removing the Regents from administrative control of SUNY and leaving them only with authority to review the Master Plans. The teachers colleges were to be given strong liberal arts programs and converted into full-fledged colleges. For universities, it foresaw creating two "graduate centers." The Heald Report was immediately followed by SUNY's 1960 Master Plan, which called for establishing four graduate centers. Rockefeller seemed committed to launching graduate centers at Stony Brook and Albany, but Buffalo and Binghamton soon joined this company. All seemed agreed at this juncture that graduate education needed to be greatly expanded in the Empire State.

Politics and geography were intermixed in the designation of the SUNY universities. Stony Brook was launched initially to fill the higher education vacuum on rapidly-growing Long Island. The absence of private-sector competitors and the contributions of local philanthropy no doubt facilitated the elevation of this campus. Its future status as a graduate center was agreed upon as early as 1960, although the scale and scope of this commitment were soon contested. In 1962 the new campus's first buildings were occupied, and SUNY at Stony Brook was born. The following year another of Rockefeller's

---

[32]Roger L. Geiger. *Research and Relevant Knowledge: American Research Universities Since World War II*. New Brunswick: Transaction Publishers, 2004.

[33]Judith Glazer, "Nelson Rockefeller and the Politics of Higher Education in New York State," *History of Higher Education* Annual, 9 1989: 87–114.

blue-ribbon committees designated Stony Brook for a medical school and health center, solidifying its university credentials. The attainment of full university status occurred during the last half of the decade under President John Toll (1965–1980), when undergraduate enrollments rose from 2,725 to 7,129, and graduate students from 120 to 1,733.

The University of Buffalo was a venerable private institution, but also on the verge of bankruptcy when it was purchased by SUNY in 1962. The Senate majority leader, Walter Mahoney, is said to have been instrumental in arranging this transaction, which included the promise to erect an entire new campus. However, the acquisition of Buffalo gave SUNY a functioning university, complete with law and medical schools, doctoral programs, and a football team.

Binghamton became a graduate center, despite little interest on the part of its core, Harpur College. Rather, the graduate center was pushed quite strongly by State Senator Warren Anderson and George Hinman, a Regent and Rockefeller confidante. After moving to a new campus in 1961, the institution officially became SUNY at Binghamton in 1965.

The Graduate Center at Albany subsumed the Albany College for Teachers, which had a good reputation among an otherwise woefully handicapped group. Rockefeller strongly favored having a state university in the capital, and once again, few private institutions were threatened. Albany was designated for university status in 1962 and began occupying its new campus in 1966.

Interestingly, only Stony Brook developed through a combination of central planning and local initiative. The other three graduate centers were largely the product of political sponsorship—from Rockefeller, George Mahoney, and Anderson/Hinman.

Although the pieces seemed to be in place by 1962 for the SUNY universities, the next two years were plagued by vacillation and indecision at the center under an acting president, J. Lawrence Murray, while national enthusiasm soared for expanded university research and graduate education. Another blue-ribbon committee, this time led by Indiana University President Herman Wells, underlined both shortcomings and challenges for SUNY. The Wells Report criticized the bureaucratic paralysis of the SUNY administration, inadequate fiscal commitment, and the lack of autonomy for the graduate centers. Above all it underlined the contemporary knowledge revolution and pointed out that "the university is the center of the knowledge process."

> High quality graduate education in scientific research—today the very keystone of educational vitality at leading universities throughout the nation—are far too little at public universities in New York.[34]

---

[34]Wells, Herman B. *The Legislature and Higher Education in New York State*. Report by the Legislature's consultant on higher education. New York: Academy for Educational Development, 1964.

The Wells Report urged the state to go much further than the existing Master Plan in "improving graduate education and research," and specifically suggested developing "three or four peaks of excellence each year at the graduate level in individual departments ...."[35] Thus, by 1964, New York finally had an unambiguous mandate to join other major states in supporting public research universities. Furthermore, the notion had been planted that excellence, as well as access, ought to be the goal of such efforts.

B.   Samuel Gould and the Take-off Years

Samuel B. Gould assumed the presidency of SUNY in September 1964. Formerly chancellor of UC Santa Barbara, he understood the importance of academic quality and the challenge of nurturing it in developing institutions. He spoke of creating an institution of "undeniable greatness," that would have a "passion for excellence." He believed, like many others at this juncture, that greatness and excellence must be built on a foundation of core academic disciplines. He established an official SUNY policy that "strong doctoral programs in the traditional arts and sciences ... shall be developed fully before a [graduate] center embarks on doctoral work in other specialized fields."[36] However, the politics of Albany and the multiple commitments of the SUNY system made it difficult to maintain a focus on greatness or excellence.

The graduate center that most fully shared Gould's initial vision was Stony Brook. As a new founding, it had harbored ambitions of attaining academic eminence from its early days, especially as it moved to its new campus. As Gould was taking office, SUNY was negotiating the appointment of John S. Toll as president of the Stony Brook campus. A University of Maryland physicist, Toll explicitly embraced these ambitions. In those negotiations he sought assurances that SUNY "intended to develop the program, faculty, and facilities on the Stony Brook campus during the next fifteen years so that it will have an excellence comparable to the present status of the Berkeley campus." He specifically identified the need for "super-scale salaries" to entice academic stars and he wanted 100 new graduate assistantships each year (increased from ten). The "comparison group" he established to measure Stony Brook's academic progress consisted of UC Berkeley, UCLA, and the universities of Illinois, Michigan, and Wisconsin.[37]

Toll made a promising start for an inchoate research university. He recruited Nobel physicist C. N. Yang to anchor a distinguished Physics Department and established ties with nearby Brookhaven National Laboratory. It was less clear, however, that the other graduate centers shared this "Berkeleyitis." SUNY's University at Buffalo clearly had high aspirations when it summoned its new president down from Valhalla—Martin Meyerson (1966–1969), who

---

[35]Gelber, Politics, quotes p. 187.

[36]Ibid., quotes pp. 189, 190.

[37]Ibid., 192–199.

had been acting chancellor of Berkeley. Buffalo managed some distinguished appointments in English, but was largely preoccupied with planning and building its new Amherst campus. Meyerson soon departed for the University of Pennsylvania. Binghamton seemed content to emphasize undergraduate education and the liberal arts foundation it had established as Harpur College. And Albany apparently had few pretentions of academic eminence. Moreover, the commitment of the SUNY administration to distinguished graduate programs wavered almost as soon as it began. Stony Brook made plans for every department to offer the doctorate by 1970, with a target population of 3,000 graduate students. However, in 1965 SUNY revised the enrollment projection downward to only 500 graduate students in 1970, which would make it scarcely worthwhile to develop doctoral programs. Stony Brook actually reached 1,700 in 1970, but inconsistency at the center made it more difficult to develop these programs.

Hence, one can only wonder how seriously SUNY was committed to developing graduate centers that would rival the University of California, or at least place New York in the forefront of public universities. Certainly the rhetoric was congenial to Gould, and before him, Nelson Rockefeller was fond of invoking the image of a great state university. No wonder that academics in far-off Stony Brook believed that their mission was to build such an institution. The campus's first two presidents looked specifically at UC San Diego, where an explicit commitment to build a leading university had included years of planning. It had been built from the top down—eminent professors and strong graduate programs first, followed by fairly small undergraduate programs.

In the event, no rival to Berkeley—or to San Diego—emerged from the SUNY colossus. But this scarcely qualifies as a failure. A more pertinent question is to ask to what extent the SUNY graduate centers fulfilled their mission? When did they join the ranks of America's research universities and how did they compare with other universities? More specifically, to what extent did a belated start and continuing vacillation in Albany retard their progress? Or conversely, what did Albany's billions in funding accomplish?

These questions have been addressed, as in Sidney Gelber's and Martin Fausold's accounts, by describing the impediments that gradually mounted against the SUNY graduate centers. By 1967, the private sector began to reassert its influence with the Bundy Commission; developments in the CUNY system then dominated the attention of lawmakers; the student revolt caused further embarrassment; the tenure of Ernest Boyer as head of SUNY (1970–1977) endured unrelieved fiscal stringency; and the Regents became more aggressive in stifling the development of SUNY, including an organized effort to suppress fledgling doctoral programs.[38] However, the larger issue of timing

---

[38]See the 1973 report: "Meeting the Needs of Doctoral Education. A Statement of Policy and Proposed Action by the Regents of the University of the State of New York." Position Paper No. 19.

has been virtually ignored. During the great post-Sputnik expansion of the university research system, established universities were far better suited to take advantage of federal largesse. By the late 1960s, as the SUNY centers were gearing up, the federal research economy was beginning to spiral downward. The peak year for federal support for academic research was 1968, followed by eight years of stagnation. Other federal programs for graduate students and developing science departments were reduced far more. Moreover, when university research began to recover in the late 1970s, the growth areas were no longer in the arts and sciences—the darlings of the 1960s and the focus of SUNY graduate departments.

C. The SUNY Record in Doctoral Education

In order to weigh the impact of all these factors, it is necessary to look at results rather than circumstances. A shorthand way of doing this is to examine trends in the awarding of doctorates. Doctoral students are an input to academic research and PhDs are an output. As an input, doctoral students are actually a scarce resource. PhD students choose the best programs that will have them and graduate programs seek to enroll the best students that they can attract. This produces a queue and overflow system nationally, so that academic quality is reflected in the number and abilities of applicants.[39] The limits of this system were scarcely visible in the 1960s, when graduate enrollments were booming and projections predicted continuing growth.[40] However, these predictions proved far wide of the mark. The relative scarcity of doctoral students became apparent in the 1970s and has persisted since. Thus, the ability of the SUNY graduate centers to attract and graduate doctoral students can serve as a rough barometer of their relative performance as research universities.

Figure 5.1 provides one answer to the question of when SUNY graduate centers matured as research universities. Until 1980, SUNY's production of doctorates was consistently rising. Particularly from 1973 to 1980, SUNY was increasing doctoral graduates, even while the national total was in decline. Thus, despite the adverse conditions faced by the SUNY graduate centers in the 1970s, the momentum of academic development sustained a growing output from doctoral programs. After 1980, however, the outperformance ceased. For the next sixteen years, doctoral production mirrored the national trend. This would imply that SUNY graduate centers collectively reached maturity around 1980. For the most recent decade, SUNY doctorates have failed to keep up with the national pattern. Still, this overall trend masks the performance of the individual centers.

---

[39]Roger L. Geiger. "Doctoral Education: Short-term Crisis Versus Long-term Challenge," *Review of Higher Education* 20, 3 (1997): 239–51.

[40]Allan M. Cartter. *Ph.D.'s and the Academic Labor Market*. New York: McGraw-Hill, 1976.

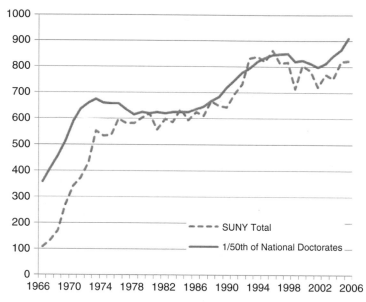

FIGURE 5.1 Number of Doctorates Awarded (1966–2006).

As shown in Figure 5.2, until the early 1970s, SUNY doctorates were largely awarded by the Buffalo campus—the sole established university. But doctorates at Buffalo ceased to grow at about the same time that national doctorates turned down, and Buffalo has not shown any growth since. Stony Brook stands out for increasing its doctoral awards from the early 1970s to the early 1990s. However, this growth faltered just when national doctorates again begin to climb. Both Albany and Binghamton do not depart much from the national trend, growing about 50 percent from the early 1980s trough to recent highs, though they only produce about 100 PhDs per year.

How does SUNY's performance compare with that of other universities? Perhaps a better question is with whom should SUNY be compared? One possibility is other Eastern states that have a low regard for public universities.

We can see in Figure 5.3 that UMass Amherst has fared poorly since 1973. Except for a burst of graduates in the early 1990s, it has become steadily less active in doctoral education.

State universities in the South were in a position that bears some similarity with SUNY's. Although long established, until 1970, segregation and the general backwardness of public life left them as marginal regional performers of research and doctoral education. So, they, too, tended to be late bloomers, if they bloomed at all. And several have.

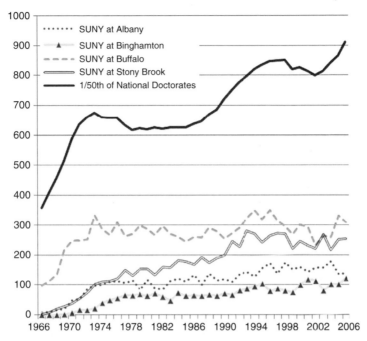

FIGURE 5.2 Number of Doctorates Awarded (1966–2006).

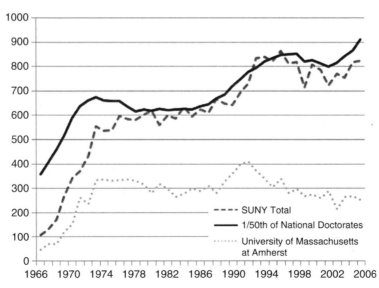

FIGURE 5.3 Number of Doctorates Awarded (1966–2006).

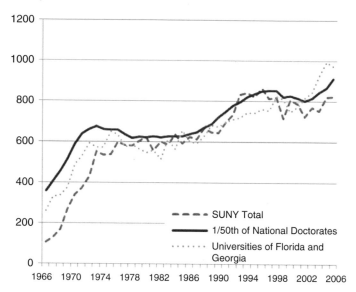

FIGURE 5.4 Number of Doctorates Awarded (1966–2006).

Florida and Georgia are two universities that experienced inconsistent state backing, with periodic efforts to advance their standings as research universities. Interestingly, except for an initial advantage, their combined output of doctorates traces that of SUNY until the end of the century (Figure 5.4). Since 2000, however, they have risen above the national trend, as state policies have been generally positive, while SUNY has fallen behind.

Considering the rhetoric that accompanied creation of the SUNY graduate centers, the University of California presents an obvious comparison. However, emulating Berkeley was never a realistic possibility. Figure 5.5 compares SUNY with the four new campuses of the UC that were founded or expanded in the 1960s: Irvine, Riverside, San Diego, and Santa Cruz. Interestingly, doctoral education at those campuses developed rather slowly and matches that of SUNY until about 1990. In the 1990s, and particularly after 2000, these campuses have pulled away from SUNY.

Considering the early aspiration at Stony Brook to emulate UC San Diego, one final comparison (Figure 5.6) juxtaposes doctoral outputs from those two campuses. Surprisingly, in light of the volume of research and the eminence of its faculty, San Diego's doctoral degrees parallel those of Stony Brook until very recently.

D.   Conclusions

This comparison of doctoral outputs suggests two kinds of conclusions, one historical and the other contemporary. Historically, it appears that SUNY's late

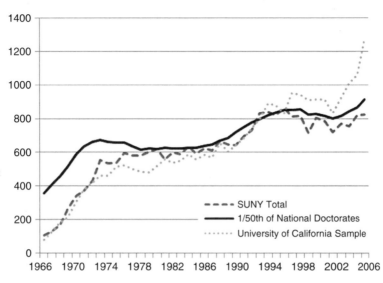

FIGURE 5.5 Number of Doctorates Awarded (1966–2006).

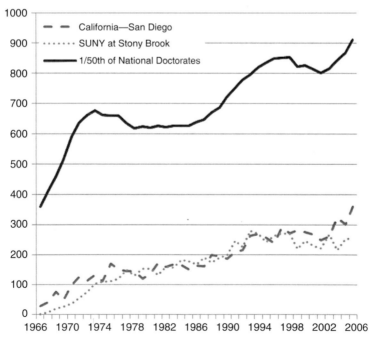

FIGURE 5.6 Number of Doctorates Awarded (1966–2006).

start was not a decisive handicap to the development of research universities. The pattern of doctorates indicates that SUNY graduate centers continued to mature as research universities and advanced their relative standing until about 1980. After that, the SUNY research campuses tracked the national trendline until the mid-1990s, indicating that they no longer exhibited characteristics of immaturity. Two factors may have been working toward this result. First, the advantage of backwardness: starting in the mid-1960s the SUNY graduate centers were able to call upon the talents of individuals who were familiar with research universities and the new research economy. John Toll certainly fit that description, and Buffalo was reorganized by Martin Meyerson during his brief tenure. Whereas other universities had learned from experience during the 1960s, the SUNY campuses were able to import these lessons. (Assimilating or implementing them was another matter, made difficult by the politics and administrative structure of SUNY itself.)

Second, in the decentralized structure of American higher education, each university possesses its own rhythms of development, which often vary from the rhythms of the overall system. Most research universities over-expanded during the golden age of the 1960s and found it necessary to engage in retrenchment during the 1970s, whereas expanding institutions, like Arizona and Georgia Tech, made great strides during that dismal decade.[41] The SUNY universities, with the momentum of their late starts, had some degree of additional expansion, as well. Despite harsh fiscal conditions, Stony Brook, for example, added 130 regular faculty and almost 300 health center faculty from 1969 to 1979. It was still getting bigger and better during those trying times.

There is nevertheless a downside to the timing factor—namely path dependency. The academic expansion during the golden age of the 1960s was extraordinarily traditional. Historically, most periods of dynamic expansion have featured new kinds of institutions and bold new experiments. Not so the 1960s. Graduate programs were multiplied and expanded in the basic arts and sciences disciplines. As a latecomer, SUNY was no exception. But, by adopting this pattern, the SUNY universities set the path for much of their futures. This did not become a problem until the 1980s, when the academic research economy began to revive, but on a different basis. Then private money, rather than federal dollars, drove the expansion, and contributions to economic development were valued more highly than articles in disciplinary journals. SUNY universities fared poorly in this competition, and seemed to be reluctant or

---

[41]Geiger. *Research and Relevant Knowledge*, 273–96.

unable to adapt. For example, their rankings for industry-sponsored research were far below their standing on other indicators, at least until recently.[42]

Some time ago, Nancy Diamond and I conducted an unpublished study of the relative advancement of research universities—using a combination of measures—from the early 1980s to the early 1990s. On the basis of relative change, Stony Brook was about 100th out of 120 universities, and Buffalo was a bit lower. Without claiming undue validity for this exercise, it provides one piece of evidence that the SUNY universities were not doing too well during those years.

The years from about 1995 to the economic disaster of 2008 were an extremely good stretch for research universities, nearly another golden age. The doctoral data in this case suggest, once again, that SUNY universities have had limited participation in this prosperity. Data on change in research share paint a more encouraging picture: Buffalo and Stony Brook are about where they were in the mid-1990s, and Albany has more than doubled its share. The doctoral data do not reflect considerable vitality in SUNY research in recent years. On the other hand, one could argue that SUNY universities were late once again to the academic research feast.

Since the 1990s, SUNY research universities have achieved greater autonomy, have emphasized distinctive identities, and appear to have a boosted morale. Binghamton University now boasts of its combination of rigorous undergraduate education and limited research programs emphasizing microelectronics. It has found a distinctive niche as a small, selective public university with a reputation for undergraduate teaching. The University of Albany has broken out of its initial path with the College of Nanotechnology and is now firmly seated on the economic development bandwagon. Stony Brook remains a fairly small university focused on the arts and sciences. The academic eminence it has always sought is no doubt limited by its size, although that makes its relative accomplishments more substantial. A close relationship with Brookhaven provides a strong presence in physics research. And the University of Buffalo has large ambitions to expand both enrollments and its economic contribution to Western New York. Thus, in the final analysis, there can be no doubt that the SUNY founding fathers were better late than never in establishing research universities.

---

[42]SUNY Albany has risen spectacularly since 2003 in ranking for industry-sponsored research and SUNY Buffalo has risen, too, since 2005. Stony Brook has remained a marginal performer of research for industry: NSF data.

The Best Laid Plans

Introduction

John Aubrey Douglass, Senior Research Fellow, Center for Studies in Higher Education, University of California–Berkeley

After the hardship of the Great Depression, and after the great conflagration of World War II, America was poised to reinvent and reinvigorate its reputation as a land of opportunity. During the war and in its immediate aftermath, governors and their appointees formed caucuses and commissions to contemplate "post-war planning." They joined federal task forces and created agendas to help imagine the post-war era and to influence federal policies toward less didactic and more supportive roles for state governments.

It is in this environment that the State of New York, including Democratic lawmakers and Republican Governor Thomas E. Dewey, ventured forth to create a state university system. Promoting educational attainment in all its forms, but in particular higher education, was a key component in virtually all respectable state post-war plans—along with expansive plans to build roads and dams, state parks, and other activities meant to curb unemployment and reduce the dole. In no small part bolstered by the attention generated by President Harry Truman's blue ribbon commission on higher education formed in 1946, and by the GI Bill passed in 1944, New York and other states plotted to expand access to higher education.

It was anticipated that the GI Bill, alone would create a surge in demand, but it was up to state governments and their network of public and private colleges and universities to actually cater to returning veterans armed with federal funds for fees and tuition. And the GI Bill was not just a moral obligation to those who fought in a prolonged and bloody war. Its intent was also to help the nation adjust to a postwar era of communities awash in returning veterans and an anticipated return to high unemployment rates.

Published in early 1947, the Truman Commission Report was hugely influential, with state governments forced in some form to reflect on their own systems of higher education. In seventeen states and the District of Columbia, the report noted, widespread segregation persisted in all phases of education,

184

almost always sanctioned by state and local laws. This needed to end. "Although segregation may not legally mean discrimination as to the quality of the facilities, it usually does so in fact."[1] The report took aim at the use of quotas, in use primarily by private institutions. But it also represented one of a number of major reports that urged states to become more proactive in expanding education opportunity—particularly after the stresses and budget cuts to education over the previous fifteen or so years of economic hardship and war.[2]

Expanding higher education access became the key post-war policy variable that states could actually do something about. Under the U.S. Constitution, state governments were, and are, the primary organizer and funders of their education systems, from pre-school to the university.

New York's system of higher education—if one could call it such—up to 1947, and as recounted in this book, was an unusual mesh of institutions that reflected New York's peculiar history. In essence, New York was very late in creating a public system of institutions that could cater to the very American notion of "mass higher education." The private institutions, many among the best in the nation and the world, dominated the political discourse, much like the rest of the northeast and along the eastern seaboard, and naturally wanted no significant public competition.

The political anomaly of New York City as virtually an entity into itself within the state, with its own system of public higher education, the City University of New York (CUNY), created a dynamic found in no other state. The microcosm of the city, with its surging immigrant population and liberal politics, ventured early into public mass higher education, in part in reaction to the biased admissions practices of the city's collection of private, elite institutions. When, in 1948, New York became one of the last states to create a state university system by placing thirty-two institutions under one umbrella, Dewey proudly noted and accurately predicted that SUNY was the state's "most important educational advance of our time." He also knew it was only a foundation, and that the building would come later.

As discussed in the chapter by Henry Steck, early efforts to chart a vision for SUNY acknowledged that it was a "limping" enterprise, forged by political forces bent on expanding access, yet, after the initial conception, always dealing with the opposition of the well-established privates and, until Governor Nelson Rockefeller's arrival, a lack of political support.

New York, similar to other northeastern states and dissimilar from much of the midwestern and western states, embarked on an effort to cobble together

---

[1]Higher Education for American Democracy," A Report of the President's Commission on Higher Education. Washington, D.C, December 1947, volume 1, 34.

[2]See John Aubrey Douglass. *The California Idea and American Higher Education*. Palo Alto, CA: Stanford University Press, 2000.

a public higher education system, as opposed to building from the ground up by creating new campuses—at least initially. That belated effort at creating a public higher education system meant that New York had no community colleges until the 1950s. In contrast, for example, California, first in this regard, had the beginnings of a network of what were then called "junior colleges" by 1910, and very soon afterward, a robust transfer function.

While there is much that is unique about New York's valiant effort to create a public higher education system, there is also much that reflects general trends in American higher education system building. Most states created public colleges and universities haphazardly, usually starting with one or two university campuses, often prompted by initial funding from the federal Land-Grant Act of 1862. New institutions resulted from local and regional politics and boosterism through constituent-driven bills passed in state legislatures. Until after World War II, there were few truly multi-campus systems; most were collections of institutions often with their own board or loosely managed by state departments of education.

As the American population grew, most state lawmakers came to realize that their ambition to expand access to higher education, both for social well-being and economic development, was growing in its costs to taxpayers. Local constituency-driven legislation to gain a state-funded campus was creating new institutions often without regard to statewide needs and resources. Hence, New York and many other states sought to create a network of institutions under a single board or with a statewide coordinating agency helping to guide state policymaking. In 1939, a total of thirty-three states had no form of state coordination of higher education; by 1969 there were only two which did not, Delaware and Vermont, both with relatively small populations. More significantly, the number of governing boards with regulatory powers over all or most public four-year colleges and universities within their states increased from sixteen in 1939 to thirty-three in 1969, including New York, North Carolina, Oklahoma, Ohio, Oregon, Tennessee, Texas, Utah, and West Virginia (see Figure 1).

States needed to make sense of their burgeoning networks of public colleges and universities. But in many instances, such as in New York, the result was not simply a single governing board charged with managing and protecting the university from the forces of unreasonable demands. It also often meant unbridled state regulatory claims that grew mightily as states expanded their public services and their bureaucracies.

These and other problems—some unique, some not—faced by SUNY academic leaders are duly recognized in the pages of this important publication—what is, in essence, the first scholarly and practitioner-oriented attempt to archive and reflect on its institutional memory. SUNY has struggled with its self-identity, with gaining a political constituency, with its internal organization, and with gaining an adequate financial model. Yet these challenges

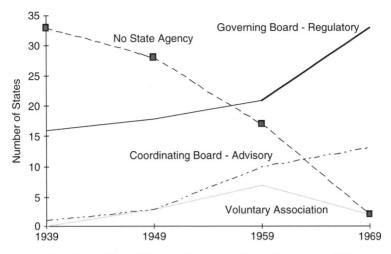

FIGURE 1 Creation of State Higher Education Coordination and Governance Boards: 1939–1969.

are ones faced by other states and now a growing effort at national systems of higher education throughout the world. In the course of building a broadly accessible and high quality higher education system, New York's efforts are relatively young, full of difficulties, but with much promise and many major successes.

A charting of the higher education enrollment growth in New York and a number of other large states validates the efforts to envision and expand SUNY. Figure 2 charts enrollment between 1918 and 1998. Between 1918 and 1948, the year of SUNY's establishment, enrollment growth was modest, and similar to other states with large and growing populations. Before World War II, the vast majority of New York's students were in private institutions, and much of the growth in enrollment occurred in New York City, largely facilitated by CUNY. After the war, very few new private institutions were established and those that were already in existence had little desire to expand their enrollment. But as Figure 2 also indicates, SUNY initially made no impact on enrollment growth after the brief upturn fostered by the GI Bill dissipated.

Capacity building began in earnest after the planning efforts of the 1960s and the strong commitment of state government—and Governor Rockefeller—to bolster higher education via the only mechanism available: public institutions. Like other states, SUNY has had its share of statewide planning and rethinking of the system to expand enrollment capacity and raise the quality of its teaching, research, and community service. These have

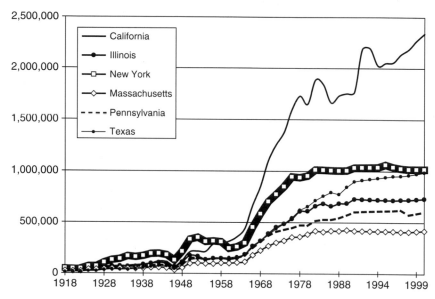

FIGURE 2 Total College and University Enrollment Growth in Six Major U.S. States.

included the 1948 Young Commission report that proposed establishing SUNY, the 1957 Blegen and 1960 Heald Reports, the 1985 Wharton Report sanctioned by Governor Cuomo, the 1991 Vision for a New Century Report chaired by Frederic Salerno and D. Bruce Johnstone, the conservatively driven 1995 Rethinking SUNY report sanctioned by Governor Pataki, and finally the recent 2008 New York Commission on Higher Education in the short-lived Spitzer era.

In the 1960s, three variables coalesced: a relatively robust economy, an ability and willingness of state government to invest in education, and political leadership in Albany that embraced higher education as a key to future prosperity. But since then, each of the subsequent statewide planning efforts noted has been largely cast in the midst of a cascading collapse in the state and national economy, and an interest by state lawmakers, often a governor, to deal with short-term needs by cutting higher education budgets.

With perhaps the exception of the Pataki's "Rethinking" report, which contains some common sense desires for greater non-government funding of the SUNY enterprise, but also displays a lack of understanding of how to build a network of public institutions that serve both public and private interests, these reports provide many solid ideas and confront many of the conundrums facing SUNY.

Both Henry Steck and John B. Clark chronicle and contemplate the similarities and differences among these important reports. Their articles explicate the common threads running through the reports: the need for logical policies to promote mission differentiation, the partially successful move toward greater deregulation and autonomy, and the need to create more stable funding commitments from state government.

As is perhaps self-evident in this collection of essays on the growth and development of SUNY, there has been no lack of good ideas or of esteemed academic leaders and visionaries, such as Thomas Hamilton, Samuel Gould, Ernest Boyer, Clifton Wharton, and D. Bruce Johnstone. But SUNY's future may be determined more by external forces, especially the economy and the emergence of lawmakers who view a healthy state higher education system as vital to future economic growth.

Without competitors and for reasons linked to America's unique democratic experiment, the US invented mass higher education. But the resolve and idealism of earlier political and academic leaders who led that revolution has largely dissolved. Economic downturns and Americans' long-held anti-government predilections have hindered the ability of state and national governments to "think big" on public higher education. As a result, American rates of educational attainment have stagnated over the last decade or so, while governments throughout the world have decided that higher levels of educational attainment are vital to creating competitive economic systems. Thus, according to the latest OECD report (2007), in about twelve short years, the US slipped from first to fourteenth in its national higher education participation rates.[3]

New York, in large part because of SUNY, has slightly out-performed much of the US, with degree completion rates just above the national average, and with the proportion of its citizens aged twenty-five to sixty-four with a bachelor degree or higher at 34 percent in 2006, compared to a national average of 29 percent.[4] But it is likely that both higher education access and graduation rates will decline in the aftermath of the recent economic collapse in New York and other states experiencing dramatic budgetary shortfalls.[5]

---

[3] I believe I was the first to articulate and analyze this trend in "The Waning of America's Higher Education Advantage: International Competitors Are No Longer Number Two and Have Big Plans in the Global Economy," CSHE Research and Occasion Papers Series, CSHE.9.06. (June 2006).

[4] National Center for Public Policy and Higher Education. *Measuring Up 2008: The National Report Card on Higher Education*, 2008.

[5] John Aubrey Douglass, "College vs. Unemployment: Expanding Access to Higher Education is the Smart Investment During Economic Downturns," CSHE Research and Occasional Paper Series, CSHE.21.2008; a version published in *InsideHE*, December 9, 2008.

With or without a strong or moderate economic recovery, the first governors and state political leaders that break out of the malaise to more fully nurture and fund an asset like SUNY will reap huge economic and, yes, social benefits.[6]

I. James Bryant Conant and the Limits of Educational Planning in California and New York

Wayne J. Urban, The University of Alabama

What little I knew about education in the State of New York before writing this essay stemmed from my experience as a high school, undergraduate, and graduate student at a variety of institutions, all in the state of Ohio in the 1950s and 1960s. Wherever I was in Ohio in that era, I was led to believe that our state was inferior in its educational accomplishments to New York State, not because of SUNY, but because of the rigorous Regents' examinations given to high school students in New York to gauge their achievement in subject matter of various kinds. These exams meant, we were told as students, that high school education was more demanding in New York than elsewhere, particularly than in Ohio, and that rigorous high school education paved the way for more rigor in higher education, particularly at the undergraduate level. What is remarkable, at least to me, about this understanding is that it dovetails rather nicely with the evaluation of secondary education in New York offered by James Bryant Conant in 1964, and which served as a basis for his recommendations for higher education in the Empire State. Before dealing with Conant directly, however, let me explain my interest in him and his work in education.

I am an educational historian whose work has been concentrated on a small number of subjects, most significantly, at least in my own mind, on teacher unions and associations.[7] In an expansion of that research, I undertook a study of the Educational Policies Commission (EPC), a body founded in 1936 under the formal sponsorship of the National Education Association (NEA) to facilitate professional educators' contributions to the consideration and development of educational policy. The EPC was composed of educational leaders drawn from college and university ranks, as well as from the

---

[6]See John Aubrey Douglass and Richard Edelstein. "Whither the Global Talent Pool?: How Can the US Remain Competitive." *Change Magazine*. July/August 2009.

[7]Wayne J. Urban. *Why Teachers Organized*. Detroit: Wayne State University Press, 1982; ibid *More Than the Facts: The Research Division of the National Education Association, 1922–1997*. Lanham: University Press of American, 1998; and ibid. *Gender, Race, and the National Education Association: Professionalism and Its Limitations*. New York: Routledge Falmer, 2000.

elementary and secondary schools which provided the bulk of NEA members. Its numerous reports weighed in on a myriad of topics in American education.[8] Its demise in 1968 was associated changes in the NEA and more broadly in the policy climate surrounding American education.[9]

My intensive study of the EPC almost immediately brought me into contact with James Bryant Conant. Then president of Harvard University, Conant was a member of the EPC for four multi-year terms from the late 1930s into the late 1950s. Conant's greatest accomplishment, however, according to his biographer, was not in education, but in his work with other scientists involved in the Manhattan Project in World War II. Further, as Harvard president, he presided over the modernization of that institution, especially in the sciences, as it moved into the powerful status it enjoyed with other major research universities as co-creators with the federal government during and after World War II of advances in science and especially in technology.[10]

Unlike his biographer, Conant himself devoted a substantial part of his autobiography to his encounter with education both at Harvard and away from Harvard, in higher education and in secondary education, and in international as well as domestic contexts. The enormity of Conant's involvement in the affairs of American schools and colleges captured my interest as I read the discussions of the EPC, marveling at the simultaneous naivety and acuity he exhibited, especially in regard to the nation's public high schools.[11]

In these discussions, Conant emerges as a truly remarkable influence. He often represented the leaders of American higher education on the EPC; there was almost always at least one university president on the EPC, and more often than not it was James Bryant Conant. The topics considered by the EPC, however, were usually devoted to the welfare of public elementary and secondary

---

[8]Wayne J. Urban, "Education for All American Youth (1944):An Educational Proposal in a Time of War and Its [Lack of] Relations to the War," International Committee of Historical Sciences, Children and War Roundtable, Sydney Australia. July 6, 2005; ibid. "Public Education and Religion: A Look at the Educational Policies Commission's Moral and Spiritual Values in the Public Schools." History of Education Society, Baltimore, MD: October 22, 2005; and ibid, "What's in a Name: Education and the Disadvantaged (1962)," *Paedagogica Historica*. January–February, 2009.

[9]My EPC work was financed through a small grant from the Spencer Foundation. For its results, see Wayne J. Urban, "The Educational Policies Commission, 1936–1968: Notes for an Autopsy," *The Sophist's Bane 3*. Fall 2005: 15–30 and ibid, "Why Study the Educational Policies Commission," *Georgia Educational Researcher*. 3,1, Spring 2005 available on-line at http://coefaculty.valdosta.edu. lschmert/gera/vol3no1-GERA-Urban-specFEAT05.pdf. Also see Urban, "Social Reconstructionism and Educational Policy: The Educational Policies Commission, 1936–1941," in K. Riley, Ed., *Social Reconstructionism: People, Politics, Perspectives*. Information Age Publishing, 2006.

[10]James G. Hershberg. *James B. Conant: Harvard to Hiroshima and the Making of the Nuclear Age*. New York: Alfred A Knopf, 1963.

[11]James Bryant Conant. *My Several Lives: Memoirs of a Social Inventor*. New York: Harper and Row, 1970.

education. Conant was willing to learn about public education from his fellow EPC members, assorted school superintendents and other administrators, a few noted professors of education, and occasional teachers who had become prominent in NEA and its state affiliates. And Conant seemingly respected his school colleagues on the EPC; at least they surely thought he respected them. William G. Carr, initially the chief NEA staff person on the EPC and later the NEA's chief staff officer, frequently mentioned the good that Dr. Conant did for American public schools through work on the EPC.[12]

Conant, educated almost completely in private schools and at private colleges and universities, learned a good bit about the problems and prospects of public schooling through his service on the EPC. More specifically, Conant was exposed to, and became a sometime supporter of, the ideology of progressive education, as least as it was manifested in the ideas of America's leading school people in the 1930s, 1940s, and 1950s. This ideology was basically student-centered rather than subject-centered, was devoted to the betterment of the nation's public schools over the welfare of the non-public sector, was concerned with extra-academic curricular emphases (such as vocational education) to meet the needs of the increasing percentage of adolescents in secondary schools that was likely not college bound, and was devoted to topics such as citizenship education, which were important for all students, college bound and non-college bound.[13]

The intellectual and curricular concerns of higher education and of elementary and secondary schools were largely unrelated, at least in the minds of most of those involved in both of those sectors. Conant was an exception to this rule, and the educators on the EPC knew it and hoped to capitalize on his exceptionality, especially when Conant retired from the Harvard presidency and embarked on an international career that culminated in his roles as education adviser, and as high commissioner and then ambassador to West Germany. Alas, at least for the school people, the positive results anticipated did not eventuate. As Conant was leaving the United States in 1963 for a final year in Germany as education advisor to the city of West Berlin, he noted in his autobiography a farewell dinner sponsored by several members of the EPC. He remarked that while the educators were praising him, he was about to enter an era of conflict with the same professional educators

---

[12]On Carr, see Conant, *My Several Lives*, 614.

[13]Ibid. Conant refers to his participation in the 1944 EPC report, Education for All American Youth, which outlined a scenario for high school development that stressed the vocational, as well as the academic, looked to meet the needs of all youth, and considered a variety of innovations geared to meeting them that went well beyond the traditional academic curriculum. Conant also learned an appreciation for public education from two of the deans of the Harvard education school who served while he was president; see Arthur G. Powell, *The Uncertain Profession: Harvard and the Search for Educational Authority*. Cambridge, MA: Harvard University Press, 1980.

from whom he had learned much, and who presumably he had taught much. Conant's account of the evening noted that the pleasure he felt was "marred by a thought which kept running through my mind. Some of the paragraphs of *The Education of American Teachers* (which was already at the printer) would not please the majority of those who were being so cordial that evening. I felt I ought almost to apologize in advance." He chose not to mention his forthcoming book and thereby "spoil the atmosphere by sounding a sour note." He uttered not a word about the education of teachers but, instead, reiterated some ideas from his earlier published book on "slum schools."[14] It is Conant's largely negative view of teacher education that is important to the rest of this account, as it laid bare the fissure that would develop between him and the educators.

In *The Education of American Teachers*, Conant joined the increasingly strident criticism of teacher education that was emanating in large part from the academic community, but also from other powerful voices in American politics and public affairs. Briefly, the criticism was that teacher education was too important to be left in the hands of a largely anti-intellectual professional education faculty that eschewed the rigor of the academic subjects in favor of the nostrums, the inanities, and insanities of progressive education. It is not the point of this paper to adjudicate that criticism, either as it came from Conant or from other noted critics, academic and non academic, such as Arthur Bestor, James Koerner, or Hyman Rickover.[15] Rather it is to reiterate what Conant said in his autobiography. Many of the ideas he expressed in *The Education of American Teachers* were critical of professional educators, in public schools and in teacher education faculties that trained public school teachers. Publication of that criticism meant that these groups could no longer look to Conant for support for their ideology and ideas. With the publication of his book on teacher education, Conant became firmly ensconced in the ranks of critics of teacher educators and the public schools that employed their graduates, a group that he coined, not favorably, as "the educational establishment" in this, and in subsequent, writing.[16]

This brings my account to a more direct consideration of the State University of New York. To get there, I need to consider directly a book Conant

---

[14]Conant, *My Several Lives*. 626.

[15]Arthur E. Bestor. *Educational Wastelands: The Retreat from Learning in our Public Schools*. Urbana, Ill.: University of Illinois Press, 1953; James D. Koerner. *The Miseducation of American Teachers*. Boston: Houghton-Mifflin, 1963; and Hyman G. Rickover. *Education and Freedom*. New York: Dutton, 1959.

[16]See James B. Conant. *The Education of American Teachers*. New York: McGraw-Hill, 1963; James D. Koerner. *The Miseducation of American Teachers*. Boston: Houghton Mifflin, 1963; and Arthur Bestor. *Educational Wastelands: The Retreat from Learning in our Public Schools*. New York: Alfred A Knopf, 1961.

published in 1964, one year after the publication of *The Education of American Teachers*. In this volume, *Shaping Educational Policy*, Conant turned his attention to the problem of the lack of a coherent national educational policy in the United States, a problem he considered to be the major educational deficiency in the United States. Conant's major difficulty in writing this volume was in getting around the visceral, and also constitutional, American belief that education was a state and local issue, not one over which the federal government should wield heavy influence. What Conant attempted to achieve in *Shaping* was to suggest a set of serious educational problems around which state educational agencies could coalesce to solve them and thus construct a *de facto* national policy through agreement on a set of rigorous, consistent state educational policies.[17]

Conant sought to accomplish this objective by beginning with an account of how education, in the war and post-war (or Cold War) years, had legitimately become a national concern. Education was increasingly becoming a key to the material prosperity and the political leadership of the United States in international affairs, he argued. No longer could American education afford the radical decentralization that existed when the nation's public schools were governed by 4,000 local school boards. Just as importantly, for Conant, the high school could no longer afford to postpone the curricular differentiation necessary for the proper pursuit of national interest and economic improvement, for the proper political socialization of all students and for the economic advancement of individual students and of the national economy.

Conant also argued that it was past the time when the United States could afford to have its educational policy determined solely by educational leaders such as school superintendents and teacher educators. Conant felt members of the "educational establishment" were out of touch with the needs of the nation, especially in areas such as the education of the gifted and talented. Conant asserted that "any amorphous unofficial body composed of public school administrators and professors of education is not now well suited to establishing policy for our public schools." Clearly, Conant included the EPC among the groups that had failed in its policy role. He remarked that he had been "a member of the [Educational] Policies Commission off and on for twenty-two years" but went on to discuss how the EPC had failed in its efforts to accommodate the educational needs of the gifted student, limiting the reach of its recommendations to only one percent of the school population when the academically-talented group in high schools was at least 20 to 25 percent of the total population. He added that because of these failings, educators "must

---

[17]The affinity between Conant's ideas and the recent dance around the adoption of voluntary national achievement standards by states in response to No Child Left Behind seems clear.

consider a drastic alteration in the ways in which educational policy for our public schools is shaped."[18]

Conant listed a number of problems in secondary education, the institutional arena in public education that he knew best, that merited attention in what he saw as the new educational policy environment. They included instructional reforms in science, mathematics, and foreign languages, an invigoration of the advanced placement program, improved instruction in English composition, adoption of new instructional media such as television and programmed teaching, and recruitment of more able students into teaching. All of these pedagogical concerns required the attention of subject matter professors, not just professional education faculty members. He was also concerned with deficiencies in the education of students of limited ability; with vocational education; with education, especially in reading, for disadvantaged students; with slum schools; and with segregated schools. He went on to bemoan the weaknesses of existing regional accreditation agencies, such as the North Central Association, another part of the educational establishment, which had failed to sponsor changes that meaningfully addressed any of the issues he had mentioned. For Conant, the antidote to these weaknesses was a drastic increase in the effectiveness of state educational authorities that integrated the views of professional educators, academics, and appropriate lay people and political leaders. More specifically, he added, "What is needed are strong state boards of education, a first-class chief state school officer, a well-organized state staff, and good support from the legislature."[19]

Conant added that existing departments of education in most states were but a shadow of what he desired. They were consciously hampered by local school administrators and professors of education in normal schools and teachers colleges who feared the incursions on their own prerogatives from empowered state education officials. A marked counterexample existed, however, in the State of New York. Conant considered developments in New York as an "example of what can be accomplished by a state to help the public schools keep pace with the educational revolution." He referred specifically to publications by the Board of Regents in New York (the state school board), which indicated the numerous changes necessary to modernize the public schools, as well as a plan for reorganization to accomplish the modernization.[20] Taken

---

[18]James Bryant Conant. *Shaping Educational Policy*. New York: McGraw-Hill, 1964; quotations pp.7, 8. Conant's concern for the gifted student was characteristic of scientists since the post–World War I era. See Jane Robbins, "The Problem of the Gifted Student: National Research Council Efforts to Identify and Cultivate Undergraduate Talent in a New Era of Mass Education, 1919–1929," Roger L. Geiger, ed. *Perspectives on the History of Higher Education*. 2005: 91–124.

[19]Ibid., 30–31.

[20]Ibid.

together with the academic rigor of the state examinations required for high school students for graduation, the phenomenon with which I began this essay, Conant believed that New York had the most advanced secondary education policies in the nation, policies that should be emulated by all states.

In a subsequent chapter on higher education, Conant bemoaned the overt politicization of state appropriations for public colleges and universities in many states, singling out Illinois, Indiana, and Pennsylvania as particularly egregious examples. Appropriations in these states were made to individual institutions on the basis of whatever political favors or pressures could be mounted by these institutions. He noted the advantages of the largest state universities with considerable numbers of alumni in the state legislatures over other state institutions, and the use of extra-educational benefits such as football tickets to aid in fund raising by those large state universities with the legislature.[21] Though the particulars of Conant's critique of higher education differed from those of his criticism of elementary and secondary education, the solution of an invigorated state educational policy constituted Conant's prescription for success in both realms.

In specifying what enlightened state education policy would look like, Conant devoted an entire chapter to "New York and California." He began this chapter with praise for the Empire State for its already mentioned rigorous governance of public elementary and secondary education and the Golden State for the efficiency of its Master Plan for higher education. California in the elementary-secondary arena, however, was distinctly inferior to New York for Conant because of the overt politicization of educational issues and the negative outcomes that this politicization led to in the educational decisions of the California state legislature. New York, on the other hand, was much more rational about its public schools. The Board of Regents and other state groups largely acted responsibly on educational concerns, weighing the issues judiciously and coming to measured conclusions that resulted in policies that were adopted for distinctly understandable, and educationally legitimate purposes, and policies that were not circumvented by the state legislature. California would gain considerably if it adopted a New York State model for elementary and secondary education, though there was little evidence that this was on the horizon.[22]

In contrast to its flawed secondary school system, California's Master Plan for higher education was a model for Conant and for other states to consider in adopting a rational policy for higher education. It broke sharply

---

[21]Ibid. Ch. 3.

[22]Ibid. Ch. 4. In discussing New York, Conant distinguished New York City from the rest of the state in its educational governance and administration as somewhat insulated from control by state authorities.

with the politicized situation in higher education in most other states. Conant exempted New York from his indictment of most states for haphazard higher education planning. New York was in the process of developing a plan for its higher education institutions that adopted the California planning model, though not the particulars of that state's Master Plan. While the New York plan for higher education was in its early stages of development, Conant noted that the basic assumptions that would undergird the plan had been agreed on. They included decentralized opportunities for a "sizable" number of full-time undergraduate students in popular fields of study in all the areas of the state with concentrated populations; even wider opportunities for access to the first two years of higher education; provision of sufficient available spaces both in popular fields and in fields necessary for economic development in private institutions, as well as in public institutions; and an expanded Regents' scholarship program to facilitate attendance by superior youth of poor financial means.

Conant asserted that only through a rigorous planning process, involving a state Office of Planning in Higher Education, and a State University Board of Trustees as influential in its sector as the Board of Regents had become in elementary and secondary education, could New York take advantage of its existing private colleges and universities while beginning to seriously develop its public institutions. Conant concluded his discussion of higher education in New York by noting that "New York is starting down the California road. One can only applaud and wish for rapid progress."[23]

One task of this article is to measure the progress that has been made along the road to a planned system of higher education for the State of New York. Conant clearly was almost mesmerized by the virtues of systematic planning and implementation of that planning at the state level. He also was seemingly unaware of the challenge that existing private higher education institutions presented, and would continue to present, to significant development and support for the State University of New York and its constituent parts. New York, for Conant, had only to implement the new SUNY structure to bring its state higher education effort into line with its efforts in elementary and secondary education. Conant's faith in planning for SUNY seems almost quaint, or at least naive, in retrospect. Yet it also represents a powerful current in education policy that continues into the present day.

Finally, I want to introduce a question about the California Master Plan which may help evaluate New York's statewide higher educational efforts. To do so, I turn to a comment on the career of Clark Kerr, author of the plan that so caught Conant's attention. Written by a professor at a California State University campus who had been an undergraduate at Berkeley during the

---

[23]Ibid. 106–08, quotation, 108.

student revolt in the 1960s, it illuminates problems that are given short shrift in considerations of the planning pioneered by Kerr and lauded by Conant. Writing from his faculty perspective, he felt that Kerr's Master Plan raised some distinct problems. First were the limitations such planning placed on institutional autonomy and on the professional autonomy of faculty in the institutions. That is, a statewide planning board, and plan, is removed from the perspective and priorities of individual campuses and, more importantly for this author, from faculty members on those campuses. Additionally, the California Master Plan, with its assignment of places at the University of California campuses for the top eighth of high school graduates, for the top third of graduates at California state university campuses, and for the rest of the high school graduates at state junior colleges, "failed to provide a college education for all who wanted it." The major reason for this failure was that the plan "contained no funding mechanism" to achieve the enrollment goals it had set. Next, the plan "secured a near monopoly over the granting of PhDs to Kerr's own system [The University of California campuses]." This situation meant that in 2004, when California had fifteen million more residents than in 1970, there were still only nine places in the state where students could get a PhD from a public institution. And the difficulties in gaining access to PhDs were exacerbated by the cost, geographical, and cultural factors at the bachelor's and master's degree levels.[24]

To sum up the critique, master planning and Master Plans such as those pioneered in California and emulated in New York State are excellent vehicles for achieving a large number of purposes and addressing numerous educational concerns. Their ability to serve the legitimate professional autonomy of faculty who serve in them, and the need for access to both graduate and undergraduate programs for students throughout the state, is not as clear.

Further, the opposition to the development of the State University of New York mounted by the private institutions of the Empire State at the time of its birth was a phenomenon that Conant, former president of Harvard University, perhaps the most prestigious private institution of higher education in the nation, gave short shrift. That opposition has not diminished much over the years since the initiation of SUNY, and it hampers productive development of public higher education in the Empire State to this day. It seems that one devoted to the virtues of planning and suspicious of unwarranted political involvement in educational development might have been more attuned to the major obstacle that private higher education presented to public higher education, in the past and in the present.

---

[24]Jeff Lustig, "The Mixed Legacy of Clark Kerr: A Personal View." *Academe* (July/August, 2004): 51–53.

II. Three Historical Moments: Contested Visions of the State University of New York[25]

Henry Steck, Department of Political Science, SUNY Cortland

Over its long and difficult history, the State University of New York (SUNY) has yet to discover or to resolve its full identity. Since its founding in 1948–49, its ongoing identity crisis has centered on two questions: What kind of university will it be, and what kind of university do the people of the state really want? One might look with envy on those states where "State U" is proudly seen inescapably as one foundation stone in the state's sense of itself. In such states, State U is the dreamed-of destination for college bound youngsters. It is the incubator for the professions and it is where future state politicians bond with each other. "Ol' Miss," the "Buckeyes," "Cornhuskers," "Crimson Tide," the "Wildcats": while the identity of "State U" may be wrapped up in school colors and the storied records of athletic teams, the universities themselves appear embedded deeply and emotionally in the state's culture. Closer to home, such a bond exists between the City University of New York (CUNY) and the city's sense of itself, its history, its personality. But even after sixty years, SUNY remains a university in search of a fixed and settled identity.

From its earliest days, SUNY's history has been characterized not simply by the recurrent challenges of growth and financing, but by a more profound disagreement over what public higher education means to New Yorkers. Within the framework of the 1985 statutory mission statement (Chapter 552, Laws of 1985), there has been no consistent, compelling, or coherent vision or policy-goals for the State University. Indeed, one might argue that it is not clear who would be responsible for fashioning such a vision: the Regents? The legislature? The trustees? The chancellor? Or the university community itself? As a member of the SUNY community, I am inclined to argue for the notion "Let SUNY be SUNY." The problem is, however, what is SUNY?

In this brief essay, I will take a look at three points on this contested terrain. I do so by revisiting three distinct visions for SUNY that were projected at three significant moments in SUNY's history. These are:

- The 1959 installation address of Thomas H. Hamilton, who served as what was then termed president of SUNY and is now called chancellor[26]

---

[25]Prepared for the SUNY 60th Anniversary Conference, SUNY and the Promise of Public Higher Education. April 3–5, 2009, Albany NY.

[26]Installation Address delivered by Thomas H. Hamilton, president, State University of New York, Albany, New York, October 29, 1959

- The 1985 Cuomo era report by the Independent Commission—*The Challenge and the Choice.*[27]
- The 1995 Pataki era trustees report, *Rethinking SUNY.*[28]

For historical importance alone, one might have turned to the founding document, the *Report of the Temporary Commission on the Need for a State University* (1948), the equally crucial Heald Report (1960), or even the all-important *Report* of the New York State Commission on Public Higher Education (2008).[29] But these three reflect the disparate visions that have guided SUNY, or sought to guide it.[30] Sixty years on, the visions described here still have much to contribute to the on-going discourse as SUNY seeks to chart its course.

A. Thomas Hamilton: Toward the Democracy of Excellence

We do not hear much about Thomas Hamilton these days. Assuming office as president of the entire system in SUNY's tenth year, he served at the hinge point between the SUNY of 1949–1959 and what it was to become during the expansive Rockefeller era. When Hamilton took up his new position in 1959, SUNY was a scattering of disparate institutions, still reflecting the hard-fought political battles surrounding its founding ten years earlier and still subject to the restrictions placed on it at its founding. It enrolled only 41,000 students. His installation address was delivered two months before Governor Rockefeller charged the Heald Committee to explore ways to meet the increasing demand for higher education in New York. In 1959, the national revolution in public higher education lay just around the corner.

In 1959, SUNY was the "limping and apologetic enterprise" that the Heald Report was to call it fourteen months later. Under the circumstances, Hamilton might have been expected to address current practical problems or

---

[27]Report of the Independent Commission on the Future of the State University, Albany NY, January 16, 1985.

[28]Rethinking SUNY. The Board of Trustees of the State University of New York, Albany NY, December 1, 1995.

[29]New York (State). Temporary Commission on the Need for a State University. Report of the Temporary Commission on the Need for a State University. Albany, NY: Williams Press, 1948. Legislative document (1948) no. 30. Committee on Higher Education (Henry T. Heald, Chairman), Meeting the Increasing Demand for Higher Education in New York Sate: A Report to the Governor and the Board of Regents. 1960. The report of the NYS Commission on Higher Education (2008) is discussed elsewhere in this volume.

[30]Over the years, individual SUNY campuses have also developed mission statements, "vision" statements, strategic plans, not least in connection with such exercises as "mission review," and the various system-campus memoranda of understanding. See an early example in SUNY Cortland, *A College Charts Its Course* (1966).

to look ahead in "bold" institutional terms to the challenge of the new decade, as a modern chancellor might be expected to do. The last thing his listeners must have expected was a philosophical discourse on the idea of a university in a democratic society.

When Thomas Hamilton rose to speak, SUNY's mission was expressed in its watchword, namely, "let each become all he is capable of being."[31] The emphasis was on the education of the individual learner in a democracy society and this is what Hamilton proceeded to deal with. He began by reminding his listeners that educational theory was a branch of "political theory." Education was thus linked to politics in the largest sense, that is, in the sense that Aristotle might have used in the *Politics* or John Dewey in his writings on education and democracy. His purpose, then, was to define the place of an institution of learning, with its emphasis on talent and excellence, within an egalitarian and mass society. This was the central challenge facing higher education.

In the context of 1959, this was not an abstract philosophical question or simply the clichéd rhetoric conventionally displayed on such occasions. This was the era when liberal and conservative intellectuals alike turned their guns on mass society and on what Newton Minow, former chairman of the Federal Communications Commission, called the "vast wasteland" of the mass TV audience. Hamilton was, then, dealing with a bedrock question of public policy: what is the mission of the state university where private universities and colleagues were so dominant and had resisted the establishment of SUNY ten years before? Without putting it into so many words, he apparently intended to expound the meaning to those words on the SUNY seal: "Let Each Becomes All He Is Capable of Being."

Hamilton called on those who, like himself, had responsibility for directing universities to "thoroughly understand and relate their own activities to the premises, to the assumptions, to the conception of humankind by which that democratic society lives." The mission of the university is, he argued, to realize "true democratic ideals." For Hamilton, the central paradox of democracy, at least in a university setting, is that it must at once be concerned with *both* the many *and* the few, or even with the solitary individual. The university must be at once dedicated *both* to advancing those of talent—the intellectual, scientific, and artistic elite—*and* those who fall short of the highest excellence. The latter, too, must "become all they are capable of being." With this, Hamilton takes dead aim on those who were, in his words, "unreconstructed neoaristocrats," namely, the Edmund Burkes and the Alexander Hamiltons of the world. One senses that he regarded these as the real enemies; perhaps he meant

---

[31]These words are found in an essay by Thomas Carlyle (1795–1881) on Jean Paul Friedrich Richter: "Let each become all that he was created capable of being; expand, if possible to his full growth resisting all impediments, casting off all foreign, especially all noxious adhesions, and show himself at length in his own shape and stature be what they may."

them to serve as stand-ins for those who, a decade earlier, had bitterly fought the creation of the state university, despite their own shabby record of quotas and outright discrimination[32] and those elitists who, 100 years after the Morrill Act, still disparaged public institutions.

Hamilton was not less easy on those levelers and egalitarians he described as "uniformitarians." Wrongly in his view, that was the position that "all students must have identical opportunities and identical treatment without regard for differences in talent and the will to achieve." They would reject equality of opportunity with its potential for unequal outcomes in favor, so to speak, of the Lake Woebegon construct, namely, that all children are above average. Uniformitarians would create, in Hamilton's view, a social order "perpetually colored the dull gray of mediocrity." Speaking against the background of right-wing populist and McCarthyite-style attacks on Adlai Stevenson as an egghead, Hamilton told his listeners "that it is not un-American to have ideas, it is not dangerous to think, it is not undemocratic to be intelligent beyond one's fellows."

For us, his critique of these positions has a distinctly contemporary resonance. On the one hand, he rejected the conservative argument that education is a private individual good whose cost should be borne not by society as a whole, but by individuals who will benefit from their investment. Should such a concept prevail, Hamilton warned, there would be "no hope for the success of the unfinished social and political experiment which this Republic of ours represents." On the other, he rejected the pure egalitarian argument that does not nourish or recognize talent, but would "extend sameness of opportunity to all, regardless of individual differences in attainment, merit or distinction or diligence." For Hamilton, both elitists and egalitarians are "opponents of true democratic values," although the former trouble him far more.

His arguments were not philosophical abstractions. University workers confront seemingly opposed values in almost everything they face: balancing quality and quantity; promoting costly programs that serve the few, while maintaining quality and access for the many; distributing diminished scholarship funds among those with more need than talent and those with more talent than need; defining, above all, the mission of a great public university. His vision was guided by a conviction that a distinction of mind is natural and normal and that the university can nurture and advance intellectual and cultural talent without impinging on social and political equality. Hamilton closed by articulating the vision of a "democracy of excellence."

---

[32] David S. Berkowitz, *Inequality of Opportunity in Higher Education; a Study of Minority Group and Related Barriers to College Admission. A report to the Temporary Commission on the Need for a State University.* Albany, NY: Williams Press, 1948. Legislative document (1948).

The goal of life in a democracy is the realization of one's capacities and aspirations; the obligation of a democracy is to see that no deserving person fails of this realization for lack of opportunity.

Hamilton struggled with big questions and he talked about things. What is particularly noteworthy in retrospect is what he did not talk about. He did not define the university as an "engine" of economic development or a partner with corporate America. He did not talk about the university's research mission, so often a euphemism for bringing in federal dollars. He did not talk about the role of scholarship or service, a sign of the extent to which in its early days, SUNY was defined primarily for its teaching mission.

We cannot but wonder whether Hamilton's talk caught the attention of Henry Heald. By October 1959, discussions must have been underway in the Executive Mansion about appointing a committee to look at the future of higher education in New York. Was Heald familiar with Hamilton's installation address? Did he attend it in the days preceding the appointment of his committee? What is not speculation is that language of the Heald Report echoed Hamilton's words:

> Over the years the people of the State of New York have been rich enough, but they have not given enough thought, perhaps, to educating their young people as they should be educated. Much more will have to be done in the future than has been done in the past. There should be goals—high goals ... What ... will be required is a new attitude toward public higher education, a new state of mind, a new desire to put some real meaning into the motto inscribed on the seal of the State University of New York which says, "Let each become all he is capable of being." If we resolve to be guided by those words, public higher education in New York will cease to be a limping and apologetic enterprise and will achieve the spirit and style which characterize the nation's great public institutions.

We can step back to take a wistful look back on Hamilton's address. He articulated a daring and challenging vision for what was then a weak second-rate university. It was a vision that policy-makers and university administrators today would do well to take to heart. Is not the democratic faith in education and the role of education for developing republican virtue a vision still worthy of our state university?

B. *The Challenge and the Choice*: Toward A Modern University System

By the 1980s, SUNY faced a political and cultural environment a world away from the Eisenhower era of the late 1950s. But as SUNY approached its thirtieth anniversary, the state and the university were confronted with the severe fiscal consequences of Rockefeller spending and of a recessionary economy.[33] The 1976 New York City fiscal crisis introduced an epoch of fiscal austerity, captured by Governor Hugh Carey's blunt message that "the days of wine and roses" were over. With this framework, we turn next to SUNY's long-range strategic planning effort, *The Challenge and the Choice* that was initiated by then-Chancellor Clifton R. Wharton Jr.

The downward curve of budgeting that began in 1974 could not have come at a more inopportune time for SUNY. As universities go, it was still young and building the quality of its teaching, service and research. Although it achieved its present configuration by the late 1970s, it was still in an expansion mode; in the 1970s, to take one example, hospital staff grew by 1,900 new positions, 1,400 at Stony Brook alone.[34] A new 500-bed hospital was added to the system as the university's commitment to the health sciences grew by leaps and bounds. While SUNY was relatively new on the national academic scene, it set its sights on becoming a national, if not world class, university. From the 1960s through the late 1970s, its motto could well have been "The Great Leap Forward." It was also flexing its political muscle as successive bad budgets forced students, faculty, staff, and administrators to mobilize politically. By the 1980s, United University Professions (UUP), the faculty-staff union, was well on its way to becoming a presence and a player in Albany political circles along with its affiliate, New York State United Teachers. Legislators were waking up to the fact that virtually every county in the state was home to one or more SUNY units and that in increasing numbers, the children of their constituents were attending SUNY schools.

As bad as the budgets of 1975–78 were, nothing prepared the university for the firestorm that was about to engulf it. In late 1979, the Division of the Budget required SUNY to slash 500 additional positions. The news was devastating. Agreeing to some vacancy freezes, Chancellor Clifton Wharton posed the question that framed the policy issue then and since:

> The five-year review and your proposed reduction raises a fundamental question of public policy: how good and how large a State University does the State of New York really want?[35]

---

[33]Between 1960 and 1974, the state budget went from $2.04 billion to $8.8 billion, while Rockefeller's ambitious capital programs, including the construction of much of SUNY's physical plant, produced the largest debt in the nation. Lynne A. Weikart. *Follow the Money: Who Controls New York City Mayors?* SUNY Press, Albany, 2009, 32–33.

[34]Letter, Chancellor Clifton Wharton to Michael Finnerty, Deputy Director of Division of the Budget. November 29, 1979.

[35]Ibid.

When the fundamental question posed by Wharton went unanswered, SUNY managers made the decision to take SUNY's future into their own hands and to trust that state policy-makers would buy into the necessary solutions. Beginning in 1980, SUNY's top officials undertook the first of several major internal efforts at long-range or strategic planning, in an attempt to bring order into conduct of its affairs. Whatever the strengths or weaknesses of these initial efforts, they proved inadequate. Within two years, moreover, the state was engulfed in a budget deficit more severe than any since 1975, indeed more severe than any in its history.[36] In early 1983, in his first budget as governor, Mario Cuomo asked for 3,000 personnel cuts, plus another 900–1,000 line reductions through voluntary furloughs and retirements. This was a cut so enormous that it equaled all positions cut in the previous eight years. To put it another way, it was the equivalent of the combined workforce of five average four-year colleges, or of the university centers at Albany and Binghamton, or of the center at Buffalo. Wharton again posed the question: "whether it is to be State policy that New York cannot permanently afford to continue supporting a State University of the current size and configuration."[37]

While this particular threat was averted, it was clear that SUNY could no longer guide itself by the ebullient gubernatorial vision of growth that had guided it in the halcyon days of Nelson Rockefeller. Nor could it simply try to deal with the successive budgets cuts that hit it year after year. SUNY's leadership could develop excellent five-year plans for a major research initiative for example, but there was no guarantee that these could be implemented. Clearly, SUNY needed to do something if it was to be a national or world class university. As permanent downsizing was not politically feasible, the remaining options were to attempt to break free of the tangle of bureaucratic red tape and legislative politics and reconfigure its mission and structural arrangements. Under these dire circumstances, Chancellor Wharton then did what shrewd executives do when they are in a fix. He turned to a commission of distinguished outsiders to provide a comprehensive solution that would appear to be more legitimate than another set of in-house plans. He charged this blue-ribbon commission—the Independent Commission on the Future of the State University of New York—with forming a plan for SUNY in an era of "constrained resources" and an "increasingly constrained regulatory environment."

---

[36]This section of the paper draws on my chapter, "Hard Times Come to Campus" in Peter W. Colby and John K. White, eds. *New York State Today: Politics, Government, Public Policy, 2nd. Ed.* Albany: State University of New York Press, 1989, 313–330. See also my chapters in subsequent editions.

[37]Memorandum. From Clifton R. Wharton Jr., Chancellor to State University Board of Trustees. February 15, 1983.

It is in this context, that the resulting *The Challenge and the Choice,* a dense seventy-eight page document, must be read.[38]

There was and is much to admire about the report. For a start, it was so elegantly done that it disarmed those who might have been critical of its recommendations. At a time when SUNY needed a morale boost, the report was a ringing endorsement of both SUNY and public higher education. It said all the things that the SUNY community had been saying for years: that the university was different from and should be administered differently from other state agencies—it was not the Department of Motor Vehicles; that the university was built from the bottom up in terms of teaching, learning, research, and service; that SUNY suffered badly due to a lack of support; that the university was suffocating in a tangle of red-tape. And to underscore its criticisms, the commission attached the requisite horror stories. The bottom line was delivered in blunt terms: "*SUNY is not yet good enough.*"

The report emphasized that SUNY suffered from the circumstances of its birth. True, it was established to "offer equal educational opportunity to qualified New Yorkers who would otherwise be denied access to higher education" and to meet the demand for enrollment arising out of social pressures and the demands of returning veterans following World War II. But it was also established on the basis of political compromises that constrained its mission. Initially, it was constructed on a scatter of state teachers colleges, and its ability to expand was restricted. It was meant to "supplement but not supplant" the state's private institutions. Above all, it was not to challenge the elite schools and the private schools that had fought the creation of a state university. Even the expansion in the Rockefeller period did not overcome all the circumstances of its birth.

As the Independent Commission pointedly noted, SUNY was handicapped by the "lowered aspirations," the "unambitious expectations," the "diminished expectations," that shaped its founding. As the commission pointedly and correctly noted, "no other state university system suffers from such crippling ambiguity concerning its place and mission." The commission thus set for itself the task of fulfilling SUNY's "unfulfilled promise." It made major recommendations across several areas. One, which will not be discussed here, was that the university be set free from the red tape and restrictions of state budgeting and control and be converted into an independent public benefit corporation. It should receive a single lump sum budget to allocate as it wished. One result of this part of the commission's work was the flexibility legislation that was enacted in 1985 and the enactment of a statutory mission statement.[39]

---

[38]Report of the Independent Commission on the Future of the State University. The State University of New York: The Challenge and the Choice, January 1985.

[39]Chapter 552, Laws of 1985.

More relevant to our purpose is the commission's core recommendation. Contending that SUNY was lagging behind in graduate research and professional education, the commission argued that SUNY needed a new mission statement that would focus SUNY's mission in the areas of research and graduate education. What is striking is a key rationale employed by the commission. Moving SUNY toward becoming a world class research institution would be, in its view, the way in which SUNY could best contribute to economic development. In sharp contrast to Thomas Hamilton's vision for the university, the commission contended that the advancement of knowledge and graduate training was linked to the very utilitarian purpose of furthering the economic well-being of a weakened New York economy.[40] "The economy of New York," the commission stated, "requires a state university that can serve, in full partnership with the independent sector and with the City University of New York, as a magnet for industry and a force for community and economic development." Advancing education is a "key cause of productivity increases." There were other recommendations, for example, the need to recruit and retain minority students, but the utilitarian focus on the importance to the economic health of New York State was central.

Beyond this, the report was strikingly notable for what it did not, at least on first reading, recommend—namely, the immediate closing of any campuses. The commission did not propose a single flagship campus, but it anointed Stony Brook and the University of Buffalo as leading research centers, co-flagships, as it were. Community colleges were given a brief, though resounding, vote of confidence without any mention of separating them. As these ideas had been widely mooted, the tone and substance of the report set those reservations to rest. Still, the commission argued for "drastic" change. It projected a vision of what might be seen as a "new model" SUNY. Its primary structure recommendation was to convert SUNY into a private benefit corporation, a proposal which, if implemented, would have weakened the link between SUNY and the legislature. Despite its insistence that it "rejected any effort to dismantle SUNY," the commission left no doubt that "reconsideration of" campus closings "will be appropriate in the future." SUNY, it made clear, had suffered from the "excessive dispersal of small" campuses. Such decisions would require

---

[40]It is worth noting in passing that the policy for arts in New York State (and nationally) commonly used much the same argument, namely, that promoting the arts brought economic benefits to the State and to communities throughout the state. Thus, both SUNY and the New York State Council on the Arts grounded policy appeals for two public goods (art, education)—goods whose price and value could not be quantified—on quantifiable utilitarian considerations. The same shift is seen in discussions of education as contributing to the pool of "human capital," rather than to a public of educated citizens. The two rationales are not opposed. The point is where the emphasis is put.

decision-making that would be vested in a Board of Trustees, free from the constraints of the political environment except for "major actions."[41]

What would a SUNY reconfigured along these lines look like? It might resemble the state university model found in the West and Midwest; it would be managed along corporate lines with stronger macro-level authority given to the trustees and to SUNY Central (or SUNY "System Administration" as it came to be called); it would enjoy autonomy from the messy arena of politics—not to create an academic ivory tower, but to free managers from the distractions of politicians, faculty, students, and division of the budget bureaucrats. Beyond this:

1. Its primary emphasis would be research and graduate/professional, rather than on liberal learning or undergraduate education. It would play a more direct role to advance the state's economic development.[42] Without moving toward the California model, each sector of the system—university centers/health science centers, colleges of arts and sciences, and two-year colleges—would be responsible for distinct missions and would, one might predict, come to serve different student clientele for different life chances.

2. It would be reorganized along technical rational lines and would include substantial (a) downsizing, perhaps in time including campus closings; (b) program refocusing; (c) selectivity among competing institutions; (d) enhanced managerial flexibility, especially with respect to "scarce public resources"; and, (e) above all, freedom from the red-tape and micro-managing of Albany bureaucrats.

3. The commission emphasized that "maximum possible deference" would be paid to campuses, faculty, and students, but it made clear that significant and decisive authority would be lodged in the trustees and administrators under the structure of a public benefit corporation.

4. Although the commission did not say this, it appears that by insulating internal SUNY constituencies from the normal constraints of politics, the public benefit corporation structure would render them less able to appeal to external legislative and lobbying allies. One must not push this point too far. In states where state universities enjoy significant autonomy, politics, and budget politics in particular, is still a feature of higher education policy.

5. SUNY might well become a more stratified, multi-tiered institution along the following lines: (a) institutions would be stratified with two quasi-flagship university centers at the top, followed by the other

---

[41]The Challenge and the Choice, 53–54.

[42]Ibid. 23.

university centers, then the four-year colleges, and then the specialized and perhaps the community colleges; (b) a stratified workforce rather than a workforce of faculty peers; and (c) stratification of the student body by class, should differential tuition be introduced.[43]

But this is speculation that takes a critical view of the *Report*. My purpose here is not to trace the subsequent history of its recommendations. Suffice it to say, *The Challenge and the Choice* did have an impact, although less than the commission wished for. The flexibility legislation enacted in 1985 gave the university far more responsibility for budget execution than it had previously enjoyed. The commission's recommendation that the university place greater emphasis on graduate research and education was realized. As noted above, a statutory mission statement reflecting the commission's outlook was enacted in 1985. *The Challenge and the Choice* was a bold and—on its own terms—visionary document. It firmly asserted the unique characteristics of a university as a corporate institution and rejected in the strongest possible terms the treatment of SUNY as just another state agency.

Freeing SUNY from the Kafka-esque world of state bureaucracy was one thing, but recreating SUNY as an independent public benefit corporation may just have been too visionary for a legislature and an executive that were not eager to give up authority over an important piece of the budget or over one of the state's key policy arenas. The former, in particular, believed that a public university should remain democratically accountable to the people through the legislature, never mind that with a campus in virtually every legislative district, SUNY was too close to the hearts and interests of legislators for them to give up their role as, so to speak, the "ultimate Trustees" of the people's university. Particulars aside, *The Challenge and the Choice* projected a vision of a very modern SUNY. It rejected the notion that SUNY was a "supplemental" or "second best" system. It looked to the transformation of SUNY from an institution created with "unambitious" and "diminished" expectations.[44] But it was a document written in the prose of humane managers, rather than the poetry of liberal learning and democratic aspirations, that had given passion to Hamilton's inaugural address.

There was, of course, a good reason for this. The times, they had been "a changing." The SUNY of the 1980s was not the SUNY of the 1950s or even the 1960s. But for those who look to a university that could fuse Newman's *The Idea of a University*, dedicated to learning for its own sake, to Morrill's vision of a university serving broad democratic values, Thomas Hamilton's words of 1959 still point to a road not taken. Perhaps they are, after all, a road sign to a destination that cannot be reached in the contemporary era.

---

[43]Steven H. London, "The Independent Commission on SUNY: The 'Excellence' of Centralization and Standardization." New York State Political Science Association Annual Meeting. 1986.

[44]The Challenge and the Choice, 16–17.

C.   Rethinking SUNY: Market Efficiencies in Service of a Neo-Liberal Vision

The final vision is that found in *Rethinking SUNY* (1995), a short plan prepared by the Board of Trustees in response to a legislative request. The point has been made that the 1980s were marked by fiscal austerity and by a shift in the prevailing paradigm of public policy. These conditions did not ease up. The fiscal and political storms that struck SUNY in the early 1990s were far more severe than even those of the 1980s.

In response, Chancellor Bruce Johnstone prepared a set of grim options that raised the prospect of radical restructuring. His options included permanent downsizing, campus closings, and increased tuition. Ultimately, SUNY avoided Johnstone's doomsday options, but only because the SUNY community knew from experience how to do with less while, Micawber-like, waiting for something to turn up.

In 1995, the incoming Pataki Administration proposed budget cuts that would have been among the deepest, if not the severest, in SUNY's history. At the same time, the new administration appointed new members to the Board of Trustees who brought to the Board a conservative ideology that charted quite a different path for the university. To simplify, we can say that the "Pataki trustees" took a path that moved along two dimensions: (a) a conservative cultural and educational ideology that was deeply critical of SUNY as an academic institution and (b) a "neo-liberal" market orientation and a commitment to a much reduced public sector. The former was undoubtedly an element in the broader "culture wars" of the time, while the latter was a reflection of the conservative project to reduce the size and importance of the public sector.[45]

Confronted with intense opposition to the first Pataki budget and frustrated at SUNY's apparent inability to bring its budget problems to resolution, the legislature directed the trustees to prepare a "multi-year comprehensive, system wide plan to increase cost efficiency." The resulting document, *Rethinking SUNY,* was presented as a plan for utilizing state resources efficiently, raising academic standards, and ensuring accountability. In so doing, it projected quite a different vision for SUNY.

In some ways, *Rethinking SUNY* is a curious document. On one level, it was not as novel as it appeared. A number of its ideas were already common currency in many national higher education circles.[46] The notion was that students should be regarded as consumers, colleges should respond to the needs of the marketplace, education was about advancing individual interests, and that

---

[45]For an example of the former, see the article by Trustee Candace De Russey, "Educational Policy Avert Educational Dissolution in New York," *Academic Questions,* Summer 1999.

[46]See, "The New U: A tough market is reshaping colleges," *Business Week,* December 22, 1997.

quality control and assessment ways of measuring "productivity" were in step with the new ways of viewing higher education.[47]

At the same time, however, the very title—*Rethinking SUNY*—announced an intention to think radically about SUNY and about reframing the SUNY vision. Consistent with this, *Rethinking SUNY* projected a new institutional architecture and basic mission for SUNY. Campus autonomy and "self-sufficiency" would replace system-wide leadership and policy direction. Undergraduate education would become SUNY's highest priority while graduate, professional, and research programs were seen as "essential"—an ambiguous formulation—for the economic vitality of the state. This presumably suggested changing the long-time balance of undergraduate, graduate, and professional education. The hospitals would be spun off from the health science centers and converted into public benefit corporations or 501(c)(3) organizations, thus severing their historic and organic connection to SUNY and to its founding in the 1940s. Differential tuition would replace the long-standing policy of uniform tuition and introduce a more pronounced hierarchy- or prestige-based dynamic into the university. With the emphasis on "productivity," readers were left with the impression that "quality" and "access" were to be balanced against cost. Some ideas in *Rethinking SUNY* were reasonable approaches to tidy management; others offered interesting possibilities for developing intellectual communities between units, something SUNY tended to lack.

Fundamentally, then, *Rethinking SUNY* was more than an administrative handbook. It advanced the view that a market approach to management would be more efficient than SUNY's more centralized architecture. A second premise was that the private sector was superior to the public and that a downsized SUNY would be a better SUNY. Clearly, SUNY could not be privatized, but SUNY campuses could be obliged to compete—more "entrepreneurially" was the way it was put—in a market environment. In time, campus presidents felt a steady pressure to manage their campuses as if they were in the private sector. To some extent, of course, this provided a welcome degree of freedom (e.g., in terms of fund-raising). As for campuses that could not compete successfully, well, perhaps, in time, they would need to be closed and, if so, it would be "the market" and not the political process that would administer the *coup d'grace*. While the trustees did not neglect quality, it was reasonable to ask whether managerial concerns were taking precedence over academic considerations or over SUNY's broad social mission.

---

[47]For an example of some of the discussion at the time, see "Towers of babble: Whatever happened to the university?" *Economist*, December 25, 1993–January 7, 1994, p.72–74. For an important early work, see George Keller. *Academic Strategy: The Management Revolution in American Higher Education*. Baltimore: Johns Hopkins University Press, in cooperation with the American Association for Higher Education, 1983).

Without reviewing all the elements in *Rethinking SUNY,* one point seems worth emphasizing. What traditionally distinguished SUNY from some of its sister state "systems" was the principle that the SUNY whole was greater than the sum of its campus parts. Views differ, of course, on whether this is a good thing. But the rejection of a flagship campus model, the absence of formal tiers *a la* California, the historic commitment to uniform tuition–these elements and more created a model that looks to a strong SUNY "brand." Whether this image and identity is one that the people of the state would come see as distinctively their own and as distinctively "New York" has yet to be decided.

Such a view was contrary to the perspective of *Rethinking SUNY.* Its vision projected a model of structural devolution, with a concomitant limiting of the role of a downsized SUNY System Administration. To some extent, this was a trend that was evident before the Trustees set their minds to rethinking SUNY. But by its emphasis on campus autonomy, self-sufficiency, and competition between campuses, *Rethinking SUNY* accelerated the spread of a market culture. The 2008 Commission on Higher Education described this result as a "'culture of devolution' that continues to this day."[48] Campuses aggressively began to promote their own individual "brand," (e.g., Binghamton University instead of SUNY Binghamton, Geneseo as an "honors college") rather than an organic link to SUNY as the state's university. The upshot of *Rethinking SUNY* was to encourage *centrifugal* forces with all their unanticipated and possibly negative consequences, rather than emphasizing those *centripetal* elements that would strengthen the university as a *university.* Moreover, as the university centers grew in size and strength and as Stony Brook and the University at Buffalo were recognized nationally as top-ranked research centers, it doubtless became difficult for SUNY Central to serve as an effective countervailing force providing vision and leadership on behalf of an increasingly large and complex system.

My point is not to examine the policies in detail or their fate, but it is worth noting that by 1998, some of its ideas (e.g., differential tuition or even cutting back on access) were abandoned or defeated. The trustees' subsequent decision to mandate a system-wide core curriculum raised the issue of the contradiction between administrative and fiscal decentralization and curricular centralization. But these are questions for another time.

To be fair, the charge to the trustees in 1995 was a circumscribed one. The legislature wanted an accountant's spread-sheet: "a multi-year, comprehensive, systemwide plan to increase cost efficiency." But there was a vision embedded in *Rethinking SUNY,* and it was not one that many in the SUNY community found uplifting. While *Rethinking SUNY* committed itself to meeting the challenges of the 21st century, it also sought to meet "the public demand for

---

[48]New York State Commission on Higher Education, Final Report of Findings and Recommendations. Albany: June 2008, p.49.

the most effective use of tax dollars." To see the shift in emphasis and direction, one need look no farther than the values embedded in the text of *Rethinking SUNY*: the word "market" appears four times; the word "efficiency" seven times, and the word "democracy," not at all.[49]

D. Conclusion

The chapters in this volume and the conference that gave birth to them provide an opportunity to look back at roads taken and not taken. Sixty years on, it is arguable that the state still does not fully know what it wants of its great state university. To reflect anew on the promise and potential of the State University of New York, the SUNY community and the state's policy makers could do no better than to return to the promise of public higher education exemplified by the Morrill Act in 1862. Surely, the purposes of the modern "multiversity," as Clark Kerr put it, can be—should be—accommodated within this uniquely American vision. The historian of "the state universities and democracy" describes this vision as follows:

> American democracy, fired by its vision, flung itself into one of the grandest works it had ever undertaken: the creation of scores of universities and colleges, on a broad model new to mankind.[50]

This is the promise and purpose of a great, coherent and unified state university. SUNY—with its companion City University of New York—owes no less to the people of New York. Surely, that should be its identity and its legacy.

III. An Assessment of the Recommendations of the NYS Commission on Higher Education

John B. Clark, Visiting Professor, Stony Brook University, and former Interim Chancellor, the State University of New York

This paper evaluates the major recommendations of the "Final Report of Findings and Recommendations of the New York State Commission on Higher Education" (hereafter referred to as simply the "Report").[51]

---

[49]I am indebted to Thomas J. Kriger for bringing this to my notice.

[50]Allan Nevins. *The State Universities and Democracy*. Urbana, Ill.: University of Illinois Press, 1962.

[51]To observe due disclosure, the author of this report was a member of the Commission. Also, "A Preliminary Report of Findings and Recommendations" was released by the Commission in December 17, 2007, and sent to Governor Spitzer so it could be used in time for his executive budget request to the State Legislature. With small exception, it differed little from the final report and the major recommendations remain unchanged.

The paper will provide brief background on the commission, the composition of its membership, a historical review of previous commissions and reports on the State University of New York, and a summary overview of the Report itself. This will be followed by a presentation of the recommendations of the commission and finally, some critical points and concluding thoughts for the reader's consideration.

It is important to note the emphasis will be on the State University of New York (SUNY), but the sister public system of higher education in the state, the City University of New York (CUNY), and New York's private colleges and universities also played important parts in the commission and are also included in the discussion.

A.   The Background of the Commission

The commission was established by Governor Spitzer's Executive Order No.14 on May 29, 2007. The governor charged the commission to complete a preliminary report by December 1, 2007, to be used in the state budgeting process and a final report to be issued on or before June 1, 2008.

The commission was composed of thirty members and chaired by Hunter Rawlings, president emeritus of Cornell University. The executive director was John Reid, who was also assistant secretary for education in the Spitzer and then Paterson administrations.[52] Of the thirty members, thirteen were from public universities—seven from SUNY, six from CUNY, and six were from private institutions of higher education. The remaining members were representatives from the unions, state government, private sector, elected officials from the state senate and assembly, and a member of the State Board of Regents. (See the Appendix for a complete listing).

The commission then formed committees that were to formulate preliminary recommendations, which would be presented before the full commission for its consideration in making the Report's final recommendations. They were composed of commission members, assisted by staff, and in frequent communication with the executive director. There were five committees:

1.   Governance
2.   Tuition/Financial Aid
3.   Workforce/Economic Development
4.   Access/K-12 Partnerships
5.   Finance/Capital

---

[52]A number of key officials of the Spitzer administration, including Dr. Manuel Rivera, deputy secretary for education, and Mr. Lloyd Constantine, senior advisor to the governor, who were not members of the commission, played influential roles in its deliberations and recommendations.

These titles foreshadow the categories of the major recommendations that would eventually emerge in the Report.

B.   Previous Commission Reports

The work of the commission and its resultant recommendations must be seen in the light of the previous commissions on higher education in New York State. From these, one can see that some of the recommendations in this Report are new; but some, unfortunately, have been noted in the reports of previous commissions, but never implemented. The following summarizes only those commissions and reports of specific interest for this paper.[53]

1.   Report of the Temporary Commission on the Need for a State University ("Young Commission," 1948)—This was the landmark commission, established by Governor Thomas Dewey and chaired by Regent Owen Young, former chairman of the General Electric Company, which recommended the establishment of a state university. The commission report formed the basis for the bills enacted by the state legislature and signed into law by Governor Dewey in 1949 that created SUNY.

2.   A Report on Research Potentials and Problems in the State University of New York ("The Blegen Report,"1957)—Dr. Theodore Blegen was commissioned by the SUNY Research Foundation to report on the state of research at SUNY. His major findings were that SUNY needed a central or "flagship" campus and with few exceptions, was oriented towards teaching, rather than research, and gave a series of recommendations to improve research at the campuses.

3.   A Report on Meeting the Increasing Demand for Higher Education in New York State (The Committee on Higher Education or the "Heald Commission,"1960)—This report was commissioned by both Governor Rockefeller and the New York State Board of Regents and the committee was chaired by Henry T. Heald, president of the Ford Foundation. It noted the projected, dramatic increase in demand for a college education in the coming years (p. 3), as well as the importance of

---

[53]A more comprehensive listing can be found in a working paper done by the staff of the New York State Commission on Higher Education dated September 28, 2007 entitled "The History of New York State Higher Education Commissions (1948–2007)," which includes summarizations of twelve commission reports. Additionally, in an unpublished paper about the history of the State University of New York delivered at the SUNY Administrators' Retreat at the Gideon Putnam Hotel in Saratoga Springs in October, 1988, University Counsel and Vice Chancellor for Legal Affairs Sanford H. Levine identified four reports as crucial to the formation and development of SUNY; Young Commission Report (1948), Blegen Report (1957), Heald Committee Report (1960) and The Independent Commission on the Future of the State University or the Wharton Report (1985). The author has added the SUNY 2000 report (1991) and Rethinking SUNY report (1995) to this group.

science and technology as fields of study in contemporary higher education. It also addressed the state's need for more "trained manpower" in its economic development needs, as well as recognizing another familiar issue, "In addition, the State University as a whole appears to have less administrative and management freedom of operation than almost any other publicly supported institution or group of institutions in the United States." (p. 17).

4. The Challenge and the Choice (The Independent Commission on the Future of the State University or the "Wharton Commission."1985)— Originated by SUNY Chancellor Clifton R. Wharton Jr., the co-chairmen were Ralph Davidson, chairman of the board at Time, Inc.; and Dr. Harold Enarson, president emeritus of Ohio State University. The report's major concerns were: "1) In research and graduate education—areas that are crucial to the future well-being of New York's economy—SUNY's achievement is well behind that of leading public universities in other states and leading independent universities in New York. 2) The commission finds that SUNY is the most over-regulated university in the nation." (p. 2) The commission also found that the "high skill level of the state's labor force" could not be maintained without investing in a "top-ranked public university system." (p.23) It also recommended investment in the university research centers and expressed the fundamental importance of increasing minority enrollment at SUNY (p. 22). The commission also emphasized the lack of financial support for SUNY and under-investment in its facilities.

5. SUNY 2000: A Vision for the New Century (A Report from the Board of Trustees and the Chancellor of the State University of New York, 1991)—Headed by Chairman Frederic Salerno and Chancellor D. Bruce Johnstone, the report has five major areas of focus; access, undergraduate education, graduate education and research, SUNY and state needs, and more efficient management of SUNY (p. 37). The report recognized that SUNY would have to make significant changes if it was to meet its basic educational mission and New York State was to remain competitive in the "global village" (p. 31) and the "information economy." (p. 32) This meant that more New Yorkers had to be college educated and SUNY had to assume a greater role by remaining affordable and accessible ,with its diversity of campuses with different missions located throughout the state. (p. 37) It also called for a predictable tuition policy (p. 61) and a reform of the student transfer system for the community colleges and baccalaureate granting institutions. (p. 39) Also, the report identified the critical importance of graduate education and research and recommended the recruitment and retention of outstanding faculty, increased sponsored research, and further collaboration with industry. (p. 44)

The report stressed the need for increased recruitment of under-represented groups (p. 44) and also emphasized SUNY's obligations to the needs of New York State in areas such as public education, health care, and economic development. (p.53) Finally, the report called for increased efficiencies in the management of SUNY. It also noted the under-funding of SUNY relative to other states, the critical need for more investment in capital infrastructure and educational technology, and increased fund-raising. (p. 57)

6.   Rethinking SUNY (a report by the SUNY Board of Trustees. 1995)—
This report was done at the request of the state legislature, which called upon the SUNY Board of Trustees to formulate a "multi-year, comprehensive, system-wide plan to increase cost efficiency" (p. 1). The report recommended the review of academic programs and the time to degree completion by students. It emphasized the importance of community colleges as "centers for workforce training" (p.4) and promoted a "seamless" transfer system between the community colleges and SUNY's four-year institutions (p. 4). It also concluded that System Administration should be made "smaller and more efficient" and "less controlling of the campus operations,"(p. 6) and argued for financial reform, including a rational tuition policy and differential tuition for the state-operated campuses. Finally, the report argued for greater autonomy and less statutory regulation for SUNY.

As one can see, these reports presented a number of major recommendations that set precedents for the current Report. With this historical background in mind, we now turn to a summary of the Report itself.

C.   An Overview of the Report[54]

Chapter One: "Cornerstones in a Foundation for Excellence: Adapting and Connecting to a World of Ideas" identifies four "cornerstones" that constitute the major problems identified in the Report—which must be corrected—and provide a foundation of excellence for New York State.

- Attracting and expanding world-class research
- Connecting faculty, researchers, and students to the contemporary world of ideas
- Developing a diverse workforce and
- Adapting quickly to change

---

[54] The full report can be found and downloaded on the commission's website www.hecommission. state.ny.us.

They were further addressed in Chapter Two: "Building on a Foundation for Excellence."

It is important to note that in addition to these four "cornerstones," the commission added three major areas which constitute the remaining chapters of the Report:

- Chapter Three: "Making Excellence Available to All," which addresses access and affordability issues.
- Chapter Four: "Organizing for Excellence," which discusses management, governance, and regulatory concerns.
- Chapter Five: "Resources Required for Excellence," which identifies funding sources needed to improve public higher education in New York State.

Consequently, there are seven major areas the commission identified as suitable and appropriate for review, analysis, and recommendations in the Report. In the next section, the Report's recommendations in each major area will be discussed.

D.   The Recommendations of the Report

First, "Attracting and Expanding Research Capacity," really reveals that one of the commission's top priorities was to promote the state's economic development through a major and concentrated investment in university research. This would include:

1. The creation of the $3 billion "Empire State Innovation Fund" to promote collaboration between and among the state's private and public universities.
2. The hiring of 2,000 full-time faculty for SUNY and CUNY over the next five years, which of special note, would include 250 "eminent research faculty."
3. In support of this faculty hiring, there would be the recruitment of 4,000 top doctoral students who would be given stipends competitive with the leading national institutions.
4. Improve the capabilities of NYSTAR (New York State Foundation for Science, Technology and Innovation) to promote greater partnership between and among higher education, government, and the business sector in building a high technology economy.
5. Also, collaboration and dialogue between and among the educational, government, and business sectors would be further encouraged in New York's scientific community by a series of programs with the New York Academy of Sciences.

Second, "Connecting Faculty, Researchers and Students to a World of Ideas" contained a series of recommendations to increase technological infrastructure across the state and provide incentives to New York's colleges and university libraries to share electronic information. There were also recommendations to increase the emphasis on international education and volunteer community service among New York's college students.

Third, "Developing a Diverse Workforce"'s one recommendation was to consolidate the various state agencies for workforce development under a single, unifying one (p. 27). Of special significance to SUNY, this section also emphasized the importance of public higher education in training a diverse workforce and specifically identified the central role of its community colleges.

Fourth, in "Adapting Quickly to Change," the sole recommendation in this section was that the processing time to approve new academic programs by SUNY and the State Education Department be reviewed and shortened considerably.

Fifth, "Making Excellence Available to All," contains a number of recommendations:

1. The commission recommended creating "Education Partnership Zones," in which colleges and universities would enter into collaborative efforts with local school districts.
2. The commission proposed funding for remedial learning programs for high schools students, especially in disadvantaged areas, to prepare them for admission into college.
3. The Report also recommended further financial relief to college students by proposing reforms to the state's Tuition Assistance Plan and the establishment of a low-interest state subsidized loan program for resident full-time students enrolled in public or private New York institutions of higher education.[55]
4. Of special significance for SUNY as a "system" of higher education was the Report's recommendation of the implementation of a "seamless" transfer system between SUNY's and CUNY's community colleges and its baccalaureate granting colleges and universities.[56]

Sixth, in "Organizing for Excellence," the major recommendation is regulatory reform and greater operational flexibility for SUNY. It also noted the establishment of a new committee of the SUNY Board of Trustees devoted to the needs of the University Research Centers and the College of Environmental

---

[55]This recommendation was actually included in Governor Paterson's State of the State address, delivered January 7, 2009, in a proposed $350 million New York State Higher Education Loan Program (NYHELPs).

[56]Note SUNY has already made substantial progress in improving the transfer and articulation system well ahead of the commission's deadlines under the collective leadership of the SUNY Board of Trustees, Office of the Provost, University Faculty Senate, and the Faculty Council of Community Colleges.

Science and Forestry, especially in the development of their research capabilities. Also, there is a recommendation for the Governor to have the SUNY Board of Trustees conduct an "outside review" of System Administration and how it can be made more effective and best support the SUNY sectors. (p. 66)

Seventh and finally, in "Resources Required for Excellence" the Report addressed the need to finance public higher education in the state. The method adopted was called "The New York Compact," an idea introduced by CUNY Chancellor Matthew Goldstein. In the Compact, there would be a broad partnership among the State, SUNY, CUNY, faculty, staff, students, alumni, industry, and private benefactors in a united effort to raise funds for public higher education, rather than SUNY and CUNY taking the usual route of asking the governor and state legislature for additional tax-supported tax assistance or an increase in student tuition and fees.

Under the provisions of the compact, the state would be responsible for the so-called "mandatory costs" of operating the public systems of higher education (e.g. personnel costs, fringe benefits, utilities, etc.) and a set percentage of additional funds to invest in SUNY and CUNY for educational purposes. SUNY and CUNY would be responsible for their portion through fundraising, commercial partnerships, and generating additional monies through savings and efficiencies on their respective campuses. Students would pay modest tuition increases on a rational and predictable basis based upon an agreed upon price index, with the important provision that no qualified student would be denied admission or matriculation to SUNY or CUNY because of the lack of financial means.

It is also important to note that the Report places special emphasis on the need for additional expenditures for critical maintenance, new capital funding, and the "greening" of SUNY's and CUNY's aging campuses. (p. 67).

E.   An Analysis of the Recommendations

From these recommendations, the Report explicitly identifies ten major ones (p. 5):

1.   Establish a $3 billion Empire State Innovation Fund.
2.   Create a low-cost New York student loan program.
3.   Establish the New York State Compact for Public Higher Education.
4.   Hiring the additional 2,000 full-time faculty including 250 eminent scholars.
5.   Reform SUNY's governance structure and System Administration and provide more support for the research campuses.
6.   Provide meaningful regulatory relief for SUNY.
7.   Develop Educational Partnership Zones in high-need school districts.
8.   Ensure that high school graduates are well prepared for college through a College Readiness Act.
9.   Strengthen and improve the articulation and transfer system throughout SUNY and CUNY.

10. Address the backlog of critical maintenance at SUNY and CUNY with a sustained program of capital reinvestment.

As you review the recommendations contained in the Report's seven major areas and compare them with the ten major recommendations of the commission, it will give you a fairly good idea of the prioritization given these areas:

1. Attracting and Expanding Research Capacity: two (2) major recommendations (I. $3 billion Empire State Innovation Fund and IV. Hiring of additional faculty, especially 250 eminent research faculty)
2. Connecting Faculty, Researchers and Students to a World of Ideas: zero (0)
3. Developing a Diverse Workforce: zero (0)
4. Adapting Quickly to Change: zero (0)
5. Making Excellence Available to All: four (4) (II. Low-Cost Student Loan Program; VII. Education Partnership Zones; VIII. College Readiness Programs; IX. SUNY Articulation and Transfer System)
6. Organizing for Excellence: two (2) (V. SUNY Structure and Mission Differentiation and VI. Regulatory Reform)
7. Resources Required for Excellence: two (2) (III. NYS Compact for Public Higher Education and X. Capital Reinvestment Program)

And while interpretation may be made difficult because of overlap and inter-connection of many of the issues and ideas presented in the Report and the varying amount and availability of funds required for each recommendation (which is another indicator), four top priorities may be identified from the above.

1. It was evident, with two major recommendations, that the Report placed a premium on research to both improve SUNY's stature among leading public universities and make major contributions to the State's economic development.
2. Also, with two major recommendations, the issue of a more efficient and effective SUNY assisted by significant regulatory reform was a leading goal.
3. And another critically important area, with two major recommendations, was the funding and financing of SUNY and CUNY, which had suffered from chronic underinvestment both in operating and capital funds.
4. Finally, with four major recommendations, accessibility to higher education must be considered the leading priority of the commission.

In summary, one can say that the Report was devoted to making recommendations that would make a marked improvement to the traditional mission of SUNY, which was providing a quality education to all New Yorkers that was accessible and affordable. Yet, at the same time, it recognized the critical importance and inter-relationship of SUNY, its research capability, and the state's future economic outlook. Furthermore, if one accepted this proposition, and New York State was to remain competitive, both nationally and internationally, SUNY would have to be a major contender with other leading universities, especially in cutting-edge research and quality faculty and students—the leaders and workforce of tomorrow's New York.

F.   A Concluding Personal Note

Finally, I want to return to those halcyon days when the commission was first founded and there was great excitement in SUNY, since we thought there were the financial resources to accomplish the goal of making SUNY one of the nation's truly great systems of public higher education. And indeed the Report refers to many of the key elements that distinguished scholars of the university have noted before: great faculty, first rate administrative team, committed student body, affordability and accessibility, superior campus facilities, sufficient funding, cutting-edge research, world-class reputation, governmental support, sense of obligation to the public welfare, and a commitment to excellence.[57]

Yet to me, the above really does not capture the true spirit of what Professor Bloom[58] would call the "soul" or Cardinal Newman[59] the "idea" of SUNY. And I will conclude with a short story which shows, in my opinion, why SUNY is already a great system of public higher education (but still sorely in need of additional funding and relief from burdensome regulations). It concerns, say, a young woman from a disadvantaged background, who for one or more reasons did not want to go to or could not gain entrance into an institution of higher education, took a few years off, worked a few odd jobs, and then decided she wanted an education and enters one of our fine community colleges. There, she encounters supportive faculty, staff, and fellow students and becomes interested in the field of health. She receives her associate's degree and then goes to one of our wonderful colleges of technology and enters the nursing program and receives another associate's degree. She receives her degree, works in a hospital for a few years, and then decides she wants to become a doctor. She then goes to one of our excellent university colleges in a pre-med program, which she successfully completes and gains entrance into one of the medical schools of our great university research centers or academic medical centers and announces she wants to be a primary care physician in those areas of New York State, either rural or inner city, in dire need of medical coverage.

---

[57]While this is discussed in many works, too numerous to mention, for a nice, concise listing see James Axtell's. *The Pleasures of Academe: A Celebration & Defense of Higher Education*. Lincoln, Neb. and London: University of Nebraska Press, 1998, in the chapter appropriately entitled "What Makes a University Great?" pp. 85–98.

[58]Allan Bloom. *The Closing of the American Mind: How Higher Education Has Failed Democracy and Impoverished the Souls of Today's Students*. New York: Simon and Schuster, 1987.

[59]John Henry Cardinal Newman. *The Idea of a University*. Oxford, UK: Clarendon Press, 1976.

And while this individual story happens to be fictional, and perhaps dramatized, real stories like it happen all the time in SUNY. And while I may agree in large part with the traditional definition of the "great" university, this story hopefully illustrates that my view of the great university is determined and measured by the number of students such as this woman it graduates, for she symbolizes the real America—the land of opportunity, but imbued with a sense of duty and responsibility, and yes, altruism and citizenship. And the value of the Report's recommendations should be seen in the light of student success and its importance for our civilized society, now threatened by financial disaster and war brought on by egoism, greed, and various external threats.

And the more students like this we can graduate, who go on to lead good, productive, and honorable lives, the greater an institution of higher education SUNY truly is.

Acknowledgments

The author would like to thank Bruce Leslie of The College at Brockport (SUNY) and Cambridge University, as well as James Ketterer, Beth Bringsjord, and Pam Sandoval of SUNY System Administration, who also served as staff to the Commission, for reviewing the paper and making very helpful suggestions and constructive comments which improved it immeasurably. As usual, any errors or shortcomings in the papers are the sole fault of the author.

Dedication

The author would like to dedicate this paper to the memory of a dear colleague and friend, Ernesto Malave, key Commission staff member and CUNY Vice Chancellor for Budget and Finance. His inspirational life exemplified the sentiments expressed about democratic education in the concluding personal note.

Appendix

Members of the New York State Commission on Higher Education

+Hunter Rawlings, President Emeritus, Cornell University, Chairman
+Stephen Ainlay, President, Union College
*Donald Boyce, President, Student Assembly of the State University of New York
+Nancy Cantor, Chancellor, Syracuse University
*John Clark, Interim Chancellor, State University of New York

Milton Cofield, Regents, New York State Board of Regents
*Lois DeFleur, President, Binghamton University, State University of New York
John Dyson, Chairman, Millbrook Capital Management, Inc.
Peter Fishbein, Special Counsel, Kaye Scholer LLP
Hon. Deborah Glick, Chair, Assembly Higher Education Committee
*Matthew Goldstein, Chancellor, City University of New York
*Carl Hayden, Chair, State University of New York Board of Trustees
+Elena Kagan, Dean, Harvard Law School
*Marcia Keizs, President, York College, City University of New York
+Abraham Lackman, President, Commission on Independent Colleges and Universities (CICU)
Hon. Kenneth LaValle, Chair, Senate Higher Education Committee
*Eduardo Marti, President, Queensborough Community College
Richard Mills, Commissioner of Education
*Myron Mitchell, Professor, College of Environmental Science and Forestry, State University of New York
*Robert Paaswell, Professor, City College, City University of New York
Hon. Crystal Peoples, Member of the New York State Assembly
Bruce Raynor, President, UNITE HERE
*William Scheuerman, President, United University Professions (UUP)
+Joel Seligman, President, University of Rochester
+John Sexton, President, New York University
*John Simpson, President, University of Buffalo, State University of New York
*Thomas Schwarz, President, Purchase College, State University of New York
*Mark Shaw, Trustee, City University of New York
*Lauren Talerman, Student, Queens College, City University of New York
Adam Urbanski, President, Rochester Teachers Association
*Public university representatives (fourteen out of thirty; seven from SUNY, six from CUNY, and President, UUP)
+Private university representatives (seven out of thirty including the President, CICU)

COMMISSION STAFF

John Reid, Executive Director; Kathy Bennett, Chief of Staff; Craig Abbey, Elizabeth Bringsjord, David Crook, James Ketterer, Ernesto Malave, Pamela Sandoval, Daniel Sheppard, Jane Sovern, Clarissa Wertman; Ryan Greer, Intern; Laura Mahoney, Intern; Glenn Pichardo, Intern.

Source: Report, p. i

"Diversity"—Demography, Culture, and Education for a Changing New York

Introduction

Pedro N. Cabán, Vice Provost for Diversity and Educational Equity, State University of New York

The History of SUNY Conference was a much-needed retrospective on the origins, current challenges, and future directions of the nation's largest comprehensive system of public higher education. The organizers of this seminal conference, keenly aware of SUNY's mission of providing educational services of quality with broad access and full representation of all segments of New York State's population, created a panel on "The Changing Face of SUNY: Diversity and Educational Equity." The panel speakers explored the function and origin of race and ethnic studies; the history and development of educational opportunity centers and programs and student retention programs; and presented an original conceptual framework for assessing the educational imperative for representational diversity.

The title of the panel was not meant to be ironic, although presenters identified the tensions between the changing racial and ethnic composition of the student body and the seemingly inalterable makeup of the SUNY professoriate and senior administration. However, the speakers did affirm that while SUNY has faithfully adhered to its institutional commitment to expand access and opportunity to economically disadvantaged and underserved communities, it has been unable to significantly diversify its professoriate and high-level academic administrators and executives.

Professor Jose Cruz's essay "Changing Demographics and Representational Dilemmas at SUNY" challenges a university committed to diversity to pursue universal representation. Universal representation pertains both to the composition of the community of scholars that make up the university, and to the content and scope of knowledge creation and dissemination. Professor Cruz adroitly avoids the issue of specifying a numerical measure of diversity, since no comparable measure for diversity of knowledge and academic human resources can be established. Nonetheless, the jarring disparity between the demographic composition of the student body and the faculty who teach, and administrators who manage the system does raise issues of SUNY's ability to fulfill its mandated mission. Implicit in Professor Cruz's argument is that academic excellence requires that universities be inclusive of new and challenging knowledge, and promote a diverse learning environment in which the experiential differences of both those who disseminate knowledge and those who are its recipients constitute a vibrant intellectual and learning community.

Carlos Medina's and Jeffrey Scott's essay "Creating Educational Opportunity for All: A Brief History of EOP and EOC" reviews the socio-economic changes and political forces that moved New York State to expand access and opportunity for economically disadvantaged students. By the 1960s, the growing economic desperation of urban youths denied educational opportunity had become a major policy issue for state governments. SUNY, which had been established as a public alternative to the state's private universities, was becoming increasingly inaccessible, precisely when New York's population most required its educational services. The educational crisis virtually guaranteed that the state's economically disadvantaged would be deprived of the opportunity for social and economic advancement. To counteract this situation, New York established the Educational Opportunity Program (EOP) and Educational Opportunity Centers (EOCs). These programs enhanced the prospects for underserved communities to receive an academic preparation that had been out of reach. The EOCs also set SUNY on a new mission to educate students for employment in a changing labor market and to prepare students to pursue a postsecondary education.

Both essays emphasize SUNY's unique attributes as a comprehensive public university. It aspires to be a people's university by providing access and creating opportunity. In fact, access, equity, and inclusion were the founding principles of SUNY when it was established in 1948. Demand for higher education increased dramatically in the aftermath of World War II, but opportunities were primarily confined to the private universities. Some of the financially well-endowed universities and colleges resisted the efforts by New York State to build a public university. These very universities fought the enactment of the Fair Educational Practices Law that sought to bar the discriminatory admissions policies they freely practiced. Prohibitive tuition denied access to untold numbers of academically prepared, but economically disadvantaged, young people and veterans. These restrictive policies preserved a social hierarchy increasingly at variance with New York's changing socio-economic and demographic realities. New York's post-World War II restructured economy demanded technically competent workers and highly educated professionals in numbers the private institutions could not possibly supply.

The higher education challenges that New York State encounters today are different from those it faced six decades ago. However, these challenges are comparably daunting and will require the visionary and determined leadership that resulted in the creation of SUNY. Two major differences are that in 1948, New York State had the financial resources and political determination to build a public university founded on the principles of access and equity. The state's current fiscal plight, marked by deterioration in revenues not experienced since the Great Depression, will severely test SUNY's ability to provide a quality education to New York's residents. Moreover, the profound demographic transformation marked by the unprecedented growth of Latino and Asian American residents, projected to significantly continue in the foreseeable future, challenges SUNY to develop cost-effective programs to enhance inclusion and representation.

In anticipation of this evolving need to develop a comprehensive approach to enhancing diversity and promoting inclusion, SUNY established the Office of Diversity and Educational Equity (ODEE). ODEE has developed system-wide initiatives to support campus efforts to diversify the university's academic human resources and to strategically invest resources to enhance academic excellence. Through various initiatives, including the Graduate Diversity Fellowship Program, the Doctoral Diversity Fellowships in STEM, the Faculty Diversity Program, the Empire State Scholars Program, Explorations in Diversity and Academic Excellence, and the Native American Initiative, ODEE contributes to enhancing diversity at SUNY. ODEE is committed to obtaining support to recruit professors, graduate, and undergraduate students from diverse backgrounds, including from groups that have historically been underrepresented in higher education, and providing them with the resources to excel. With appropriate funding ODEE will support curriculum reform that promotes diversity, support new research directions, and finance and organize regionally based multi-campus faculty diversity research initiatives. It will seek additional funding to expand ongoing system-wide diversity efforts and to develop new initiatives to promote cross-campus collaboration on public policy issues of critical importance to the state. ODEE may well be the only one of its kind in a public higher education system, and support for its proposal for a series of integrated initiatives to advance diversity system-wide is novel, if not unique. In the late 1980s, SUNY emerged as a national leader in creating programs to enhance access and equity, particularly for historically underrepresented students. In establishing the Office of Diversity and Educational Equity with system-wide responsibilities, SUNY created a unique opportunity in public higher education and reaffirmed its historical mission of providing access to a quality education.

In these troubled times, the tendency is to think of diversity as a luxury. Yet it is precisely at this moment in history that it is incumbent on SUNY to move creatively and forthrightly on diversifying its academic human resources and supporting diversity related research initiatives. Success for SUNY's students in the fast paced, internationally competitive world depends on developing their analytical and technical abilities, cognitive skills and cultural competence to respond to new opportunities and challenges propelled by the forces of globalization. Those universities that conceptualize diversity as critical to their academic mission will very likely succeed in creating an intellectual climate that fosters respect for differences, stimulates innovation, and encourages collaboration. Students educated in this environment will be prepared to live and work productively in our multiracial and multiethnic democratic society. In short, diversity is critical, not only for attaining academic excellence in the extremely competitive higher education environment, but SUNY's contribution to New York State will be more substantial and enduring if it diversifies its academic workforce and student population and promotes the integration of diversity-related research and teaching.

I. Changing Demographics and Representational Dilemmas: Latinos at SUNY and CUNY Meeting the Diversity Challenge

José E. Cruz, Political Science & Latin American, Caribbean, and U.S. Latino Studies, University at Albany

The only time I ever thought of racial and ethnic diversity as a potential weakness was when I returned to New York City a month after the September 11 attacks on the World Trade Center had interrupted a research sabbatical in the city. I remember being scared out of my wits as I heard my taxi driver speaking in Arabic to someone on his cell phone immediately after the radio announced that a plane flying out of JFK airport on route to the Dominican Republic had crashed after takeoff. Later that day, walking down Madison Avenue and 68th Street looking for a place to have lunch, I was more aware than ever of the people surrounding me and the incredible diversity of phenotypes. I remember thinking, "If all that Homeland Security agents have to go by are visual cues, how can they tell who's a suspect in this kaleidoscope of faces?" Shortly after September 11, a friend of my son told him, "Your father looks like a terrorist!" I remembered that as well and thought, "Seeing what I'm seeing now, that kid would probably think that New York City is full of terrorists."

In 2007, a *Boston Globe* article reported on the shocking claim by Robert Putnam that the correlation between diversity and trust in social life was negative. The report brought back my post-9/11 experience in New York. Michael Jonas wrote: "Harvard political scientist Robert Putnam—famous for 'Bowling Alone,' his 2000 book on declining civic engagement—has found that the greater the diversity in a community, the fewer people vote and the less they volunteer, the less they give to charity and work on community projects. In the most diverse communities, neighbors trust one another about half as much as they do in the most homogenous settings."[1]

When I first read reports of Putnam's new research, I was skeptical. Then I was reassured by an important caveat: lack of trust in diverse settings is only an initial reaction that, under the right conditions, is overcome in time. As I write this, eight years after the events of September 11 and two years after Putnam's revelations, urban life in New York City thrives amidst diversity of all kinds and trust in our political system and in the hope of America has been renewed as a result of the election of Barack Obama, our first non-white president. All across America, numerous signs suggest that "social divisions can eventually give way to 'more encompassing identities' that create a 'new, more capacious sense of 'we,'" as Putnam suggested in response to both liberals who decried his findings and conservatives who embraced them. But this was not emphasized in 2007. Putnam's conclusion that "increasing diversity in America is not only inevitable, but ultimately valuable and enriching," was also underemphasized.[2]

In light of that conclusion, I want to suggest that SUNY and CUNY—the latter must be considered, given that it is the second half of the state's public higher education system—must not just acknowledge the inevitable diversity created by demographic changes in New York, but respond to this new diverse environment by reflecting it among its students, administrators, staff, and faculty. In this essay I am specifically interested in racial and ethnic diversity, with a focus on Latino faculty.

A.   Latinos in New York State

Between 1990 and 2007, demographic change in New York was marked by sustained and significant increases in the number of Latino residents. In 1990, the U.S. Bureau of the Census counted 2,214,026 Latinos in the state or 12.3 percent of the total population. By 2000, their proportion of the total population had climbed to 15 percent and their numbers reached 2,867,583, a 30 percent change from 1990. Between 2000 and 2007, the Census estimated that another 255,818 Latinos had become state residents, for a 9% increase since the last official count. No other population group in the state compares to Latinos in terms of both absolute and relative demographic growth. By 2007, the non-Hispanic white population had lost 76,000 residents. In that year, African Americans were the largest racial minority in the state, but their numbers had decreased by 0.3 percent since 2000.

---

[1]Michael Jonas, "The downside of diversity," *The Boston Globe*, August 5, 2007. http://www .boston.com/news/globe/ideas/articles/2007/08/05/the_downside_of_diversity/ <Accessed June 12, 2009>

[2]Ibid.

Traditionally, Latinos have concentrated in New York City. In 2007, Latinos in the city made up 72 percent of Latinos in the state, but the city was not the area of greatest demographic growth. The counties where growth was most dramatic between 2000 and 2007 had small Latino concentrations, thus leaving New York City as the most significant Latino enclave in the state. With the exception of Orange County, where Latino growth was dramatic proportionally—44 percent—and Latino numbers were high as well, at 57,147 residents—the counties where Latino population increases were notable still had small concentrations. For example, from 2000 to 2007, the Latino population in Putnam County grew by an astonishing 62 percent, but this amounted to only 9,680 Latinos; Seneca County experienced a 53 percent increase and Saratoga County saw Latino numbers grow by 48 percent, but Latino numbers there were 1,005 and 4,182, respectively.

The highest concentrations of Latinos outside New York City were in Westchester and Suffolk counties, where their numbers grew by 22 and 26 percent, for a total of 175,405 in Westchester and 188,756 in Suffolk. If the 2007 Census estimate is any guide, Puerto Ricans will continue to be the majority Latino group in the state in the foreseeable future, followed by Dominicans, South Americans, Mexicans, Central Americans, and Cubans.[3] Thus, if SUNY and CUNY really value diversity, the rapid and significant demographic growth of the state's Latino population poses a representational challenge that the system must confront head on. This challenge was recognized and embraced early on by SUNY's former chancellor, John Ryan. Whether it will be met or not by his successor remains to be seen, but the establishment in 2007 of the Office of Diversity and Educational Equity (ODEE) headed by Dr. Pedro Cabán is a serious step in the right direction.[4]

SUNY was established to provide affordable quality education to New York State residents. If it is true that SUNY was created as an alternative to parochial and discriminatory private institutions, it follows that it had to be founded on principles of equity and access. But how inclusive should SUNY be as a university? To answer this question, I focus on the representation of Latinos within SUNY faculty. Nevertheless, my argument is applicable to students, administrators, staff, and other groups, as well. My basic premise is that diversity requires universal representation. I also suggest that the appropriate measure of representation is excess, rather than parity. Parity is an important parameter, but it is not enough. Even though my views are not wholly

---

[3]See "Latinos in New York State: Demographic Status and Political Representation," NYLARNet Policy Report, Spring 2009 and Latinos in New York: 2000–2007, NYLARNet, Spring 2009. Available at http://www.nylarnet.org.

[4]For an account of the genesis of ODEE see "NYLARNet Goes to the University of New Mexico," *Enlaces Latinos*, Newsletter of the New York Latino Research and Resources Network. Spring 2007.

idiosyncratic, I do offer this essay as a personal reflection intended to generate discussion, rather than as a work of social science research.

B.   The Idea of University: Exclusion and Inclusion

The idea of exclusivity is anathema to the idea of the university. That which is exclusive cannot by definition be universal. In that sense, it is logical to think of the university as, in the words of John Henry Cardinal Newman an "assemblage of strangers from all parts in one spot." Newman defined the university as a school of universal learning, a place where you could find "professors and students for every department of knowledge."[5] In his view, great cities were virtual universities simply because there, anyone could find the intellectual environment that leads to universal knowledge and learning: "The newspapers, magazines, reviews, journals, and periodicals of all kinds, the publishing trade, the libraries, museums, and academies there found, the learned and scientific societies, necessarily invest [cities] with the functions of a University."[6]

According to Newman, "You cannot have the best of every kind everywhere."[7] And extending his metaphor of the city as university he added: "You must go to some great city or emporium for it."[8] In cities, one could find pretty much everything under the sun:

> ... the choicest productions of nature and art all together ... All the riches of the land, and of the earth ... the best markets ... the centre of trade, the supreme court of fashion, the umpire of rival talents, and the standard of things rare and precious. It is the place for seeing galleries of first-rate pictures, and for hearing wonderful voices and performers of transcendent skill. It is the place for great preachers, great orators, great nobles, great statesmen. In the nature of things, greatness and unity go together; excellence implies a centre.[9]

And as cities went, so did universities:

> It is the place to which a thousand schools make contributions; in which the intellect may safely range and speculate, sure to find its equal in some antagonist activity, and its judge in the tribunal of truth. It is a place where inquiry is pushed forward, and discoveries

---

[5]John Henry Cardinal Newman. "What is A University," in Essays and Sketches, V. II. New York: Longmans, Green and Co., 1948, p. 280.

[6]Ibid., p. 286.

[7]Ibid., p. 288.

[8]Ibid.

[9]Ibid., pp. 288–289.

verified and perfected, and rashness rendered innocuous, and error exposed, by the collision of mind with mind, and knowledge with knowledge.[10]

In Newman's description, the notion of exclusivity is implicit, even in a context of universality. Why? Because you cannot have the best of every kind everywhere. Excellence must have a center, Newman tells us. Thus, the moment boundaries are established, the stage is set for a dynamic of inclusion and exclusion. The question then becomes, who is to be included and who is to be left out? What criteria do we use to regulate access?

If the university must have students and professors from every department of knowledge, does that mean that it must have students and professors from every department of life? I would argue that such is the case, except in cases where inclusion is counterproductive or destructive. No one in his/her right mind would make an argument for the inclusion of idiots or criminals within the university. Just as biodiversity is essential for the sustainability of human life, sociopolitical and intellectual diversity is essential to the sustainability of human society. Yet, if it is acceptable to stunt the growth and eradicate the presence of noxious plants and organisms from ecosystems to insure their vitality, it should be acceptable to deny legitimacy within the university to ideas and practices that are clearly and unequivocally antithetical to generally accepted and cherished societal values such as freedom, equality, civic virtue, and democratic participation. Is there a contradiction there? Only if we believe in absolute freedom and equality and only if we agree that it is legitimate to destroy democracy through democratic participation.

C. Disembodied Knowledge and Representation

The written word allows us to acquire knowledge with autonomy from physical presence. So long as students from, say, the University of Virginia, read my books and articles, my physical presence there is not necessary for them to learn about Puerto Rican or minority politics in the United States. In other words, a diverse faculty is not a *sine qua non* condition for a diverse curriculum. Descriptive representation may not be necessary to have all departments of knowledge and even all departments of life represented within the university. The field of Latino studies, for example, has enriched our understanding of liberal democracy, of imperialism and modernity. There is no reason why this enterprise had to be carried out by Latino scholars but, for the most part, it has been. Why? Because their Latinidad has provided the impetus to address the kinds of questions that have come about in light of their own experiences as Latinos. Segregation has also played a part, as well as historical happenstance.

---

[10]Ibid.

At SUNY, the record suggests that, just as in the political sphere, the best predictor of substantive representation is descriptive representation; the sure way to make the experience of mutual education diverse is by having a diverse faculty. If we want Latino studies, it is almost imperative to have some Latino faculty. For the system as a whole the question is, how many Latino faculty? New York State is currently 16 percent Latino. Should 16 percent of SUNY faculty also be Latino? Alternatively, should the standard for SUNY be the Latino population outside New York City? In this case, the benchmark would be only 6 percent for Latinos as a whole—this represents the 707,029 Latinos that were counted in the fifty-seven counties outside New York City in 2000. In the state, Puerto Ricans are the majority group among Latinos. Should they be the majority group among Latino faculty at SUNY?

How many Latino faculty should CUNY have? In New York City, Latinos were 27 percent of the population in 2000. Puerto Ricans were 10 percent of the total and 37 percent of Latinos in the city. Dominicans were 5 percent, Mexicans were 2 percent, Cubans were 0.5 percent, and the second largest category, "Other," representing groups from Central America, South America, and Spain, was a smaller proportion than Puerto Ricans at 9 percent of the total population. Should Puerto Ricans be the majority of Latino faculty at CUNY as well?

What about diversity within the Latino population? Should it be reflected and if so, how? Puerto Ricans are 6 percent of the state population, but a much smaller proportion of the population outside New York City; Mexicans are a little over 1 percent of the state population; Dominicans are 2.3 percent and Cubans are less than 0.5 percent. Outside New York City, these groups, along with those in the "Other" category, are invisible.

Any demographic parameter would represent a significant recruitment challenge at CUNY. At SUNY, even if the system were to use the proportion of the state population outside New York City that is Latino or Puerto Rican to guide its recruitment efforts, the same would be true. In 2005, only 3 percent of the full-time tenured and tenure track faculty at SUNY was Latino. In that year, Latinos were 2 percent of full professors and 4 percent of associate professors.[11] Currently, SUNY has no published data about Puerto Rican faculty within the system.

In New York City, representation is not much better. At CUNY, the historical trend has been Latino population growth, increasing Latino and

[11]Office of Diversity and Educational Equity, Office of the Provost and Vice Chancellor for Academic Affairs, "Keeping Pace: Racial/Ethnic Diversity of Students and Faculty at the State University of New York," 2009, pp. 3–6. In 2005, the combined Latino, African American, Asian or Pacific Islander, and Native American cohort of full professors at SUNY was 13 percent and it was 16.3 percent of associate professors. According to Census Bureau estimates, by 2007 African Americans, Latinos, Asians, and American Indian/Alaska Natives were 38.8 percent of the state's population.

decreasing Puerto Rican faculty representation. Between 1970 and 1974, Puerto Ricans experienced a significant increase in proportional representation among instructional staff at CUNY. But during the period 1981–2002, the full-time Puerto Rican faculty declined by more than 20 percent. The growth of Latino faculty during this period shows the need to pay attention to diversity within population groups. In this case, increases in Latino representation occurred while the majority Latino group remained significantly underrepresented.[12]

At 16 percent of the state's population, Latinos at SUNY are obviously underrepresented. Even if we use the lower benchmark of 6 percent, the problem remains. In New York City, the situation is even worse. Latinos make up 27 percent of the city population, but only 7 percent of the full-time faculty at CUNY. The representation of Puerto Ricans, the largest Latino group in the city, is also low. In 2002, they were 2 percent of the full-time faculty in CUNY's senior colleges and the Graduate Center, 4 percent of the full-time faculty in the system's community colleges, and only 3 percent of the full-time faculty in the system as a whole.[13] While within SUNY, Latino representation has increased over time, between 2000 and 2005 the proportion of Latino full-time faculty increased only by eight-tenths of 1 percent, from 2.2 percent to 3 percent.[14] At CUNY, as we have seen, increases in the number of Latino faculty have been not just low relative to population, but have also obscured the unequal treatment of Puerto Ricans.

Just as labor produces surplus value, that is, value that exceeds what is necessary to reproduce it, these meager levels of representation have had what we could call surplus impact in terms of service, teaching, and research at SUNY and CUNY. Like the ant that can carry a grain of corn ten times its own weight, at SUNY Albany, the Department of Latin American, Caribbean, and U.S. Latino Studies sponsors and produces MAs and PhDs—the latter through a doctoral track in cultural studies officially ascribed to the Department of Languages, Literatures, and Cultures—in greater numbers than one would guess based on its resources. Despite setbacks in terms of faculty representation, the Center for Puerto Rican Studies at Hunter College continues to have a significant presence and growing impact after thirty years of uninterrupted activity.

Without descriptive representation, the likelihood of a Latino intellectual presence at SUNY and CUNY would be nil because disembodied knowledge

---

[12]Felipe Pimentel. "The Decline of Puerto Rican Fulltime Faculty at the City University of New York (CUNY) from 1981–2002." NYLARNet Policy Paper, Fall 2005, pp. 1, 2, 4, 6.

[13]Ibid., pp. 2–3.

[14]The proportion for 2000 is from B. Runi Mukherji and Paul Brodsky. "The Changing Face of Diversity: Minority Enrollment Trends in the State-Operated Campuses of SUNY." Report of the University Faculty Senate, State University of New York, April 2000, p. 58.

has no will of its own. At the macro level, social and political agitation have been instrumental in achieving descriptive representation. The Center for Puerto Rican Studies at CUNY and the Department of Latin American, Caribbean, and U.S. Latino studies at SUNY are cases in point. At the micro level, descriptive representation is often the only reason for substantive intellectual presence. My own Political Science Department at SUNY offers courses on race and ethnicity in American politics and Latino politics in the United States only because I am a member of the faculty. In contrast, ever since my Latin American colleagues left the department in the 1990s, one to retire and the other to pursue a different career, the course on Latin American politics they had taught has not been offered. In the absence of any institutional push, the department has made little effort to hire someone to cover the politics of Latin America. This leads me to think that the moment I leave or retire, the Latino presence in the departmental curriculum will disappear as well.

D. Increasing Representation

The number of Latinos receiving doctorate degrees has grown steadily during the last twenty years. Yet the Latino academic pool is still small and the disciplinary distribution of PhDs is skewed. According to SUNY's Office of Diversity and Educational Equity, the university system "does not appear to be keeping pace with the national publics and New York State privates with respect to underrepresented faculty hiring."[15] This is, in part, a reflection of the limitations of the pool. Given the tendency within Academia to hire from the outside, New York State private institutions are in a better position than SUNY to hire Latino PhDs in the social sciences and the humanities because SUNY produces more Latino doctorates than the privates in those areas. Only in the professions does SUNY graduate fewer Latino PhDs than private universities in the state, thereby having more options for recruitment.[16] Going beyond New York State could help offset pool limitations except that data for the top twenty-five institutions awarding doctorate degrees to Latinos shows that the total number is small: only 842 in 2006–07 or 7 percent of the U.S. total. In contrast, in 2000, Latinos were 13 percent of the U.S. population. In addition, during that period, 30 percent of all Latino doctorates were awarded by universities in Puerto Rico.[17] SUNY and CUNY could easily target Latino doctorates from Puerto Rico for recruitment, but since competition

---

[15]Office of Diversity and Educational Equity, Op. Cit., p. 7.

[16]Ibid., p. 8.

[17]Deborah A. Santiago. *The Condition of Latinos in Education: 2008 Factbook*. Washington, D.C.: Excelencia in Education, 2008, p. 14.

for Latino PhDs is not only fierce but continuous, the initial conclusion may stand: the recruitment pool is small.

One important consequence of this fact is that oftentimes, accomplishing the goal of diversity becomes a zero-sum game. In 2006, CUNY, for example, established the CUNY Puerto Rican Faculty Recruitment Project in response to the publication of *The Decline of the Puerto Rican Full-Time Faculty at the City University of New York (CUNY) From 1981–2002*, a NYLARNet policy paper authored by Hostos Community College Professor Felipe Pimentel. The primary functions of this project, subsequently renamed the CUNY Latino Faculty Initiative, are to conduct outreach and recruitment activities to fill faculty positions in all disciplines at CUNY and to work with CUNY colleges to connect Latino candidates with positions available within the CUNY system. So far, the project has been a case of robbing Peter to pay Paul. Professors hired by CUNY through the project have been simply recruited away from other universities.

What is the alternative? One possibility is to target high-achieving Latino college graduates, as some have suggested for minorities in general, to encourage and promote their choice of an academic career.[18] Another option is to focus on best practices to improve recruitment, evaluation, hiring, mentoring, and retention of Latino faculty. Acknowledging that institutional practices do not evolve in a vacuum, the proponents of the best practices approach also suggest a host of ancillary changes ranging from calling for a fully inclusive constitutional convention to produce a U.S. Constitution of broader vision, to the elimination of academic tracking in junior and high school.[19] A third view suggests that leadership—through faculty agency, interdisciplinary collaboration, and organized mobilization—is a key factor in the dual task of dismantling environments hostile to diversity while building the institutional setup that will promote it systematically.[20]

The CUNY experience is also suggestive. How do we explain the growth in Puerto Rican faculty during the 1970s? What do we make of the fact that Puerto Rican professors began to decline precisely as more Puerto Rican doctorates were available? Pimentel notes that "during the 1970s, at a time when the pool of Puerto Ricans holding doctorates was much smaller [than during the 1980s and 1990s], CUNY did implement a proactive recruitment policy that expanded considerably the number of [Puerto Rican] faculty members."[21] Thus, while in 1973 the proportion of Puerto Rican doctorates

---

[18]See Stephen Cole and Elinor Barber. *Increasing Faculty Diversity*. Cambridge, Mass.: Harvard University Press, 2003.

[19]See JoAnn Moody. *Faculty Diversity*. New York: RoutledgeFalmer, 2004.

[20]See Winifred R. Brown-Glaude, ed. *Doing Diversity in Higher Education*. New Brunswick, NJ: Rutgers University Press, 2009.

[21]Pimentel, Op. Cit., p. 5.

was 0.1 percent, Puerto Ricans were 2.2 percent of CUNY's instructional staff.[22] Alas, once Puerto Rican faculty retired or left for other institutions, they were not replaced.[23]

These decisions were made in specific contexts. CUNY's affirmative action is only part of the story because the institution was also responding to grassroots pressure. For example, while the 1973–78 campaign to save Hostos Community College from closure resulted in a short-term loss of faculty resources, in the long run, the result was growth in terms of both faculty and students, as well as institutional expansion. The administration at CUNY was responsive because the pressure coming from students, faculty, community organizations, and some elected officials forced its hand.[24] Once the protesters were placated, the pressure waned. In that context, it was easier to stop hiring; and without oversight from below, the decline in Puerto Rican faculty occurred unnoticed.

What happens when there are no strategies in place from the top and no sustained pressure from below? At SUNY, the Office of Diversity and Educational Equity notes that international scholars are a growing percentage of SUNY's faculty, and the office rightfully wonders whether diversity at SUNY is to be achieved through the internationalization of the academic pool of candidates.[25] Instead of turning to the domestic pool of Latino academics, are we to promote Latino representation by hiring nationals from Central America, South America, and Spain? Given the problem with the pool of Latino doctorates noted above, this may be an inevitable strategy. But even if the pool was substantial, in an increasingly globalized world, does it make sense to distinguish between international and domestic faculty? In the case of Latinos, how do we count Puerto Rican scholars from the island? If we think of Puerto Rico as a colonial possession of the United States, would they count as international? If we accept the idea of Puerto Rico as a U.S. Commonwealth, do their inhabitants count as Latinos? Either way, Puerto Rican scholars from the island are American citizens and yet, they only "belong to, but are not a part of, the United States."[26] Does the solution to our diversity problem lie in focusing on

---

[22]Ibid.

[23]Pimentel, Op. Cit. p. 3.

[24]See Gerald Meyer. "Save Hostos: The Struggle for a College in the South Bronx," Centro XV: 1. Spring 2003, pp. 72–97.

[25]Office of Diversity and Educational Equity, Op. Cit., p. 7.

[26]This is how the U.S. Supreme Court defined Puerto Rico, and by extension, Puerto Ricans, over a century ago in the Insular Cases. In these cases, decided between 1901 and 1904, the court established the parameters for application of the federal constitution to the islands of Hawaii, Puerto Rico, Cuba, the Philippines, and Guam.

racial and ethnic categories in general, or should we consider race and ethnicity only in their national/domestic context?

The solution to this dilemma may be a matter of priorities. Just as during World War II Puerto Ricans were favored over Jamaicans to fill labor market shortages on account of citizenship, the recruitment of diverse faculty at SUNY should favor the native-born, the naturalized, and the foreign-born, in that order. Regardless of how the U.S. Supreme Court may define their citizenship, once in the continental United States, Puerto Ricans are native-born. We may live in a global village, but a salient feature of globalization is that the sovereign nation-state is the operating political reality, even in the context of collapsing socioeconomic boundaries. Transnational citizenship, while an observable phenomenon, remains a bottom-up process without formal or legal validation. The closest thing to formal-legal validation of transnational citizenship we have is the recognition by some nation-states of dual citizenship. Even so, dual citizenship presupposes the existence of sovereign nations and the first order of business for nation-states is to tend to the needs of their nationals.[27]

E. Diversity and Mutual Education: Race and Ethnicity

According to Newman, the university fulfilled a basic human need: mutual education. And in the process of mutual education, books stand as a special instrument. Books, he suggested, raise the question: why do we need to go up to knowledge [to the university] if knowledge comes down to us through the proliferation of all kinds of texts—not just books but also pamphlets, periodicals, tracts, even newspapers. "Such certainly is our popular education," he wrote in answer to this question, "and its effects are remarkable." He added:

> Nevertheless, after all, even in this age, whenever men are really serious about getting what, in the language of trade, is called 'a good article,' when they aim at something precise, something refined, something really luminous, something really large, something choice, they go to another market; they avail themselves, in some shape or other, of the rival method, the ancient method, of oral instruction, of present communication between man and man, of teachers instead of learning, of the personal influence of a master, and the humble initiation of a disciple, and, in consequence, of

---

[27]Scholars of transnational citizenship define it as dual engagement, without any reference to legal-formal recognition as a definitional requirement, and distinguish it from concepts such as post-national or global citizenship. See Michael Peter Smith and Matt Bakker. *Citizenship Across Borders*. Ithaca: Cornell University Press, 208, p. 185.

great centres of pilgrimage and throng, which such a method of education necessarily involves.[28]

In other words, they go to universities where "if we wish to become exact and fully furnished in any branch of knowledge which is diversified and complicated, we must consult the living man and listen to his living voice."[29]

In Newman's formulation, the "living voice" of the teacher is abstract; it has no color or ethnicity (although in the language of the day it has a gender—male). Newman wrote in the nineteenth century and from the perspective of an Englishman. He could write today and still ignore race and ethnicity. This is because color-blindness and post-ethnicity work only when one color or ethnic group is demographically and politically dominant; only then can these categories be taken for granted and only then can the dominant color or ethnicity pass as "objective" and "neutral."

Today, should we think about the "living voice" in mutual education in abstract terms? If not, how do we justify the insertion of suspect categories such as race and ethnicity as criteria for inclusion? The standard argument for faculty diversity is built on the shoulders of the argument for a diversified student body. The main assumption is that diverse students need diverse faculty as mentors, role models, and sympathetic advocates. In addition, the argument goes, a diverse faculty signals redress for past exclusion and a greater likelihood, if not a guarantee, that the curriculum will also be diverse. Diversity in higher education is also justified because it prepares students for diversity in the "real" world.[30]

Another argument for diversity in the university is that there are racial and ethnic ways of learning and producing knowledge. This is a controversial proposition. Concerning race, Jacques Barzun has stated that "genes … help account for so-called white skin, not for socialism, genius, dipsomania, or delinquency,"[31] meaning that learning is learning and knowledge is knowledge regardless of race. The same thing could be said of ethnicity: there is no "Latino way" of learning or producing knowledge. So, if this is the case, how do we justify descriptive representation as a means to achieve diversity?

Using Newman's vocabulary, we could say that the process of mutual education that the university represents, which requires a meeting of strangers, ought to consider and include all the possible categories that define strangeness.

---

[28]Newman, Op. Cit. pp. 281–282.

[29]Ibid., p. 282.

[30]See Cole and Barber Association of American Colleges and Universities, American Pluralism and the College Curriculum: Higher Education in a Diverse Democracy, Washington, D.C. 1995. Op. Cit., pp. 1–3;

[31]Jacques Barzun. *Race: A Study in Superstition*. New York: Harper & Row, 1965, p. xii.

If mutual education requires comparison, there is no reason to exclude any of the possible ways in which comparisons are made. And there is no reason why the elements of comparison should not be embodied by the participants in this process of mutual education. To play on the title of a popular feminist self-help health book from the 1970s, our bodies are also our texts. Except that in this case, the bodies in question would be historical rather than biological, historical in the sense of being rooted in a particular ancestry or background, in a particular culture and set of experiences.

But how is this not racism? It depends on the answer to this question: Are moral and intellectual qualities rooted in biology? The answer is NO. Our racial and ethnic makeup is relevant to our knowledge and therefore is part of the process of mutual education, to the extent that it provides a framework for comparison and a set of diverse experiences according to which we interpret reality. In the abstract, no one would question the relevance of lived experience and interpretation to the development of ideas, to the creation of discursive frameworks, the analysis of reality, and the prescription of action. To question the validity of lived experience and interpretation when filtered through the lens of ascriptive categories makes sense only insofar as these ascriptive categories are historically suspect; their exclusion is justified only if the intention behind their use is to exclude rather than include, if it serves invidious rather than remedial purposes.[32] Fortunately, it is no longer necessary to make the case for diversity (racial, ethnic, or otherwise) solely on the basis of what should not happen. The available research evidence showing the multiple ways in which campus diversity has a positive impact on the college experience, both from the point of view of students as well as faculty, is not sufficient to end the discussion but it certainly helps cast the conversation in a brighter light.[33]

F. Meeting the Diversity Challenge

If education requires embodied knowledge, diversity is not just about equity. Equity, meaning a fair distribution of opportunities and resources that brings material gain to those with previously limited access to those opportunities

---

[32]See Randall Kennedy. "Persuasion and Distrust: The Affirmative Action Debate," in Nicolaus Mills, ed. *Debating Affirmative Action*. New York: Delta Trade Books, 1994, pp. 48–67.

[33]See, for example, Mitchell J. Chang "The Positive Educational Effects of Racial Diversity on Campus," pp. 175–186; Sylvia Hurtado, "Linking Diversity and Educational Purpose: How Diversity Affects the Classroom Environment and Student Development," pp. 187–204; Kermit Daniel, Dan A. Black, and Jeffrey Smith, "Racial Differences in the Effects of College Quality and Student Body Diversity on Wages," pp. 221–232; Jeffrey F. Milem, Increasing Diversity Benefits: How Campus Climate and Teaching Methods Affect Student Outcomes," pp. 233–250; and Roxane Harvey Gudeman, "Faculty Experience with Diversity: A Case Study of Macalester College," pp. 251–276, in Gary Orfield, ed. *Diversity Challenged*. Cambridge, MA: Harvard Education Publishing Group, 2001.

and resources, is important but it is not sufficient to meet the challenge of diversity. If going up to knowledge means not just listening to a living voice but to a mixture of distinct living voices, the inescapable conclusion is that the process of mutual education requires representation of all the possible dimensions along which these living voices can make comparisons. From this vantage point, more than a representational dilemma of what SUNY and CUNY face is a representational *imperative*. Why? Because representation produces vessels for the creation and the dissemination of knowledge. To achieve diversity, the university cannot rely just on disembodied knowledge. Even disembodied knowledge requires agents to make its way into the curriculum. It is possible for non-diverse faculty to bring diversity into the process of mutual education, but experience suggests that this does not happen as often as it should.

All too often, descriptive representation is decried as extraneous to the real article, a false proxy for substance or qualifications. This itself is a false dichotomy. We are not individuals in the abstract. Barzun is right when he argues that "generalities about groups, even when true, tell us nothing about the individual, and … it is the individual we must judge."[34] Yet our group identity is never completely absent from our definition of self. I cannot separate my individuality from my Puerto Rican-ness, even though I can certainly differentiate myself from the average census bureau Puerto Rican who has no college degree, speaks mostly Spanish, is a blue-collar worker, and does not own a house. Thus, while it is possible for a white North American to teach about Puerto Ricans, the advantage I have is that I can do it from the inside out while also being objective because I do not embody the universality of Puerto Rican experience. In *Faculty of Color*, American Studies Professor Adrian Gaskins tells a story that speaks to this issue. He recalls being questioned about his objectivity concerning the teaching of slavery in the United States because he is African American. "Would you assume the objectivity of a white professor talking about slavery, or would you ask her the same question?" Gaskins asked the skeptical student. "It would never have occurred to me to ask that question if you were white," was her answer.[35] Both in the student's question and her reply to his, Gaskins saw racial bias. But it is possible that the student simply assumed that objectivity is compromised if the subject matter of instruction is descriptively represented by the teacher. Thus, while Gaskins was right to confront the student with her potential bias, he should also have noted that his objectivity was possible, given that he had never been a slave.

---

[34] Barzun, Op. Cit., p. xiv.

[35] Adrian Gaskins, "Putting the Color in Colorado: On Being Black and Teaching Ethnic Studies at the University of Colorado-Boulder," In Christine A. Stanley, ed. *Faculty of Color*. Bolton, Mass.: Anker Publishing Company, Inc., 2006, pp. 142–143.

The example of the census bureau Puerto Rican raises another question: if in the process of mutual education, all perspectives must be considered, how do we incorporate the point of view of those whose primary language is not English, who rent rather than own property, and who pick up our garbage, build our buildings, and grow our food? If we decide to go beyond rescuing the working-class from the "condescension of history," as historian E. P. Thompson put it, how is that to be done?[36] This is a thorny question. I cannot possibly answer it here except to suggest that in order to remove class as an obstacle for higher education, and further, to bring class into the diversity equation, we may need more than just a fiscal climate that makes college affordable to everyone who belongs there. True democracy may be necessary, as a way of life rather than as a mere system of governance. But what does democracy as a way of life mean? I believe Walter C. Parker is on the right track when he suggests that it is a process of nurturing the qualities that define citizenship among everybody, *everywhere*, within the university and without. And what qualities are these? The minimum set, Parker tells us, include a sense of the inescapability of mutuality, practical judgment, shared civic knowledge, shared civic know-how, and a thirst for justice, for oneself and for others. To these, he adds a disposition to counter hatred with love.[37]

If Parker is right, having students and professors from every department of knowledge, as well as from every department of life in the university, may turn out to be a rather modest proposal. Modest or not, the goal of diversity requires it and the limit should not be parity. At SUNY and CUNY, a greater representation of Latinos among students and faculty would contribute to that goal. As a measure of diversity, descriptive representation, Latino or otherwise, must find its template in demographic realities, Latino or otherwise. This is not "turning prejudice upside down,"[38] so long as the match is inclusive and/or remedial in nature. I find it interesting that such a staunch critic of race-thinking as Barzun himself would provide an excellent justification for a match between demography and representation when he writes that "in social judgments the mind's eye must vividly see a crowd of diverse persons."[39] The question then is, what constitutes a crowd? How much diversity is enough? If Latinos are 16 percent of the population, do we stop hiring Latinos once the faculty at SUNY is 16 percent Latino? Parity should be the starting point of

---

[36]E. P. Thompson. *The Making of the English Working Class*. London: V. Gollancz, 1963, p. 13.

[37]Walter C. Parker. *Teaching Democracy, Unity and Diversity in Public Life*. New York: Teachers College Press, 2003, pp. 23–24.

[38]Barzun, Op. Cit., p. xv.

[39]Ibid., p. xvii.

assessment not the final objective. For, as William Blake put it: "You never know what is enough unless you know what is more than enough."[40]

II. Creating Educational Equity: A Brief Look at the History and Development of the SUNY EOCs and EOP

Carlos N. Medina, Assistant Provost, SUNY Office of Diversity and Educational Equity, and Jeffrey Scott, Grant Development Specialist, SUNY Office of Diversity and Educational Equity

While the history of SUNY is certainly a rich one, it would not be complete without telling the story of its Educational Opportunity Centers (EOCs) and Educational Opportunity Program (EOP). These two major initiatives have not only stood the test of time, but are needed just as much today, if not more, than when they were first conceived in the 1960s. Now, over forty years later, these programs continue to make a tremendous contribution to New York State and wherever its graduates decide to live and do business. The impact, however small, can be felt throughout the nation and, for that matter, the world.

Since its inception, SUNY has pledged to "Let Each Become All He Is Capable of Being," and made a commitment that "every student capable of completing a program of higher education shall have the opportunity to do so."[41] The EOCs and EOP are programs with transformational power and an incredibly interesting history that speaks volumes about social justice and equality. This chapter will outline the origins and shared history of the EOCs and EOP, describing their creations and developments both together and separately, and conclude with a discussion of the impact of these opportunity programs.

A. Historical Development of the "Special Programs"

As high school graduate numbers grew and expansion in an increasingly technological society demanded highly-skilled personnel, the enlarged demand for higher education and its tremendous expansion in the 1950s and 1960s animated the need for a more diverse student population and professoriate.

---

[40]William Blake, "Proverbs of Hell," in William Blake. *Collected Poems*, edited by W.B. Yeats. London: Routledge, 2002, p. 167.

[41]State University of New York, A General Plan for the Organization, Development, Coordination and Operation of the Educational Opportunity Programs of the State University of New York. This was submitted to the Board of Regents in compliance with Education Law §6452 as amended in 1970. Criteria for determining economic disadvantagement were established by the Board of Regents and was the same as for Higher Education Opportunity Programs at the private colleges. Policy Title: Guidelines for the Operation of Educational Opportunity Program (EOP), Document Number 3600. Effective Date: January 01, 1970).

Dramatic changes that began to change the scope and purpose of public higher education in the early 1950s resulted from increases in governmental funding that prompted more supervision of admission and accessibility policies, curriculum, and the general operations of institutions. The *Brown v. Board of Education* decision, the civil rights movement, and the social reform movements of the 1960s energized efforts to address the exclusionary nature of higher education in the United States and necessitated greater inclusion in public higher education. Through its "War on Poverty" and "Great Society" programs, the Johnson administration addressed social ills and provided financial support for education as well as housing, jobs, and social programs. Predominantly black colleges and universities had already created programs to assist financially and academically disadvantaged students, with the Morgan State College program serving as a prime example of an influential initiative. In the early 1960s, predominantly white colleges and universities also began efforts to admit a broader range of students, thus reflecting growing concern with inequality and social responsibility. Democratic principles merged with an increased desire for social mobility among the underserved.

SUNY was founded on the principles of inclusion, equity, and access. The accessibility of higher education for traditionally underrepresented groups was cited as a reason for developing a public system: "some members of New York's large minority groups have had difficulty in securing access to educational facilities on an equal basis with college level but on the professional and graduate school levels as well. This discrimination is repellent to the American spirit and must be eliminated."[42] The creation of the nation's largest public comprehensive university was New York State's progressive response to urgent social and economic needs. To this day, SUNY strives to realize its foundational mission to "provide to the people of New York educational services of the highest quality, with the broadest possible access, fully representative of all segments of the population" and to "meet the needs of both traditional and non-traditional students and to address local, regional and state needs and goals."[43] SUNY's performance is tied, in large part, to its ability to recruit and retain students, faculty, and administrators that reflect various aspects of human difference among the people of New York, and its capacity to create knowledge of benefit to society and educate new generations of students for leadership positions in our culturally diverse and globalized environment.

---

[42]State of New York. Report of the Temporary Commission on the Need for a State University. Legislative document number 30. (Albany, NY: Williams Press, 1948), p. 15. Because the first mention of minority or disadvantaged students did not occur until sixteen years later in the 1964 State University Master Plan, Wallace (1980, p. 211) notes that "one of the very principles upon which the State University was built was ignored until the 1960's."

[43]SUNY Mission Statement, 2009.

1.   Common Origins and Shared History

In the early 1960s, just before opportunity programs were developed, there were only a few compensatory education programs in New York State and nothing existed on a system-wide level. There was also national concern due to the plight of the urban youth for whom the opportunity of specialized training and higher education was a remote possibility. It was clear that not enough was being done in the area of recruitment, admission, and retention of historically underrepresented students in New York State's colleges and universities.

The significant expansion of public higher education in New York State was a result of public desire for more educational access, the belief of the state legislature in quality post-secondary education, and the resolve of Governor Nelson Rockefeller. New York State's interest in expanding higher education opportunity prompted two studies: The Heald Committee on Higher Education reported to the governor and the Board of Regents in 1960 that enrollments in New York's colleges and universities would double in ten years and triple in twenty five; and the New York state legislature's report by Herman Wells in 1964 that aimed to help the legislature better understand Rockefeller's higher education proposals and develop its own. In the early 1960s, several reform-minded legislators, most of whom were from New York City, were elected to the legislature. They were sensitive to the wretched socioeconomic conditions that increasingly hampered inner-city populations across the country, and their ambitions for liberal progress lessened Republican domination of the legislature.[44] The Wells study forcefully stated, "the magnitude of the challenge is now so great that only the New York State Legislature can help the public universities meet it adequately ... [and] provide the educational opportunity needed by New Yorkers [to] reach new heights of excellence."[45] Of particular relevance to this chapter's focus, Wells also suggested "special programs" by way of the development of "youth colleges" for the socioeconomically disadvantaged.

A recognition of the need for and commitment to providing greater educational equity for historically underrepresented groups was made in the 1960s by both the Board of Regents and SUNY trustees. The Regents' goals emphasized "[e]qual and open educational opportunity beyond high school ... unrestricted by race, creed, or national origin, and to be available until each person's needs for economic and social self-sufficiency are met" and "educational opportunity available in each economic-geographic region so that factors of cost and

---

[44]In 1964, the Democrats gained control of the traditionally Republican legislature for the first time in thirty years. Although the Democrats had lost control of the Senate in 1966, they maintained a majority in the assembly.

[45]Wells (1964), p. 11.

accessibility are more even throughout the state."[46] SUNY's 1964 revision of its Master Plan, which recognized the vulnerability of the disadvantaged and the need for two-year colleges to "develop the skills, study habits, and social behavior required for a fuller and more productive life," also expressed an aspiration that "many of the disadvantaged who undertake these programs will eventually be trained as technicians. Others will be encouraged to continue their studies in four-year colleges and graduate schools."[47]

As early as 1960, New York State had created several small compensatory educational initiatives to provide greater access to higher education for the disadvantaged. One of the most comprehensive was the pre-baccalaureate program established at the City College of the City University of New York (CUNY) in 1965. The success of this program led to the development of a program known as SEEK (Search for Education, Elevation, and Knowledge) in 1966. Its success also led to a state legislative mandate, sponsored by CUNY, to provide higher educational opportunity to disadvantaged students in impoverished areas of New York City. Only a year after its inception, however, SEEK found it had been left out of CUNY's budget for the coming year. This led to public hearings of the Joint Legislative Committee on Higher Education, and further investigation found that funding to continue SEEK also was not in the governor's executive budget. Students enrolled in the SEEK program testified at the hearings, emphasizing the positive impact of SEEK and their desire to continue their education. After much political debate and lengthy compromises, funds were eventually secured to continue SEEK within CUNY.

First-year Assemblyman Arthur Eve from Buffalo became impressed by the positive impact SEEK had on students at a hearing of the Joint Legislative Committee on Higher Education, and decided to bring the SEEK program to upstate New York, in hope that it would address the needs of the Buffalo community, in particular. Along with Senator Earl Bridges of Niagara Falls, Eve's efforts were instrumental in obtaining funds to begin the program. In 1967, the Joint Legislative Committee on Higher Education requested funds to support SEEK in areas outside of New York City. $500,000 was appropriated to SUNY under Chapter 170 of the Laws of New York in 1967. Because Eve had worked so hard to support the legislation to expand SEEK, it was decided to allot the entirety of the funds to establishing a program in Buffalo. Buffalo State College became home to the first upstate program, establishing it as the first effort on the part of SUNY to provide higher educational opportunities to the disadvantaged at the four-year college level.

---

[46]The Regents Statewide Plan for the Expansion and Development of Higher Education, 1964. Albany: The State University of New York and The State Education Department, 1965, p. 28.

[47]The SUNY 1964 Master Plan entitled: Stature and Excellence: Focus for the Future, pp. 15–16, 13.

In May of 1967, Buffalo State College announced eligibility requirements for SEEK and set the first application deadline for August 1. SEEK students would be non-matriculated, given special teachers, courses, and tutoring, as well as free books, tuition waivers, and modest financial support as needed. Successful applicants would enter a pre-baccalaureate program and after one year, the students would apply to the college for matriculation and degree status. The admissions process for SEEK was separate from the college's standard admissions office. Meetings were held with local schools and community groups, posters were printed and distributed, and radio and television ads were utilized. A Community Advisory Council was also formed to recommend specific students for consideration. The program's initial curriculum included non-credit remedial courses taken by all students.

There was a widely recognized urgent need to develop appropriate opportunities for young people who were beyond the normal reach of colleges. The need for higher education by the youth of New York State was so great that community colleges were unprepared for this demand and in effect, denied access for the socioeconomically disadvantaged who could not afford the required tuition.[48] The Wells study called for a new setting in which to educate the state's disadvantaged youth by urging the legislature, SUNY, and CUNY to tackle the problem using more "socially and culturally acceptable settings" than community colleges.[49] In a report commissioned by the SUNY Board of Trustees, before establishing what would, in effect, be another type of two-year college in the state university system, consultant Dorothy Knoell noted that New York State's commitment to post-secondary education had not resolved the question of which agencies or institutions would extend opportunity to the most disadvantaged high school graduates. With three types of two-year colleges (independent junior colleges, local community colleges, and state-administered agricultural and technical colleges) the need for a new two-year institution, vocational in nature and serving, among others, disadvantaged youth became the basis of Knoell's study. In the introduction to this work, SUNY Chancellor Samuel Gould stressed that the greatest number of young people who could profit from further education "are largest and opportunity least abundant in the urban areas, particularly for the economically and educationally disadvantaged, and it is their plight which prompted this study … [which] involves research into some of the realities of expanding educational opportunity in the State University, and an examination of the philosophic commitment of the State to the provision of universal opportunity for education beyond the high school."[50]

---

[48]See Martens 1985.

[49]Wells 1964, p. 35.

[50]Samuel B. Gould, "Introduction," in Knoell, 1966, p. vii.

Knoell concluded that, from an institutional perspective, the "State University should look to its present two-year colleges to expand opportunity before seriously considering the creation of a new type of institution."[51] She also stressed the need for expansion in order to provide a full spectrum of occupational and liberal education programs leading to certificates of completion and degrees, including remedial or developmental work, and appropriate to the diverse needs and abilities of the people to be served. The study concluded that "New York State has far to go before all such disadvantage [related to race, social class, quality of high school preparation, motivation, or place of residence] is removed or even alleviated. To provide more of the same type of opportunity now offered is to do little to remove the educational disadvantage."[52]

The result was the creation of four "Urban Centers" under the administration of associated community colleges. Soon after, many community colleges took part in the SEEK program[53] and even more participated in a new program of open-door admission, counseling, and developmental education known as "full opportunity."[54]

2. *The Educational Opportunity Centers (EOCs)*

The EOCs, then known as Urban Centers, got their start in 1966. They were based on a recommendation from Wells' report, which focused on the importance of serving the disadvantaged by providing educational opportunity, particularly to those in urban settings. He called for the creation of "youth colleges" to provide a combination of work experience and organized instruction fit to individual needs. The "special programs," as they were known at the time, began as a direct result of the 1960s recognition that segments of the population were not being adequately served by traditional educational methods. Each center was to not only offer vocational training and college preparation, but also services aimed at all surrounding residents and their communities.

As the story goes, while giving a tour of Harlem to Queen Wilhelmina of the Netherlands, Governor Nelson Rockefeller noticed that many young and able adults were loitering on the streets, idle and unemployed. He called attention to the plight of urban youth "for whom neither the regular four-year

---

[51]Knoell 1966, pp. 201. See also pp. 193 and 205–16.

[52]Knoell 1966, p. 204.

[53]State University of New York, A General Plan for the Organization, Development, Coordination and Operation of the Educational Opportunity Programs of the State University of New York. This was submitted to the Board of Regents in compliance with Education Law §6452 as amended in 1970. Criteria for determining economic disadvantagement were established by the Board of Regents and was the same as for Higher Education Opportunity Programs at the private colleges.

[54]See Chapter 708 of the 1973 Laws of New York State.

nor the community college now provides the answer."[55] Upon Rockefeller's authorization, a study was conducted that recommended the establishment of experimental centers in four locations to provide needed vocational training to economically disadvantaged populations. After reviewing Wells' report, Rockefeller suggested to Chancellor Samuel Gould that he look at the possibility of creating these urban colleges to serve young adults in programs combining liberal arts and technical subjects. In the fall of 1966, four community colleges were invited to cooperate with SUNY in establishing the Urban Centers: Borough of Manhattan Community College, New York City Community College, Hudson Valley Community College, and Erie County Community College. Directors at the centers procured funds from the federal Vocational Education Act to purchase equipment for training programs appropriate to the region's training and employment demands. The Urban Centers emphasized developing occupational training to prepare students for employment, but it was also found that many of the students who attended the Urban Centers were adults who had not completed a high school education. Therefore, student interest in obtaining a high school degree and going beyond training programs into college prompted the Urban Centers to develop high school equivalency and college prep programs. SUNY followed the national trend of providing opportunities for the disadvantaged through training programs and two-year colleges without anything planned beyond entry-level initiatives. An unexpected student demand for education beyond training programs led to the establishment of the Cooperative College Centers in 1969 as a bridge program for outreach, skill development, and preparation for entry into the EOPs that were being developed on several SUNY campuses.

In September of 1973, the Urban Centers and the Cooperative College Centers were consolidated, reducing the total number of centers from thirteen to ten. This merger reduced duplication and formally established the EOCs. The newly created EOCs were placed under the supervision of the Office of Special Programs at SUNY System Administration and involved coordination with various state agencies. The primary function of the EOCs was to develop occupational and educational skills to meet the needs of disadvantaged youths and adults in metropolitan areas. Academic offerings included college preparatory courses, credit-potential courses, job training courses, and high school equivalency courses. In addition, education-related services included tutoring, academic advisement, and career counseling. As an initial thrust of SUNY's efforts to empower the disadvantaged, the development of these urban occupational and college preparatory programs played a major role in the development of the EOP.

---

[55]Cited by Kenneth T. Doran (associate executive for two-year colleges) in the Foreword to Knoell, p. ix.

3.   The Educational Opportunity Program (EOP)

The development of the "special programs" was a direct result of the political pressure and will in New York State at the time. The impetus for state-funded programs to assist minority and disadvantaged populations originating within the New York state legislature, particularly came from the black and Puerto Rican legislative caucus, including New York City politicians such as Percy Sutton, Charles Rangel, Basil Paterson, Shirley Chisholm, and Bobbi Garcia. The eventual inclusion of the EOP in SUNY at the four-year college level did not come from within the system, but was imposed from the outside.

On the heels of those efforts, which had established the SEEK program at CUNY in 1966, Assemblyman Arthur Eve gave further force to the principles of access and opportunity by spearheading the effort and developing the appropriation bill that created the EOP program within SUNY in 1967. Modeled on CUNY's SEEK program, the first SUNY institution to operate an EOP program was Buffalo State College and the enrollment for that first class was a respectable 249 students.

In the following year, Assemblyman Eve was able to obtain sufficient funding to permit expansion to ten campuses. In 1969, EOP was codified in Education Law §6452, which formally established the provisions of all the higher education opportunity programs: SEEK, EOP, and the Higher Education Opportunity Program (HEOP) for independent colleges and universities.[56] This demonstrated a recognition that programs for disadvantaged students should be an integral part of New York State's plan for higher education, rather than an appendage. In the 1970–71 academic year, thirty campuses enrolled more than 4,600 EOP students.

In 1972, the SUNY Faculty Senate Committee on Expanding Educational Opportunity published a model for EOP that integrated SEEK programs into the existing structures of the university system and brought EOP students directly into the college setting with all other students. The new EOP model did not emphasize remediation or skill development as much as the SEEK model and students were expected to carry a full course load of regular classes. In addition, EOP revised the guidelines for the academically disadvantaged and financial eligible.

On July 1, 2007, EOP was officially renamed the "Arthur O. Eve Educational Opportunity Program" in recognition of the former deputy speaker of the assembly for his foresight and commitment to educational equity that opened the doors of higher education to so many New Yorkers.

---

[56]Chapter 917 of the Education Law of 1970 separated the public institutions from the private colleges and universities in regard to administering SEEK. All funding for post-secondary education programs for the disadvantaged (including SEEK/EOP/HEOP, the Urban Centers, the Cooperative Colleges, and the College Discovery Program) was still covered by a single appropriation in the mid-1970s. See Wallace (1980), pp. 121–24.

B. The Impact and Advancement of Educational Equity

Today ten EOCs and two Outreach Career Counseling Centers serve over 15,000 students annually. EOCs are still under the supervision of SUNY System Administration out of the University Center for Academic and Workforce Development (UCAWD), which assumed oversight in 1997. Each center is affiliated with a sponsoring campus within the SUNY or CUNY system. All are committed to providing access to higher education and employment to the most underserved and economically disadvantaged populations in New York State. They offer state-of-the art technology labs and a host of innovative academic and vocational programs and services that lead to certificates of completion, state-level certification, and/or a GED. Graduates of EOC have moved into jobs in business and industry, health, and governmental service either directly or after further education for which they were prepared at the EOC.

The EOP, which is the second oldest program of its kind in the country and is also directed within System Administration by the Office of Opportunity Programs, serves approximately 11,000 students a year on forty-three campuses across the SUNY system. At 84.5 percent, first-year retention rates for SUNY EOP students outrank the national public average by 11.5 percent; six-year graduation rates for SUNY EOP students, 62.6 percent at doctoral degree-granting institutions, outpace the national average by more than seven percent. Additionally, more than 2,200 EOP students maintained a 3.0 cumulative average and received honor certificates in the spring 2007 semester.[57] EOP combines access, academic support, and supplemental financial assistance to make higher education possible for students who have the potential to succeed despite poor preparation and limited financial resources. EOP remains at the forefront of highly successful programs that increase the college attendance, persistence, and success of low-income and first generation college students. To date, the program has graduated over 55,000 students. The alumni represent the entire spectrum of licensed professions, including: civil service, entrepreneurs, politicians, journalists, and even a college president.

Several other programs administered by UCAWD and the Office of Opportunity Programs provide access, support, training, technology, and financial aid to hundreds of thousands of educationally and economically disadvantaged New Yorkers. UCAWD's mission is to promote the socioeconomic well-being of its disadvantaged citizens by creating and sustaining high quality education and workforce initiatives. The statewide network of centers has pioneered providing urban communities with innovative academic programs leading to higher education and vocational training programs leading

---

[57]State University of New York, "SUNY Educational Opportunity Program Celebrates 40 Years: Graduation and Retention rates Outpace National Average." Press release: November 2, 2007.

251

to gainful employment. In addition, UCAWD serves disadvantaged students through: 1) the Bridge Program, which uses performance measures consistent with the Workforce Investment Act, validated skill standards, and continuous improvement concepts towards the outcome of gainful employment for students; 2) the Advanced Technology Training and Information Networking (ATTAIN) program, a statewide technology initiative with over thirty locations that provides communities access to new technologies, education, and technology training that increase employment opportunities and wage prospects; and 3) the Jobs for Youth Apprenticeship Program (JFYAP), which prepares "at-risk" economically disadvantaged in-school and out-of-school youth for entry into skilled occupations, apprenticeships, or post-secondary education.

Within the Office of Opportunity Programs, EOP provides access, academic support, and financial aid to students who show promise of mastering college-level work but may not otherwise be admitted. Offered primarily to full-time students who are New York State residents, EOP serves students who meet economic and academic qualifications and reached over ten thousand students in 2008–09. The Office of Opportunity Programs also serves historically underrepresented students through the Graduate Opportunity Program and Economically Disadvantaged First Professional Study, which provide tuition waivers for economically disadvantaged students to undertake graduate level study, and Gaining Early Awareness and Readiness for Undergraduate Programs (Gear Up), which create the aspiration for higher education among 4,000 at-risk eighth grade students in New York State and provide them with the guidance, incentives, skills, and knowledge that will aid them in gaining admission to college and succeeding once they are there.

Both UCAWD and the Office of Opportunity Programs report to the Office of Diversity and Educational Equity (ODEE) established in August 2007.[58] ODEE provides leadership and strategic direction to all SUNY campuses for developing and implementing a portfolio of diversity programs. Its fundamental academic mission is to help SUNY fulfill its responsibility to create knowledge that will benefit society and prepare a new generation of civic and corporate leaders, as well as a highly skilled and technically proficient workforce that can work effectively in a culturally diverse environment. Through the creative marshaling of resources, strategic investments, and consultation with chief diversity officers system-wide, ODEE develops a focused approach to enhance access, success, diversity, and academic excellence at SUNY.

New York State is currently facing a historic economic crisis at the same time it struggles with dramatic demographic changes. The combination of state budget cuts to SUNY and increasing applications to SUNY colleges

---

[58]Much of the information on ODEE here is derived from the office's Mission Statement and 2009 report "Keeping Pace: Racial/Ethnic Diversity of Students and Faculty at the State University of New York," particularly pp. 3–4 and 16–18.

and universities due to their affordability relative to private institutions has made it harder for the economically disadvantaged and other historically underrepresented groups to access a postsecondary education, continue in their studies, and graduate. New York State faces the "unsustainable paradox of a public higher education system that was originally established to maximize access and equity but may be driven by economic necessity to implement policies that contradict its foundational principles."[59] New York is undergoing another demographic transformation and will continue to experience significant growth in minority groups, especially the Hispanic community, with the consequent socio-cultural effects and greater educational needs. However, the composition of the SUNY faculty and student body has not kept pace with these changes. ODEE was established in large measure to respond to this challenge. By creating new opportunities that enhance academic excellence through strategic investments in diversity and inclusion, SUNY can make a significant contribution to New York State as it adjusts to demographic and economic changes. With a mandate to act holistically for the inclusion of students and faculty from diverse backgrounds, ODEE is integral to SUNY's mission and responsibility to New York State.

The EOCs and EOP continue to have a major impact on the lives of so many New Yorkers. Indeed, these programs have transformed lives. This is true for thousands of academic alumni and skilled laborers and clearly illustrated by the sixteen outstanding graduates honored by the EOC Distinguished Alumni project in 2005 and celebrated at EOP's fortieth anniversary in 2007. The spirit of the EOCs and EOP is shaped by the diversity of people it brings together as community. It is a force that leads its members through struggle to achievement, creates strength of mind and character, and empowers both the individual and the community.

References

Knoell, Dorothy M. *Toward Educational Opportunity for All.* Albany: State University of New York, 1966.

Martens, Freda R. H. "The Historical Development of the Community Colleges of the State University of New York." SUNY Community College Topical Paper Number 1. Albany: SUNY Office of Community Colleges, 1985.

Office of Diversity and Educational Equity. "Keeping Pace: Racial/Ethnic Diversity of Students and Faculty at the State University of New York." Albany: April 2009.

---

[59]"Keeping Pace," p. 3.

Wallace, Jeffrey Joseph. *Historical Development of the Educational Opportunity Programs in the State University of New York.* Ph. D. dissertation, State University of New York at Buffalo. Ann Arbor: UMI, 1980. 8104251.

Wells, Herman. The Legislature and Higher Education in New York State: A Report by the Legislature's Consultant on Higher Education. New York: Academy for Educational Development, 1964.

SUNY in and of the World

Introduction

James Ketterer, Deputy Provost, State University of New York

Universities are perhaps the most international of institutions. With a built-in mandate to exchange people and ideas across borders and cultures, and a mission that transcends geopolitical limitations, universities embody the spirit and practice of what we now call "globalization." There is a tendency to think that globalization is a new phenomenon, which is not true except perhaps in worldwide, high-speed communication. Global connections have existed in ebbs and flows for the entire span of human existence—and for much of that time universities have also existed; this is no coincidence.

Yet the internationalization of a university, particularly a system as large and complex as SUNY, does not happen without determined effort. Academic leaders must make it a clear priority, policies must support internationalization, resources must be put in place, and an openness to "all things international" and a serious emphasis on international programs must be inculcated on campuses. As with all policy goals, to truly be an international institution requires translating grand ideas into concrete action and doing so through sustained effort. This chapter addresses how that has happened—and might continue to happen—at SUNY.

There is a yawning gap in comparative analysis in international education. John Halsey brilliantly fills that gap with his paper on "SUNY from an English Perspective." He notes the deep differences between English and American universities in general, and SUNY's comprehensive system of higher education in particular. In terms of access, size, and mission, SUNY at its founding in 1948 was large and ambitious compared to the small and elite universities in the England. However, the governments of Prime Minister Tony Blair invested a great deal of financial resources and political capital in widening access to higher education. John Halsey notes that the effects would have been better had the English heeded lessons from SUNY's history

255

and he identifies areas in which SUNY can learn from England's recent experience. That, after all, is the power of comparative analysis and Professor Halsey is right to remind those on both sides of the Atlantic that our two nations and our respective university systems have much to learn from one another.

Carla Back's paper in this chapter highlights the history of international education at SUNY. She makes the interesting point that a number of institutions that became members of the system were already engaged in international activities before SUNY's creation in 1948. She lays out the key details of international activities on SUNY's campuses and the policies undertaken by the SUNY Board of Trustees and at SUNY System Administration. She also makes the important observation that the internationalization of SUNY (or any university) is more than a collection of study abroad programs, as important as those programs might be. University partnerships, research exchange programs, the attraction of international students to SUNY, and the establishment of SUNY programs overseas each play a key role in how SUNY engages the world beyond the borders of New York State. In addition, the internationalization of SUNY's curriculum and advances in the teaching of international affairs are important recent components of how SUNY is ensuring that the citizens of New York State become citizens of the world.

International education is no longer something that can be contained in a small office in the basement of a campus. It is central to the university's mission and involves the entirety of faculty, staff, students, and alumni. This chapter makes an important contribution to understanding where international education has come from at SUNY and where it might go next.

I. SUNY's Strategic Role in International Higher Education

Karla Back, SUNY College of Technology at Alfred

"Perhaps the greatest power of educational exchange is the power to convert nations into peoples and to translate ideologies into human aspirations."—Senator J. William Fulbright

SUNY's engagement with the world has varied origins. Sensaburo Kodzu of Japan, a member of the class of 1877 at the New York State Normal School at Albany, was the first documented international student at one of SUNY's future campuses. Other foreign students, such as Christian Ringwald of Germany, who studied at Oneonta in 1905, came to the campuses over the decades on individual informal bases.[1] In turn, in the summer of 1953, SUNY first offered credit for overseas international study programs, some thirty years after many other colleges had taken the plunge. Early pioneers included Marymount College and the University of Delaware, which established French language programs for juniors to study abroad in 1923. Two years later, Smith College and Rosary College followed in Paris and Fribourg and by 1926, Marymount had established a program in Rome.[2] International programs soon proliferated around the country.

A number of future SUNY campuses were involved in international education well before the system was even established. For instance, SUNY Oneonta reported that an early 1930s student International Relations Club (IRC) was established and popular; a number of Oneonta students and faculty attended international education conferences at Syracuse University and St. Lawrence University and presented and studied "Regional and Cultural Groupings as Factors in World Peace," "The Clashing of Ideologies," and "The Maintenance of Peace." Oneonta alumni reported Russian and German students studying on campus during 1935–38.[3] Faculty, as well as student exchanges, developed after World War II with countries such as China, Syria, England, and India.

A.   International Programs and Initiatives in the 1950s

In the summer of 1953, SUNY became the first multi-campus college system in the United States to offer credit for "student participation in institutionally backed overseas activities."[4] Unfortunately, this early venture in overseas study caused a stir when an external agent was involved in the coordination of the summer trip abroad and an airline stranded one of the study groups in London.

These approved programs were travel tours which were arranged by a travel agent and one or more SUNY faculty. An incident occurred in the summer of 1953 that focused a spotlight on the new and emerging SUNY sponsored educational tours. A group of sixty-six students and faculty from the Crane School of Music at the Teachers College at Potsdam were stranded at the airport in

---

[1]Pierce, Lisa Ann. *The History of Foreign Students at the State University College at Oneonta*. Oneonta, NY: SUNY, 1981.

[2]Freeman, Stephen A. "Undergraduate Study Abroad: U.S. College Sponsored Programs." In *Undergraduate Study Abroad: U.S. College Sponsored Programs*, by Stephen A. Freeman, 6–7. New York: Institute of International Education, 1966.

[3]Pierce, Lisa Ann. *The History of Foreign Students at the State University College at Oneonta*. Oneonta, NY: SUNY, 1981.

[4]Dean, Larrie John. "The Development of Policy for the Centralized Administration of the Overseas Academic Programs of the State University of New York: A History," Syracuse, N.Y.: Syracuse University, April 14, 1974.

London. The Flying Tigers Airline in London returned the SUNY students and faculty to the United States three days later after a member of the SUNY Board of Trustees intervened to ensure their safe and timely return home. The negative attention from this incident challenged these newly-approved educational tours and much more stringent regulations were developed for governing all future similar international education ventures.

The first written record of SUNY system-wide involvement in international education was a memorandum from Hermann Cooper, executive dean for teacher education, on November 16, 1953 approving a series of "educational tours."[5]

This inauspicious beginning led to a review of the incident by System Administration and President Carlson's decision that the state university would not continue to support the type of existing programs, essentially "educational tours."[6] In 1955 a Committee on Foreign Study was established, including presidents of all SUNY institutions sponsoring overseas study. This group developed the first set of governing principles for the SUNY system-wide international program activities.[7]

Included in the resulting "Memo of Regulations Governing the Operation of Foreign Study Programs" were a number of guidelines that indicate how the early international education programs were designed. Significant regulations included:

- All educational programs in foreign countries were university-wide programs sponsored by the system and operated under the direction of the president of SUNY.
- The president of SUNY shall approve all operated unit programs, and they were responsible to the president. No college or university of the system could receive any financial gain from any foreign study programs ... any surplus was to be paid to the state university.
- Any student in any unit of SUNY could enroll in any of the foreign study programs. Credit was to be recognized by all state-operated units.
- Students from colleges outside of SUNY could enroll, as well, in a SUNY foreign study program on a full-time or part-time basis.[8]

---

[5]Cooper, Hermann. "Memorandum from Hermann Cooper" Albany, NY: SUNY, November 16, 1953.

[6]Carlson, William S. Summary of Syracuse Symposium. Albany, NY: SUNY, 1954.

[7]Dean, Larrie John. "The Development of Policy for the Centralized Administration of the Overseas Academic Programs of the State University of New York: A History." Syracuse, NY: Syracuse University, April 14, 1974.

[8]Committee on Foreign Study. Appendix B Regulations Governing the Operation of Foreign Studies Programs. Albany: SUNY, 1955.

To avoid further problems with these summer programs, the summer of 1956 found SUNY participating in the Experiment in International Living, an established program based in Putney, Vermont.[9] During the Depression, Donald Watt, a personnel director for Syracuse University, had hit upon a simple idea to improve understanding across nations and cultures through summer programs that included the experience of living with a family in the host country. The first Experiment in International Living contingent departed New York in June, 1932, on a ship bound for Germany; the twenty-three students on board were trailblazers for thousands who have followed in their footsteps, building friendships and crossing cultural divides. Over the last seventy-five years, programs have changed the lives of more than 100,000 people, many witnessing first-hand the impact of refugee crises, poverty, and conflict. From 1957–65, all SUNY summer programs were coordinated and organized in conjunction with the Experiment in International Living Program.[10] The decision to use this well-established program demonstrated System Administration's concern about Overseas Study Programs after the debacle in 1953.

Early SUNY faculty also became involved in the international educational arena as Fulbright Scholars beginning in the 1950s and continuing today, with more than ten SUNY faculty on global scholar assignments for the 2008–09 school year.

B. International Programs and Initiatives in the 1960s

In 1961, the trustees approved a proposal by Thomas Hamilton, the third president of SUNY, and Mort Grant, the director of the SUNY Research Foundation, establishing the first International Education Center within SUNY.[11] The center was designed to coordinate and encourage SUNY programs overseas. Within the year, SUNY Fredonia and SUNY Buffalo inaugurated overseas study with programs at the Royal Academy of Fine Arts and the Royal Flemish Conservatory of Music. Soon the University of Buffalo offered overseas courses in Italian history, Italian language, Italian renaissance art, and studio art courses in painting, ceramics, and sculpture.[12]

---

[9]Croce, Marianne Della. "American Studies Collection: Your Rugged Constitution." Institute of International Education (IIE). Oyster Bay, NY: Planting Fields Foundation, October 10, 1958.

[10]Dean, Op cit.

[11]SUNY Board of Trustees. Minutes of Meetings of the Board of Trustees, State University of New York. Albany, NY: SUNY, 1961.

[12]SUNY Board of Trustees. Annual Report of the Board of trustees, SUNY, 1963–1964. Albany, NY: SUNY, 1964.

In 1964 President (soon-to-be Chancellor) Samuel Gould took the helm of SUNY, having been appointed by Governor Nelson Rockefeller to consolidate the state's loose federation of campuses into a unified institution. Gould oversaw creation of the Center for International Studies and World Affairs (ISWA), which opened at Planting Field near Oyster Bay, Long Island, in August 1965 and was headed by the first executive dean for International Studies. In the spring of 1966, President Samuel B. Gould told the campus chief administrative officers that "students needs that are so varied that no single campus can respond fully even to its own students' interests. We must therefore look toward inter-campus or university-wide undertakings."[13]

SUNY's enrollment grew sharply from 48,000 in 1960 to 139,000 in 1968 and international involvement grew apace. Before Gould, the international programs had been shrinking; whereas in 1954–55, there were eight programs sponsored by five campuses with 144 participants, by 1961–62 there were only six programs with eighty-five participants. Gould's impact was dramatic. By 1968–69 fifteen campuses sponsored forty-two enrolling 749 participants.[14]

The Scholar in Residence Program was founded in the mid-1960s. Notably, in 1967–68 the program included distinguished global scholar Edvard Hambro, a Norwegian, who lectured on international law, economics, and business administration. He became president of the U.N. General Assembly in 1970–71.

Campus programs flourished. For instance, in 1967, Oneonta created an Office of International Education, which soon launched an Israel Summer Program and exchange programs with West Germany, jointly sponsored with the University of Albany. Programs then followed with universities in England and Austria. A later director of International Studies at Oneonta, Allen Caswell, noted that students from underdeveloped countries often stayed for four years to complete their degrees, while European students tended to stay for one or two semesters just to experience the educational system and American culture.[15]

In late 1967, SUNY issued "Policy Recommendations for International & Study Abroad Programs in SUNY,"[16] which noted the need for more specific regulations and processes due to the rapid growth and changes within SUNY in the mid 1960s. Its educational objectives focused on quality control,

---

[13]Gould, Samuel B. "SUNY President." Memorandum from Samuel B. Gould, President of SUNY to Campus Chief Administrative Officers. Albany, NY: SUNY, April 8, 1966.

[14]Dean, Op cit. Putnam, Ivan, Brochure on Overseas Academic Programs Administered by State-Operated Campuses of the State University of New York. Albany, NY: SUNY, 1976.

[15]Pierce, Lisa Ann. *The History of Foreign Students at the State University College at Oneonta.* Oneonta, NY: SUNY, 1981.

[16]SUNY: International Studies and World Affairs. Policy Recommendations for International & Study Abroad Programs. Planting Fields New York: SUNY, 1967.

transferability of credit across the system, and a system of classification of study abroad programs. It established program criteria in proficiency in relevant foreign languages, provision for cultural immersion, guarantee of development in the students' chosen field of study, and use of instructional staff from the host country when possible. It also sought to increase education feedback to the home campus and to SUNY administration.[17]

C.   International Programs and Initiatives in the 1970s

The 1970s was a turbulent decade for international education programs. ISWA was moved to Albany in early 1971 after it was decided to use its Long Island facilities and office space as a temporary site for the Old Westbury campus. ISWA staff was reduced substantially, the title was changed to the Central Office of International Programs, and its functions were limited to policy coordination and services in the areas of study abroad and foreign student and faculty exchange programs.[18]

Despite these cutbacks, by 1973, the enrollment of foreign students studying at SUNY campuses had risen to 4,441, a dramatic increase from 545 in 1960. Between 1960 and 1973, foreign student enrollment in SUNY had averaged 1.41% of the total of SUNY's full-time student population. In 1974, the University of Buffalo enrolled the largest number of full-time foreign students, sixteenth in the nation.[19]

During the mid-1970s the popularity of SUNY's overseas academic programs continued to rise. Programs diversified in their locations abroad and fields of study offered and educational exchanges became much more popular.[20] By the mid-1970s at least eighteen campuses were actively involved in study abroad programs, including: Albany, Binghamton, Brockport, Buffalo College (Buffalo State today), University of Buffalo, Cobleskill, Cortland, Delhi, Fredonia, Geneseo, New Paltz, Old Westbury, Oneonta, Oswego, Plattsburgh, Potsdam, Purchase, and Stony Brook.[21]

---

[17]Dean, Op cit.

[18]Central Office of International Programs Division of Educational Services. International Education in the State University of New York: Background for a Report to the Board of Trustees. Albany: SUNY, 1977.

[19]SUNY: International Studies and World Affairs. Policy Recommendations for International & Study Abroad Programs. Planting Fields, NY: SUNY, 1967.

[20]Central Office of International Programs Division of Educational Services. International Education in the State University of New York: Background for a Report to the Board of Trustees. Albany, NY: SUNY, 1977.

[21]Putnam, Ivan. "Brochure on Overseas Academic Programs Administered by State-Operated Campuses of the State University of New York." Albany, NY: SUNY, 1976.

And the 1976 Master Plan promoted international education expansively:

> Recognizing the growing interdependence of the nations of the world, and emphasizing the great educational and cultural value of international contact among students and faculty, the University will continue to advance its substantial commitment to international education.
>
> The public university in the nation's most internationally-minded state ... has a unique obligation and opportunity to establish, within limited resources available, a thoughtful, effective program of international education in order to maintain adequate communication in the world of scholarship and to provide sufficient educational opportunities for those students who should be trained in programs and cultures beyond the United States.
>
> Only a great university can be most helpful to this State, and no university can be truly great which is not international in its attitudes, its research, and scholarship. The University will continue with even deeper conviction its efforts to develop exchange programs with the universities of other nations and will seek new ways of interacting with institutions across the seas.[22]

The SUNY Board of Trustees included in their response to the 1976 Master Plan recommendations that SUNY expand international education to community colleges, expand the number of foreign students on SUNY campuses, and expand opportunities for SUNY students to earn academic credit overseas.[23] The Master Plan also urged campuses to make their courses and programs more international at all levels, general education, undergraduate majors, and graduate degrees.

SUNY also promoted an interesting two-way flow of information among SUNY leaders, faculty, and staff who focused on further developing the international education commitment by the SUNY System. Chancellor Boyer set a pattern on his visits to Japan, the Soviet Union, China, Israel, and his study in England. A number of college and university presidents were given leaves by the Board of Trustees in the 1970s to study abroad. In turn, a number of foreign senior higher education leaders made formal visits to SUNY during this decade, including the rector of Moscow State University, the pro rector of Leningrad University, five French University presidents, the president of the University of Wurzburg in Germany, and the president of the University of Haifa in Israel.

---

[22]SUNY. The 1976 Master Plan of the State University of New York. Albany, NY: SUNY, 1976.

[23]Ibid.

But these expansive plans were soon restricted by the national and state economic problems of the mid-1970s. Budgets across the state were reduced because of the dire nature of the New York State budget and the imminent threat of New York City's bankruptcy.[24] Across the university system, this financial crisis had a tremendously negative impact, especially on the growth and development of international education at SUNY. Sadly, the ambitious 1976 SUNY Master Plan's "Charter for International Education" would be reined in.

D. International Programs and Initiatives in the 1980s

During this decade, the senior leadership in System Administration, as well as the Board of Trustees, sought to enhance the level of commitment, as well as visibility for SUNY in international education. The strategic aim of the international education programs within SUNY was "to enable our constituent institutions to offer students in every discipline and professional area; the opportunity to achieve international competence, the ability to understand, communicate, and work with people of different societies and cultures, is a fundamental need of every citizen. We at SUNY are responsible for educating and training the citizenry." There was recognition of the need for more coordination from System Administration, but an envisioned SUNY Institute of International Studies died on the drawing board.[25]

SUNY Chancellor Clifton R. Wharton Jr. lent his considerable support, touting success in strengthening the international perspective through language and area study departments, while other SUNY faculty added an international perspective to teaching and research in history, social science, and the arts. He highlighted the need to bridge a persistent communication gap between traditional international program areas such as foreign languages and area studies like Asian history or European social systems and international development. Wharton also called for stronger bridges between development programs and business, physical science, and engineering.[26]

In its 1983 Annual Report, SUNY's Office of International Programs plaintively cried that "we are increasingly being drawn into a world in which the myths of nationalism and sovereignty have less and less meaning, and we must prepare ourselves to accept and function in the new reality of global

---

[24]Gelber, Sidney, *Politics and Public Higher Education in New York State*. New York: Peter Lang Publishing, 2001, pp. 286–287.

[25]SUNY Office of International Programs. Annual Report. Albany, NY: State University of New York, 1984.

[26]Wharton Jr., Clifton R. "Development, Language, and the Area Studies The Challenge of Working Together." Albany, NY: SUNY International Education Quarterly, 1984.

interdependence."[27] But attempts to enhance international ventures repeatedly ran into economic problems on the campuses and at System Administration. It was difficult to implement new programs in such an environment. Students were less interested in going overseas when they were worried about finding employment after graduation. Research funding for faculty members focused on international studies was drying up. Retrenchment and hiring freezes limited faculty initiative.

Steven Sample, president of the University of Buffalo in 1985, documented a need for an increased emphasis on international programs in research universities. Sample noted the "need to broaden the international knowledge of our students at all levels—undergraduate, graduate, and professional—must be a high priority of every institution with the SUNY system."[28] Major study abroad initiatives were also taken by campus officials, notably by John Perry at Brockport, Willi Uschald at Cortland, Gerhard Hess and Howard Berry at Rockland Community College, and James Preston at Oneonta.

E. International Programs and Initiatives Since 1990

In the 1990s, support for international education fluctuated. In the early part of the decade, the International Education study areas reported that fewer students from New York State-based institutions were going abroad to study than there were international students studying in the state. In 1993–94 there were 47,278 foreign students enrolled in colleges and universities in New York State, with fewer than 10,000 students from New York State's institutions studying abroad.[29]

In 1994 New York State Assemblyman Edward C. Sullivan obtained funds in the 1994 New York State Budget to establish the New York State Task Force on International Education. Assemblyman Sullivan touted economic, financial, and global business development as the drivers that make study abroad experiences imperative for "future generations to function in the global community and the developing international marketplace."[30]

The task force's December 1995 report identified a number of findings and recommendations. It highlighted the barriers to increasing the number

---

[27]SUNY Office of International Programs. Annual Report. Albany, NY: State University of New York, 1984.

[28]Sample, Steven B. "International Programs in the Research University." International Programs Quarterly, Fall 20, 1984: pages 8–11.

[29]New York State Taskforce on International Education. "Overcoming Barriers to Study Abroad: The Case of New York State." Ithaca, NY: Taskforce on International Education, 1995.

[30]Letter by Assemblyman Edward Sullivan on Support for SUNY International Study Abroad. Albany, New York: The Assembly of the State of New York—Albany, December 13, 1995.

of students in study abroad programs, including inadequate foreign language training, on-campus curricular requirements, limited information, and lack of funding. To address these problems, it urged campuses to integrate education abroad into their programs by expanding foreign language instruction, cooperating more fully with other SUNY institutions, facilitating financial aid, and coordinating information across SUNY. Most ambitiously, it proposed setting a goal of ten percent for student participation in study abroad programs.

The 1995 task force concluded:

> The status of international study in New York can be likened to a family computer with a 286 processor. It was fine for its original purpose, but it no longer meets the current needs of word processing and it is unqualified to meet future needs. International study in SUNY also works, but it has not adapted rapidly enough to the challenging realities of the USA and the rest of the world; it too needs to be strengthened and expanded to enhance the quality of its workforce.[31]

However, on December 1, 1995, Governor Pataki was presented with a report from the SUNY Board of Trustees entitled, *Rethinking SUNY*.[32] This strategic document created by the SUNY Board of Trustees did not mention international education or study abroad. The primary focus of this plan was the need to focus on a "multi-year, comprehensive, system-wide plan to increase cost efficiency." But despite "Rethinking SUNY's" silence on international education, major programs with Turkey, Russia, China, and a number of other countries were either established or continued, and the Levin Institute was created.

Interesting campus international program initiatives continued. For instance, in the early 1990s, the University of Buffalo developed international education initiatives with Poland. Its School of Management also took a lead role in SUNY's USAID-funded management education and development program in Hungary, aiding that country's efforts to reform its economy and promote private enterprise. This initiative led to the establishment of an exchange program between the University of Buffalo and the Technical University of Budapest. Buffalo also collaborated with Riga Technical University and the University of Latvia to develop the Riga Business School, which has since become the leading premier western-style business school in the Baltic.

---

[31]Ibid.

[32]The Board of Trustees, State University of New York. "Rethinking SUNY." Albany, NY: SUNY, 1995.

An example of internationalizing a campus is Marleigh Grayer Ryan's work at SUNY New Paltz, where she taught Japanese language, Japanese literature in translation, and courses on Japanese aesthetics, including theatre and film. From 1990 until her retirement in 1998, she chaired the Asian studies program, with particular attention to developing opportunities for students to live and study in Asia. The courses she developed at New Paltz included Beauty in Japan, Japanese Fiction, Japanese Poetry, Japanese Theatre and A Historical Study of Asian Americans with Particular Emphasis on their Artistic Achievements.

Currently, SUNY's leadership in the international education arena includes an Office of International Programs at SUNY System Administration, with the mission to promote and advance international education throughout SUNY. It works alongside the state university's Center for International Development (CID) to expand SUNY's outreach across the world and to create partnerships with international governments, institutions, and organizations. It began in 1986 and has designed and implemented more than $140 million in development projects on four continents."[33] The center is currently located at the University of Albany's Rockefeller College of Public Affairs and Policy. The SUNY CID is unique because of its history as a university-based center. In particular, the SUNY CID is well known globally today for its work in collaborating with legislatures to strengthen their operational, as well as oversight, roles and responsibilities.[34]

F.   Concluding Thoughts

If the State University of New York is truly to become a world class institution, this paper has argued that, among other worthwhile programs, it must have the administrative and governmental support for a first-rate international education program with sufficient funding.

Frequent changes in SUNY's leadership have robbed international education programs of a consistent vision. Over the course of the past sixty years, the system has had seventeen individuals leading the system as permanent presidents (later "chancellors") or as temporary leaders. On average, leadership of SUNY has changed every three-and-one-half years. This constant change in senior leadership has contributed to inconsistent vision, support, and resource allocation for international education over the years.

---

[33]SUNY, Office of International Programs. International Programs Mission Statement. November 1, 2008. http://suny.edu/International Programs/MissionStatement.cfm?navLev=1& navLevel=1 (accessed August 10, 2008).

[34]Russell-Einhorn, Malcolm, interview by SUNY website. SUNY Center for International Development Announces New Director (September 9, 2008).

Clearly, numerous short-term and long-term challenges face international education at SUNY. For more than sixty years, many people have recognized the value and importance of international education and learning for SUNY's students and faculty, citizens of New York State, and students and scholars from around the world. Today's challenges are similar in some ways to those of the past. Periodic economic crises presented significant challenges and future economic crises are highly likely. SUNY should expect to face periodic contractions in funding for all programs, with international education programs likely to be among the first to be cut, as in the past.

SUNY and its international programs also face some unique challenges. In addition to a global economic crisis, there are changes in leadership at the state level as well as at SUNY, global unrest (e.g., Iraq and Afghanistan Wars, current violence in the Gaza Strip, challenges in Darfur, etc.), structural changes in the global economy, and President Barak Obama's stated goal of changing global perceptions of the United States. All of these will affect the need for and nature of international education.

This historical review lends itself to two specific recommendations to deal with these challenges:

First, further develop a system-wide knowledge management system that tracks all international education program initiatives, innovative ideas and solutions, future planning ideas, and campus-specific solutions. This recommendation was made in 1984 by then Associate Vice Chancellor Wilbert J. LeMelle when he called for a "documentation depository."[35] This knowledge management system would integrate all relevant information, including early documents currently archived at many of the campus libraries, as well as archives (such as the SUNY Collection from The Planting Fields and Coe Foundation Archives), system level annual reports, Master Plan documents, and other system-wide reports. An integrated knowledge management approach would involve "the discovery and capture of knowledge, the filtering and arrangement of this knowledge, and the value derived from sharing and using this knowledge throughout the organization."[36]

Second, leverage the capabilities available through free standing, system-wide institutes within SUNY. Models like the Levin Institute provide the flexibility, continuity, and international recognition that is needed to sustain and grow international education at SUNY.

In the years to come, SUNY, as well as the state of New York and the country, will be faced with an increased demand for global competence across

---

[35]SUNY Office of International Programs. Annual Report. Albany, NY: State University of New York, 1984.

[36]Milam, John. "Knowledge Management for Higher Education." *ERIC Digest*. January 1, 2001. http://www.ericdigests.org/2003-1/higher.htm (accessed December 13, 2008).

many subject areas. As the world becomes more interdependent, individuals, organizations, and nations will become even more dependent on educated and trained graduates with international experience and skills to lead us forward.

Acknowledgments

A special thank you to Joe Petrick, SUNY at Alfred State College's director of technical services for the Hinkle Memorial Library. Also, thank you to Heather Heyduk and Kasandra Smith at the James M. Milne Library at SUNY Oneonta and Special Collections and reference/instruction librarian Liz Argentieri at SUNY Geneseo. Finally Professors Calista McBride and Amal Rowezak worked their magic with words and graphics.

Appendix: Timeline of Enrollment Growth

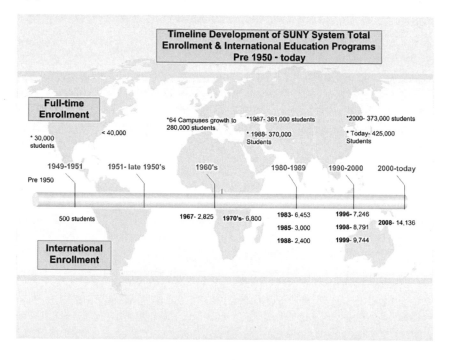

II.   SUNY from an English Perspective

John Halsey, The College at Brockport, SUNY & Brunel University, England

In the discussions leading to the creation of SUNY in the 1940s, few people made reference to English higher education. There would have been no point in doing so. Three centuries earlier, the Massachusetts settlers had based Harvard on Cambridge, the only model they knew; and anglophiles had continued to have an influence on American private higher education. But the public sector of higher education was distinctly American, and the creation of SUNY owed little to England. The GI Bill, the Truman Report, and Mayor LaGuardia's "Committee on Unity" report into discrimination by private colleges in New York, were all home grown. Governor Dewey's vulnerability in the 1948 election as the governor of the only state without a state university did not depend on international comparisons, and neither did the more local pressure in the opposite direction from supporters of New York's private universities and colleges.

Higher education in England was small and based on the assumption that very few people had the capacity to benefit from it. In the late 1940s, a New Yorker was twelve times more likely to be in higher education than an Englishman was. In 1949, England had a population of around forty-two million, but there were fewer than 62,000 students in higher education. In New York, in the year before SUNY was founded, the total population was just under fifteen million, and there were 269,000 students (181,000 full-time, and 88,000 part-time).

This paper will argue that England's rapid passage in the 1990s from elite to mass higher education would have been more successful if it had learned from SUNY and created a unitary organization. A clearly-differentiated structure would have enabled English universities to focus their activities more effectively and to play distinctive roles in a coherent system. This would have produced a number of benefits and three will be discussed. First, SUNY's community colleges play a much clearer role than the English further education colleges. Second, the university college model would have provided a model for a viable institution of higher education that was not research-intensive. And third, the establishment of a nationwide credit transfer system would have given students more flexibility and choice as they negotiate their route towards a degree.

Successful mass higher education depends on broad public support, which in turn depends on the perception that institutions of higher education are accessible. Although the English attempt to introduce mass higher education without a clear break with the past has reduced its effectiveness, the government's emphasis on making higher education more socially inclusive has led to some innovative strategies. The paper will also suggest that despite the lack of a coherent *structure* in English higher education, SUNY could draw on some of the *policies* developed in England to widen access.

The contrast between attitudes to higher education in America and those on the other side of the Atlantic is vividly illustrated by the contrast between America's GI Bill and Britain's 1944 Education Act. The latter scarcely mentioned higher education. World War II had revealed the deficiencies of the education system in England, with almost a quarter of the conscripts aged sixteen and seventeen illiterate. It was clear that the urgent educational need in Britain was to reform and expand the provision for its school-age children. The 1944 Act's raising of the school leaving age from fourteen to fifteen was seen as quite ambitious enough.

In the United States, the idea that education, including higher education, was a way of tackling social class divisions goes back at least to Horace Mann in 1848. The massive expansion of higher education in the United States in the second half of the nineteenth century reflected the idea that an inclusive society needed an inclusive system of higher education. In England, it was generally assumed that different sorts of young people needed different sorts of education, which would be provided in separate schools. Education tended to magnify the social and psychological distance between social classes. In the 1950s and 1960s, advocates of secondary education reform argued that comprehensive schools would help reduce social divisions. But the idea that higher education could play a similar role was not a serious part of the debate in England until the 1990s. As traditional social class lines weakened and the language of class division no longer resonated, demand for higher education increased. The Labour party under Tony Blair turned its attention to higher education and sought to make universities more inclusive.

A.   Is More Worse?

When millions of veterans used the GI Bill to enroll in higher education, it was clear how much demand for higher education there was. President Truman's Presidential Commission on Higher Education advocated even more growth, proposing that huge sums of money should be available to publicly-funded colleges and universities with the goal of doubling total enrollment by 1960. The Truman Report's title is also very un-English: "Higher Education for Democracy." The idea that higher education could help make democracy more effective was central to the Truman Report; it is almost entirely absent from English discussions of higher education.

To link higher education with democracy is to place higher education at the centre of American culture in a way that has not happened in England. It is true that at SUNY's star-studded 1950 "First Symposium" some voices sounded like English defenders of elitism, especially among the supporters of the private sector. Several speakers argued that the university needed to be defended from the demands of the modern age. Robert M. Hutchins, president and later chancellor of the University of Chicago, even suggested that it would be a good idea to emulate the medieval University of Paris. The influx of veterans was said by some to threaten academic standards, in much the same way as Kingsley Amis was to say famously fifteen years later in England, "More Means Worse." And some New York elitist educators who feared that if you increased liberal arts education for the public you would create a dissatisfied population, and thus "undermine the established order of society," sounds very English, too.[37] In England, the elitists believed that although universities were crucial for the cultural health of the nation, the rarefied air within them wasn't suitable for most people. Higher education was like a lifeboat: if too many people got in, it would no longer be able to do what it was designed to do. But higher education was firmly in the mainstream in America by 1950; the publication of the proceedings of the symposium ends with a description of SUNY as "an institution providing equal opportunity to all—irrespective of race, color, creed, or national origin ... a modern university, a true example of democracy in action."[38] American elitists were on the defensive in a way that English ones wouldn't be for another twenty, some might say forty, years.

When English higher education abandoned its elitist past, or at least when it increased the number of students dramatically, extraordinarily, it did not look to the United States in general, or to SUNY in particular, for a model of how to make mass higher education work. SUNY was curiously ignored by politicians and policymakers. The influential Robbins Report of 1963 referred briefly to SUNY, mainly to criticize its bureaucratic procedures. Neither the 1997 Dearing Report nor the 2004 Schwartz Report said much about SUNY. The 2003 White Paper implicitly drew on American comparisons, but instead of SUNY, it was the California State University system's twenty-three campuses that were picked out. Given Californian "mission creep" and the deep dissatisfaction in some of the California state colleges about not having doctoral programs, SUNY would have been a better choice. The largest comprehensive public higher education system in the United States could surely have taught the English some useful lessons in effective popular mass public higher education.

B.   A Differentiated System

SUNY was formed from existing universities and colleges that differed widely from one another, as well as new institutions created to fill particular needs. English universities were more homogeneous. The history of higher education in England until 1992 was dominated by the Oxbridge model. Although not all the newer universities used the one-to-one tutorial teaching method, they used much of the language of Oxbridge, and sought to replicate many of its elements. With some exceptions, such as the University of East Anglia and Keele University, it was as though there was only one way to do higher education in England, only one way to be a proper university, and an institution's prestige,

---

[37]Sidney Gelber. *Politics and Public Higher Education in New York State.* New York: Peter Lang, 2001, 34. *Functions of a Modern University*, Albany, NY: SUNY, 1950.

[38]Ibid. *Functions of a Modern University*, 359.

and even its self-esteem, depended on looking as much like Oxbridge as you could manage.

What would have served England better is a clearly-differentiated system that would have enabled English universities to focus their activities more effectively. The lack of such a system meant that the fiction had to be maintained that all higher education institutions were playing the same role. If SUNY had been taken as a model, the tripartite division between universities with doctoral programs, four-year colleges, and community colleges would have enabled the less selective, less research-intensive universities to develop an identity which would have better served the interests of their students and their communities.

In fact, Britain has moved in the opposite direction. For twenty-five years it had a "binary system," with universities on the one hand, and polytechnics on the other. Both universities and polytechnics were publicly-funded, although by separate funding bodies. Both taught degree courses, but university degrees were traditionally academic, while the polytechnics offered more vocational courses, particularly in professional areas such as business, health, and welfare. Then the 1992 Further and Higher Education Act unified higher education in England and Wales, as did the corresponding act in Scotland. A new single funding structure for universities and polytechnics was introduced, and polytechnics were allowed to use the title "university." The opportunity to create a system based on a model like SUNY was missed.

A key reason for the lack of clear differentiation is the confusion about whether English universities are public or private. In the United States, the distinction between the public and private sectors of higher education is clear. In England the picture is mixed, and seems to combine the worst of both worlds. Gareth Williams argues that since 1993, the whole of post-secondary education has been "in a real sense private."[39] Universities have always been private institutions; in 1989 the polytechnics were given similar full legal independence, and in 1993, the same status was accorded to further education colleges.[40]

But financially, English universities depend heavily on funds from the public purse. In Stéphan Vincent-Lancrin's wonderfully paradoxical phrase,

---

[39]Gareth Williams. "The market route to mass higher education: British experience 1979–1996," *Higher Education Policy* 10 (1997): 286.

[40]Further education (FE) colleges provide post-compulsory courses. Until 1993 they were controlled by local government, and since then, they have been funded nationally. The courses are mainly vocational, but FE colleges also offer more academic classes, including some higher education classes. As I argue later, they are similar to American community colleges, but are not integrated into a state system such as SUNY.

they are "government-dependent private."[41] Before the expansion of higher education, the University Grants Committee managed the relationship between the state and the universities in a way that suited universities very well. The scale of government support to higher education was discussed over gentlemanly dinners between academics and ministers or civil servants, many of whom had been educated at Oxford or Cambridge and who, in some cases, aspired to return to Oxbridge at the end of their government career as master of this college or that.[42] But this comfortable arrangement depended on the marginal position of universities. It could not survive the move to mass higher education.

Because universities are financially dependent, it is difficult for them to ignore government policies. When Ken Clarke was the minister in charge of health in Mrs. Thatcher's government, he said that if he wanted the doctors to read something, he wrote it on a check. Despite, or rather *because of*, the legal independence of universities, the government uses financial incentives to encourage them to support its higher education policies.

The position of English universities, then, is very different from anything either public or private American universities would recognize. Although they depend on the state, the individual universities are free to make their own strategic decisions on the basis of institutional self-interest. What no government has been willing to do is to establish clear lines of differentiation, such as a SUNY-style tripartite model of public higher education.

As Maurice Kogan put it, in England, "academic strategies are thus formed according to the possibility of achieving financial rewards or of avoiding financial punishments."[43] In the absence of a differentiated structure, universities jockey with one another seeking to maximize institutional self-interest, often with an eye on the annual league tables published by various newspapers. A Brockport colleague once described SUNY to me as being like "a Canada made up of nothing but Quebecs," but the description applies far better to English higher education.

Indeed, there is a paradox. Social-democratic England, where the state plays a major role in many areas of public life, has a higher education sector with a central element of free market competition between universities. There is no *system* of higher education in England, rather a collection of institutions that compete or cooperate on the basis of judgments about institutional

---

[41]Stéphan Vincent-Lancrin, "The 'Crisis' of Public Higher Education: A Comparative Perspective," *CSHE* 18.07, Research & Occasional Paper Series (electronic journal): November 2007; University of California, Berkeley. http://cshe.berkeley.edu/

[42]Sir John Wolfenden, "Great Britain" in James A. Perkins (ed) Higher Education: From Autonomy to Systems. New York: International Council for Education, 1973.

[43]Maurice Kogan et al. *Transforming Higher Education: a comparative study*. London: Jessica Kingsley, 2000, 138.

self-interest. America is famously committed to the free market, but New York has a centrally-guided state system with system-wide policies, in which institutions have clear roles.

It is the argument of this paper that a more straightforward and unembarrassed state system of higher education in England would have served the country's educational needs more effectively. What was there to stop Tony Blair saying to the universities "in Order to form a more perfect University system, We the People of the United Kingdom, do ordain and establish a State University. We recognize that universities are independent institutions, and it is entirely up to each of them whether or not they choose to join. But if they choose not to, they will need, over a period of time, to wean themselves from dependency on state funds."

If any universities had decided not to join the State University of England, the money the government saved could have been used to fund the state system more generously. Whether or not a new, truly independent sector had developed, a differentiated structure could have been established. Such a state system would also have meant that higher education was more fully embedded into the mainstream of English society, a matter for public political discussion and debate as much as any other national institution paid for by the people. England would have benefitted if, like SUNY, it had a clearly differentiated system in which not all colleges were research-intensive. A system that provided higher education in a way, and at times and places, convenient for students at all stages of life, would have served the needs of its people better, by enabling higher education to escape the pernicious legacy of elitism.

I shall briefly discuss three advantages an English state system modeled on SUNY would have had.

C.   Lesson #1: The Community Colleges

The community colleges have been a key element in SUNY from the very beginning. The chair of the Truman Commission, George Zook, was a committed supporter of junior colleges, as they had been called, but the report carefully used the term community colleges instead, to signal a broadening of their role. As well as educating students for transfer to four-year institutions, they would offer vocational courses, and indeed the line between the two kinds of course was porous: there was nothing to prevent students from switching between them.

New York's community colleges helped meet the high demand for higher education after World War II. In England, the doubling of the higher education participation rate from 15 percent in 1988 to 30 percent in 1994 was largely achieved without the further education colleges.

Burton Clark sees community colleges as exemplifying the inclusiveness of American higher education:

> With community colleges guaranteeing entry without regard to qualification, and with many four-year colleges and universities, public and private, also generous in whom they admit, especially when applicants are in short supply, students coming out of secondary schools have second, third, and fourth chances in a fashion unimaginable in most other systems of higher education.[44]

Brint and Karabel describe the community colleges as exemplifying America's pragmatic and utilitarian educational tradition.[45] In England, universities have been slow to develop relationships with the colleges of further education. The divide between higher and further education is wide, and they are financed by different funding bodies. But increasingly, higher education courses are taught in further education colleges, and the 2003 White Paper indicated that the expansion of higher education would take place largely in further education institutions, by means of the foundation degree. The foundation degree is somewhat like the associate's degree in the United States. It is both a transfer qualification, which enables the student to progress to the last year of a bachelor's degree, and a terminal qualification, designed with the needs of employers in mind. However, unlike the associate's degree, it is offered by both further education colleges and universities. The 2007 Further Education and Training Act gave further education colleges the power to award foundation degrees themselves, rather than having to work with universities to design and approve them. This change was attacked by Universities U.K., the group representing the university sector. For them it was unwelcome competition. This is a marked contrast with SUNY, where the community colleges are an integral part of an articulated system.

D.   Lesson #2: The University College Model

The tripartite structure is deeply-rooted in the United States, but not widely understood in Britain. John Douglass says that the structure, which was formalized in California as early as 1910, has "proven a remarkably durable and flexible system for expanding educational opportunity and for meeting

---

[44]Burton Clark (ed). *The School and the University: an International Perspective.* Berkeley: University of California Press, 1985, 315.

[45]Steven Brint and Jerome Karabel. *The Diverted Dream: Community Colleges and the Promise of Educational Opportunity in America, 1900–1985.* New York: Oxford University Press, 1989, 221.

the growing and evolving training and research needs of California."[46] The development of New York's university colleges was based on a commitment to broaden educational opportunity and an assessment of the demand for higher education. The College at Brockport, for example, developed from a teachers college into a liberal arts college as a result of statewide policies combined with local innovations. At the heart of Brockport's remarkable growth in the late 1960s was the realization of how much locally unmet need there was, together with the efforts of inventive academic staff willing to develop ways of meeting the demand. At their most successful, university colleges combine the local and the cosmopolitan: faculty members whose professional lives are informed by cosmopolitan academic communities, teaching courses, and programs to meet local and regional needs.

In England, there have, from time to time, been proposals to concentrate research funds in fewer universities, but most universities have reacted with horror to the prospect of becoming "non-research-intensive." In England, almost all universities offer at least some doctoral degrees and there are no counterparts to the well-established American model of non-doctoral colleges, private and public. In the absence of a strong central system, the response of most English universities to such suggestions has been to say that research is central to what they do, and to resist any suggestion that they should concentrate on teaching. In SUNY's colleges the fact that teaching is the priority does not prevent faculty members from being involved in scholarly activity: they still engage in research, publish, edit journals, and take part in national and international academic conferences. If English higher education policy-makers had looked more carefully at SUNY they would have been able to provide convincing evidence that it was possible to have a satisfactory academic life without granting doctorates.

E.   Lesson #3: Credit Transfer

A third, and even stronger, example of a way English higher education could have gained from SUNY's experience as it moved to mass higher education is the establishment of a nationwide credit transfer system. From an English perspective, it is striking that the 2008 Report by Governor Spitzer's New York State Commission on Higher Education was critical of the difficulties faced by transfer students in New York. It recommended that there should be statewide legally mandated transfer policies, to give students greater flexibility as they negotiate their way to a degree. The report was using New York's "peer states" such as Florida and Texas as exemplars: their state systems even have common course numbering. But imperfect though it may be, the ability of

---

[46]John Aubrey Douglass. *The California Idea and American Higher Education: 1850 to the 1960 Master Plan*. Stanford: Stanford University Press, 2000, 10.

students within the New York state system to transfer from one institution to another without losing the credits they have gained is very different from the experience of students in England.

On paper, English universities have a system of credit accumulation and transfer, but in practice it is far more rarely used than credit transfer within SUNY. English academics have a horror of anything that smacks of standardization. Different institutions have different admission policies and standards. To take one example, few students studying in institutions within the University of London ever transfer their credit from one college to another, despite being in the same city and part of the same federal university. Credit transfer simply isn't part of the culture of English universities.

From time to time there are calls to embrace it, but few English commentators seem to grasp how widespread and well-established the practice is in the United States. In February 2008, the universities secretary, John Denham, asked the higher education sector (including vice-chancellors, government advisers on science and technology, and funding bodies) how it should change in the next ten to fifteen years. Among other ideas, these sages suggested that students should be able to mix and match courses across departments, and indeed across institutions, and switch between part-time and full-time study. What they failed to say, of course, was that all this had been happening in SUNY and other U.S. state systems for years.

One of the key goals of the European Bologna Process was to facilitate student mobility between the participating countries. Higher education across Europe was increasingly organized in a three-cycle, bachelor-master-doctorate structure, which improved the comparability of qualifications. But the Bologna Process did not have a great impact on the frequency or ease with which students moved from institution to institution within England.

F.   English Lessons for SUNY

It is perhaps counterintuitive to argue that the English, having come so recently to mass higher education, could teach SUNY anything about how to make higher education more widely accessible. But successive British governments, especially since 1997, have invested considerable political capital in expanding the number of disadvantaged young people going into higher education, and their policies have been successful to a significant extent.

The expansion of English higher education was an important part of the Labour party's "modernization" policy, as it sought to appeal to middle England. At the 1999 Labour Party Conference, Tony Blair, then Prime Minister, said that he expected 50 percent of people to have benefited from higher education by the time they were thirty. This target was to be achieved by 2010, and it was clear that hitting it would depend on many things, not least increasing participation rates among lower-income students. Modernization required that more young people should become graduates; social justice and cohesion required that previously under-represented social groups should enter the university fold.

However, this expansion of higher education could not be paid for wholly from the public purse. Labour was keen to repudiate its reputation as a big spender, and in any case there were more politically-attractive demands for government resources. Students had not previously had to pay university tuition fees; the Blair government introduced a standard annual fee of £1000. However, even if it was inevitable that the cost of the expansion of higher education would have to borne partly by the students themselves, it would be self-defeating if the introduction of tuition fees were to discourage less well-off students from aspiring to higher education. There was also a political dimension to the issue. Within the Labour party, the introduction of tuition fees was bitterly opposed by some on the left, who saw no difference in principle between free higher education and free primary or secondary education. One way to reduce this bitterness was to try to make higher education more accessible. For both practical and political reasons widening participation was central to English policy.

Five policies were at the heart of what became known as "the widening participation agenda."

One was tuition fees, which were centrally regulated. The £1000 standard annual fee was replaced by a variable fee of up to £3000, although in practice, almost all universities decided to charge the maximum. To mitigate the effects on the poor, non-repayable grants were reintroduced and student loans were expanded so that no tuition had to be paid until a graduate's income reached a threshold.

The second was university admissions. No English government would think of telling any university what its admission policies or procedures should be, of course. But a great deal can be achieved by exhortation and monitoring. Each year the government minister responsible for higher education policy writes a public letter to the Higher Education Funding Council for England (HEFCE). (This is, incidentally, a good illustration of the way the British government uses the universities' financial dependence to persuade them to accept government policy.) The second priority in the 2006 letter was:

> ... widening participation in HE for low income families, where in spite of the recent progress we have made we do not perform well enough. Low rates of participation in HE among the lowest socio-economic groups represent entrenched inequality and in economic terms a waste of human capital. I am therefore asking the Council to explore options for additional support in widening

participation in 2006–07, building on the work that has already been done in understanding the costs to institutions.[47]

Universities were given financial rewards for successfully recruiting students from the most deprived areas. They also had to publish an annual document describing their admission and widening participation policies, and showing the measures taken to help ensure accurate and fair policies.

Third, government policy encouraged closer links between schools and universities. In 2007, the National Council for Educational Excellence was created in order to help achieve the government's aspirations for children and young people's education. Among its recommendations was that every primary school work to raise student aspirations to take up a place in higher education by various means, including pupil visits to higher education campuses. It is British government policy that every university should have strong links with local state schools. When the New York State Commission Report looked at the link between higher education and K-12 schools, it proposed the creation of Educational Partnership Zones (EPZ) in high-need school districts. The goal would be to improve access to higher education through partnerships between such school districts and higher education institutions. But it was only anticipated that there would be one such EPZ in each region of the state. English policy is across the board. In October 2007, the secretary of state for universities, John Denham, defended the policy from the accusation that this was "social engineering," saying that in order to spot talent effectively, universities needed to form deep-rooted partnerships with schools.

Fourth, the aspirations of young people from social groups that are underrepresented in higher education were addressed directly. The government set up and financed a program called AimHigher, designed to encourage young people to think seriously about going to university, using road shows, campus visits, open days, and residential schools.

Fifth, HEFCE sought to improve the quality of information, advice, and guidance, especially in the areas with the lowest proportion of young people going into higher education.

The evidence suggests that a central government that puts widening access at the heart of its higher education policy can make a significant difference. Not that it is possible to eliminate the disparity between the experiences of young people in communities with high levels of university-bound school leavers and those in communities with low levels. Research by HEFCE showed that the likelihood of someone getting into higher education was established well before

---

[47]Quoted by David Watson, "How to think about widening participation in UK higher education." Discussion paper for HEFCE, July 2006, page 10.

school-leaving age.[48] There are still disadvantaged areas in England where the proportion of school-leavers going into higher education is one sixth that in nearby places. It is unlikely that Britain could easily leave behind its deep-rooted and complex inheritance of social class differences. But there has been dramatic change: the proportion of those going to university from the lowest occupational rank in 2008 was higher than the proportion of anyone going in the late 1980s.

G.   Conclusion

Looked at from an English perspective, SUNY is comprehensive, inclusive, and impressive. The subjects it embraces are as varied as New York itself. Its scale is enormous and students are studying at all levels from remedial courses to post-doctoral studies. Almost everyone in the state is within reach of one of its campuses, and for those who are not, there are facilities for studying at home. But even more impressive is the fact that it all takes place within a single policy framework. There is little mission creep; each institution is different, but they all fit into a coherent overall structure, and students can transfer between colleges and universities in ways that suit them best.

The English journey from elite to mass higher education has been recent and rapid. Elitism has been rejected and mass higher education embraced. The Blair governments devoted economic and political capital to support policies to enable and encourage under-represented groups, especially the least well-off, to apply to institutions of higher education, to gain admission, and to graduate. Higher education came to reach parts of English society that would previously have been unthinkable, and some of the policies that achieved this could provide useful lessons for SUNY.

However, the effectiveness of English expansion was weakened by the attempt to graft new models onto the elitist patterns of the past. There was no SUNY-style central structure, no attempt to create an articulated system of institutions, each with a clear role and mission. The pretence that all universities were doing the same thing robbed the nation of distinctive institutions of higher education that valued teaching without ignoring research. The provision of higher education in England was not as inclusive or as convenient as in New York. The journey to mass higher education would have been faster and smoother if England had used the state university route map developed in New York.

---

[48]"Young Participation in Higher Education." January 2005: HEFCE 2005/03.

The View from the SUNY Tower: Two Chancellors Look Back

Editors' Note: The following two keynote speeches were delivered by former Chancellor Clifton R. Wharton Jr. (1978–87) at dinner on April 3, 2009, and former Chancellor D. Bruce Johnstone (1988–94) at a luncheon on April 4, 2009, at the SUNY 60th Anniversary Scholarly Conference held at the University at Albany, April 3–5, 2009.

I.   Historical Vignettes of SUNY: A Personal Sampling

Clifton R. Wharton Jr.

The invitation to participate in SUNY's sixtieth anniversary was most welcome. I also spoke at SUNY's fiftieth anniversary, so I don't want to repeat myself.

The other problem is that I have been writing my autobiography. People who write their life story rarely tell you the true reason why they do it. Most say that the autobiography is for their children and grandchildren. The secret real reason is the author's anxiety that history will forget who they were and what they did. Hence, my greater challenge this evening is not to let any admission of such vanity cross my lips.

As soon as this conference was announced, I began to receive letters and e-mails asking me what I planned to say. So, I decided to use some of these questions as the basis for my remarks this evening. The advantage is that they give me a good excuse to offer a personal sampling of SUNY vignettes that might add to the sixty year scholarly conference review. The questioners' names have been changed to protect the guilty.

Dear Dr. Wharton,

When you became Chancellor in 1978 after the demise of the Rockefeller "Golden Years," did you have a specific vision of what SUNY might become?

Mr. John Peoples, New York Association for the Improved Funding of SUNY and CUNY

I did not develop a vision for SUNY until after visiting all sixty-four campuses in my first ten months in office. Capitalizing on the rich diversity of SUNY as a system was my first vision. Virtually every field of knowledge could be found somewhere in the SUNY system, an enormous academic treasure. During my visits, I saw numerous cases where linkages between campuses could provide opportunities for complementary and supplementary relationships. For example, I was struck by a course at Erie Community College on principles of offset lithography covering plate preparation, paper handling, and ink, as well as related materials. These key components of Erie's program in graphic arts and communications technology could have benefitted students majoring in art at the Buffalo State College or at the College at Purchase. Reciprocally, the students at the community college could have benefitted from linkages with the two state operated campuses.

Whether it was the incredible SUNY Fashion Institute of Technology in New York City, or the nationally famous SUNY School of Ceramic Engineering and Materials Science at Alfred University [Editors' note: Today officially known as the New York State School of Ceramics at Alfred University], the system abounded with phenomenal and distinctive academic riches that collectively were probably unmatched by any other university in the nation. I was convinced that if this awesome range of curricula could be effectively harnessed and made more evident to New York citizens, SUNY could become recognized as a vital resource for the state and its development.

From these visits emerged my other priority initiatives, such as pushing for a public service or a campus education extension dimension which was lacking; reducing excessive bureaucratic oversight by the state and pressing for greater administrative flexibility; promoting private fund-raising as a new component at all colleges and universities; strengthening research and graduate studies; increasing support for community colleges;[1] and protecting SUNY's original commitment to diversity and promoting women and minorities to senior administrative positions.

A vision alone is not sufficient; you must also have two other components to enable strong execution. First, I served under a superb, non-partisan board of trustees. During my tenure there were hardly ever instances of political ideological posturing, or of intruding beyond policy into the roles of management. Each trustee fully believed that their role was as a fiduciary for the well-being of SUNY. They worked extremely hard and were totally supportive of achieving the best for SUNY. Second, I had the good fortune of great top

---

[1] Neal Robbins, then associate chancellor for community colleges, Bob Brown, then president of Ulster County Community College, and Stuart Steiner, president of Genesee Community College, were key promoters of this effort.

executives and staff in the central administration who, despite regular cuts by the state, continued to operate efficiently and with an unwavering commitment to every SUNY campus. A chancellor's leadership is highly dependent upon an outstanding board of trustees and committed administrative colleagues.

Dear Wharton,

I wasn't a professor at SUNY during your nine years as chancellor, but my colleagues who were here then always say that your era was very positive. Do you agree, and if so, why do you think it was true?

Professor Socrates Sagacious, SUNY College at Cooperstown

Such assessment is flattering, but not always true. You win some battles and lose others. Let me give two examples where I did not make as much progress as I wanted.

In October 1980, I pushed for the development of a multi-year planning and budgeting process for all state operated campuses designed to facilitate campus future plans and SUNY Central's ability to respond.[2] Like the movie "Casablanca," the plan was devised by the cast of SUNY's "usual suspects"— co-chaired by President Clifford Clark and Associate Chancellor Tom Freeman, and including such leaders as Presidents Clifford Craven and Bruce Johnstone, plus central staff such as Bill Anslow and Mike Reynolds.[3] The SUNY "multi-phase rolling plan" (MRP) produced a major change in the academic planning and budgeting process of the university.

The academic dimension of the plan consisted of three parts: 1) intra-campus program changes; 2) inter-campus program trades and affiliations; and 3) campus mission changes and system reconfiguration. The first two areas were an attempt during severe fiscal stress to encourage campuses to exchange or transfer similar programs between two campuses or to affiliate duplicate programs. Only a few campuses did so, which led to a net savings in cost and strengthening of the remaining programs.

The budget aspect of the MRP program required that each campus prepare, during a current operating year, the next year's budget request—a year in advance—and include a five-year projection of their academic and capital

---

[2]Clifton R. Wharton Jr., "A 'Multi-Phase, Rolling Plan' for the State University of New York: Coping with the New Austerity," SUNY Administrators' Retreat, Saratoga Springs, NY October 1, 1980. See also, Thomas M. Freeman, "The Meshing of Planning and Budgeting Through an Annual Evaluation and Report Process: Concepts for Review," SUNY memo, October 15, 1980.

[3]"A Multiphase 'Rolling Plan' for the State University of New York," SUNY memo, November 1, 1980; Clifford D. Clark and Thomas M. Freeman, "Report of Multiphase Rolling Plan: Committee on Planning and Budgeting," SUNY memo and letter, May 1, 1981.

plans.[4] This enabled a more systematic assessment of campus immediate needs and a better anticipatory evaluation of their future goals and aspirations. The first year of the plan became the basis for the annual budget request. These projections were then "rolled" forward each year. Well-thought-out short and long-term plans meant that each new or final budget request did not require major change, since it was based upon the rolling forward of the prior long-range planning.

This new process enabled the SUNY system and the campuses to move from a one-year budget focus, including a longer view, so that each succeeding state budget was based on campus and system five-year plans. As a result, SUNY was better prepared for more effective use of the system and its campus resources. This process was a revolution in university and New York State budget planning.

Although the ambitious plan did have an impact, it was only partially successful. I am not certain that the plan is still used, perhaps because of its awkward name. Everyone made it a garish sounding "MRRRP!" Some even used it humorously as a verb—"to MRP."

Second, my efforts to build SUNY as a system did prove itself during a crucial budget battle. The 1980 national recession created severe stress for New York. Governor Hugh Carey made large cuts in the SUNY budget, which would have had major negative impacts on the system. When the legislature restored many of the cuts, Governor Carey vetoed their action. With the concurrence of the trustees, I decided to fight for restoration. My strategy hinged on convincing SUNY campuses to act together as a unified system. I called on each campus president to launch a local campaign with his or her campus council, alumni, the media, and local elected officials, using their own campuses as examples of the fiscal needs, but always as a way of demonstrating why the entire system warranted better fiscal support. I argued that we could amass incredible political clout and collectively be more persuasive than individual campuses promoting only their single campus interest. Campus councils were energized; the faculty union joined in with its considerable power; even the umbrella SUNY student organization participated. Editorials supporting SUNY appeared all over the state, from Long Island to Buffalo and Albany to Binghamton.

On April 30, by unanimous votes in both the Senate and the assembly, $22.3 million was restored[5] to the SUNY budget and for the first time in a

---

[4] For example, in preparing for the 1983–84 budget request, each campus submitted its updated mission and resource allocation plans for review by the chancellor in preparation for a July 1982 academic and support plan/budget hearing. Then in August/September 1982, each campus submitted its final 1983–84 budget document, which included an outline of its 5-year academic plans. All this for a budget fiscal year that would begin in July 1983.

[5] "Albany Legislators Vote Aid for State University," *New York Times*, May 1, 1980.

quarter-century, the legislature overrode a New York governor's veto.[6] Because 1980 was an Olympic games year, Hy Rosen, cartoonist for the *Albany Times Union*, drew a hilarious sketch of Carey and me running a track race as I was giving him a hot foot—adding a bit of levity to a serious event.

The most positive outcome was not the financial relief, but the reaction of the SUNY presidents; they saw tangibly the direct benefits of acting as a system, giving far greater strength than any of them could have achieved individually. As President Virginia Radley of SUNY Oswego told me, "You proved to all of us that we could win as a system."

Regrettably, the understandable centrifugal forces of the individual campuses eventually worked against my concept of a "system." My efforts to include SUNY in the title of each campus as a system symbol had limited success. After I left SUNY, many campuses reduced their system linkages and returned to their earlier separatist labels. Academic institutional independence is a powerful force.

Dear Wharton,

What were your biggest problems and what were your greatest legacies?

Peter Q. Scribe, Author, *SUNY: Yesterday, Today, and Tomorrow*

My biggest problems are hard to select because there were so many. One was trying to combat the negative image of SUNY and to deal with the public versus private battles over state funding. The northeast region's conventional wisdom is that any private university is higher quality and more prestigious than any public university. Some private colleges encouraged this negativism, even though I regularly argued that our different, but complementary, missions could be a source of collective strength for the state, especially if we worked together. I was not always successful.

A particularly galling example was when the private colleges and universities went to Washington, D.C. to block our attempt to secure funds to build a state-wide system of small business development centers involving both public and private universities. They succeeded in killing our request. But we went ahead without them. Today, the program is a network of twenty-four regional centers, and since its founding in 1984, has provided high quality counseling and training to 292,602 business clients.

The SUNY image problem was not helped by news reporters, who seemed to have a special key on their typewriters or computers which they hit to write

---

[6]The next legislative override of a gubernatorial veto would not take place until Governor George Pataki's veto of the proposed state budget, enacted by the legislature without his involvement, was overridden. (Al Baker, "State Legislature Overrides Pataki on Budget Vetoes," *Albany Times Union*, May 16, 2003.) This time it was the entire state budget, not just the SUNY portion.

automatically, "The sprawling overgrown 64 campus SUNY system." SUNY "sprawl" and "overgrown" always went together. Another key would automatically say, "SUNY's failed attempts to achieve top-tier status." Never mind that two campuses are members of the prestigious Association of American Universities: Buffalo (1989) and Stony Brook (2001).

I spent considerable energy promoting SUNY's great strengths, whose excellence was unrecognized or underappreciated by too many New York citizens and by some state government officials. I invariably shocked audiences when I stated that the quality of entering freshmen at SUNY Albany and SUNY Binghamton ranked those campuses as fourth and fifth among all U.S. public universities. Also, I visited editorial boards of major newspapers across the state once a year—such as the *New York Times*, *Newsday*, the *Buffalo News*, the *Rochester Democrat* and *Chronicle*, and the *Albany Times Union*.

I probably made some progress in changing perceptions of SUNY, but the anti-public higher education bias and the drumbeat of private elitist superiority and excellence was a tough long-standing virus.

Ironically, today's fiscal crisis may have a silver lining in that more college applicants are seeking value for money in their higher education institutions and thus, are increasingly choosing SUNY campuses. That's the good news. The bad news is that it is uncertain whether SUNY and CUNY will benefit significantly from the new Federal stimulus program's education segment compared with other states. If New York State leaders fail to protect the higher education portion, the public campuses will have to limit enrollment precisely when they face an increase in demand for their services.

Probably my most frequently mentioned legacy is the Independent Commission and its sequel, the SUNY flexibility legislation. After five years as chancellor, I thought that the time was propitious to attempt a reform of the grossly over-regulated state university.[7] After approval by the SUNY trustees, we created an independent commission to study the matter. I wanted a group of distinguished individuals that was genuinely independent, with its own funding and staff, and whose recommendations would be respected and not easily ignored.

I approached Ralph P. Davidson, chairman of Time Inc., and Harold K. Enarson, president emeritus of Ohio State University, to be co-chairmen of the commission. Next, I assembled a highly-diverse group of persons from New York State and nationally, representing business, labor, finance, government, plus public and private higher education. SUNY chairman Don Blinken, served as an *ex officio* member, representing the Board of Trustees.

---

[7]In late 1978, my first year, I signaled this problem in a speech entitled, "Administrative Flexibility: Accountability's Point of Diminishing Returns," (Annual Regional Conference, American Society for Public Administration, Albany, NY, October 6, 1978). But I knew I had to bide my time.

The commission visited eighteen SUNY campuses, which profoundly influenced subsequent deliberations. Each person returned with examples of bureaucratic red tape, such as the famous incident at Upstate Medical Center, where a $5,000 kidney transplant had been held up by the state Audit and Control Bureau due to the failure to secure a competitive bid from other possible kidney donors. The commission held six plenary sessions in 1984,[8] and interviewed officials of the legislature, state agencies, private universities, SUNY presidents and faculty associations, trustees, and other organizations dealing with higher education.

The report, *The Challenge and the Choice*, was issued on January 16, 1985, with extensive media attention across the state from the front page of the *New York Times* and *Newsday* to the *Binghamton Press* and *Time*,[9] followed by generally positive editorials. The commission found that, compared with ten other states, SUNY had the least administrative flexibility and was the victim of "a tradition of over-regulation originating from the initial conception of SUNY as just another state agency."[10] The language accompanying its twenty-nine recommendations was blistering: "No great university, and no very good one, has been built or can be built under the state rules that presently govern the administration of SUNY ..." Ironically two decades later, another commission appointed by the Governor repeated many of the same prescriptions for SUNY reform.[11]

Doubts were expressed that such sweeping recommendations could be passed before the Legislative session ended in five months. I disagreed. We shifted into high gear and began drafting proposed legislation embodying the commission recommendations.

The New York Senate and assembly chairs of the committees on higher education held four joint public hearings around the state. I will spare you the week-by-week battle that was waged for the next three months involving key officers such as Herb Gordon, Sandy Levine, Jerry Komisar, Harry Spindler, Bill Anslow, Al Ballard, and Irv Freedman. A key stumbling block was the proposal to convert SUNY into a public benefit corporation. When blocked, we

---

[8]February 8, March 21, July 25, September 19, October 25, and December 14, 1984.

[9]Edward B. Fiske, "Panel Suggests SUNY's System Be Reorganized," *New York Times*, January 17, 1985; "Panel says state strangling SUNY; urges restructuring," *Binghamton Press*, January 16, 1985; John Hildebrand, "Rules Strangle SUNY, Panel Says," *Newsday*, January 17, 1985; "SUNY Red Tape, A Study urges a freer structure," *Time*, January 28, 1985.

[10]David Ernst, "Key Panel Calls On State to Ease Grip on SUNY," *Buffalo News*, January 16, 1985.

[11]Clifton R. Wharton Jr. and Donald M. Blinken, "SUNY needs swift, dramatic changes," *Times Union*, January 17, 2008. SUNY Chairman Carl Hayden and former Interim Chancellor John Clark, conveners of this 60th SUNY conference, were members of this Spitzer Commission which issued its preliminary report on December 17, 2007.

re-drafted legislation, which achieved most of the benefits without the name. The end result was passage of the flexibility bill on June 29, 1985.

There are many other developments of which I am quite proud, such as the creation of the Nelson A. Rockefeller Institute of Government, despite strong opposition and zero funding for its first year of operation. The institute was spawned by a conversation I had with Nelson Rockefeller three months before his death. He and I were confident that because most think-tanks on government dealt with federal issues, an institute concentrating primarily on state issues was strongly needed. Today, under the superb leadership of Richard Nathan, the Institute has far exceeded all the ideas which Nelson and I had discussed thirty years ago.

Dear Chancellor Wharton,

If you were fifty years old again today and were beginning as Chancellor all over again, what would you do differently?

Nancy Topnotch, Retired SUNY administrator and TIAA-CREF Annuitant

First, I would begin my tenure with the same sixty-four campus visits I made in 1978, just as the new incoming chancellor Nancy Zimpher has proposed. Organized and led by Murray Block, I learned that there is no substitute for direct inspection and contact at the campus level to improve understanding and management—and I soon knew every single campus. Today at age eighty-two, I would still do it, but it might take me a full year!

Second, I would explore the burgeoning examples of distance learning or mobile programs and internet courses which might be created *within* the SUNY system.[12] Interestingly, this concept is not new—when Samuel B. Gould was chancellor during the Rockefeller years, many campuses developed state-of-the-art technological broadcast facilities. Given today's massive national and state fiscal crisis, the situation cries out for creative methods of greater utilization of the incredible range and diversity of courses and curricula that could be engaged. The new technologies and the Internet offer unparalleled opportunities for greater efficiency, cost savings, and even greater range of offerings. On-line education is burgeoning. Many colleges and universities are experimenting with various approaches and models. For example, twenty public and private universities in Indiana have formed a partnership to work together to offer courses from a central repository. These developing new approaches may not be panaceas, but clearly the centuries-old model of higher education is under challenge.

---

[12]See, Randy Angiel, "Higher Education Goals and Geography in NYS: The Regents, SUNY and the Mobile Future," presented at SUNY 60th Anniversary Conference, April 3, 2009. The paper may be read in the online Conference Working Papers, http://www.sunypress.edu/Conference Proceedings.aspx.

Third, I would stress the unique fragility of maintaining the excellence of a university. Building a top tier department takes many years; wiping it out due to weak or inadequate funding can destroy it almost instantly. I am reminded of a December 2008 news report that the SUNY Upstate Medical Center lost its twenty-five member team of heart-rhythm researchers to the University of Michigan.[13] Rebuilding this academic capacity will probably cost the university and the state even more than it would have to match the Michigan offer.

Dr. Martin Sorin at the New York State Department of Health recently analyzed the National Institute of Health (NIH) research funding for New York public universities. His analysis showed that from 1981 to 2007, the level of grants in real dollars remained virtually the same, while that for California's schools increased 2.5 times.[14] This is no accident, given the continued under-funding of SUNY. Great and strong universities require sustained long-run support to attract funding and to achieve excellence.

Finally, let me repeat one of my old themes on why the state should invest in SUNY. Particularly in these days of unprecedented fiscal crisis, state funded and operated colleges and universities face a special challenge to protect their survival and special mission.

Economic studies have found that education creates a public or social benefit which we all receive and which is not captured by the individual as personal income. Education is an investment which society makes and from which society receives additional benefit, beyond professional or trained persons. In other words, education is society's investment in itself—and its future. The taxpaying public must look at this spending as a means of empowerment and not a luxury or consumer product. Until society recognizes the fact that higher education contributes to future growth, we will continue to neglect this decisive key to our nation's future.

At a recent commencement,[15] I concluded my speech saying, "Colleges and universities are the creators of America's greatest asset—its human capital …. This human capital is the source of economic growth and social, as well as personal advance …. In today's shrinking globe, we ignore this fact at our lasting peril. Remember what we do about education in the 21st century will be of paramount importance in meeting the major challenges which will affect the way you and your descendants will live."

SUNY has met this challenge for the last sixty years. I am confident it will do so even more for the next sixty years.

---

[13]Kristina Martino, "Heart research team to depart for Michigan," *CNY Business Journal*, Dec. 28, 2007.

[14]Martin D. Sorin, Letter to CRWJr., September 25, 2008.

[15]Clifton R. Wharton Jr., "Human Capital and Education," Commencement Address, Excelsior College, Albany, NY, July 13, 2007.

II. The State University of New York: Memories and Perspectives

D. Bruce Johnstone

I am delighted to be back in Albany at a SUNY event after nearly fifteen years. As the past is always a useful prologue, I am especially delighted to be able to share some thoughts in this very important scholarly retrospective of the history of our state university. For my part, I will make a few comments about some challenges I faced as chancellor, at least as I recollect them from a distance of fifteen to twenty years. There were challenges then, and there are challenges now: to the chancellor, to the trustees, to all of the campus leaders, and to the faculty and staff. And while each time has its own special challenges—and the current ones are genuinely formidable—I suspect that the ones that Clifton Wharton and I faced, and the ones looming before Chancellor-designate Zimpher have more in common than in difference. Many of these challenges are deeply rooted in SUNY's history, and this is why we must learn from each other and why this scholarly conference on SUNY's history is so important. In keeping with my current role as a professor of higher and comparative education at the University at Buffalo, I will attempt to set them in a broader national and international context.

August 1988. My first week on the job. At least students were no longer picketing on the SUNY lawn, protesting the selection of a new chancellor who believed small, predictable, annual increases in tuition were entirely appropriate. But Governor Cuomo was exceedingly cranky about a letter he had received (well before I was on board) giving all of the reasons why SUNY should not be asked to cut back like the other state agencies in light of New York's then fiscal crisis—which, unsurprisingly, Mario did not buy. His *Budget Call Letter*, as we called it then, came out requesting a plan for SUNY to cut $80 million dollars. And we were off.

We persevered, although almost every year was a budget cut, and sometimes two. I do not believe that SUNY came out stronger for the cuts. But I do believe that we became stronger in spite of them because of a great Board of Trustees, a great system staff, an extraordinary group of presidents and campus leaders, and most of all because of the quality of the faculty and staff on every one of our diverse campuses.

Building on Clifton Wharton's wise and courageous start in throwing off some of the shackles of state regimentation, we added a few more:

- Ending the silly Office of Budget and Management practice of holding down spending simply by mandating vacant lines. (We suggested cutting budgets if they really had to cut—but letting us and the campus presidents find the ways to cut with the least damage to our academic missions.)

- Ending the practice of stipulating the job title of every hire (a proper campus responsibility, if ever there was one).
- Eliminating the *research overhead tithe*: the state's practice of confiscating a portion of federal indirect cost overhead on faculty research grants (a research disincentive, if I ever heard one).
- Continuing the movement toward a budget allocation process that recognized the appropriate differences in costs between research universities and colleges, between graduate and undergraduate programs, among the costs of instruction in science, engineering, and some of the social sciences, and between labor costs on Long Island and in the North Country ... and that was transparent to all ... and that attempted, even in the financial hard times, to move the campuses toward a kind of equity, however perverse, in *relative under-funding*.
- And persuading the trustees in 1992 to adopt a far-sighted policy, which continues even today to be resisted by the New York state legislature, that would allocate the inevitably increasing costs of instruction—driven mainly by the governor's negotiated increases in wages and salaries—among the taxpayers of the state (who rightfully contribute the largest share) and students and families through modest annual increases in tuitions commensurate with these increased costs.

Of course, we never got this. Rather, we got a lot of theatre about how tuition was the one price that should never increase, punctuated by the periodic legislative realization that since the state was usually not fully paying for the wage and salary increases either, and since SUNY was therefore getting smaller and even a bit shabbier—even as it was continually expected to do *more and more* with our *less and less*—that a really big tuition increase was due. But this is a worldwide phenomenon, more about which I shall say in a moment.

There were also, as I recollect, other steps along the pathway to a greater state university, as well as the steps simply of further unshackling ourselves from the tentacles of the state bureaucracy. True legacies are for the historians to figure out. But what I would hope that future historians of SUNY might call a legacy of the Johnstone chancellorship (and I am assuredly in the right place to make this suggestion) is the central theme of *SUNY 2000: A Vision for the New Century* that the trustees and I released in September of 1991. Like all strategic university plans, this one had a lot of goals, many of which, like the better stewardship of the state's resources, would be found in the plans of any public university system. But what I thought was special to SUNY 2000, and what was in many ways a reflection of the late and contested birth of SUNY as we have been hearing about at the conference, was the goal of the more effective *meeting of state needs*. This was far more than a ritual homage to the old Wisconsin idea of public universities and state service. This was a statement that New York's major agencies that were charged with the people's welfare—very specifically for *health care, public education, economic development, environmental conservation*, and *social services*—had never formed the habit of turning to New York's state university for the consultation, advice, research, or service these agencies constantly required. Rather, they too often, in my opinion, turned to out-of-state firms or consultants or universities. To me, brought up in Minnesota where the University of Minnesota was at the table and probably the first port of call when the state's Departments of Education or Health or Commerce had a need for research or special training, the failure of our New York state agencies to think of the State University of New York was a waste of their resources and ours.

But it was also an understandable omission, given our history. And it had to be turned around not with rhetoric or pleading to be better recognized and appreciated. Rather, it had to be turned around with concrete policies and mechanisms that brought together, on a permanent basis, formalized task forces of top officials from these responsible state agencies with top system officers and—most importantly—senior academic leaders and faculty from our SUNY campuses to discuss the needs perceived by these agencies and the concrete ways in which more of these needs could be met by the faculty and departments and campuses of the State University of New York. So we formed task forces that met, set goals and time tables, and named names—all the stuff of concrete action and progress.

Alas, my departure and a brand new board that seemed to want little to do with past agendas, together with a new governor and new state agency leadership, effectively buried *SUNY 2000* and all of the SUNY state agency task forces. Perhaps this was inevitable in New York State politics when a new party takes the governorship. And perhaps the momentum of these specific policies and procedures would have slowed anyway. But the attempt to better meet state needs—and to create concrete mechanisms to better do so—was the essence of this plan, which I would hope might someday return with a new champion, under a different name, and with different policies and procedures, but with the same ultimate end of better meeting the needs of New York State and working in closer association with our state agencies to do so.

Beyond the state's sluggish economy in the late 1980s and early 1990s and our state government's continuing, albeit lessening, passion for control, there were challenges of image and misperception, which were then very much a function of the history you are uncovering through this conference. Three misperceptions seemed then particularly salient.

The first was the myth that SUNY had irresponsibly and foolishly been overbuilt by Rockefeller during its early days. This myth or misperception was—at least then, and I expect to some degree today—held without realizing that public colleges and universities throughout America were expanding in the 1950s and 1960s. They expanded first to accommodate our returning GIs, then the sheer expansion of college participation of our growing nation, and then the demographic bulge of the baby boom. The expansion in New York State of our SUNY *research universities* was greater than in most states, for the simple reason that New York State *had never before had* a public research university. It was the last state in the union to do so with the creation of SUNY. And of course, the growth of SUNY was larger than in most states because New York State in the 1950s was still the largest state in the union. Finally, unlike other states such as California, Illinois, and Texas, New York State had—wisely I believe—created a *single system*, rather than the multiple public systems of those other large states, which made SUNY *look* large; this in spite of the fact that California's state college system *alone* (the equivalent of our SUNY four-year colleges) claims to enroll today slightly more students than all of SUNY, and the enrollment of California's community college system alone is almost *six times* the enrollment of all of SUNY. So SUNY is the *right size* for this state—or arguably too small—as New York State continues, relative to most other states, to be so oriented to *private* colleges and universities.

Second was the misperception—which became politically convenient during the great downsizing of the system that I experienced—that New York State could not afford its state university. In fact, as I pointed out countless times to politicians, the press, and anyone else who might listen, New York actually spent less—as a percentage of its budget or relative to its per-capita income—than almost every other state, save only, as I recall, Vermont, New Hampshire, Massachusetts, and perhaps, New Jersey. In fact, public higher education—SUNY and CUNY combined—was then and I believe still is the only major state expenditure that the New York state taxpayers spend *less* on than other states. New York taxpayers are, admittedly, heavily taxed. But if we are seeking a correction, we should look first not to public higher education but to the expenditures on which we spend *more* than most states—in some cases much more: corrections, for example, on health, or elementary and secondary education, or most especially the cost of state and local government itself.

A third misperception that I heard so frequently was that there is something amiss with SUNY because it does not have the longstanding academic reputation of the University of California, or the Universities of Michigan or Wisconsin, or for that matter, many of the great midwestern or western so-called flagship or land grant universities. This claim, whatever its merits or demerits, has to do only with SUNY's research universities, not the colleges of arts and science or technology or the community colleges. And in some respects it is true: the great public universities of the West and Midwest were undisputedly world class—along with the great private universities of Harvard, Yale, Cornell, Columbia, Johns Hopkins, and Stanford—at the turn of the 20th century, when they banded together to form the Association of American Universities. This was a full half-century before New York's public research universities of Buffalo, Stony Brook, Albany, and Binghamton were even being formed. And it was nearly a century after Ezra Cornell had managed to funnel New York's land script—which was to build great public land grant universities in forty-eight of the fifty states (all except New York and Massachusetts)—into his dream of a great private university. And great it is, along with Columbia and the private civic universities of Syracuse, Rochester, and Buffalo, and dozens of other private colleges and universities. But the New York State government simply missed the need—later realized—to form a true state research university until the long and turbulent gestation of SUNY in the 1950s and 1960s. And during that gestation, the early visionaries of a true public state university in New York had to fight against the powerful New York State Board of Regents, the formidable private college and university lobby, and even the New York state legislature, all of which—at that time—were against SUNY's aspirations for genuine scholarly distinction, the raising of private revenue, and Division I athletics.

Is this simply an excuse for not being Berkeley or Michigan? I don't think so. For one thing, the increasing, now worldwide, mania for ranking universities by long standing academic reputations, federal research dollars, and numbers of Nobel Prize winners, misses so many other valid measures of excellence—including teaching quality, student learning, and service to their communities, against which measures the universities of SUNY rank high. But even on the traditional measures, our research universities have grown to be great centers of advanced study and scholarship, granting well over 13,000 graduate and advanced professional degrees in 2008 and with sponsored research approaching $800 million. (According to the 2007–08 RF report, the number is $788 million.) And our comprehensive, specialized, and community colleges are, without question, as fine as can be found anywhere. The State of New York is better off for its great and venerable private universities, as well as its plethora of fine private colleges, and the great and unique City University of New York. But New Yorkers can be very proud of their state university system and the distinct institutions from which it is formed—and I think these misperceptions are indeed fading.

As I have spent the last ten years mainly in examination of higher education in the rest of the world, I wish to conclude these remarks with a few comments on five largely *underappreciated* features of the State University of New York, and indeed of all American higher education, that make our higher educational enterprise—public and private, colleges and universities—the envy of the world.

First, public colleges and universities in America are governed not by governmental ministries, as in most countries, but by governing boards composed of caring and competent volunteers who are appointed by governors or directly elected, but who have an obligation to serve not the appointing governor, but the interests of the people of the state and its university. Public governing boards in America properly stand a little to the side, communicating and bringing their influence in two directions: first to their governors and legislatures on behalf of the universities or systems they serve and shielding their universities from some of the slings and arrows of politics, but at the same time communicating to, and steering the universities toward, the greater welfare of the students and the state. This feature of American university governance is generally accompanied by a relatively greater measure of *university autonomy* than is found elsewhere in the world. This autonomy is designed not to please management or to further the parochial interests of single institutions, but to make our public colleges and universities more efficient and more accountable ultimately to professionalism and academic integrity than to regulations and bureaucrats. Neither the supposedly de-politicized governing board, nor the principle of institutional autonomy always work as they are supposed to—in New York or other states. But these features remain beacons for the rest of the world.

Second and like unto the first, most public colleges and universities in America are governed by *system boards*. Far from simply adding another layer of bureaucracy, as they are sometimes portrayed, system boards bring to a state's total array of public colleges and universities the same supposed depoliticization of the essential issues of individual campus missions, the selection of campus leaders, and the intercampus allocation of public resources that would, in the absence of a system board, have to be determined either by state legislatures or governors (and thus in many ways by their political staffs), with local politics or political clout being the determining factor. Again, these critical decisions in most countries are either set in a national constitution, never to be altered, or in the mercurial politics of national governments and ministries of higher education. System leaders and trustees must never lose sight of the fact that all of the teaching and all of the research are carried out on the campuses. At the same time, the American public university systems, when they work, can be—for the students and for their states—much more than the sum of their institutional parts. And so it has been and should continue to be for SUNY.

Third, contrary to the conventional—and generally incorrect—notion, SUNY colleges and universities, like American colleges and universities generally (both public and private) are significantly *more attentive* to teaching and learning and to the needs of students—even to undergraduates—than universities in most countries of the world. This is not because the American college and university leaders or faculty are more noble or inherently more interested in, or better at, teaching. Rather, this feature is a function of the vastly greater inter-campus competition for students, upon which is based both campus reputations and public resources. This competition, in turn, is fueled by the dependence of both public and private colleges and universities on tuition, further fueled by abundant financial assistance that is fully portable among institutions, and then, even further fueled by the ease of transfer. In America, a student can take his or her credits to another institution if the quality of teaching or the availability of the desired program is better met elsewhere. European systems are only now trying to emulate these features via what they call the "Bologna process," the points of which are both to better serve the European student and to create the climate of competition that will ultimately better serve the European university.

Fourth, the State University of New York—again like colleges and universities throughout America—is noticeably more committed to genuine equality of opportunity and to the goal of widening higher educational access than the colleges and universities of most other countries. Elsewhere (no more so than in Africa, where I have spent much of my recent scholarly attention), accessibility is too often thought of as flowing naturally from free tuition, free room and board, and pocket money—even though no country (least of all in Sub-Saharan Africa) can afford this without greatly limiting both the capacity and quality of their college and university offerings. And the consequence to the severe limitations on capacity is that there is room only for those who pass very rigorous entrance examinations, which in turn is possible mainly for those who have had the advantages of extensive tutoring and private secondary schools. The consequence, of course, is free higher education mainly to the wealthy, who could and would pay at least some tuition if they had to, and very little opportunity to the poor, the isolated, or ethnic and linguistic minorities. In the State University of New York, as in public systems in all states, we expand our resources and our capacity with the combination of state tax revenues and modest public tuitions. But we also expand *opportunities* with abundant means-tested financial assistance, admissions practices that are sensitive to backgrounds and the nature of our diverse secondary schools, special programs of counseling and academic assistance for the educationally disadvantaged, a range of initial opportunities differing in academic selectivity, and second chances—all designed to lessen the essentially unmerited simple transmission of opportunities from privileged families to their children.

Fifth and last, the State University of New York, like all American higher educational institutions and systems, public and private, provides more higher education for the taxpayer dollar than arguably any other country. This is not because we are leaner, or more efficient, or harder working than our academic counterparts in the rest of the world (even though I also think we are as efficient and as hard working—although not necessarily leaner—than the best of them). The reason, rather, is that U.S. higher education draws so heavily on tuitions and other fees—particularly through our extensive private sector, but extending also to America's public colleges and universities—and also on private philanthropy and other forms of non-governmental support that are the envy of colleges and universities in every other country. In short, and comparatively speaking, American higher education is one of the truly good deals to the American taxpayer.

Let me conclude by once more thanking the trustees, the System Administration, and all of the participants for the foresight to plan this celebration of SUNY history. We need a strong state university now—even, or perhaps especially, in the face of the current economic woes—more than ever. I am proud to have played a small part in SUNY's history, and I look forward to the pleasure of observing, as an emeritus professor and emeritus chancellor, its continuing growth in both academic excellence and significance to this state.

Telling SUNY's Tale: Historians Look Back and Forward

Introduction

Chris Ward, New York State Archivist and Chief Executive Officer of the Archives Partnership Trust

This chapter focuses on the documentation of SUNY—its component campuses and System Administration, the heart of the system—and on the histories that have been, and are yet to be, written. Historians are dependent upon an institution's primary sources to make sense of its past, to chronicle, analyze, and evaluate what went before.

We are connected to the past through those primary sources, through records. They embody the history of an institution and make possible the passage of that institution's legacy from generation to generation. They are the institutional memory and support a systemic connection with a history that is important to the individuals whose lives are intertwined with, and affected by, that institution.

Properly managed, records that provide the basis for writing history can be easily found. A proactive records management program is key to identifying important institutional records that need to be preserved for posterity in an archival setting. Lesser records, as well, are identified for destruction on a timely and legal basis, adding to the efficiency of the institution's business operations and ensuring that only those records that have long-term legal, administrative, fiscal, or historical value are retained.

An institution's archive identifies and incorporates those records that have enduring value to the institution and to its legacy. A professionally-managed archive ensures that the institution's records are permanently preserved and accessible for research, analysis, interpretation, and dissemination. Without such an archive, the institution's connection to its history cannot endure and its legacy cannot be sustained.

The authors of articles in this, the last chapter of this SUNY retrospective, bear testament to the importance of archival documentation and its role in understanding, interpreting, and conveying our history, and in establishing a connection to the past in order to better understand the present. Both Bruce Leslie and Joel Rosenthal discuss the critical role records play in writing the history of an institution. Rosenthal's piece rejoices in a plethora of histories of SUNY college campuses, most undoubtedly underpinned by the availability of primary resources lovingly saved throughout the years. Leslie, on the other hand, decries the dearth of available records documenting the establishment and evolution of the great SUNY system, whose unexpurgated history has yet to be written. Geoff Williams' survey of archival and records programs on the campuses provides us with excellent information on the status of records dispersed throughout the system, while noting the lack of an archival program at the system level and the inability of scholars to access SUNY System Administration records. Unfortunately, one reverberating theme throughout this chapter and, indeed, an underlying current throughout the conference itself, is the lack of access to archival resources that would provide the raw material for writing the definitive history of the SUNY system.

The records of the state university system are public records, subject to provisions of the archives statute as well as the Freedom of Information Law. The question of their condition and long-term preservation, as well as their appropriate management is a concern, given their public nature and great importance. As Geoff Williams points out, there has been significant progress in developing records management and archival programs at the various SUNY campuses, but the lack of progress in establishing standards for the professional stewardship of SUNY's System Administration records is troubling.

New York's state university system has a rich legacy and a proud heritage. Its records are significant resources for the history of higher education not only in this state, but the nation. The records of SUNY undoubtedly contain key archival resources that would provide critical insight for the study of statewide higher education policy and practice, including for the formative and influential postwar period. There is reason to anticipate that with the impetus of the sixtieth anniversary conference and this resulting publication, a movement to ensure the long-term preservation and accessibility of some of New York State's most important public records will emerge.

Working together, those of us with a stake in the university's documentation—the state archives, the SUNY system institutions, SUNY System Administration, and individuals including archivists, records managers, librarians, faculty, administrators, and researchers—can meet the challenges and obstacles to tracing the history of the various campuses and of SUNY as a system to ensure a lasting legacy for the State University of New York system.

I. The State of Archives on SUNY Campuses: The Good, the Bad, and the Unaccounted

Geoffrey Williams, University Archivist/Campus Records Officer SUNY - Albany

A. Purpose of the 2009 SUNY Campus Archives Survey

Why survey SUNY archives now? We are celebrating the sixtieth anniversary of the SUNY Board of Trustees' assumption of administrative control of the original 32 members of the SUNY system. The presidents and heads of the original institutions met in Albany on the morning of April 4, 1949, with their new leaders, Chairman of the Board of Trustees Dr. Oliver C. Carmichael, and SUNY President Dr. Alvin Eurich. What better time to investigate whether SUNY institutional archives are preserving and providing access to the system's historical records? We are also deeply into a transition from paper to electronic records, and it is essential for the future of SUNY archives and for researchers that we understand how SUNY archives are reacting to this transition.

The intent of the survey, which was sent to 66 SUNY archival/institutional records holders, was to discover which institutions have an archive and if so, how they operate; what they accession/collect; whether they have a records management function; how they are dealing with electronic records, either born digital or digitized; what needs they have in dealing with digital records; and how to bring education to campus archivists. I conducted a similar survey in 1996. Aside from the number of archives reported (26 schools in 1996, versus 45 with archives in 2009), the results of the two surveys are remarkably similar. Institutions with archives in 1996 and 2009 collect the records of major administrative offices, governance bodies, official publications, student publications, faculty papers, and alumni memorabilia. Many schools then and now also hold local history collections, and servicing those local history collections may take more staff time than servicing the institutional archive. Few schools then or now have written accessioning/collecting policies, a real problem. Most archives then and now are serviced by part-time archivists with little formal archival training. One very positive sign is that while no one was dealing with electronic records in 1996, today 25 institutions are making an effort to deal with electronic records.

B. Questions and Answers

1. Basic Findings

Who responded? (54 responses)

Respondents: 25 of 30 community colleges, 12 of 13 liberal arts colleges, 5 of 6 statutory colleges, both medical schools and the college of optometry, 6 of 8 technical colleges, and 3 of the 4 university centers. Interestingly, almost the same number of institutions responded to the 2009 (54) as to the 1996 survey (51). First the good news; in response to the question: *Do you have an archive?* 45 institutions stated they have an archive (2/3 of SUNY institutions), while 4 said they only held memorabilia collections, and 3 community colleges indicated they were planning to create an archive. Four additional institutions responded, but only gave their contact information (which means they have records of some sort, and/or are the official contact person), but didn't describe their holdings as an archive, or even a memorabilia collection. This is a marked improvement over the 1996 survey, when only 28 schools (44 percent of SUNY institutions) indicated they had an archive.

Which confirmed having an archive? (45 responses)

> Arts and sciences colleges = 11 of the 13
> Community colleges = 17 of the 30 (3 are considering developing an archive)
> Health sciences centers = 2 of 3 (college of optometry is the third; the academic medical centers at Stony Brook and Buffalo were not surveyed to see if they have an archive independent of the university center archive)
> Statutory colleges = 5 of 5 (2 have an institutional archives, while three are served by Cornell's Archives and Records Management program)
> Technical colleges = 6 of 8
> University centers = 4 of 4 (Stony Brook lists an archive on its Web page, but the archivist did not respond to this survey. I have included them in the count as having an archive).

All the health-related institutions and university centers appear to have an archive, while the community colleges are most in need of archival development. Unfortunately, community colleges are also the institutions whose libraries have the fewest staff members, and thus the least ability to use librarians part-time to service an institutional archive.

If there is no archive, is there contact information for the location of the institution's records? (4 responses)

One community college reported keeping many of its records in the county records center (Rockland, with an undefined Rockland Room in the library, which may include some college memorabilia but from conversations with local staff appears to be mainly a local history room), and three of the community colleges reported college records held in the library director's office (Adirondack Community College), in campus offices (Westchester Community College), or in the president's office (Schenectady Community College). Columbia-Greene's librarian reported there was no archive.

How long the archives had been in existence? (41 responses)

In my 1996 survey, SUNY Maritime had the oldest archive, founded in 1946. Unfortunately, Maritime didn't respond to this survey, leaving the statutory colleges at Cornell University with the oldest continuous archives. Cornell's archive, which originally serviced all of the statutory colleges, was created in 1951. Most archives in the system were founded in the 1970s and 1980s.

Why was the archive established and does it have a written mandate? (41 responses)

> 86.8% (33 institutions) said the archive was created as part of a traditional library function
> 18.4% (7 institutions) credited a presidential mandate with creating the archives
> 2.6% (1 institution) credited a SUNY mandate from Provost Joseph Burke in the early 1990s with creating the archive.

Three respondents didn't know why their archive was founded, one institution reported that the archive was founded by an interested librarian, and one institution reported that their archive was founded by the alumni association.

Is there an official accessions policy? (49 responses)

More importantly, only 40.8% (20 institutions) said they had a written mandate that defines what the archive accessions/collects, while 59.2% (29 institutions) said they had no written mandate. Most said the librarian and/or archivist decided what they should accession/collect, though a number reported working on a collections policy, often with the aid of an archive advisory committee.

What type of official records does the archive accession/collect? (48 responses, in order of accessioning importance)

> President's office = 87.5% (42 schools)
> Public Relations = 87.5% (42 schools)
> Institutional publications = 87.5% (42 schools)
> Academic affairs/provost = 81.3% (39 schools)
> Board records = 75.0% (36 schools)
> Academic Departments= 75.0% (36 schools)
> Alumni Affairs/Association = 73.9% (35 schools)
> College/University Senate = 68.9% (31 schools)
> Student Affairs = 64.6% (31 schools)
> Research office = 60.4% (29 schools)
> Budget Office = 35.6% (16 schools)
> Personnel Office = 35.6% (16 schools)

Only 8.9% (4 schools) accession the institutional website—probably the most consulted public resource of SUNY schools in the digital age, and surely an institutional publication.

Beyond official records, what do SUNY archives collect? (48 responses, in order of collecting importance)

Historical artifacts/memorabilia = 89.6% (43 schools)
Student publications = 85.4% (41 schools)
Faculty papers = 70.8% (34 schools)
Alumni papers = 41.7% (20 schools)
Students group records = 39.6% (19 schools)

Who uses archive/historical records collections? (47 responses, in order by use, most to least)

Public relations office = 72.3% (34 schools)
Alumni and alumni office = 66.0% (31 schools)
Student researchers = 63.6% (28 schools)
Institutional offices = 53.2% (25 schools)
Outside researchers = 48.9% (23 schools)
President's office = 48.9% (23 schools)
Institutional library = 23.4% (11 schools)

Does the archive perform records management for the institution, and if so, what schedules do they follow? (46 responses)

Yes = 17.4% (8 institutions, and 4 of those were at Cornell)
No = 82.6% (38 institutions)

Only 4 institutions outside Cornell answered the questions regarding schedules and they use a combination of the 1977 *SUNY Records Retention and Disposition Schedule* and the *General Retention and Disposition Schedule for New York State Government Records*, 2008 available at: http://www.archives.nysed.gov/a/records/mr_pub_genschedule.shtml

While much of what an archive accessions/collects is not mandated by officially sanctioned state schedules, the core of what we must accession is mandated by those schedules. Records management is critical to identifying records that should be transferred to an archive and what can safely be discarded after the appropriate retention period.

How many institutions also collect regional or local history, and how much time do they spend on that activity? (34 responses)

Thirty-four schools collect local history, though 82.4% (28) spent less than 25% of their time on these collections, 5.9% (2) spent between 26 and 50% of their time on these collections, 8.8% (3) spent between 51 and 75% of their time on local history collections, while one institution spent more than 76% of its time on local history collections.

Electronic Records

How are SUNY institutions dealing with electronic records: Do they accept them, in what formats, and do they preserve them? (46 responses)

> Accessioning e-records = 23 institutions
> Do not accession e-records = 23 institutions

Of those accessioning e-records, most accept information in the most common electronic formats: 95.8% (23 institutions) and 87.5% (21 institutions) reported accepting records on CD and DVD respectively. Much lower percentages were accepted from disk (66.0%), the server (54.2%), and flash drive (41.7%).

Do they make electronic records available to the public? (40 responses)

27.5% (11 institutions) have procedures in place to make electronic records available to the public, 72.5% (29 institutions) had no procedures in place to make e-records available.

Do archives store their records in a formal electronic records repository such as D-Space? (37 responses)

> Yes = 21.6% (8 institutions)
> No = 78.4% (29 institutions)

How are archives storing e-records? (26 responses, some listing more than one format)

> 17 (65.4%) stored the records in the format received
> 5 (19.2%) backed e-records up on CD
> 6 (23.1%) on DVD
> 7 (26.9%) on a hard drive
> 5 (19.2%) on the library server
> 10 (38.5%) on the institutional server

Are SUNY archives/records repositories cooperating with institutional information technology staff to preserve, insure the authenticity of, and make accessible e-records? (43 responses)

Only 11 institutions are working with their institutional technology staff to store, preserve, and authenticate their electronic records.

A key issue for the future of archives is the next question—namely, are campus offices providing access to digital archival records they create or receive, and by-passing archives where such records would ordinarily be stored? (45 responses)

> Yes = 33.3% (15 institutions)
> No = 26.7% (12 institutions)
> Don't know = 40.0% (18 institutions)

What kind of training do institutional records holders need to deal with e-records? (44 responses)

    Preservation = 86.4% (38 institutions)
    Access = 77.3% (34 institutions)
    Metadata = 77.3% (34 institutions)
    Accessioning = 59.1% (26 institutions)
    Appraisal = 54.8% (24 institutions)

Are archives digitizing paper archives and putting them online? (48 responses)

    Yes = 23 institutions
    No = 25 institutions

Does web access exist for institutional archival holdings? (33 responses)

    To archives = 39.4% (13 institutions)
    To collection descriptions = 48.5% (16 institutions)
    To collection finding aids = 57.6% (19 institutions)
    To whole collections = 3.0% (1 institution)
    To selected items from collections = 63.6% (21 institutions)
    To exhibits = 33.3% (11 institutions)

Are the archival holdings listed in the institution's catalog? (49 responses)

    Yes = 16.2% (8 institutions)
    No = 40.8% (20 institutions)
    Some = 42.9% (21 institutions)

In other words, from the answers to the two previous questions regarding reporting holdings to potential users, the answer to the question "*How are we doing?*" is, not all that well!

2. Staffing Levels at SUNY Archives

Who has full-time professional archival staff? (48 responses)

    Less than one = 72.9% (35 institutions)
    One = 16.7% (8 institutions)
    Two = 10.4% (5 institutions)

Staffing levels are, on the whole, are quite low. Chronic underfunding of archives is a continual problem. As campus archives are placed in campus libraries, the functioning of the library will always come first, with staffing for an archive (which is often seen in the library as serving administrators and not "library patrons") will come second.

What is the actual time professional staff spend working in the archives? (37 responses)

1–20% FTE = 78.4% (29 institutions)
21–40% FTE = 10.4% (4 institutions)
41–60% FTE = 5.4% (2 institutions)
61–80% FTE = 2.7 % (1 institution)
81–100% FTE = 2.7% (1 institution)

Does the archivist have clerical support? (49 responded)

Yes = 46.9% (23 institutions)
No = 53.1% (26 institutions)

How much FTE clerical support does the archivist have? (23 responded)

1–20% = 73.9% (16 institutions)
21–40% = 4.3% (1 institution)
41–60% = 8.7% (2 institutions)
61–80% = 0.0%
81–100% = 13.0 (3 institutions)

Does the archive use temporary service students, interns, and volunteers? (22 responses)

Uses temporary service students = 86.4% (19 institutions)
Uses interns = 63.6% (14 institutions)
Use volunteers = 27.3% (6 institutions)

How many hours per. week of student, intern and/or volunteer labor do you use? (23 responses)

Temporary service students: 1–5 (10 institutions), 6–10 (3 institutions), 16–20 (4 institutions), 21–25 (1 institution), 30 or more (1 institution)
Interns: 1–5 (6 institutions), 6–10 (4 institutions), 11–15 (3 institutions), 31 or more (1 institution)
Volunteers: 1–5 (5 institutions), 11–15 (1 institution)

Who staffs archives? (37 responses)

Teaching faculty = 2.7% (1 institution)
Library faculty = 81.1% (30 institutions)
Staff = 16.2% (6 institutions, all statutory colleges)

3. *Archival Education and Training*

What is the level of archival training? (46 responses)

M.L.S./M.S.I.S./M.I.S. with archival concentration = 17.4% (8 institutions)
M.L.S./M.S.I.S./M.I.S. = 63.0% (29 institutions)
Other = 19.6% (9 institutions)

Few SUNY archivists have formal graduate archival training.

Where archivists would go to seek additional archival training? (33 responses)

Library conferences = 69.7% (23 institutions)
Archival conferences = 60.6% (20 institutions)
NYS Documentary Heritage Program (DHP) workshops = 54.5%
     (18 institutions)
NYS local government workshops and webinars = 39.4% (13 institutions)

How many archivists have certifications as archivists or records managers? (4 responses)

Certified archivists = 4
Certified records managers = 0

What archival/records management organizations do you belong to? (16 responses)

Society of American Archivists (SAA) = 11
Mid-Atlantic Regional Archivists (MARAC) = 13
New York Archives Conference (NYAC) = 8
Capital Area Archivists (CAA) = 1
Long Island Archivists (LIA) = 0
New York City Archivists Round Table (NYCART) = 2

What library organizations do you belong to? (32 responded)

State University of New York Librarians Association (SUNYLA) = 25
American Library Association (ALA) = 15
Association of College and Research Libraries (ACRL) = 14
New York Librarians Association (NYLA) = 7

Which professional organization or organizations are you most likely to turn to for archival education? (34 responses, top 4 choices listed)

First choice (in order of preference)
SAA = 41.2% (14 institutions)
SUNYLA = 14.7% (5 institutions)
NYAC = 11.8% (4 institutions)
MARAC = 8.8% (3 institutions)

Selected general comments received:

- Think it would be valuable if SUNY offered some archival training and helped to coordinate archives management across all campuses.
- I would benefit from "archives boot camp," that is, a day-long professional training on the essentials of archives management for libraries without an archivist! (A community college librarian)
- We need to organize both the physical and electronic archive.

C.   Conclusions

The good news is that there is an increase in the number of archives in SUNY institutions from 28 institutional archives in 1996 to 44 in 2009. Also on the plus side is evidence that archives are accessioning a broad spectrum of administrative records, faculty papers, and student and alumni papers. The bad news is that lack of funding and staffing is a system-wide problem. The pressures are especially severe at the community colleges, and some need assistance to upgrade or create archives.

Another disturbing sign is the divorce of records management from the archival function. Records scheduling can lead to stronger archives by identifying records that should be turned over to the archive by campus offices.

Despite the existence of a larger number of archives in the SUNY System, the fact remains that most archives are staffed only part-time. Over 90% of the 48 institutions answering staffing questions reported their archival staff worked less than 40% FTE. The implication is that most SUNY archivists are primarily functioning as librarians. Somewhat encouraging is the use of temporary service student assistants, interns, and volunteers to supplement archival professional staff, but again, fewer than half of the reporting institutions received any student or volunteer help.

Also disturbing is the comparative lack of such fundamental archival administrative tools as written mandates (which would give archives administrative support) and written collection development policies, though a number of institutions reported that they were developing written policies, occasionally with the assistance of archival advisory committees.

Regarding electronic records, there are indications that archives in the SUNY system are beginning to respond to the challenge of the digital age. The future of archives and research is bleak if campus offices put all of their records on-line rather than send them to the institutional archives. There is no guarantee that campus offices will maintain their archival records on the server as the cost of its space rises and the information is increasingly out of date (witness NASA's overwriting the moon landing tapes to save space and money), or that they will provide open access to those records. Fifteen respondents believe records that they formerly accessioned are now by-passing the archive, and more disturbingly, eighteen institutions didn't know whether campus records are being maintained by their offices in electronic format. While archives may not have the server space, archivists can ensure permanent electronic records are identified, described, preserved on servers, verified as to authenticity, migrated to new formats, and made accessible.

Fifty percent of the responding institutions reported that they were accessioning electronic records, a marked improvement over 1996. On the down side, only half the institutions that accepted electronic records had procedures in place to make those records available to the public. An even smaller number,

8 institutions, had a formal electronic records repository. Eleven institutions report working with their institutional IT staff to deal with electronic records, a positive sign.

Also disturbing is the lack of public notice about the records the SUNY archives hold. Only 8 institutions list their archival holdings in the library catalog, while 28 indicate that some of their holdings are listed in the catalog. Web access to collection descriptions and finding aids is only available at 16 and 19 institutions, respectively.

Clearly, continuing archival education is needed both for librarians serving as archivists, and for archivists facing the new age of electronic records. Most SUNY archivists are librarians working very part-time in the archive, and twice as many belong to library organizations as to archival organizations. Many SUNY archivists also report attending New York State DHP workshops and NYS local government workshops and webinars. Ideally, outreach to SUNY archives will involve SUNYLA, NYAC, and traditional New York State Archive sponsored educational tools such as the local government and DHP workshops.

It is hoped this survey will lead additional SUNY institutions to create an institutional archive; that institutional archivists will recognize the need to develop policies that strengthen documentation of their institution; that more SUNY archivists will begin dealing with electronic records, the *lingua franca* of the twenty-first century; that institutional archives will report their holdings so that researchers can find them; and that appropriate means will be found to address the continuing educational needs of SUNY archivists.

II.   Pride and Identity: The College Histories of the SUNY Campuses*

Joel T. Rosenthal, State University of New York at Stony Brook

Writing college histories—and the number of such volumes runs to legion—can be thought of as one of the many cottage industries we encounter when we survey the landscape of scholarly and popular writing. Though college histories rarely reach a high level of popularity or bring their authors much fame, such histories are—and have been for some two centuries and more—perennials in the garden of U.S. academia. For those who write them—almost always someone writing about her or his own college—the words of John Nash in the forward to a history of Carleton College ring loudly: "To found a college is an act of faith. To write its history is a labor of love."

---

*Author's Note: For reasons of space, this paper is presented without notes. Most of the material is taken from items listed in the bibliography of SUNY campus histories in this volume that Bruce Leslie and I compiled.

Many of the public institutions of higher learning in and of New York State—that string of jewels on the glittering necklace of SUNY—can be put forward as subjects or recipients of such a study, or of more than one study, when we tally the ranks of historical memorialization. Someone has turned his or her hand to chronicling the fortunes of many of the components of the SUNY system. This is true for quite a few of the older institutions—those antedating the magic year, 1948—as it is also the case for some of the newer branches of the state university. And while SUNY as a system is a relative newcomer to the higher education scene—a mere sixty years to set against Harvard, founded in 1636, or William & Mary, from 1693, or even Columbia, from 1754—we know that age, like size, is not all that matters. A college's history does not need centuries of accomplishments to be worth telling; pride and a sense of identity can grow in a matter of decades. Furthermore, while some of our SUNY case studies cover the entire waterfront of the campus, we also have institutional histories with a narrower focus: industrial arts at Oswego, music at Fredonia, student protests at SUNY Buffalo.

To add historical depth to the picture of SUNY as a unit of the government of the State of New York, let us turn to some of its component institutions. The details of college histories—when written and by whom—are detailed in the SUNY Campus Histories bibliography (pp. 332–340). This list of college histories is impressive, some of the dates of publication a reminder of older, pre-SUNY institutional lives and academic fortunes. A peculiar aspect of higher education in New York State is that while most of the plums of the Morrill Act of 1862 just happened to fall on the Cornell campus, the Normal School Act of 1866 came along soon afterwards to give both moral and tangible support to many of our older brothers and sisters in what is now the SUNY system. Moreover, while the creation of SUNY in 1948 was a major triumph of populist government, carried out under the ambivalent aegis of Governor Thomas Dewey, the legislation of 1948 created no new schools and carried no battlefield promotions for those seeking to climb the ranks from technical or normal schools to four-year, degree-granting colleges. Many components of SUNY had been going about their business in an efficient and admirable way for almost three-quarters of a century before 1948, proud of their own traditions and well ensconced in their own communities.

Old campuses or new, what about those college histories that are the bread and butter of this paper? As the bibliography indicates, and as I said at the start, they are legion. As a genus of historical writing, such narratives (to offer a wide sweeping generalization) are apt to concentrate on the glories of the good old days and shine much of their light on the men (and occasionally on the women) who helped raise the bricks and then hold the fort. Often they have a multi-purpose agenda, focusing in good part on the importance and support of the local community, while also making much of the institution's role on some larger stage—be it statewide, national, disciplinary, or professional. A college history is something we offer as proof of the idea that the school has come of age and is hereby proclaiming its maturity. Its roots are now firmly planted, its accomplishments and contributions sufficient in both quantity and quality to merit their own tale. And beyond this parochial purpose, these volumes can be read as case studies toward a synthetic over-view of the history of higher education in the republic. If their tales tend to be rose colored, they compensate by offering—and helping to preserve—a wealth of inside knowledge and a full measure (and sometimes an overabundance) of details about people, buildings, and events. If they are usually a version of top-down history, they do keep in mind the importance of faculty, scholarship, student life, and the political economy of public higher education.

The bibliography we offer gives an idea of how many units of the SUNY system have been the subjects of such memorialization. The goodly number is, perhaps, a pleasant surprise; most of the older units of the system make at least one appearance, as do some of the newer ones. Furthermore, in assembling the bibliography we suspected that there is a good deal more out there, could one beat all the bushes and search all the shelves. However, neither databases nor SUNY professors know everything and library catalogues take little heed of typed or word-processed manuscripts, of oral histories, and oral history projects (be they transcribed or still on tape or disk), of personal memoirs that stop short of proper publication, of departmental histories written for in-house circulation, or of scurrilous parodies and personal scribbles best left for private circulation, if such exist amidst the ivy.

The early history of many nineteenth century institutions of higher education is often a cloudy one—and not just for schools in New York State— and their failure rate is much like that of small businesses on today's main street. Because many of the oldest branches of what would become SUNY had a rocky start in the wilds of upstate New York—debt, bankruptcy, wooden buildings that burned, waning local support after the initial enthusiasm, serious mistakes regarding both personnel and investments, too few students and/ or faculty, etc—it is hard to say which SUNY schools are the very oldest ones of all. But certainly a trolling of the educational profile of the state just before the outbreak of the Civil War would show a college at Albany or at Potsdam, along with what would grow up to become Downstate Medical Center. And if we shift our gaze to the landscape in the years after the Civil War we find our numbers are growing. How well have our oldest units been served in terms of institutional histories? Not too badly, I am pleased to report, though, as we might expect, most college histories only appeared some years after the institutional doors had been declared open. We can turn to a history of the college at Albany published in 1944, one for Brockport in 1969, one for Geneseo in 1971. And as an exception to the gap or interval between the date of institutional origin and that of its first chronicle, the innovative teacher-training institution at Oswego began telling the tale of its accomplishments as early as

1888, a mere twenty-plus years after it had set up shop. And since 1888, and certainly since 1948—to use that year as our dividing line between the ancient and the modern—many authors, covering many schools, have gotten on track; Carey Brush for Oneonta in 1965, Richard Bancroft on the music program at Fredonia in 1972, Camille Howland for Canton 1976, to pull just a few names, schools, and dates off the list.

Who actually sits down and writes these college histories? If I had to offer a modal answer to cover the bulk of the cases, the answer is an aging or retired faculty member or administrator, now thinking back amidst the mellow glow of long service and regular paychecks upon what had gone before, upon what was going on now, and perhaps upon what might go on in the future. This authorial formula is a pretty good guarantee of a volume with a lot of on-the-spot information—mixed, in most instances, with a very respectable level of objectivity about people and policies. Devotion need not be at odds with critical faculties, though the general tone of a college history is almost always a positive one. Some volumes tilt toward the perspective of the administration and its problems, while others lean more toward faculty and academic issues; almost all pay some passing notice to student life and athletics.

Some of our authors who have turned their hand to a college history have given us a study that is but one of their books, while for others such devotional labor was their only foray into the ranks of historians. An academic historian like myself is inclined to say that writing history is a skill best developed through a long and tough disciplinary apprenticeship and that neophytes and lay authors do not do as well. But this is mostly partisanship and I suspect that honors are about even when we talk of a nose for information and for readability. Wayne Mahood, chronicler of Geneseo, also wrote on the Civil War; Dorothy Rogers, historian of the college at Oswego, was extremely enterprising as the author of *Adolescents and Youth* as well as *Highways across the Horizon, with photographs by Rogers and Louis Osberg,* among other works. Melvin Bernstein, historian of the College of Ceramics at Alfred, wrote to encourage interest in "a more accurate history of taste in the U.S.," rather than from a great commitment to a small college in the western tier. But others were taking a maiden voyage, at least as historians, when they signed on for the trip; neither Stephen McIntire, who covered Harpur College in the Bartle Era, nor Eugene Mindell, concerned with the history of orthopaedic surgery at Buffalo, seem to have put a foot into historiographical waters at any other time.

Whatever their credentials and experience, most of our authors were quite candid about their affection for the task and for the institution they were memorializing. William and Florence French said in their co-authored volume on Albany: "We are writing primarily for the thousands of alumni, hoping to bring back to them [an] equally clear memory of 'normal' or 'state'." Dedman was emphatic about the importance of "the continuing reciprocal relationship between the . . . College and the community of Brockport," and Sidney Gelber dedicated his book to "those who contributed to the creation of Stony Brook as a pre-eminent university and to the generations of students who will continue to be its principal beneficiaries." Sometimes the volume's title is sufficient to proclaim this theme: *From Vision to Excellence, From the Ground Up*, or *In Honor and Good Faith.*

This whole topic of writing college history is a rich and intriguing area, at least for those who find it rich and intriguing. There are many more directions in which I could extend this survey, this effort to analyze college histories. We could enlarge on the way in which they, as case studies of institutional individualization, can be seen as tiles in the historical mosaic of higher education in this country. The tale of teacher education in the U.S. would have to give honorable space to our colleges at Albany and at Oswego, the latter coming forward as the "mother of normal schools." A study of music teaching would look at the Crane College at Potsdam; one on arts and crafts would look at Alfred; one on medical training would touch both Upstate and Downstate; one on the building of research universities could take SUNY Buffalo and SUNY Stony Brook as book end cases; one on diversity of mission could look at Purchase, Old Westbury, or Empire State; and one on public services, for which SUNY rarely gets credit, at Maritime, Optometry, or FIT. That some of these institutions still await their own historian only drives home my point about how case studies—apart from their inherent interest—have a role to play in the full pageant.

But I do not want to close with a focus on the half-empty portion of the glass. Just the process of writing this paper brings home the way in which we become boosters of enterprises in which we have participated. It would be appropriate to end by issuing a call for college histories—particularly for those schools not mentioned in the bibliography; perhaps t-shirts emblazoned with "every college deserves a history" would help convey the message. But we know there are many agendas and many priorities, whether we look at headquarters or at the separate campuses, and the encouragement and/or support for some of those great enterprises of college history writing that we find on the shelves, most of it from efforts in an earlier era, may be hard to conjure up. On the other hand, Sidney Gelber got help from Stony Brook for a study that delves heavily into early workings of the SUNY system, as well as into the growth of one of the new campuses, and Geneseo was generous to Wayne Mahood when he became its chronicler. Though tastes may change and costs invariably spiral upward, and there is only so much sex and violence one can pack into the pages of the story of the alma mater, the topic does seem to remain of interest. Even if no one today is apt to match the orgy of self-congratulation my alma mater at Chicago indulged in on its twenty-fifth birthday in 1916, or the time and money that Harvard expended in 1936 to celebrate its 300 years, new studies appear regularly and it will be interesting to see what Harvard coughs up for when 2036 rolls around. Many examples and precedents remind us that this is serious business. The University of Missouri, in the course of its 150 years, has been the subject of three or four general histories, plus separate studies of journalism, forestry, athletics, agriculture, the library, and the school of mines. Perhaps these, and innumerable other volumes and projects, reflect the commitments of a less complex world; flagship state universities, affluent alumni support for "state college," a university press, and a state legislature eager to wave the flag. It seems safe to say that Thomas Clark's four volumes on Indiana University, with one volume just for documents, is a model no one in SUNY, or elsewhere, is likely to follow.

As I move to conclude, I am mindful of the problems of institutional histories, they being parochial in scope and more inclined to see trees than the forest. They are easily dismissed as being of limited appeal, let alone of sales, in a world where print culture fights to hold its own against the visual and the electronic. Nor do university presses rush to encourage such volumes as they once seem to have done. Furthermore, a book—even one of limited scope and of modest quality (let alone quantity)—is hard to write. We all know colleagues who talk of the projects to which they will get around to when . . . though I trust none of our authors are to be found in the ranks of the procrastinators. But against these sober reflections we can pose some sanguine alternatives. Though the college histories being published by Arcadia Press focus more on a pictorial tour of a campus, rather than with the social and intellectual minefields of higher education, they clearly have a market: Brockport, Canton, Farmingdale, Oneonta, Stony Brook, and Downstate Medical Center have already been covered in the series. Furthermore—and now I speak as a medieval historian—there is something challenging about writing a history in which one has had a personal commitment and perhaps even a personal role. Every institution in our society, but especially one devoted to the preservation of culture and tradition, has rich potential regarding the tale of its own past: institutional archives, people alive and dead, buildings, town-gown relations, economic impact, student culture, alumni achievements, and so much more. The old movie classic told us that there were eight million stories in the Naked City. I am not sure if SUNY's deep well of historical narration could match this lofty total, though there is little question but that there are a lot of stories waiting to be told about the public university of the state of New York. Anytime you wish, you can just turn on your word processor and join the ranks.

III.   The Strange Career of SUNY's History

W. Bruce Leslie, The College at Brockport, SUNY

For all its bright achievements, SUNY sits low on scholars' and New Yorkers' horizons. Its late start, its low athletic profile, and the rich array of well-known private colleges and universities in New York, all contribute to a relative lack of scholarship on SUNY. But the wound is partially self-inflicted—SUNY has failed to effectively project its history to scholars and its heritage to New Yorkers. A recent book review commenting on the "surprisingly sparse scholarly literature" on SUNY attests to a void that this book attempts to fill. For instance, SUNY barely figures in Roger Geiger's trilogy on research universities. SUNY's relatively low profile in national scholarship on higher education stems partially from the limited historical scholarship that scholars can draw upon for writing national studies.[1]

In-state, SUNY fares little better. Milton Klein's imposing 734-page standard history of New York, *The Empire State,* devotes less than one page to a system with 2,500,000 alumni. Adding insult to injury, several index references confuse SUNY with USNY.[2] SUNY rates only four accurate index references while Columbia, Cornell, and Alfred garner a total of seventeen. More inexplicably, Richard Norton Smith's definitive and lengthy biography of Governor Dewey devotes only one page to SUNY. Similarly, in *Imperial Rockefeller,* Joseph Persico records that Nelson Rockefeller regarded SUNY as "his crowning achievement as governor," yet spends less than one page (and much of that to a hostile encounter with Binghamton students as vice president) describing his former boss' favorite legacy, and does not mention Rockefeller's favorite chancellor, Samuel Gould.[3]

A.   How to Tell a State System's Tale?

In fairness to SUNY, telling the history of a state system is neither straightforward nor a strategy for writing best-sellers. And relatively few try. The author of the historic California Master Plan of 1960, Clark Kerr, later lamented that there has been "almost complete neglect" of multi-campus state systems.[4]

Historians are more comfortable writing campus histories and national histories, both well-developed genres. Campus histories abound, but they leave the history of higher education dominated by prestigious research universities and elite liberal arts colleges with deep pockets. And the focus on individual campuses leaves many dots disconnected. While national policy provides a

---

[1]Nancy Diamond, review of *Politics and Public Higher Education in New York: Stony Brook—A Case Study* by Sidney Gelber, *History of Education Quarterly* 43 Spring, 2003, 148–151. See especially, Roger Geiger. *Research and Relevant Knowledge.* New York: Oxford University Press, 1993.

[2]The University of the State of New York, which includes all educational organizations in New York State under the auspices of The Board of Regents.

[3]Milton Klein. *The Empire State.* Ithaca: Cornell University Press, 2005. Richard Norton Smith. *Thomas E. Dewey and His Times.* New York: Simon & Schuster, 1982, 472–3. Joseph E. Persico. *Imperial Rockefeller: A Biography of Nelson A. Rockefeller* 1982, 201.

[4]Clark Kerr. *Great Transformation in Higher Education, 1960–1980.* Albany: State University of New York Press, 1991.

sufficient conceptual basis for histories of higher education in most countries, national histories are less useful in de-centralized American academe.

The state level provides a critical intermediary stage for the American historical narrative. Since World War II, state systems have provided the building blocks for the American experiment in mass higher education. At the end of the war, public and private institutions enrolled similar numbers. Today, three-quarters of American students attend public colleges and universities, virtually all in state systems. Unfortunately, for all of their critical importance to American higher education, state systems do not easily fit into historians' research agendas. Telling their tale is a complicated mix of state politics, economics, demography, culture, and educational policy. The possibilities and limitations are suggested by looking at how it has been done in other states.

B. The State of the Art: What We Can Learn from Other States

Studies that have attempted to deal with academe at the state level have taken different tacks, most centering on an individual or an issue. Arguably the most effective is John Douglass's *The California Idea*, which situates the evolution of higher education in California within the state's political context as a prologue to Kerr's Master Plan. Volumes by Kerr himself, sociologist Neil Smelser, and others make California's systems the best-studied in the country.[5]

William Link's biography of William Friday echoes Douglass's highlighting of Kerr, focusing on the crucial figure in shaping the North Carolina system, though without the same long historical vantage. And David Sansing's excellent examination of a single issue—racial integration, in this case—across Mississippi's higher education system in *Making Haste Slowly* provides another model.

Only a few works have examined the history of higher education across a state. The best is Richard Freeland's highly-regarded study of Massachusetts higher education in the quarter century after World War II, *Academia's Golden Age*, which examines a state that shares much in common with New York. He anchors his work in a series of case studies. Unfortunately for our purposes, only one (and perhaps, tellingly, the last) engages the public sector. But Freeland provides a model for understanding the emergence of a public system in a state with powerful private colleges and universities.

Thus, understanding higher education at the state level and the evolution of state systems has not fit easily into the historical narrative.[6] But finding

---

[5]John Douglass. *The California Idea*. Stanford: Stanford University Press, 2000. Neil Smelser. *Public Higher Education in California*. Berkeley: Univ. of California Press, 1974. Clark Kerr. *The Gold and the Blue*. Berkeley: Univ. of California Press, 2001.

[6]For other examples, see the bibliography "Histories of State Systems of Higher Education (except SUNY) pp. 339–340.

appropriate vehicles for transporting them into our historical understanding is necessary for a scholarly understanding of American higher education since World War II, and for public higher education to gain respect, especially in states it shares with formidable private institutions.

C.   Six Decades of Trying to Tell SUNY's Story

Even considering the difficulties, the story of SUNY's engagement with its past is disappointing. It began vigorously, with considerable attention to its difficult birth amid the bruising battles among the various warring parties. In the succeeding decade, Oliver Carmichael Jr. published a detailed examination of the birthing process, Frank Abbott wrote a history of the Regents with two chapters on SUNY, Amy Gilbert examined ACUNY, and Theodore Blegen's ill-fated report detailed early SUNY. In total, it was an impressive outpouring.[7]

But then the stream dried up. SUNY commissioned a 10th anniversary volume by Carl Engelhart, an English professor at Plattsburgh, but Board of Trustees Chairman Frank Moore rejected the 250-page manuscript, only recently rediscovered in the Plattsburgh archives.[8] Recently Geoff Williams, University at Albany archivist, unearthed an intriguing critique by one of Moore's staff that painstakingly dissects Engelhart's lengthy "warts and all" tome. The staff report characterized Engelhart's manuscript as "an educational bombshell ... a kind of revised edition or sequel to the much-publicized Blegen Report" that "brings up all of the unpleasantries that have occurred to State University during the past decade" and will "alienate many of State University's past, present and future public." In total, the analysis continued, "from first page to final page, the report fails to take a public relations approach."[9] Academic sensibility and administrative imperative had collided.

Unfortunately, further unpublished histories and frustrated projects have followed. Robert Spencer and Martin Fausold wrote extensive histories that remain typescripts. Spencer's "Origin & Development: State University of New York" fundamentally consists of a summary of reports and proposals and provides a useful compendium of basic policies and developments through

---

[7]Oliver Carmichael Jr. *New York Establishes a University*. Nashville: University of Nashville Press, 1955. Frank Abbott. *Government Policy and Higher Education*. Ithaca: Cornell University Press, 1958. Amy M. Gilbert. *ACUNY: The Associated College of Upper New York: a Unique Response to an Emergency in Higher Education in the State of New York*. Ithaca: Cornell University Press, 1950. Theodore C. Blegen. "The Harvests of Knowledge: A Report on Research Potentials and problems in the State University of New York." Albany: The Research Foundation of the State University of New York, 1957.

[8]Carl Engelhardt. "The State University of New York: A Decade of Growth." Unpublished manuscript: SUNY Plattsburgh Archive, 1958.

[9]"A critique on the public relations implications of the 10-year history of the State University of New York," Frank C. Moore Papers, Dept. of Special Collections and Archives, University of Albany.

1976. Fausold's "A Draft History of the State University of New York" offers an insightful synthesis of previous work.[10]

Writing in 1988, Fausold was recording the state of the art as background for the SUNY History Project. He launched this major effort to record and disseminate SUNY's history, which focused on creating an accessible SUNY archive and launching academic conferences. A conference was held in Brockport in spring 1991 with the expectation of holding annual scholarly meetings leading up to the fiftieth anniversary. But when expected support was withdrawn, the efforts faltered. Instead, the fiftieth passed with a ceremony witnessed by few and left no historical footprints. SUNY continued without an accessible "useable past" or archives through its sixth decade. Thus, the sixtieth anniversary offered an important opportunity to reflect on SUNY's history and inspire new archival collections and scholarship.

It should be noted that a cottage industry of Rockefeller studies briefly flourished. Although the biographies of Governors Thomas Dewey and Nelson Rockefeller (mentioned above) barely mention the system they influenced so fundamentally, more specialized works on Rockefeller offer insights on SUNY. Robert Connery and Gerald Benjamin's *Rockefeller of New York* offers a wide-ranging analysis of Rockefeller's place within SUNY's history and New York higher education, with particular attention to the political context. Samuel Bleeker's *The Politics of Architecture: A Perspective on Nelson A. Rockefeller* intelligently discusses SUNY architecture (featuring the University at Albany, University at Buffalo's Amherst campus, several Colleges of Technology, Fredonia, Old Westbury, and Purchase) in the context of Rockefeller's dreams for SUNY and of his innovative funding mechanisms. Both volumes followed closely in the wake of the Rockefeller juggernaut.[11]

The last quarter century has produced only a trickle of works relevant to SUNY history, making the fate of Fausold's history project and the continued failure to create accessible archives more lamentable. The most significant publication in recent decades, and the closest imitation of a published history of SUNY is Sidney Gelber's *Politics and Public Higher Education in New York*. Although subtitled *Stony Brook–A Case Study*, it casts a wide net, locating the campus's evolution in the context of SUNY's evolution and the larger higher education battles in New York State from the 1940s through the 1970s.[12]

---

[10]Robert Spencer. "Origins & Development: State University of New York," (typescript, 1977). Martin Fausold, "A Draft History of the State University of New York," (typescript, 1988).

[11]Robert H. Connery & Gerald Benjamin. *Rockefeller of New York, Executive Power in the State House*. Ithaca: Cornell University Press, 1979. Samuel Bleeker. *The Politics of Architecture: A Perspective on Nelson A. Rockefeller*. New York: Rutledge Press, 1981.

[12]Sidney Gelber. "Politics and Public Higher Education in New York: Stony Brook—A Case Study." *History of Schools & Schooling*, Vol. 11. New York: Lang, 2001.

Over the last quarter—century, Henry Steck has contributed a series of excellent articles in successive volumes of *Governing New York* that provide the most accessible introduction to SUNY's fate since the Rockefeller years.[13] But overall SUNY's history has been in the doldrums, while the system has suffered a decade-and-a-half of internal conflict and short-lived chancellorships.[14]

D.　Prospects for the Future

Colleges and universities are past masters at creating "invented communities" cemented by historical perception. Histories of state systems cannot hope to create such warm and fuzzy feelings, but they can help stake a claim to state pride and public and scholarly respect.

We all know from George Orwell that controlling history is a powerful tool for controlling the present. For instance, former Chancellor Johnstone has commented that when new trustees appointed by Governor George Pataki wanted to change SUNY's direction, some "seemed to want to dismiss at least the then recent history of SUNY" in "their determination to 'set things right.'"[15]

The SUNY 60th Anniversary Scholarly Conference and this volume express the faith that an intelligent understanding of the past will usefully inform discussions of SUNY's future. Unfortunately, the limited knowledge of—and access to—SUNY's archival holdings remains a barrier to scholars. It is absolutely essential that both increased funding and unfettered access to SUNY's archives be a top priority so that our past is preserved and made available for future generations of scholars, enabling them to tell the intriguing story of this complex institution. SUNY's approach to educating literally millions of its citizens and generating knowledge for the world deserves to be better known.

Luckily, there are already enough untapped sources for a bevy of scholars to mine elsewhere. In particular, a growing collection in the special collections at the University at Albany includes such valuable materials as the Frank Moore Papers mentioned above and Martin Fausold's invaluable interviews with over thirty-five SUNY "movers and shakers" from the Dewey, Harriman, and Rockefeller years. They and other collections are a "mother lode" waiting for prospecting graduate students.[16]

---

[13]Steck is a Distinguished Service Professor of Political Science at SUNY Cortland. All five volumes (1985, 1989, 1994, 2001, 2006) have been published by SUNY Press with a number of editors. First published as New York State Today, the title changed to Governing New York State with the 1994 edition.

[14]I apologize for omissions and urge readers to apprize me of some overlooked gems.

[15]D. Bruce Johnstone to author, e-mail, March 9, 2009.

[16]M.E. Grenander Dept of Special Collections & Archives: http://library.albany.edu/speccoll/collections.htm

Several topics beg to be studied. Chancellor Samuel Gould, a major figure enshrined on a *Time* magazine cover, has been ignored. Governor Rockefeller has hardly been ignored, but a study focusing on his remarkable impact upon New York State higher education is long overdue. As noted, John Douglass' *The California Idea* provides one model for chronicling the flowering of a system of higher education within a state's broader history.

Luring scholars into writing about the last three decades may be more difficult. Periods of institutional foundings, rapid growth, and heroic figures are more attractive than times of economic stringency, mature stability, limited scope for charisma, and internal bickering. Still, the years of the Boyer, Wharton, and Johnstone chancellorships would reward study. Controversial proposals by a few influential trustees nominated by Governor Pataki fomented debates over SUNY's structure and purpose; their recounting will make enlightening and lively reading.

As reflected in articles in this book and detailed in Joel Rosenthal's paper, SUNY's campuses are coming of age and the resulting search for identity is driving numerous historical projects across the system. The recent historical activity at community colleges is especially laudable, as they are the forgotten giants of American higher education. Such flowering of historical interest on SUNY campuses is heartening.

But is the whole larger than the sum of the pieces? Coordinating the existing literature, preserving the archives, and inspiring new work could help SUNY win the "hearts and minds" of New Yorkers and raise SUNY higher on the academic horizon. Its sixtieth anniversary and this book have created an opportunity to bring this history to prominence. Hopefully it will inspire historians to tell SUNY's tale, as well as twist its tail once in a while.

Conclusion

Some Concluding Thoughts about SUNY
and the Promise of Public Higher Education
in New York

This book is a direct outgrowth of the SUNY 60th Anniversary Scholarly Conference held at the University at Albany on April 5–7, 2009, in commemoration of its founding in 1948 and launch the following year. The conference was inspired by the deeply felt need by the SUNY community that its history had to be told and preserved for future generations of scholars and students.

More importantly, during fiscally challenging times, it was a unique opportunity to celebrate the accomplishments of a major national institution of higher education that has not received the scholarly attention it deserves. Indeed, as the reader has probably found, SUNY is so vast and complex that the full range of its activities, past and present, could not be even fully-treated in the papers collected in this book.

Consequently, this collection serves a number of inter-related purposes. The first, and most straightforward, is to provide a wide-ranging introduction to the history of the State University of New York. The second is to present in some detail the wide scope of academic, healthcare, economic development, and social programs which SUNY undertakes in support of the State of New York and its citizens. The third is to offer a critical examination of SUNY, by scholars from both within SUNY and those from institutions throughout the country. And, hopefully, the fourth is to stimulate future scholarly interest in SUNY.

As is now apparent, SUNY has indeed had a distinctive history through its six decades. Through ten chapters and twenty-seven articles, we have explored the evolution of a unique venture in higher education, born out of America's wartime cultural politics and postwar sensibilities. After World War II, New York was the nation's largest state and the only one lacking a state university, a condition rectified by combining an odd assortment of teachers colleges, agriculture and technical schools, medical schools, and specialized colleges into what was called—but obviously, was not in fact—a "state university," at least as the phrase was normally used by Americans of the mid-century.

In time, SUNY evolved. That initial collection of teachers colleges (later transformed into comprehensive institutions), agricultural and technical institutes, and specialty colleges, was soon joined by community colleges and medical schools. Then, in the 1960s, SUNY dramatically added doctoral centers and tens of thousands of students, resulting in an emerging system that grabbed significant national attention. But beginning in the 1970s and continuing through the next decade, the state's growing budget woes and changing political priorities, as well as personalities, left the hopes for a great public university system unrealized. Despite the new realities, during the remaining decades of the 20th century, SUNY went about its mission of educating millions of New Yorkers, producing research and scholarship, often world-class, and serving New York State in an impressive, literally and innumerable, variety of ways. In its mere sixty years, the state university has bestowed more than 3 million degrees on approximately 2.5 million graduates from its sixty-four campuses.

While the preceding chapters cover many aspects of SUNY's history, much is also missing. Even with our more than two dozen articles, the absence of many important topics and perspectives means this book is more suggestive of what we need to know than a comprehensive retelling of the SUNY story. For example, the period of dramatic growth under Governor Nelson Rockefeller, and especially during the "golden years" of his partnership with Chancellor Samuel Gould, deserve a detailed accounting of their own, as do the economics of SUNY, with its direct and indirect impacts on communities across the state, and its inconsistent funding patterns that have been enmeshed in New York State politics. So, too, does a broader analysis require assessments of the influence of private institutions, especially since during most of the past century, New York has provided more direct aid to its private colleges and universities than have all other forty-nine states combined.

As discussed in a number of papers in this book, SUNY has been a creature of Empire State politics from its very beginning. We need an analysis of the complex relationship between SUNY and the executive and legislative branches of government on one hand and various state entities, such as the Office of the Attorney General, the Division of the Budget, the Department of Education, and the Board of Regents on the other. Also, SUNY's role as a vehicle of upward social mobility is another topic worth close attention, as is its complex relationship to CUNY, the other—and first—public higher educational system in the state. Finally, any discussion of universities without a very long, detailed look at students and changes in student life misses the point of the enterprise, especially for a public university.

Despite these obvious gaps in our knowledge, these far-ranging papers allow us to venture some tentative conclusions about SUNY's first six decades and offer some thoughts about the future. Although American colleges and universities are captivated by domestic institutional rankings, and those in other countries are fixated by international league tables, these offer little help in evaluating SUNY. Not only do they rank individual institutions, but they focus to a large extent on reputation, usually earned by private liberal arts colleges with long traditions, or research universities. Despite progress in the past decades, no SUNY research center yet ranks with the most prestigious state flagships or the most distinguished private universities. The University of California system, which is the most obvious comparison, is composed solely of doctoral institutions, with Berkeley and UCLA having long-honored historical roots in the state. In contrast, SUNY, with so many different kinds of institutions in a single system, by definition serves many different purposes with a much more diverse student body, including tens of thousands of adults returning to pursue their education part-time.

Yet, consideration of relative college and university ranking schemes does raise two specific issues that have been at the core of the discussions about SUNY in the past decade. First and obviously, SUNY is a system rather than a university, which means that as a collection of campuses, it has necessarily attempted to enforce some large degree of common planning, which individual campuses often resisted as too great a constraint on their initiative. So the balance between system and campus, and the range of authority given each, has been and remains a critical issue.

A second issue implicit in rankings, with their emphasis on incoming student criteria, is the perplexing tension between access and excellence. "Democratic higher education," which is devoted to both the betterment of the individual and society is an idea with a history that could be argued to have begun with Plato's academy and the Greek *polis*, and been embodied in our land-grant universities and given its most compelling American exposition in the work of America's leading educational philosopher, John Dewey. However, today, this democratic ideal of "education for the masses" remains, sometimes inappropriately, at odds with notions of academic excellence.

While there is no perfect answer to the tension between access and excellence, SUNY, unique among the systems in the country, has yoked the various levels and types of institutions into a single organization, one that from the very beginning was designed to provide unlimited opportunity and access through community colleges and an effective transfer system into a geographically-dispersed network of baccalaureate colleges and university centers. In addition, the SUNY system has fostered honors programs at every level, honors societies, and undergraduate research, which together embody within a single entity the three great principles of democratic education: academic excellence, accessibility, and affordability. Its comprehensive institutional structure, along with these three principles, have been an important source of SUNY's continuing potential.

These collected essays offer several other themes to ponder. As we have learned, and as those in SUNY have experienced throughout its sixty years, New York's state university is closely tied to its state politics. It was so in the immediate post-World War II period, during the expansions of the 1960s, during the contractions of the 1970s and 1980s, and so it continues to the present day. The university's various governmental relationships, as noted before, have meant that long-term planning for SUNY is difficult at best, for the plans are subject to annual budgetary priorities (which in New York have usually been K-12 education, public safety, and health care) and the longer-term economic cycles of the state. In fact, after a decade of disinvestment in public higher education through the late 1980s and early 1990s, New York's per capita support had reached the bottom quarter of all states.[1] Moreover, unlike other state universities, SUNY's distinctive treatment as a state agency has meant that it, like all other governmental departments, has been subjected to a bewildering series of state regulations, covering almost every purchase or proposed utilization of existing resources.

As for the future, the current struggles the university faces as a function of state government probably will not cease; there is too much at risk for legislators and bureaucrats to let go of the reins. Yet, focusing on the limitations of the ties to state government obscures the much more hopeful possibilities of the role the public university in the Empire State can play as we move further into the 21st century. If part of the mission of a public university is to address the great public policy issues of the time, in the spirit of the early 20th century's "Wisconsin Idea," then SUNY can leverage its political connections and value by re-directing part of its teaching and research agenda to address specific social needs. SUNY's unique configuration of institutions is an ideal base from which to find common ground between the pressing needs of public policy and promise of a public university.

For example, New York's educational pipeline, which loses 38 percent of the student population between 9th grade and high school graduation, is among the more undependable in the country. This figure compares unfavorably to both those of surrounding states, New Jersey (9 percent), Vermont (17 percent), Connecticut (22 percent), and Pennsylvania (24 percent), and to the national average (30 percent).[2] However, SUNY offers the possibility of working through the issues much more directly than other states,

---

[1] See "Chapter 5: Resources Required for Excellence" of the Final Report of the New York State Commission on Higher Education (June 2008) for a detailed discussion of New York State's disinvestment in its State University.

[2] Gordon K. Davis, "Setting a Public Agenda for Higher Education in the States; Lessons Learned from the National Collaborative for Higher Education Policy." The National Collaborative for Education Policy, December 2006; http://www.highereducation.org/reports/public_agenda/public_agenda.pdf.

as its community colleges in urban areas are working with local school districts, both in terms of educational policy and in inducing the aspirations for underrepresented populations. In addition, possible synergies exist between the comprehensive colleges, which educate a large proportion of the state's teachers, and the graduate schools of education, which are actively engaged in research on the enduring problems of contemporary modern American education. Having these very different institutions, with their distinctive missions, within a single institutional framework offers a unique possibility for ongoing collaboration for change through a built-in network that can disseminate the results quickly and effectively.

Much the same is true for two other areas of pressing social concern, health care and energy sustainability. In health care education, SUNY educational resources run the complete gamut of educational needs for health care practitioners, with medical technology and nursing programs in community, technology, and comprehensive colleges and physician assistant and doctoral programs in medicine at the medical schools and health science centers. Health care professionals come to the state university for their education, training, and certification in every specialty. Again, the potential for cooperation among SUNY's educators, the local communities, and public officials is unparalleled in the nation.

Whatever the issue that we as a society face, from workforce education and training to the development of new technologies for more sustainable energy generation and utilization, it is SUNY's sixty-four campuses, with its unique and diverse colleges and universities, divided into distinct sectors based on institutional missions, spread throughout the breadth of the state, that offer unparalleled advantages for the future. In addition, these colleges, universities, and specialized colleges add immeasurably to the quality of life for both their almost half-million currently-enrolled students and the localities in which they have been sited. Despite its humble beginnings and the constraints mandated by the politics of the time, the State University of New York is now poised to fulfill the promise implicit in its founding over sixty years ago.

It is the hope of the editors that this book becomes the beginning of a new body of scholarship focusing on the history of the State University of New York and the critical importance of public higher education to the future of New York State, in particular, and to our national democratic culture, in general.

Appendices

Appendix 1

Presidents and Chancellors of the State University of New York

Executive	Title	Term
Alvin C. Eurich	President	January 1949–August 1951
Charles C. Garside	Acting President	September 1951–March 1952
William S. Carlson	President	April 1952–September 1958
Thomas H. Hamilton	President	August 1959–December 1962
J. Lawrence Murray	Acting Chief Administrative Officer	January 1963–August 1964
Samuel B. Gould	President Chancellor	September 1964–January 1967 January 1967–September 1970
Ernest L. Boyer	Chancellor	October 1970–March 1977
James F. Kelly	Acting Chancellor	April 1 1977–November 1977
Clifton R. Wharton, Jr.	Chancellor	November 1977–January 1987
Jerome B. Komisar	Acting Chancellor	February 1987–July 1988
D. Bruce Johnstone	Chancellor	August 1988–February 1994
Joseph C. Burke	Interim Chancellor	March 1994–November 1994
Thomas A. Bartlett	Chancellor	December 1994–June 1996
John W. Ryan	Interim Chancellor Chancellor	July 1996–April 1997 April 1997–December 1999
Robert L. King	Chancellor	January 2000–May 2005

Executive	Title	Term
John R. Ryan	Acting Chancellor Chancellor	June 2005–December 2005 December 2005–May 2007
John B. Clark	Interim Chancellor	June 2007–February 2009
John J. O'Connor	Officer-in-Charge	December 2008–May 2009
Nancy L. Zimpher	Chancellor	June 2009–present

Appendix 2

Governors of New York State in the State University of New York Era

Thomas E. Dewey	1943–1954
W. Averill Harriman	1955–1958
Nelson A. Rockefeller	1959–1973
C. Malcolm Wilson	1973–1974
Hugh L. Carey	1975–1982
Mario M. Cuomo	1983–1994
George E. Pataki	1995–2006
Eliot L. Spitzer	2007–2008
David A. Paterson	2008–

Appendix 3

SUNY Campus List by Alphabetical Order / Institutional Sector

A   Adirondack / Community College
Albany / University Center and Doctoral Degree Granting Institution
Alfred State / Technology College
Alfred University, NYS College of Ceramics / University Center and
    Doctoral Degree Granting Institution

B   Binghamton / University Center and Doctoral Degree Granting Institution
Brockport / University College
Broome / Community College
Buffalo, University at / University Center and Doctoral Degree Granting
     Institution
Buffalo State College / University College

C   Canton / Technology College
Cayuga / Community College
Clinton / Community College
Cobleskill / Technology College
Columbia–Greene / Community College
Cornell, NYS College of Agriculture & Life Sciences / University Center
     and Doctoral Degree Granting Institution
Cornell, NYS College of Human Ecology / University Center and Doctoral
     Degree Granting Institution
Cornell, NYS College of Veterinary Medicine / University Center and
     Doctoral Degree Granting Institution
Cornell, NYS School of Industrial and Labor Relations / University Center
     and Doctoral Degree Granting Institution
Corning / Community College
Cortland / University College

D   Delhi / Technology College
Downstate Medical Center / University Center and Doctoral Degree
     Granting Institution
Dutchess / Community College

E   Empire State College / University College
Environmental Science and Forestry (Syracuse) / University Center and
     Doctoral Degree Granting Institution
Erie / Community College

F   Farmingdale State / Technology College
Fashion Institute of Technology / Community College
Finger Lakes / Community College
Fredonia / University College
Fulton-Montgomery / Community College

G   Genesee / Community College
Geneseo / University College

H   Herkimer County / Community College
Hudson Valley / Community College

J   Jamestown / Community College
Jefferson / Community College

M   Maritime College / Technology College
Mohawk Valley / Community College
Monroe / Community College
Morrisville State College / Technology College

N   Nassau / Community College
New Paltz / University College
Niagara County / Community College
North Country / Community College

O   Old Westbury / University College
Oneonta / University College
Onondaga / Community College
Optometry / University Center and Doctoral Degree Granting Institution
Orange County / Community College
Oswego / University College

P   Plattsburgh / University College
Potsdam / University College
Purchase / University College

R   Rockland / Community College

S   Schenectady County / Community College
Stony Brook / University Center and Doctoral Degree Granting Institution
Suffolk County / Community College
Sullivan County / Community College
SUNYIT / Technology College

T   Tompkins Cortland / Community College

U   Ulster County / Community College
Upstate Medical University / University Center and Doctoral Degree
      Granting Institution

W   Westchester / Community College

Note: The above listing of SUNY's sixty-four campuses does not include the Levin Graduate Institute of International Relations and Commerce, located in New York City.

Bibliographies

The History of SUNY & of Higher Education in New York State

Frank C. Abbott. *Government Policy and Higher Education: A Study of the Regents of the University of the State of New York, 1784–1949.* Ithaca: Cornell University Press, 1958.

George Anker. "State University of New York Community Colleges: Summary of Operating Aid Formula." On CD-ROM: Robbins, "SUNY Community Colleges."

William C. Barba (Ed.). *Higher Education in Crisis: New York in National Perspective. Garland Studies in Higher Education.* New York: Garland Publishing, 1995.

Donald E. Barr. *SUNY, CUNY, & the Independent Colleges & Universities: Conflict in New York State Higher Education.* Albany: Rockefeller Institute of Government, 1985.

Gerald Benjamin and T. Norman Hurd. *Rockefeller in Retrospect: The Governor's New York Legacy.* Albany: Rockefeller Institute, 1984.

Samuel Bleeker. *The Politics of Architecture: A Perspective on Nelson A. Rockefeller.* New York: Rutledge Press, 1981.

Theodore C. Blegen. *The Harvests of Knowledge: A Report on Research Potentials and Problems in the State University of New York.* Albany: The Research Foundation of the State University of New York, 1957.

Kathy Reeves Bracco and Yolanda Sanchez-Penley. "New York: Politics and the Funding of Higher Education." In *Public and Private Financing of Higher Education: Shaping Public Policy for the Future,* ed. Patrick M. Callan. Westport, Conn.: Greenwood, 1997.

Oliver C. Carmichael. *New York Establishes a State University: A Case Study in the Processes of Policy Formation.* Nashville: Vanderbilt University Press, 1955.

Robert H. Connery and Gerald Benjamin. *Rockefeller of New York, Executive Power in the State House.* Ithaca: Cornell University Press, 1979.

Carl W. Engelhart. "The State University of New York: A Decade of Growth." Unpublished, 1958.

Martin Fausold. "A Draft History of the State University of New York." Unpublished, 1988.

———. "Funding SUNY: The Historic Interaction of Budgets and Politics." Unpublished, undated

———. "SUNY Past as Prologue: Six Anecdotes." Unpublished, undated.

Bibliographies

Thomas E. Finegan. *Some of New York's Contributions to the Development and Standardization of State Normal Schools.* Oswego: 1914.

James Folts. "History of the University of the State of New York & the State Education Dept, 1784–1996." Unpublished, 1996.

Sidney Gelber. *Politics and Public Higher Education in New York: Stony Brook—A Case Study. History of Schools & Schooling,* Vol. 11. New York: Lang, 2001.

Amy M. Gilbert. *ACUNY: The Associated College of Upper New York: a Unique Response to an Emergency in Higher Education in the State of New York.* Ithaca: Cornell University Press, 1950.

Judith S. Glazer. "Nelson Rockefeller and the Politics of Higher Education in New York State." *History of Higher Education Annual* 19. 1991: 87–114.

Samuel Gould. *Today's Academic Condition.* Hamilton, N.Y.: Colgate University Press, 1970.

Hugh Davis Graham and Nancy Diamond. *The Rise of American Research Universities: Elites and Challengers in the Postwar Era.* Baltimore: Johns Hopkins, 1997.

Ronald Gross and Judith Murphy. "New York's Late-Blooming University." *Harper's.* Dec. 1966: 87–95.

D. Bruce Johnstone. *Central Administrations of Public Multi-Campus College & University Systems.* Albany, 1992. CD-ROM.

Sanford Levine. "SUNY'S Community Colleges: an Introduction to Legal Resources." CD-ROM: Robbins, "SUNY Community Colleges."

Freda R. H. Martens. "Decision Making for Higher Education in New York State." PhD diss., Harvard University, 1966.

———. "The Evolution of the State University of New York Community College Funding Formula." CD-ROM: Robbins, "SUNY Community Colleges."

———. "The Historical Development of the Community Colleges of the State University of New York." CD-ROM: Robbins, "SUNY Community Colleges."

———. "Governance of the State University of New York Community Colleges." CD-ROM: Robbins, "SUNY Community Colleges."

———. "Students, Faculty and Programs in State University of New York Community Colleges." CD-ROM: Robbins, "SUNY Community Colleges."

J. Hillis Miller and John S. Allen. *Veterans Challenge the Colleges: The New York Program.* New York: 1947.

New York Times. June 29–July 3, 1981 (5 part series).

Karen K. Noonan. "New York Higher Education Policy System, 1940–1980." PhD diss., University of Buffalo, 1986.

Christine Ogren. *The American State Normal School.* New York: Palgrave MacMillan, 2005.

Todd Ottman. "'Government that has both a heart and a head': The Growth of New York State Government During the World War II Era, 1930–1950." Dissertation: University at Albany, 2001. See Ch. 4 "Creating a State University: New York's Education Policy, 1910–1948."

Joseph E. Persico. *Imperial Rockefeller: A Biography of Nelson A. Rockefeller.* New York: Simon and Schuster, 1982.

Cornelius V. Robbins. *SUNY Community Colleges: an Oral History of the First 30 Years.* Albany: State University of New York, 2006. CD-ROM.

Sixty-four Campuses: The State University of New York to 1985. Albany: 1985.

Richard Norton Smith. *Thomas E. Dewey & His Times.* New York: Simon & Schuster, 1982.

Robert W. Spencer. "Origin & Development, State University of New York." SUNY Albany Archives, unpublished, 1977.

Henry Steck. "Contested Futures: Public Higher Education and the State University of New York." In *Governing New York State, 5th ed.* Robert Pecorella and Jeffrey Stonecash, 289–331. Albany: SUNY Press, 2006. See also, Steck's articles in the four earlier volumes, titled "New York State Today" (1985 and 1989) and under the same title (1994 and 2001).

Jeffery Stonecash. "Politics and the Development of the SUNY System: The Persisting Issue of the Private Sector." Paper given at The Coming of the State University of New York Conference, Brockport, April 19, 1991.

SUNY Campus Histories

ALBANY, UNIVERSITY AT

Kendall Birr. *A Tradition of Excellence: The Sesquicentennial History of the University of Albany, State University of New York, 1844–1994.* Virginia Beach: Donning Co., 1994.

Steven Black. *Guide to the Sources of Historical Information about the University of Albany.* Albany: Friends of the University of Albany Library, 1994.

David Boroff. "Albany State: A Teachers College in Transition." *Saturday Review of Literature* Jan. 20, 1962, 2–43, 59–60.

William Marshall and Florence Smith French. *College of the Empire State: A Centennial History of The New York State College for Teachers at Albany, N.Y.* Albany: 1944.

Edward C. Oetting. "University Libraries: State University of New York at Albany, from Normal School Library to Research Libraries." SUNY Albany University Archives, 1982.

H.P. Salomon. *Greed & Corruption: The Downfall of Humanities at SUNY Albany, 1995–2003.* Braga, Portugal: Edicoes Appacdm, 2003.

W. Paul Vogt. "The State University of New York at Albany, 1844–1984: A Short History of the State University of New York at Albany." Unpublished manuscript: University of Albany Library Special Collections, 1984.

ALFRED STATE COLLEGE

Alfred State College: Celebrating the past 100 years: 1908–2008. Alfred, N.Y.: 2007

Elaine Hritz. *The First Sixty Years, 1909–1969.* SUNY Alfred, 1971.

ALFRED UNIVERSITY, NYS COLLEGE OF CERAMICS AT

Melvin Bernstein. *Art and Design at Alfred.* Philadelphia: Art Alliance Press & Associated University Presses, 1986.

Anna E McHale. *Fusion: A Centennial History of the New York State College of Ceramics, 1900–2000.* Virginia Beach: Donning Co., 2003.

John Norwood. *50 Years of Ceramics Education: A History.* Alfred, N.Y.: SUNY College of Ceramics, 1950.

Barrett G. Potter. *From Roofs to Rockets and Beyond: Ceramic Engineering and Materials Science at Alfred University, 1900–2000.* Lulu.com, 2008.

BINGHAMTON UNIVERSITY

Morris Budin. *Memoirs of an Optimistic Sisyphus.* Vestal, N.Y.: Emprise Publishing, 1997.

Christian Gruber. Harpur College into Binghamton University: A Personal Narrative, 1994.

Karen Hammond. *From Vision to Excellence: A Popular History of Binghamton University.* Virginia Beach: Donning Co., 1996.

Michele McFee. *The Cornerstone: From Depth through Breadth to Perspective: A History of Harpur College.* Binghamton: Binghamton University, 2002.

Stephen W. McIntire. *Harpur College in the Bartle Era* and Stephen Hambalek. *Alma Mater: A Popular History of Harpur College, 1946–1964.* Binghamton: Foundation of the State University of New York at Binghamton, 1975.

Tim Schum. *From Colonials to Bearcats: A History of Binghamton University Athletics, 1946–2006.* Virginia Beach: Donning Co., 2007.

SUNY BROCKPORT

W. Wayne Dedman. *Cherishing This Heritage: The Centennial History of the State University College at Brockport, New York.* New York: Appleton-Century-Crofts, 1969.

Mary Jo Gigliotti, Bruce Leslie, and Ken O'Brien. *State University of New York at Brockport.* The Campus History Series. Portsmouth: Arcadia Publishing, 2006.

BROOME COMMUNITY COLLEGE

Broome County Chamber of Commerce. *The Binghamton Area: A Presentation to the State of New York Temporary Commission on Institutes of Applied Arts and Sciences.* Binghamton, N.Y.: Broome County Chamber of Commerce, 1946.

Erwin Charles Hamm. "Broome County Technical Institute: Its Development and Present Status." Ithaca, Cornell University, MS thesis, 1955.

Harold S. Lazar. "Broome Technical Community College History, 1946–1953: Report to Albany." New York State Temporary State Technical Institute Board, 1953.

BUFFALO STATE COLLEGE

New York State Teachers College at Buffalo: A History, 1871–1946. Buffalo: 1946.

BUFFALO, UNIVERSITY AT

Ronald E. Batt et al., (Eds.). *Another Era: A Pictorial History of the School of Medicine and Biomedical Sciences, SUNY, Buffalo, 1846–1996.* Virginia Beach: Donning Co., 1996.

Ronald Elmer Batt (Ed.). *A Pictorial History, 1846–1966: School of Medicine and Biomedical Sciences, University at Buffalo.* Virginia Beach: Donning Co., 1996.

Warren Bennis. *The Leaning Ivory Tower.* San Francisco: Jossey-Bass, 1973.

Clifford C. Furnas. *Inputs and Overtones.* Unpublished manuscript, undated.

Wm. R. Greiner and Thos Headrick. *Location, Location, Location.* Buffalo: Center Working Papers, 2007.

Arthur Levine. *Why Innovation Fails.* Albany: SUNY Press, 1980. Ch. 5.

Patricia A. Maloney. "Presidential Leadership, Change, and Community: SUNY Buffalo from 1966 to 1981." PhD diss., University at Buffalo, 2002.

Eugene Mindell. *History of Orthopaedic Surgery at the University of Buffalo.* Buffalo: 2001.

Julian Park. *The Evolution of a College: A Centennial of Higher Education in Buffalo.* Buffalo, University of Buffalo Studies, Vol. 3, May 1938.

———, *A History of the University of Buffalo, 1846–1917.* Buffalo: Buffalo Historical Society, 1918 [reprinted by Cornell University Library Digital Collections, 1994].

Taher A. Razik. "State University of New York at Buffalo: Case Study of Teaching and Research." In Victor. G. Onoushkin (Ed.), *Planning in the Development of Universities—IV* (103–212). Paris: UNESCO, 1975.

Robert Schaus. *University at Buffalo Law School: 100 years, 1887–1987: a History.* Buffalo: 1992.

Lille Sentz and Richard Batt (Eds.). *Medical History in Buffalo, 1884–1996: Collected Essays.* Buffalo: 1996.

Barbara J. Shircliffe. "History of a Student-Run Women's Studies Program." Ph.D. diss., State University of New York at Buffalo, 1996.

Richard Siggelkow. *Dissent and Disruption: A University Under Siege.* Buffalo: Prometheus Books, 1992.

Connie Stofko, *SUNY Buffalo School of Medicine & Biomedical Sciences: A Pictorial History.* 1996.

Woody Vasulka and Peter Weibel (Eds.). *Buffalo Heads: Media Study, Media Practice, Media Pioneers, 1973–1996.* Cambridge, Mass.: MIT Press & ZKM/Center for Art and Media Karlsruhe, 2008.

SUNY CANTON

Camille Howland. *Seventy Years Of Change: A History of the State University of New York Agricultural and Technical College at Canton.* Ogdensburg, N.Y.: Ryan Press, 1976.

Bibliographies

Douglas Welch. *State University of New York Canton*. The Campus History Series. Portsmouth, N.Y.: Arcadia Publishing, 2000.

CAYUGA COMMUNITY COLLEGE

A.T. Skinner. *A History of Auburn Community College During Its Founding Period, 1953–1959*. Ann Arbor, Mich.: Xerox University Microfilms, 1962.

SUNY COBLESKILL

Freeman Ashworth. "A History of Cobleskill College." Unpublished manuscript, 1989.
———, *History of Cobleskill College*. Klamath Falls, Or.: Free-Mark Company, 2004.

COLUMBIA-GREENE COMMUNITY COLLEGE

Carl Nabozny. "Founding Columbia-Greene CC: A Documentary on the birth of C-GCC produced on the occasion of C-GCC's 40 anniversary." DVD.

CORNELL UNIVERSITY, NYS COLLEGES

Malcolm Carron. *The Contract Colleges of Cornell University, A Cooperative Educational Enterprise*. Ithaca: Cornell University Press, 1958.

CORNING COMMUNITY COLLEGE

William P. Thompson. *Focus on Excellence: Corning Community College–A Half-Century of Educational Service, 1957–2007*. Corning, N.Y.: Corning Community College, 2007.

SUNY CORTLAND

Cary Wentworth Brush, "The Cortland Normal School: Response to Changing Needs & Professional Standards." PhD diss., Columbia University, 1961.
Bessie L. Park. *Cortland—Our Alma Mater: A History of Cortland Normal School and State University of New York Teachers College at Cortland, 1869–1959*. Cortland, N.Y.: 1960.
Leonard Ralston. *Cortland College: An Illustrated History*. Cortland, N.Y.: 1991.

SUNY DELHI

Eleanor H. Smith, *Delhi Tech: The First Half Century*. Delhi, N.Y.: Alumni Council, 1970.

SUNY DOWNSTATE MEDICAL CENTER

L.C. Chesley. *Evolution of the Department of Obstetrics & Gynecology at Downstate, 1860–1980*. Brooklyn: 1980.

Downstate Medical Center. *Medical Education in Brooklyn: The First Hundred Years, 1860–1960.* Brooklyn: 1960.

Jack Termine. *Downstate Medical Center.* The Campus History Series. Portsmouth, N.Y.: Arcadia Publishing, 2000.

Dutchess Community College

Dutchess Community College: The 50th Anniversary. Poughkeepsie, N.Y.: Dutchess County Historical Society, 2007.

F. Kennon Moody and Ann Winfield. *The Founding of a College: Dutchess Community College, 1957–2007.* Poughkeepsie, N.Y.: Netpublications, 2007.

William Nichols, Joe Meehan, and Arnold Toback. *A History of Dutchess Community College: 1957–1997.* Poughkeepsie, N.Y.: Dutchess Community College, 1997.

Empire State College

Richard Bonnabeau, *The Promise Continues: Empire State College, the First 25 Years.* Virginia Beach: Donning Co., 1996.

Environmental Science & Forestry, College of

George R. Armstrong. *Forestry College.* Syracuse: Syracuse Alumni Association, State University College of Forestry at Syracuse, 1961.

Hugh O. Canham. *An Update on the History of the SUNY College of Environmental Science and Forestry: The Last 25 Years.* Syracuse: SUNY College of Environmental Science & Forestry, forthcoming, 2011.

Farmingdale State College

Frank J. Cavaioli. *State University of New York at Farmingdale: The Campus History Series.* Portsmouth, N.Y.: Arcadia Publishing, 2005.

Daniel S. Marrone, "Theodore Roosevelt, His Family, Long Island, and Farmingdale State College," *Humanities/Aitia* 27. Winter 2008, pp. 20–53.

SUNY Fredonia

Richard B. Bancroft. "The Historical Development of the Music Department of the State University College at Fredonia." Unpublished manuscript, 1972.

William Chazanof. *From Academy to University: Fredonia's Story 1867–1967.* Fredonia, N.Y.: 1968.

Frederick McKee, "Threshold." Fredonia, N.Y.: 1967.

John F. Ohles. "The Historical Development of State University of New York College at Fredonia as Representative of the Evolution of Teacher Education in the State University of New York." Diss., SUNY Buffalo, 1964.

Bibliographies

Joanne Schwiek. "The Lanford Decade" (Fredonia, N.Y.: 1999) and "Reflections of the Women of Fredonia" (Fredonia, N.Y.: 2001) and "The Beal Years" (Fredonia, N.Y.: 2002).

SUNY GENESEO

Rosalind R. Fisher. *A Stone Strength of the Past.* Geneseo: 1971.
Wayne Mahood, et. al. *SUNY Geneseo: From Normal School to Public Ivy, 1871–2007.* Virginia Beach: Donning Co., 2008.
Clayton Mau. *Brief History of the State University Teachers College, Geneseo.* Geneseo: 2001.
John Rorbach. *History of the Geneseo State Normal School.* Geneseo: 2002. [Reprint of original published by the Livingston County Historical Society in 1897].

JAMESTOWN COMMUNITY COLLEGE

Jamestown Community College–A Fifty-Year Journey. Jamestown, N.Y.: 2000.
William H. Schlifke. *The Development of Jamestown Community College.* Jamestown, N.Y.: 1979.
Dolores B. Thompson. *Jamestown and Chautauqua County: an Illustrated History.* Jamestown, N.Y.: 1982.

MARITIME COLLEGE

Norman J. Brouwer. "Centennial History of the SUNY Maritime College at Fort Schuyler, 1874–1974." Unpublished thesis, 1977.
Fred C. Hess. *Fort Schuyler and Me.* New York: Fort Schuyler Press, 1996.

MONROE COMMUNITY COLLEGE

Marlene Ledbetter and Susan Moline. *Building on Community, Monroe Community College.* Rochester, N.Y.: 1998.
Patrick Rausch. "Politics, Education, and Myths: Founding Monroe Community College, 1950–1968." Master's thesis, SUNY Brockport, 2003.

SUNY MORRISVILLE

William M. Houghton. *History and Development, 1908–1968: State University of New York, Agricultural and Technical College.* Morrisville: 1969, Donald G. Butcher Library.

NASSAU COMMUNITY COLLEGE

Celebrating 50 Years of Success. (2009) http://www.ncc.edu/About/Office%20of%20 Institutional%20Advancement/50th.htm

SUNY NEW PALTZ

Elizabeth & Robert Lang. *In a Valley Fair: A History of the State University College of Education at New Paltz*. New Paltz: 1960.

NIAGARA COUNTY COMMUNITY COLLEGE

C. Arnold Dutton. *From Paperback to Leather Binding: the Founding and Early Days of Niagara County Community College*. Sanborn, N.Y.: 1973.

Graham Millar. *Niagara County Community College: a Brief History*. Sanborn, N.Y.: Niagara County Community College, 1982.

———, *Just a Giant: the First Twenty-Five Years of Niagara County Community College*. Sanborn, N.Y.: Niagara County Community College, 1987.

ORANGE COUNTY COMMUNITY COLLEGE

Elizabeth Bushey, Editor. "The First 50 Years: Keepsake Journal." Middletown, N.Y.: Orange County Community College, 2001.

Sara M. Morrison. *Orange County Gets a College: An Anecdotal History of Orange County Community College*. Unionville, N.Y.: Royal Fireworks Publishing, 2000.

SUNY ONEONTA

David Brenner. *State University of New York at Oneonta*. The Campus History Series. Portsmouth, N.Y.: Arcadia Publishing, 2002.

Carey W. Brush. *In Honor and Good Faith: A History of the State University College at Oneonta*. Oneonta: Student-Faculty Association, 1965.

SUNY OSWEGO

William Aber. *The Oswego State Normal School*. New York: Appleton, 1893.

Mary Sheldon Barnes (Eds.). *Autobiography of Edward Austin Sheldon*. New York: Ives-Butler Co., 1911.

Ned H. Dearborn. *The Oswego Movement and American Education*. New York: Teachers College, 1925.

Eugene Fink. "Development of Industrial Education and Industrial Arts Education in the Oswego State Normal School." Master's thesis, New York University, 1933.

Historical Sketches Relating to the First Quarter Century of the State Normal Training School. Oswego: SUNY College at Oswego, 1888.

History of the First Half Century of the Oswego State Normal and Training School. Oswego: Radcliffe Press, 1911.

Dorothy Rogers, *SUNY College at Oswego: Its Second Century Unfolds*. Oswego: SUNY College at Oswego, 1988.

———, *Oswego: Fountainhead of Teacher Education, A Century in the Sheldon Tradition (1861–1961)*. New York: Appleton-Century-Crofts, 1961.

Bibliographies

SUNY PLATTSBURGH

Frank A. Cooper. *The Plattsburgh Idea in Education, 1889–1964.* Plattsburgh: 1964.
Douglas Skopp. *Bright with Promise: From the Normal and Training School to SUNY Plattsburgh, 1889–1989: A Pictorial History.* Norfolk: Donning Co., 1989.

SUNY POTSDAM

William D. Claudson. *The History of the Crane Department of Music: The State University of New York, College of Potsdam, 1884–1964.* Evanston, Ill.: 1965.
First Quarto-centennial History of the State Normal and Training School, Potsdam, N.Y., 1869-1894. Potsdam: 1895.
W. Charles Lahey. *The Potsdam Tradition: A History & A Challenge 1816–1966.* New York: Appleton-Century-Crofts, 1966.
State University College at Potsdam. *First Quarto-Centennial History of the State Normal and Our Goodly Heritage Potsdam, N.Y.: State Normal School.* Albany: J.B. Lyon Co., 1934.
Ralph Wakefield. *A Brief History of the Crane School of Music.* Canton, N.Y.: St. Lawrence County Historical Association, 1986.

ROCKLAND COMMUNITY COLLEGE

Jamie Kempton. *Rockland Community College: The Early Years.* Virginia Beach: Donning Co., 2000.

SCHENECTADY COMMUNITY COLLEGE

Erma Ruth Chestnut. "The Involvement and Influence of Voluntary Community Organizations in the Development of a Community College: the Schenectady Community College." Thesis, SUNY Albany, 1973.

SULLIVAN COMMUNITY COLLEGE

"The Miracle in the Mountains—First 20-Year History of Sullivan County Community College," DVD.

"STATE COLLEGE" [ANONYMOUS]

Alan R. Sadovnik. *Equity & Excellence in Education: The Decline of a Liberal Educational Reform.* History of Schools and Schooling, Vol. 35. New York: Lang, 2004.

STONY BROOK UNIVERSITY

Sidney Gelber. "Politics and Public Higher Education in New York: Stony Brook—A Case Study History of Schools & Schooling," Vol. 11. New York: Lang, 2001.

Kristen Nyitray and Ann Becker. *Stony Brook: State University of New York.* The Campus History Series. Portsmouth, N.Y.: Arcadia Publishing, 2002.

Joel Rosenthal. *From the Ground Up: A History of the State University of New York at Stony Brook.* Port Jefferson, N.Y.: 116 Press, 2004.

SUNY IT

John Swann. *From the Mills to Marcy: The Early History of the State University of New York Institute of Technology at Utica/Rome.* Utica, N.Y.: SUNY Institute of Technology at Utica/Rome, 2006.

ULSTER COMMUNITY COLLEGE

Gordon Kidd. "A Cow on a Doormat: A History of the Forces that went into the Development of a Community College in Upstate New York Ulster County." Kingston, N.Y.: mimeograph, 1989.

Rosanne M. Yetzer. "Organizational Culture, Saga, and Change: A Case Study of a Rural New York State Community College." PhD diss., SUNY Albany, 2004.

UPSTATE MEDICAL UNIVERSITY

Eric Luft. *SUNY Upstate Medical University.* Syracuse: 2005.

Kenneth Wright. *Foundations Well and Truly Laid: A History Leading to the Formation of the State University of New York Health Science Center at Syracuse.* Syracuse: 1994.

WESTCHESTER COMMUNITY COLLEGE

Flynn, John. "Address: The College at Sixty." Westchester Community College Convocation, Sept., 13, 2006.

Westchester Community College. *Westchester Community College Report Card.* Valhalla: Westchester Community College, 2002.

Histories of State Systems of Higher Education (except SUNY)

Robert O. Berdahl. *Statewide Coordination of Higher Education.* American Council of Education. Washington, D.C.: American Council on Education, 1971.

M.M. Chambers, *Higher Education in the Fifty States.* Danville, Ill.: Interstate, 1970.

John A. Douglass. *The California Idea & American Higher Education: 1850 to the 1960 Master Plan.* Stanford: Stanford Univ. Press, 2000.

Willis Frederick Dunbar. *The Michigan Record in Higher Education: A History of Education in Michigan, v. 4.* Detroit: Wayne State University Press, 1963.

Cameron Fincher. *The Historical Development of the University System of Georgia, 1932–1990.* Athens, Ga.: Inst. of Higher Education, 1991.

Bibliographies

Richard M. Freeland. *Academia's Golden Age: Universities in Massachusetts, 1945–1970.* New York: Oxford Univ. Press, 1992.

Donald Gerth and James Haehn. *An Invisible Giant: The California State Colleges.* San Francisco: Jossey-Bass, 1971.

Hugh Davis Graham. "Structure and Governance in American Higher Education: Historical and Comparative Analysis of State Policy," *Journal of Policy History,* I (1989): 80–107.

Clark Kerr. *The Gold & the Blue: A Personal Memoir of the Univ. of California, 1949–1967.* Berkeley: Univ. of California Press, 2001.

————, *The Great Transformation in Higher Education, 1960–1980.* Albany: SUNY Press, 1991.

Eugene Lee and Frank Bowen. *The Multicampus University: A Study of Academic Governance.* New York: McGraw Hill, 1971.

Wm. A Link. *William Friday: Power, Purpose, & American Higher Education.* Chapel Hill, N.C.: University of North Carolina Press, 1995.

Richard Richardson, Jr. & Mario Martinez. *Policy and Performance in American Higher Education: an Examination of Cases across State Systems.* Baltimore: Johns Hopkins, 2009.

Saul Sack. *History of Higher Education in Pennsylvania, 2 vol.* Harrisburg, Pa.: Pennsylvania Historical and Museum Commission, 1963.

David G. Sansing. *Making Haste Slowly.* Jackson: University Press of Mississippi, 1990.

Neil Smelser and Gabriel Almond (Eds.). *Public Higher Education in California.* Berkeley: University of California Press, 1974.

Ron Story (Ed.). *Five Colleges, Five Histories.* Amherst, Mass.: University of Massachusetts Press, 1992.

John Wahlquist and James Thornton. *State Colleges & Universities.* Washington, D.C.: Center for Applied Research in Education, 1964.

Walker Wyman (Eds.). *History of the Wisconsin State Universities.* River Falls, Wis.: River Falls State University Press, 1968.

List of Contributors

Karla M. Back is a professor of business in the School of Management and Engineering Technology at Alfred State College. She teaches business management, including courses in principles of leadership, organizational behavior, and managerial communications. Dr. Back has extensive experience in international education. While on the faculty of the College of Technology at the University of Houston, Dr. Back worked with the Southern Caribbean Project Management Institute to develop a common project management education framework at the University of Trinidad. She has been involved in executive management development programs at the University of Houston, including programs for public officials from the city of Zhejiang, China, and executives with China's aerospace industry. Dr. Back has also worked as a consultant to international teams from companies such as Shell, Exxon, American Express, American Petroleum Institute, and Saudi Aramco. She has presented at international conferences for the International Federation of Training and Development Organizations (IFTDO) in Taipei, Taiwan, Hamburg, Germany, and the Project Management Institute (PMI) international conference. Karla holds a PhD from Texas A&M University in innovative learning systems in business and industry; an MA from the University of Houston Clear Lake; and a BA in political science from the University of Houston.

Pedro Cabán is the vice provost for diversity and educational equity at the State University of New York and a professor of Latin American, Caribbean, and U.S. Latino studies at the University at Albany. As vice provost, Dr. Caban oversees various programs designed to enhance SUNY's diversity profile.

He received his undergraduate political science degree from the City College of New York and a PhD in political science from Columbia University. He has held tenured appointments at Fordham University, Rutgers University, and the University of Illinois. He has also held teaching appointments at Columbia University and Cornell University. Dr. Cabán served as chairman or director of various departments and programs in race and ethnic studies.

Cabán is the author of *Constructing a Colonial People: Puerto Rico and the United States, 1898-1932*. He has published dozens of articles, book chapters, and review essays on the political economy of Puerto Rico, Latinos in the United States, and race and ethnic studies.

Hugh O. Canham is professor emeritus at the State University of New York College of Environmental Science and Forestry where he taught and conducted research in forest and resource economics for over thirty years. At present, he consults and serves as historian for the New York Society of American Foresters.

Hugh has done extensive research in forest land ownership. His dissertation was a landmark study which was then adopted as the model by the U.S. Forest Service for its ongoing nationwide forest owner studies. His teachings embrace land-use economics, the economics of non-market goods, and integrated forest management. He has served as consultant to the New York State Department of Environmental Conservation, Northern Forest Lands Council, Tug Hill Commission, United States Department of Agriculture, and the New York City Catskill Watershed Agriculture Council. He is the author of five articles in the *Encyclopedia of New York*, several entries in the *Encyclopedia of American Forest and Conservation History*, and a history of the 100-year-old Empire State Forest Products Association. In addition, he has published in several refereed journals and has several monographs dealing with forest resources and the forest products industry, both in New York and the United States.

Dr. Canham is a member of the New York Forest Owners Association, a fellow in the Society of American Foresters, and an honorary member of the Empire State Forest Products Association. He and his wife reside in North Syracuse.

John B. Clark is acting executive director of the City University of New York's Office of Business and Industry Relations and former interim chancellor of the State University of New York. He also served as interim president for four SUNY colleges (Plattsburgh, Brockport, Alfred State, and Optometry) and as SUNY interim vice chancellor for enrollment management and university life.

José E. Cruz is an associate professor of political science and U.S. Latino studies at the University at Albany, SUNY. He is also director of the New York Latino Research and Resources Network (NYLARNet), a research consortium based at UAlbany, and of the Latino Political Barometer (LPB), an annual regional survey of political values, attitudes, and behavior of Latinos. His publications include *Identity and Power: Puerto Rican Politics and the Challenge of Ethnicity* (Philadelphia: Temple University Press, 1998) and *Adiós Borinquen Querida: The Puerto Rican Diaspora, Its History and Contributions*, with Edna Acosta-Belén et al. (Albany, NY: CELAC, 2000). Cruz is also the editor of *Latino Immigration Policy: Context, Issues, Alternatives* (Albany, NY: NYLARNet, 2008). His paper "Pluralism and Ethnicity in New York City Politics: The Case of Puerto Ricans" received the Best Faculty Paper Award from the New York State Political Science Association in 2009.

Christopher C. Dahl is president and professor of English at SUNY Geneseo. A scholar of nineteenth-century British literature and intellectual history, he is also the author of a critical study of the American novelist Louis Auchincloss (Frederick Ungar, 1985). He was an editor of *The Union List of Victorian Serials* and, for many years, a contributor to the annual *Victorian Bibliography* of the Modern Language Association. He has also published widely on topics in higher education. Under his leadership, Geneseo has achieved national recognition as a highly-selective public liberal arts college. On the national scene, Dahl has served as president of the Council of Public Liberal Arts Colleges and chair of the board of the Association of American Colleges and Universities (AAC&U). He currently serves on the board of the American Council on Education. As president of Geneseo, he continues to teach courses in nineteenth-century British literature.

Nancy Diamond is research associate professor in the College of Education and Social Services and special assistant to the vice president for research and graduate studies at the University of Vermont. She has been engaged in the study of research universities for more than a decade, following a period of professional administrative service in higher education. As co-author of *The Rise of American Research Universities* (Johns Hopkins Press, 1997), she has studied how institutions can expand research capacity and works as a consultant to universities that seek to advance their research/graduate education portfolio. She has also proposed alternative ways for evaluating and ranking research achievement and served as a reviewer for the National Research Council's forthcoming assessment of research-doctorate programs. Current research projects include a study of women in positions of academic leadership funded by the Andrew W. Mellon Foundation, a study of doctoral education in the California State University system, and an ongoing inquiry of faculty achievement at research universities in the United States.

John Aubrey Douglass is senior research fellow for public policy and higher education at the Center for Studies in Higher Education (CSHE) at the University of California-Berkeley. He is the co-editor of *Globalization's Muse: Universities and Higher Education Systems in a Changing World* (Public Policy Press, 2009), and author of *The Conditions for Admissions* (Stanford Press, 2007) and *The California Idea and American Higher Education* (Stanford University Press, 2000; published in Chinese in 2008). He is the founding principle investigator for the Student Experience in the Research University (SERU) Consortium—a group of major U.S. and international research universities developing new data sources and analysis focused on improving undergraduate education. He is also the editor of the CSHE Research and Occasional Paper Series (ROPS) and sits on the editorial board of a number of international higher education journals. Recent scholarly publications include articles in *Higher Education Policy and Management* (OECD), *Higher*

Education Policy, Inside Higher Education, Perspectives (UK), *Change Magazine, California Monthly, Minerva, The Journal of Policy History, California Politics and Policy, History of Education Quarterly, The American Behavioral Scientists,* and the *European Journal of Education.* For more information on his research and professional activities see http://cshe.berkeley.edu/people/jdouglass.htm.

Gary Dunham is the executive director of the State University of New York Press and the former director of the University of Nebraska Press. He holds a doctorate in anthropology. He is the co-editor of *Powwow.*

Roger L. Geiger has written widely on the history of American higher education, American research universities, and academic science policy. He is distinguished professor of higher education at Pennsylvania State University and former head of the Higher Education program. His most recent book, on universities and economic development with co-author Creso Sá, *Tapping the Riches of Science: Universities and the Promise of Economic Growth,* was published by Harvard University Press (2008). Additional writings on this subject are provided at http://www.tappingtherichesofscience.info.

He is also an editor of *The Future of the American Public Research University* (2007), where he contributed, "Expert and Elite: the Incongruous Missions of Public Research Universities." He contributed "The Ivy League" to *Structuring Mass Higher Education* (2009). His study, *Knowledge and Money: Research Universities and the Paradox of the Marketplace* was published by Stanford University Press in 2004.

His volumes on American research universities in the twentieth century, *To Advance Knowledge: the Development of American Research Universities, 1900-1940* and *Research and Relevant Knowledge: American Research Universities Since World War II,* were published in new editions by Transaction Publishers (2004). He has edited *Perspectives on the History of Higher Education* since 1993, and is senior associate editor of *The American Journal of Education.*

Marjorie Glusker is the vice president and dean of continuing education at Westchester Community College in Valhalla, New York. She leads the largest community college continuing education division in the SUNY system. Her portfolio includes the English Language Institute, the Professional Development Center, older adult programs, community services, eleven extension centers, workforce development programs, K- 12 collaborations, and the new Gateway Center (opening in summer 2010), which will house interdisciplinary programs and services for both immigrants and native-born students.

Previously, Dr. Glusker was the Hudson Valley district director for Cornell University/The New York State School of Industrial and Labor Relations where she developed, administered, and taught both credit and non-credit programs for women, labor, and management.

She received her doctorate from Columbia University's Teachers College and holds two master's degrees, one from Teachers College and one from Queens College of CUNY. She has consulted widely, taught diverse audiences, and received numerous honors and awards including the Dr. Carol S. Russett Award from the ACE/National Network of Women Leaders in Higher Education.

Dennis Golladay is currently the vice chancellor for community colleges at the State University of New York. He served as sixth president of Cayuga County Community College from July 1996 through November 2007 and was honored with the title of president emeritus. He previously served as vice president for academic affairs at Anne Arundel Community College in Maryland and as dean of the school of humanities and professor of American history at Pensacola Junior College in Florida.

A native of Virginia, Dr. Golladay earned his BS degree from Madison College and MA and PhD degrees in American history from the University of Virginia. He was a National Endowment for the Humanities (NEH) Summer Seminar Fellow at Johns Hopkins University in 1985 and an NEH Summer Fellow in 1981 at the University of Virginia.

Publications to his credit deal with topics in American history, politics, and law. Among these are "Sidestepping Due Process: Federal Grand Juries and the Unindicted Co-Conspirator" (*Judicature*, February 1982), "A Second Chance: Cary Nicholas and Frontier Florida" (*Florida Historical Quarterly*, October 1985), and "John Nicholas: Virginia Congressman, New York Quid" (*New York History*, January 1979).

John Halsey is a graduate of the University of East Anglia, where he took his first degree in sociology and philosophy, and also an MA in sociology and literature. John Halsey received his doctorate in sociology from Exeter University. He is English and lives in London, where he is based at Brunel University. He is resident director of SUNY Brockport's London Program, with responsibility for Brockport's twenty-one programs in Britain, including its nine London programs. He has published a number of articles on the sociology of education and has co-authored several reviews and articles with W. Bruce Leslie. His current research interest is the interaction and comparison between higher education in England and the United States.

Philo A. Hutcheson is associate professor of educational policy studies at Georgia State University. He received his PhD (1991) in higher education from the University of Chicago. His publications include "The Truman Commission's Vision of the Future," *Thought and Action* 23 (Fall 2007): 107-115, "Setting the Nation's Agenda for Higher Education: A Review of Selected National Commission Reports, 1947-2006," *History of Education Quarterly* 47 (August 2007): 359-367, a co-authored article, "National Higher

Education Policy Commissions in the Post-World War II Era: Issues of Representation," *The Sophist's Bane* (Fall 2003), and *A Professional Professoriate: Unionization, Bureaucratization, and the AAUP* (Vanderbilt University Press, 2000). He is nearing completion of a book on the 1947 President's Commission on Higher Education.

D. Bruce Johnstone was chancellor of SUNY from 1988 to 1994, president of Buffalo State College from 1979 to 1988, and vice president for administration at the University of Pennsylvania from 1977 to 1979. Johnstone, an internationally-known expert on comparative higher education finance, governance, and policy, directed the International Comparative Higher Education Finance and Accessibility Project, an eight-year study of the shifting balance of higher education costs from governments and taxpayers to parents and students. He holds a BA in economics and MAT from Harvard University, a PhD in higher education from the University of Minnesota, and several honorary doctorates. Johnstone is SUNY distinguished service professor of higher and comparative education emeritus at the State University of New York at Buffalo.

John W. Kalas completed his doctoral studies at the University of Chicago and Columbia and then taught philosophy at Queens College of CUNY and Lake Forest College. His first administrative position was as director of special projects for the Office of Economic Opportunity, the federal anti-poverty program. He was then a senior administrator at two small private colleges. In 1974, he joined SUNY System Administration, first in its Washington D.C. office, and then years later in Albany, as associate provost, with responsibility for campus support and policy formulation in research, economic development, continuing education, and international programs. These duties were interrupted with an assignment as acting provost and interim president at SUNY Potsdam. He then served as special assistant to the president of Empire State College.

He is the author of *The Grant System* and numerous articles on research administration and government regulation and support of higher education. Although he is formally retired, Dr. Kalas continues to teach in the fields of higher education administration and policy in the School of Education at the University at Albany.

Maryellen Keefe is a member of the order of St. Ursula and teaches in the Humanities Department of SUNY Maritime College in Throgs Neck, New York. She teaches courses on world literature and business and technical writing. She is Maritime's representative on the University Faculty Senate and serves on several university committees. She is also on Maritime's Executive Committee and is a member of the Assessment Committee. She holds a BA in English from the College of New Rochelle, an MA in English from Fordham University, and a PhD in English from the University of Delaware.

Her specialty is American and Irish literature. Her most recent research is on Sally Benson, author of *Meet Me in St. Louis*, writer for *The New Yorker* and fifteen Hollywood screenplays.

Before coming to Maritime, Professor Keefe taught English at Iona College and was director of the Iona Success Center. She taught for several years on the secondary level in New York, Maryland, Massachusetts, and Delaware. She is a graduate of St. Angela Merici School and the Academy of Mt. St. Ursula in the Bronx. She has also published a children's book on St. Angela Merici and translated several books from French into English.

James Ketterer is the deputy provost at the State University of New York (SUNY). In that capacity he serves as chief of staff of the Office of Academic Affairs and University Wide Programs and served as staff to the Governor's Commission on Higher Education. He was previously director of the SUNY Center for International Development.

Ketterer has extensive experience in international affairs and government and served on the National Security Council staff, as a policy analyst at the New York State Senate, a project officer with the Center for Legislative Development at the University at Albany, and as an international election specialist for the United Nations, the African-American Institute, and the Organization for Security and Cooperation in Europe. He has also held teaching positions in International Politics at the New School for Social Research, Bard College, SUNY New Paltz, the University at Albany, Russell Sage College, and the College of Saint Rose. He was a Boren National Security Educational Program Fellow in Morocco, an Ambassadorial Scholar at the Bourguiba School of Languages in Tunisia, and studied Arabic at the King Fahd Advanced School of Translation in Morocco. He received his education at Johns Hopkins, New York University, and Fordham University.

W. Bruce Leslie is professor of history at the College at Brockport, SUNY. He is the author of *Gentlemen and Scholars: College and Community in "The Age of the University"* and of *State University of New York at Brockport* (with Mary Jo Gigliotti and Kenneth P. O'Brien).

Sanford H. Levine was professor emeritus and adjunct professor, educational administration and policy studies, University at Albany, SUNY. Active in the practice of higher education law for more than forty years, Professor Levine was the former university counsel and vice chancellor for legal affairs for the sixty-four campus State University of New York system. He served as president of the National Association of College and University Attorneys and participated frequently in national higher education conferences and seminars. A member of the New York Bar, Professor Levine was a life fellow of both the American Bar Foundation and the New York Bar Foundation. He was also a fellow of the State Academy for Public Administration.

Wayne Mahood grew up in Illinois. He received his BA, MA, and PhD degrees at Hamilton College, the University of Illinois, and Syracuse University, respectively, before teaching at SUNY Geneseo from 1969 to 1994. He taught in Illinois, chaired the Department of Elementary and Secondary Education at SUNY Geneseo, and served as president of the Geneseo Central School Board and president of the New York State Council for Social Studies.

He has authored and/or co-authored eight books and published articles and book reviews in such journals as *Social Education, The Social Studies, The Clearing House, Civil War Times, Civil War Regiments, North & South,* and *New York History*.

In addition to the SUNY Chancellor's Award for Excellence in Teaching, he was named a SUNY Distinguished Service Professor. In addition, he was the New York State Council for the Social Studies Distinguished Social Studies Educator for 1984 and is listed in *Who's Who in America*.

He and his wife, Bobbi Mahood, have two sons (Bruce and David), two daughters-in-law, and four grandsons.

Patricia Maloney is the president of Higher Education Consulting and Research in Washington, D.C. She is a researcher and practitioner with a background in higher education policy and management at public and private colleges and universities, state systems of higher education, associations, and research organizations.

At the American Council on Education, she managed the Presidents' Network for the Education of Teachers and a publication series on distance learning. At the University System of Maryland, she was project manager for the Change and Sustainability Project of the National Science Foundation Math Science Partnerships.

She was principal research scientist at the American Institutes for Research in Washington, D.C. She was also external evaluator for the Global Policy Fellows Program, a project of the Institute for Higher Education Policy. She is engaged in research on STEM college faculty engagement in K-16 partnerships, higher education opportunity, and leadership.

She received a PhD in higher education from the University at Buffalo, an MS in journalism from Boston University, and a BA in English from the University at Buffalo.

Carlos Medina is the assistant provost for diversity and educational equity at SUNY. Mr. Medina is responsible for assisting the vice provost with promoting and advancing SUNY's diversity goals and ensuring that they are properly captured within all university policies and procedures. He is involved with implementing and sustaining programs dedicated to serving underrepresented and economically disadvantaged students, faculty, and staff, and promoting inclusion, student success, and excellence within SUNY.

Mr. Medina has served as the director of student support services for SUNY's Center for Academic and Workforce Development and managed a $12.5 million budget as director of the Bridge Program (SUNY's flagship Welfare to Work Initiative). His work for the New York State Education Department from 1989 to 1997 included managing a host of teacher preparation, math and science enrichment, educational opportunity, and professional development programs across the state. Mr. Medina received the Mayor's Community Development Service Award from the City of Albany in 1994.

He received his BS in education from the State University of New York's College at Cortland and his master's degree in professional studies from Cornell University. Mr. Medina has more than twenty-five years of progressive responsibility in state government, with proven experience in leadership, management, and staff development.

Tim Nekritz is the associate director of public affairs at SUNY Oswego and director of the Oswego History Project. He is currently writing a book on the college's upcoming sesquicentennial in 2011, spearheading an oral history project, and building related resources for future historians. He previously authored "Oswego's Public Library: A History," which chronicled the state's longest-operating library and helped raise funds for the historic building's renovations.

When not looking back at the college's rich history, Nekritz serves as chief content editor of Oswego.edu. He has spearheaded the college's foray into social media, recruiting, and supervising student bloggers, plus creating and maintaining Oswego's official Facebook fan page and Twitter presence.

He holds a master's degree in history from SUNY Oswego and a bachelor's in communications from SUNY Brockport. He keeps a blog on writing, words, and the Web at http://insidetimshead.wordpress.com.

Kenneth P. O'Brien is associate professor of history at the College at Brockport, SUNY. He currently serves as president of the SUNY University Faculty Senate and is the co-editor (with Lynn Hudson Parsons) of *The Home-Front War: World War II and American Society.*

Tod Ottman holds a PhD in history from the State University of New York at Albany (2001). His research focuses on the growth and development of New York State government during the first half of the twentieth century. He served as an assistant managing editor of the *Encyclopedia of New York State* (2005).

Joseph Petrick has been the technical services coordinator at the Walter C. Hinkle Memorial Library at the State University of New York College of Technology at Alfred since 2000. Currently a doctoral student in the Communication Department at the University at Buffalo, he holds an MSLIS from Clarion University of Pennsylvania (1998) and a BA in English from Hobart College (1978). In 2007 he received the SUNY Chancellor's Award for Excellence in Librarianship and has been the university faculty senator from Alfred State College to SUNY University Faculty Senate from 2005 to the present.

Joel Rosenthal came to the Stony Brook History Department in 1964 as an assistant professor of medieval history and worked his way up through the ranks, retiring in 2006 as a distinguished professor. Along the way he also chaired the History Department three times and the Stony Brook University Senate. Most of his writing has been on the European Middle Ages, focusing in large part on the social history of 13–15th century England. He has worked on family history, women, children, widows, old age, popular religion, and family structure. Rosenthal published a bit on the medieval university, wrote a history of SUNY Stony Brook (*From the Ground Up* 2004), and gradually became interested in the wider topic of writing college and university histories—a large and flourishing body of literature of interest to historians of education and social historians, as well as to legions of loyal alumni and faculty.

Jeff Scott is the grant development specialist with the Office of Diversity and Educational Equity (ODEE) at the State University of New York (SUNY). Dr. Scott works to create new opportunities that enhance academic excellence through strategic investments in diversity-related curriculum, pedagogy, and research, and to diversify SUNY's student body and professoriate by promoting equal access and success for underrepresented and economically disadvantaged populations.

Before coming to ODEE, Dr. Scott was the executive director of the Hudson Mohawk Association of Colleges and Universities, a consortium of public and private higher education institutions in New York, Vermont, and Massachusetts. Prior to that, he worked with the Africa Division of Human Rights Watch in New York City, taught philosophy at the University at Buffalo, and served as a Peace Corps agro forestry volunteer in Sierra Leone and Togo. Dr. Scott earned a BS in geology from Union College and a PhD in philosophy from the University at Buffalo, where he was awarded the Hourani Fellowship for Outstanding Graduate Work in Ethics. He has authored and contributed to several works on human rights. Dr. Scott's current research interests include the connections between diversity in higher education, socioeconomic justice, and civic engagement.

Douglas R. Skopp is Distinguished University Teaching Professor of History emeritus and college historian at SUNY Plattsburgh. He received his PhD in 1974 from Brown University. In 1985-86 he received a Fulbright scholar/teacher award and was a guest professor at Universitaet Hannover in the Federal Republic of Germany, during which time he researched medical ethics and practices in Germany between 1880 and 1945. In 1989, he published *Bright With Promise: From the New York State Normal and Training School to SUNY Plattsburgh, 1889-1989—A Pictorial History*. During his thirty-four years at SUNY Plattsburgh, Skopp taught aspects of the history of education, medieval and modern European history, focusing on Germany, the World Wars, the Holocaust, and the theory and practice of history. In 1998, he was an inaugural fellow in SUNY Plattsburgh's Institute for Ethics in Public Life; since then, even in his retirement, he has participated in the Institute's "guided inquiry" seminars for each semester's faculty fellows, focusing on curricular development with special attention to ethical concerns. He has published on the history of education, the professions in Germany, and medical practices under the Nazis. Skopp's historical novel, *Shadows Walking*, about medical practices and ethics in Germany before and during the Nazi era, will be published in spring 2010.

Henry Steck is a Distinguished University Service Professor and professor of political science at SUNY Cortland. He has been on the Cortland faculty since 1963 and regards himself as one of the generation of builders who came to SUNY as it was entering its growth period. His BA is from Kenyon College and his PhD from Cornell University. He has been the director of the Clark Center for International Education at SUNY Cortland and the coordinator of Cortland's International Studies Program. He is the coordinator of the SUNY Cortland Project on Eastern and Central Europe. The holder of several grants in the international area, his current scholarly interests are on higher education. He has published on higher education, including, most recently, "SUNY in the 1990s: Politics, Budgets & the Democracy of Excellence" in *Governing New York State*, 5th ed. J. Stonecash, ed. (SUNY Press, 2006).

Wayne Urban is Paul W. Bryant professor of education, associate director of the Education Policy Center, professor of higher education, and coordinator of the Higher Education Program at the University of Alabama. Prior to his arrival in Tuscaloosa in January of 2006, he was Regents' professor of educational policy studies and professor of history at Georgia State University in Atlanta, Georgia, where he had been on the faculty since 1971. In addition, he has taught at the University of South Florida at Tampa, Monash University in Australia, the University of Alabama in Birmingham, the University of Florida, the University of Virginia, the University of Wisconsin in Madison, and Kent State University. In 1999, he served as a Fulbright Senior Lecturer at the Krakow Pedagogical University in Poland. In the fall of 2004, he was the Distinguished Fulbright scholar at York University in Toronto, Ontario, Canada.

He is the author of *More than Science and Sputnik* (in press for 2010), *Gender, Race, and the National Education: Professionalism and Its Limitations* (2000), *More Than the Facts: The Research Division of the National Education Association, 1922-1997* (1998), *Black Scholar: Horace Mann Bond, 1904-1972* (1992), and *Why Teachers Organized* (1982); editor of *Exceptionalism and Its Limits: Essays in the History of Twentieth Century Education* (1999); co-author of *American Education: A History* (1996, 2000, 2004, and 2008) and *Accountability in American Education: A Critique* (1974); and co-editor, with Ronald Henderson and Paul Wolman of the NEA, of *Teacher Unions and Education Policy: Retrenchment or Reform* (2004).

Christine Ward is the New York State archivist and chief executive officer of the New York Archives Partnership Trust, the fundraising arm of the archives. Throughout her career, Ms. Ward has published and lectured extensively on topics concerning the archives profession and has provided expert advice to national organizations on the management of preservation programs, administration, and strategic development for cultural organizations. Ms. Ward has taught at the graduate level and in several continuing education programs, and most recently, has written on the topics of archives and education and archival advocacy. She is a fellow of the Society of American Archivists, the archival profession's highest honor. She was commencement speaker for the University at Albany's History Department in 2007 and for the University's College of Computing and Information in 2005. In 2006, the University at Albany honored her with their Distinguished Public Service Award and the university's College of Arts and Sciences named her a fellow that same year. Ms. Ward is a fellow of the New York Academy of History.

Benjamin Weaver is executive assistant for academic affairs and administration in the Office of the Provost at the State University of New York at Albany. He completed his doctoral studies at the University's School of Education, where he focused his research on the history of the State University of New York community colleges. His dissertation, "Bringing the Colleges to the Communities: An Historical Analysis of the Siting of the State University of New York Community Colleges," examines the factors involved in the decisions—at the state, system, and local levels—of where to locate the system's community colleges, geographically, throughout New York State.

Dr. Weaver graduated with honors from Winona State University of Minnesota in 2001 with a BA in Spanish. He also holds a master's degree in city and regional planning from the Edward J. Bloustein School of Planning and Public Policy at Rutgers University. Dr. Weaver is a double alumnus of the State University of New York at Albany, having earned his Master's degree (2006) and PhD (2008) from the higher education program at the Department of Educational Administration and Policy Studies. He resides in Guilderland, New York.

Harold Wechsler is professor of education at the Steinhardt School, New York University. He writes on access, governance, and the formation of curriculum and disciplines in American higher education. His books include: *The Qualified Student: A History of Selective College Admission in America*; *Jewish Learning in American Universities: The First Century* (with Paul Ritterband); and *Access to Success in the Urban High School: The Middle College Movement*. He is currently writing a history of minority access to U.S. higher education.

Clifton R. Wharton Jr. was the longest-serving chancellor of the State University of New York System (1978–1987). Dr. Wharton has been a Black pioneer in philanthropy, foreign economic development, higher education, and business. He has served as president of Michigan State University (1970–1978) and chairman and CEO of TIAA-CREF, as well as serving six presidents in foreign policy roles, including appointment by President Clinton as Deputy Secretary of State in the U.S. Department of State. He holds a BA honors degree in history from Harvard, an MA from the School of Advanced International Studies at Johns Hopkins University, a PhD in economics from the University of Chicago, and has received sixty-three honorary degrees.

Geoffrey P. Williams has been university archivist/campus records officer at the University at Albany, SUNY since June 1987. He holds BA in history and government from Colby College, and an MLS and an MA in European history from the University of Illinois at Urbana-Champaign. He is currently co-chair of the New York State Historical Records Advisory Board (1996–present); serves on the New York State Local Government Records Advisory Council (2004–present), chairing their Program Committee; and has chaired, co-chaired, and/or served on the program committees of the Lake Ontario Archives Conference/New York Archives Conference and the Mid-Atlantic Regional Archives Conference.

Nancy L. Zimpher became the 12th Chancellor of the State University of New York by unanimous vote of the SUNY Board of Trustees on June 1, 2009. A dynamic and nationally-recognized leader, Chancellor Zimpher is known as an effective agent of change in higher education. The Chancellor began her career as a teacher in a one-room schoolhouse in the Ozarks and has never lost her passion for providing accessible, quality education for every student. As the first academic in recent memory to be appointed Chancellor, she is also the first woman to serve in this capacity in the system's 60-year history. Prior to coming to SUNY, she served as the President of the University of Cincinnati, Chancellor of the University of Wisconsin-Milwaukee, and Executive Dean of the Professional Colleges and Dean of the College of Education at The Ohio State University. She has authored or coauthored numerous books, monographs and academic journal articles on teacher education, urban education, academic leadership, and school/university partnerships. Chancellor Zimpher also chairs the Coalition of Urban Serving Universities Board, is a past chair of the Association of Public and Land-grant Universities Board of Directors, and is a member of the National Board for the Fund for the Improvement of Postsecondary Education.

Index